SUSTAINABILITY MANAGEMENT

Global Perspectives on Concepts, Instruments, and Stakeholders

RÜDIGER HAHN

First edition: 2022

ISBN 978-3-9823211-0-3 (paperback)
ISBN 978-3-9823211-1-0 (ebook)

Published by Rüdiger Hahn, c/o Block Services, Stuttgarter Str. 106, 70736 Fellbach (Germany)
www.sustainabilitymanagementbook.com

If you are an instructor at an institution in a country from the UN list of least developed countries, please write an email to info@sustainabilitymanagementbook.com in case you want to use this book in your course. You are eligible to receive an individualized digital copy of this book for free distribution to your students.
If you are a student at an institution in a country from the UN list of least developed countries, you should have received this book for free from your instructor. In case you were charged for this book via any other channel than an official book store, please write an email to info@sustainabilitymanagementbook.com.

SUSTAINABILITY MANAGEMENT

Global Perspectives on Concepts, Instruments, and Stakeholders

Contents

List of features

Faces of sustainability

Features from this section introduce thought leaders in sustainability from all areas of society.

Sustainability in society

Features from this section illustrate practical challenges, ideas, and concepts of sustainability from a societal point of view.

Sustainability in business

Features from this section provide examples of sustainability and unsustainability in business practice.

Sustainability in research

Features from this section provide a recap on seminal research articles which influenced the field of sustainability management in different ways.

Abbreviations

B2B	Business to Business
B2C	Business to Consumer
BCI	Better Cotton Initiative
BoP	Base/Bottom of the Pyramid
C2C	Consumer to Consumer
CDR	Corporate Digital Responsibility
CO2	Carbon Dioxide
CO2e	Carbon dioxide equivalents
CSR	Corporate Social Responsibility
DSJI	Dow Jones Sustainability Indices
ELCA	Environmental Life Cycle Assessment
EMAS	Eco-Management and Audit Scheme
ESG	Environmental, Social, and (Corporate) Governance
EU ETS	European Emissions Trading System
FSC	Forest Stewardship Council
GAAP	Generally Accepted Accounting Principles
GOTS	Global Organic Textile Standard
GRI	Global Reporting Initiative
HDI	Human Development Index
IASB	International Accounting Standards Board
IFRS	International Financial Reporting Standards
IIRC	International Integrated Reporting Council
LCA	(Environmental) Life Cycle Assessment
LCC	Life Cycle Costing
LCSA	Lify Cycle Sustainability Assessment
MSC	Marine Stewardship Council
MWh	Megawatt hours
NGO	Nongovernmental Organization
OECD	Organisation for Economic Co-operation and Development
P2P	Peer to Peer
PRI	Principles for Responsible Investment
RSPO	Roundtable on Sustainable Palm Oil
SASB	Sustainability Accounting Standards Board
SBTi	Science Based Targets initiative
SLCA	Social Life Cycle Assessment
SGD	Sustainable Development Goals
TCFD	Task Force on Climate-Related Disclosure
UN	United Nations
UNDP	United Nations Development Programme
UNEP	United Nations Environment Programm
UNGC	United Nations Global Compact
UNGP	United Nations Guiding Principles on Business and Human Rights
WBCSD	World Business Council for Sustainable Development
WCED	World Commission on Environment and Development
WRI	World Resources Institute
WWF	World Wide Fund for Nature

Acknowledgments

Writing a textbook is a major endeavor in an academic career and I am deeply grateful for the support of a great number of people who provided guidance, feedback, and other types of help in the process. Apart from a huge "thank you" to my family, I would also like to thank (in alphabetic order of first names):

Aissa Djalo, Alexandra May, Andrew Crane, Anne Darcis, Carolin Waldner, Christian Kabengele, Christian Klein, Daniel Reimsbach, Dario Foese, Deike Schlütter, Dirk Matten, Elisabeth Jäger, Erik Hansen, Florian Lüdeke-Freund, Frank Schiemann, Hannah Trittin-Ulrich, Martin Müller, Jakob Roessling, Laura Marie Edinger-Schons, Lena Schätzlein, Marius Wehner, Nils Krauthausen, Rainer Source, Regina Hahn, Stefan Gold, Stefanie Fella, Victoria Rosada, and Lisa Trierweiler. My special thanks go to Dagmar Neumann, who always has my back in the office and without whom I would not know how to navigate all the "A38s".

Feedback is always highly welcome. Please send your comments to
info@sustainabilitymanagementbook.com

About the author

Rüdiger Hahn holds the Henkel-Endowed Chair of Sustainability Management at the Heinrich-Heine-University Düsseldorf (HHU), Germany. Previously, he held positions as Full Professor (University of Hohenheim, Germany), Associate Professor (University of Kassel, Germany), and Assistant Professor (HHU), all in the area of sustainability management and corporate social responsibility.

Prof. Hahn teaches sustainability management and corporate social responsibility for more than 15 years. He has won several awards for teaching excellence and his courses are highly praised by his students. Apart from his passion for teaching, Prof. Hahn is a highly recognized scholar in the field. He regularly publishes in high-ranking and internationally recognized journals.

Additional online resources

This textbook is supported by various online resources for students and course instructors: www.sustainabilitymanagementbook.com

For students

Students can access a variety of additional online resources on the website using the password: "sustainabilitytextbook". These resources include, for example:

- Introductory screencasts for all chapters: These short videos (5 to 15 minutes each) provide an overview of the respective chapters' content. The QR codes and links at the beginning of each chapter will guide you to these videos.
- Flash cards for all glossary terms and concepts to support your learning
- Selected single-choice questions for each chapter to evaluate your learning success

For instructors

Teachers can access all resources for students. Furthermore, upon registration (see instructions on the website), teachers can access the following additional resources:

- Full inspection copy
- Exemplary course outlines with different emphases and of varying lengths to create custom-made syllabi
- Full slides for all chapters
- Ready-made introductory screencasts for all chapters and for digital, blended, and flipped classroom approaches
- Extensive set of single-choice questions for all chapters
- Annotated recommendation of (free) case studies
- Suggestions for semester assignments for undergraduate, graduate, and MBA classes
- Numerous didactical features for lively in-class discussions

A. Introducing sustainable development and sustainability management[1]

Over the last few decades, the idea of sustainable development has been acknowledged and supported by many actors in modern society. Companies, as central economic players, are increasingly pressured by a wide range of actors to not only engage in sustainability management but also contribute toward sustainable development. Against this background, in Part A of this book, we first introduce the general idea and illustrate the historic roots of sustainable development as a normative-anthropocentric concept. We then move on to critically illuminate the status quo of sustainability in our modern society. Beyond the most basic and broad definitions of sustainable development, which we introduce in the beginning, there are many different but related concepts and ideas surrounding sustainability. Consequently, it is not always clear what sustainable development and sustainability management truly mean. Because definitions and meanings can vary greatly between different groups and individuals, so can the means of achieving sustainable development. We therefore highlight different perceptions and finer concepts of sustainability and sustainability management to arrive at a deeper understanding of what they really encompass. Furthermore, there is no universal law of nature dictating that societies, companies, or individuals inevitably have to behave sustainably—despite the potentially dire consequences of ignoring sustainable development. Instead, societies and their individual actors are free to choose (not) to engage in sustainable development. We, therefore, discuss ethical and moral reasons as to why sustainability and sustainability management are often regarded as valuable ideas for individuals, companies, and entire societies. We also examine the business case for sustainability management by highlighting how it may pay off financially to act sustainably, and we critically discuss the limits of business case thinking. Finally, we introduce three base strategies to achieve sustainability (i.e., eco-efficiency, eco-effectiveness, and sufficiency), detailing their opportunities and limitations.

1 A few elements in Part A of this book draw on a text that was written by the author and published under the CC BY 4.0 International License as subchapter 8.2 (pp. 249-259) in "Urban, K., Schiesari, C., Boysen, O., Hahn, R., Wagner, M [Moritz], Lewandowski, I., Kuckertz, A., Berger, E. S. C., & Reyes, C. A. M. (2018). Markets, Sustainability Management and Entrepreneurship. In I. Lewandowski (Ed.), Bioeconomy - Shaping the transition to a sustainable, biobased economy (pp. 231–286). Springer International Publishing. https://doi.org/10.1007/978-3-319-68152-8_8".

A.1 History and status quo of sustainable development

LEARNING GOALS

After reading this chapter you will be able to...

- ... describe the historic roots of sustainable development.
- ... characterize sustainable development based on the concepts of intra- and intergenerational justice.
- ... critically reflect the status quo of intra- and intergenerational justice.
- ... explain why achieving sustainable development is a wicked problem.
- ... explain how different actors are relevant for achieving sustainable development.

Introduction to Chapter A.1: Screencast
Watch an introduction to the chapter here:

A.1.1 A short history of sustainable development

The general idea of sustainable development is centuries old. An often-mentioned historic source is Hans Carl von Carlowitz, dating back to the year 1713. As chief miner of Saxon Erzgebirge, a German mountain range rich in mineral raw materials, von Carlowitz was responsible for securing supplies for the mining industry. One of the most important materials was wood, which was used mostly as an energy source but also to secure the tunnels. In his book about forestry, he coined the idea of sustainable logging, that is, using only as much wood from the forests as could be regenerated and regrown, thus allowing wood to be cultivated continuously (von Carlowitz, 1713; 2009). The book was published in times of resource shortages, especially of wood, due to the increasing energy needs of a growing European industry and population. This reveals that the historic understanding of sustainability was already anthropocentric, that is, human-centered. The sustainable use of resources was a means to achieve the broad goal of human prosperity and, for von Carlowitz, the even narrower goal of the preservation of productive capacities.

Today, the idea of sustainable development extends beyond narrow aspects of (natural) resource utilization for immediate productive purposes. It encompasses not only the needs of current society but also those of future generations and includes social aspects (such as fair labor practices and fair distribution of resources). All these aspects are covered in perhaps the most widely cited contemporary characterization of sustainable development, the so-called "Brundtland definition." This definition originated in the 1987 report of the United Nations (UN) World Commission on Environment and Development (WCED; also called the Brundtland Report after the chairperson of the commission, then Norwegian prime minister Gro Harlem Brundtland): "Sustainable development is development that meets the needs of the present without compromising the ability of future generations to meet their own needs" (WCED, 1987, p. 41).

This broad characterization covers the two main pillars upon which our modern understanding of sustainable development rests: Intra- and intergenerational justice (see Figure 1). Meeting the needs of the present (i.e., within today's generation) verbalizes the idea of intragenerational justice. This idea of justice within today's generation is often less prevalent in many discussions around sustainable development, although it was a central concept in the WCED report. In fact, the report highlights the overriding priority for needs of the poor and gives voice to the large group of underprivileged individuals in the world. Fulfilling these needs—for example, in terms of providing enough food, clean drinking water, sanitation, or minimum social security—is a cornerstone without which sustainable development cannot be achieved. Simultaneously, the idea of sustainable development gives future generations a voice through the idea of intergenerational justice, which calls for preserving societal and ecological systems in a way that does not inhibit future generations in their own development. As such, it extends beyond the historic understanding of continuous resource utilization, which focused mostly on the productive capacities of that time (and not necessarily on future generations). Both elements of justice illustrate that sustainable development is a normative (i.e., relating to an ideal standard or model) and anthropocentric (i.e., relating to the influence of human beings on nature) concept.

Sustainability in society 1: Unsustainable resource use – The historic example of Easter Island

Easter Island, far off the coast of Chile in the Pacific Ocean, is most famous for its almost 1000 monumental stone figures. It also serves as an example of the unsustainable use of resources. Once covered by extensive palm tree forests, Easter Island today is largely deforested. This primarily human-driven deforestation rendered the island uninhabitable centuries ago and began a chain reaction by causing, for example, soil erosion, which not only resulted in declining agricultural productivity but also robbed inhabitants of the ability to build vessels for fishing. According to one theory, many of the island's trees were felled to move the enormous stone statues from the quarry to the final position they have occupied for centuries. While the reasons for the deforestation might be manifold, it is likely that human inhabitants themselves caused or at least amplified many of them, making Easter Island a prototypical example of an unsustainable form of living.

Sources: Diamond (2006); Hunt (2006); VanTilburg (1994)

(Photo by Yerson Retamal (Voltamix), CC SA 4.0, https://commons.wikimedia.org/wiki/File:AhuTongariki15Moais.jpg)

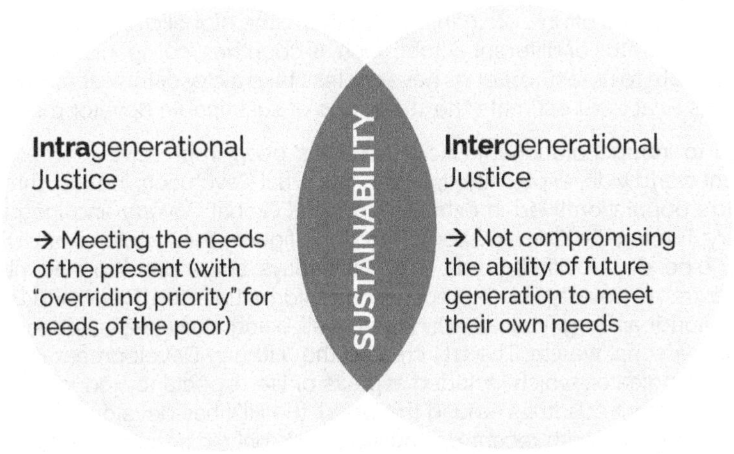

Intragenerational Justice

→ Meeting the needs of the present (with "overriding priority" for needs of the poor)

SUSTAINABILITY

Intergenerational Justice

→ Not compromising the ability of future generation to meet their own needs

Figure 1: Main elements of sustainable development according to WCED (1987)

Since the seminal report of the WCED was published in 1987, the UN has convened a series of high-profile conferences and meetings that have advanced the topic. At these conferences, UN member states have discussed the most pressing sustainability issues such as climate change, biodiversity, food security, and human development, while trying to move from consciousness-raising to agenda-setting to agreement on action. While there has certainly been an increasing awareness of sustainable development, thanks to these UN conferences, summits have also shown that it is extremely difficult to bring humankind together on a joint road to sustainability. Take the example of combating climate change as an issue of paramount importance for sustainable development. The general influence of carbon emissions on global warming has been known for more than a century. Arrhenius (1896) published an article "On the Influence of Carbonic Acid in the Air upon the Temperature of the Ground," followed 15 years later by Molena's (1912) "The Effect of the Combustion of Coal on the Climate – What Scientists Predict for the Future." More than 100 years later, there is vast scientific consensus on human caused climate change (Lynas et al., 2021) and at the 2015 UN Climate Change Conference held in Paris, the global community agreed on the goal of limiting global warming well below 2°C compared to pre-industrial levels. However, responsibilities were unclear, commitments remained vague, and important countries refused to ratify the agreements, with many observers agreeing that valuable years had been lost in combating climate change (Nordhaus, 2020).

Sustainability in society 2: Bioplastics and biofuels – Challenges of aligning intra- and intergenerational justice

Intra- and intergenerational justice may not be difficult to understand but they are often difficult to achieve, especially simultaneously. This makes achieving sustainability a very challenging task. Take the example of biofuels or bioplastics made from renewable energy sources such as plant material. From an intergenerational perspective, such products are often favorable because they potentially allow for carbon-neutral products, which have no or, at least, negligible impact on climate change compared to conventional fuel sources or plastics. However, the production of the renewable agricultural raw material for the bio-based products might lead to a crowding out of staple crops on limited cultivable surfaces. This could have detrimental effects on intragenerational justice if food prices increase or if, in extreme cases, food supply is limited (also known as the food vs. fuel debate; see, e.g., Kuchler & Linnér, 2012).

A.1.2 Status quo of sustainable development

It is difficult to determine whether or not a society is on a path of sustainable development as there is no generally accepted set of indicators that could clearly delineate a status of sustainability from one of unsustainability. Therefore, the global status of sustainability, as well as the exact status of different actors, such as countries, companies, or individuals, is almost impossible to measure. Let us nevertheless take a closer look at some figures and developments to at least estimate the status quo of sustainable development.

With regard to intragenerational justice, there has been impressive progress in human development worldwide, especially since the Industrial Revolution. In 1820, three-quarters of the world's population lived in extreme poverty ("Global Poverty and Inequality in the 20th Century: Turning the Corner?," 2001); in today's figures that would mean living on less than USD 1.90 per day (Jolliffe & Prydz, 2016). Nowadays, only around 10 percent of humankind live in extreme poverty (for the most recent information, see The World Bank data at https://data.worldbank.org/indicator/). Human well-being, however, is not only expressed in income or personal wealth. The UN created the "Human Development Index (HDI)" as an aggregated indicator, which included aspects of life expectancy, education, and standard of living. In most countries around the world, the HDI has developed positively since its introduction in 1990, with recent downward trends only in countries embroiled in (civil) war such as Yemen, Syria, or Libya (see UN Human Development Data Center at http://hdr.undp.org/en/data for most recent data). While these developments are certainly impressive, other figures vividly illustrate that this progress has not yet reached millions of individuals around the world. Some 600 million people (roughly twice the population of the United States) have less than USD 1.90 per day at their disposal, there are almost 1 billion illiterate adults, and more than 2 billion people do not have access to basic sanitation services (see The World Bank Database). Moreover, there are striking relative differences and massive inequalities in human development across the world. The entire region of Sub-Saharan Africa, with a growing population that already exceeds 1 billion people, for example, still scores low on the HDI. The difference in average life expectancy between countries with a low to medium HDI and those with a high HDI can easily reach 15 years or more. The same inequalities can be seen in educational indicators, such as years of schooling (UNDP, 2019). In terms of economic measures, less than 10 percent of the world's population accumulate almost 85 percent of total wealth, and the majority share of income increase in the last decades went to the already wealthiest people on the planet (Stierli et al., 2015).

While the status and development of intragenerational justice is ambiguous, the status quo of intergenerational justice seems to be more clear-cut. Each year, the Global Footprint Network calculates the Earth Overshoot Day. This marks the exact day in each year when humanity's demand for ecological resources exceeds the Earth's regenerative capacity—from that day on, humanity lives at the expense of future generations (see https://www.overshootday.org). In recent years, the calculated date was in August, leaving four remaining months of the year during which the Earth's resources were unable to meet the exigencies of humankind. Moreover, some interesting insights for intragenerational justice result when comparing different regions of the world. In North America, for example, the Overshoot Day has recently been calculated to be in March, showing a gross overconsumption of natural resources, while many Sub-Saharan countries do not exceed their "share" of Earth's biocapacity at all. Furthermore, the current lifestyle of many people in developed countries exacerbates the environmental situation in many countries of the Global South. Deforestation in various countries in Africa, South America, or Asia, for example, is a significant threat to biodiversity that is mainly accelerated not by local consumption but by global demand for commodities (Hoang & Kanemoto, 2021).

Overall, the state of intergenerational justice can be summarized in a few disturbing facts: Compared to pre-industrial levels, human activities until today are estimated to have caused about 1.0°C (or roughly 1.8°F) rise in global warming with further rising temperatures expected in the years to come (Allen et al., 2018). A rise in global warming by just 1.5°C will result in severe consequences due to rising sea levels, shifting rainfall patterns, or increasing extreme events, such as floods, droughts, and heat waves. This has already led to some irreversible consequences, which will not only affect future generations, but may also exacerbate intragenerational (in)justice. Many plants, animals, and insects have vanished due to climate change and other issues induced or influenced by humankind, such as deforestation or desertification. Currently, around one million species face extinction (IPBES, 2019). This is not merely an annoyance but may well prove critical for several aspects of human life as "nature plays a critical role in providing food and feed, energy, medicines and genetic resources and a variety of materials fundamental for people's physical well-being and for maintaining culture" (IPBES, 2019, p. 10). In their seminal study, Steffen et al. (2015) identified seven planetary boundaries which, if crossed, bear a high risk of destabilizing the Earth. Of these seven boundaries, two (biosphere integrity and biochemical flows) have already been exceeded according to scientific standards, while two others (climate change and land-system change) are marked with an increasing risk. Thus, the need to act is urgent if sustainable development is a favored goal. In sum, when considering the current state of the world, it seems fair to say that—so far—neither intra- nor intergenerational justice has been achieved.

Faces of sustainability 1: Greta Thunberg

For many, the climate activist Greta Thunberg is the voice and face of a generation. Thunberg, born January 3, 2003 in Stockholm, Sweden, constantly challenges world leaders, from the fields of politics and business, to fight climate change. Even in early childhood, she vividly expressed her concern for the environment. At the age of 15, as a lone protester, she began what rapidly evolved into a worldwide movement: the "Skolstrejk för klimatet" (school strike for climate). Her protests were first held outside the Swedish parliament in August 2018 and soon students from other communities and countries all over the world joined Greta Thunberg in what became known as the Fridays for Future movement. Having received numerous prestigious awards and honors, she has become an icon of the environmental movement while also raising her voice for global social justice issues. Business leaders and politicians once again came to realize that civil society also has a strong voice and that power is not always directly connected to money or voting rights.

Sources: Crouch (2018); Laville and Watts (2019); Part (2019); Watts (2019)

(Photo by Anders Hellberg, CC BY-SA 4.0, https://upload.wikimedia.org/wikipedia/commons/9/97/Greta_Thunberg_01.jpg)

A.1.3 Sustainable development as a wicked problem

These aspects of intra- and intergenerational justice illustrate that sustainable development is indeed a wicked problem (Brønn & Brønn, 2018; Pryshlakivsky & Searcy, 2013), that is, a problem that is difficult to solve due to its complexity and/or incomplete and potentially contradictory requirements. Let us reconsider intra- and intergenerational justice to illustrate potential tradeoffs in achieving both these justice aspects of sustainable development. The Earth Overshoot Day illustrates that human development is currently somehow positively correlated with the consumption of natural resources; in other words, if we try to improve the living situation, especially of the world's poor based on the current production and consumption patterns, it seems likely that such an improvement would involve further pressure on Earth's regenerative capacity (see graphically, for example, UNDP, 2019, p. 18). In sharp contrast to Western lifestyles, consumption patterns of the world's poor have significantly less environmental impact due to low-income and lower meat consumption per capita, low levels of private car ownership, and more frugal use of resources.

China's development over the last decades is a vivid example of potential tradeoffs between intra- and intergenerational justice. Following intensive economic growth, the share of the population living in extreme and moderate poverty was reduced drastically from almost 90 percent in 1990 to less than 10 percent today. However, carbon dioxide (CO2) or emissions of carbon dioxide equivalents (CO2e) emissions per capita simultaneously tripled (see The World Bank Data at https://data.worldbank.org/indicator/ for most recent data). Improving living standards of not only the world's poorest but also the growing global middle class will increase demand for food, water, energy, and other resources, thereby further increasing pressure on the natural environment, which may limit opportunities for future generations and intergenerational justice. However, denying (formerly) poor people the right to increase their consumption by spending their newly acquired wealth is hardly an option.

Nevertheless, poverty alleviation as one element of improved intragenerational justice, on the one hand, and a reduction of environmental burden to secure intergenerational justice, on the other hand, can at least potentially be closely linked. For example, the world's poor are often especially reliant on their immediate ecological environment. They need fertile land to not only grow food for subsistence farming but also to generate income; they rely on wood as their primary source of heating energy or live in shanty towns that are especially exposed to climate-induced extreme weather events such as floods. Consequently, they suffer disproportionately more from environmental problems such as climate change or deforestation. Reducing, or even reversing, the loss of the respective natural resources could contribute to their poverty alleviation.

Sustainability in society 3: The COVID-19 pandemic as wicked problem of sustainability

The outbreak of the global COVID-19 pandemic at the beginning of 2020 vividly illustrated the difficulties in pursuing sustainable development. During the pandemic, global economic activities declined, in some parts, dramatically (Liu et al., 2020). With this, greenhouse gas emissions also decreased significantly and the global Earth Overshoot Day 2020 was three weeks later than it was in 2019. While this may sound positive at first, especially for intergenerational justice, a closer look reveals some caveats. First, because modified economic activities (e.g., less air travel, meetings via video-conferences, buying fewer clothes) were largely forced upon people and organizations, they had no lasting effects (International Energy Agency, 2021). Second, the pandemic had dire consequences for intragenerational justice not only in the form of direct effects in countries with less established health care systems but also with equally dramatic indirect effects. For example, many people, especially in the Global South, lost their livelihood when supply chains broke down as several of these rely on necessity entrepreneurship or low paying jobs. In sum, global poverty increased significantly during the pandemic (Lakner et al., 2021).

Unfortunately, achieving a positive alignment of both aspects of justice is not an easy task as we will discuss throughout this book. There are not only the mentioned conflicts between intra- and intergenerational justice but also many actors (individual citizens, companies, governments, etc.) with potentially conflicting interests. To steer the world society in the direction of sustainable development, multiple actors need to play their parts (see Figure 2). Politicians need to recognize the need to embed sustainability goals and principles into rules and regulations at different levels, consumers need to recognize how their behaviors add up and contribute to or hinder sustainability, and civil society organizations need to recognize their influence on other players and advocate different elements of sustainability. Not least, of course, companies, as central and powerful players in modern society, need to contribute their share using various elements of sustainability management, either by reducing their environmental and social footprint or by actively and positively contributing to sustainable development with sustainability-oriented business models, goods, and services. Sustainability management can be characterized by the collective efforts of a company to contribute to sustainable development. It is insufficient, however, for one single group of actors to ensure sustainable development. This is because regulators and politicians are usually restricted by their national borders, customers often do not know or do not care about the consequences of certain purchase decisions, and companies might feel the pressure of market forces if stricter environmental regulations do not pay off financially.

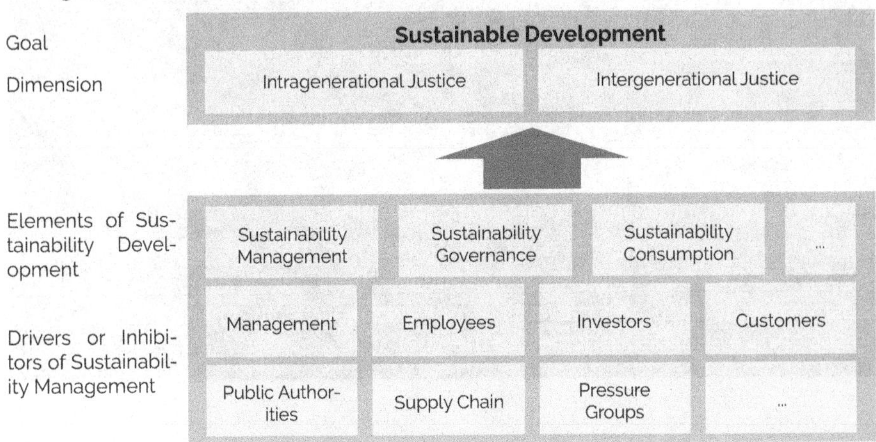

Figure 2: Elements and actors of sustainable development and sustainability management

In Part B of this book, we will approach the topic of sustainable development and sustainability management from a stakeholder perspective and discuss the (potential) influence of various stakeholder groups on sustainability and on companies' sustainability efforts. To make a company more sustainable (or less unsustainable), the management needs to balance a multitude of interests and have the backing of various actors. Certain types of investors or stockholders, for example, might pressure a company to actively pursue the idea of sustainability while others fear that measures of sustainability management are costly and could reduce their earnings. Many potential employees nowadays expect their future employer to be socially responsible, while still other do not see the need to change their own behaviors, such as switching off computer monitors when leaving the office. Although customers often claim to value sustainability, and the market for organic and Fairtrade products is constantly growing around the world, the willingness to pay a higher price for fair and sustainable products is often still limited. Supply chains and networks of most goods and services are extremely complex and easily cover thousands of suppliers, which makes it difficult for companies to monitor sustainability performance. Simultaneously, many pressure groups actively advocate better working conditions and environmental standards. In sum, the management of sustainability is a complex endeavor.

Task A1-1

"Climate change jeopardizes intragenerational justice!" – find arguments supporting this claim!

"Intragenerational justice jeopardizes the fight against climate change!" – find arguments supporting this claim!

On a metalevel: Why do you think that modern understandings of sustainable development include intra- and intergenerational justice simultaneously? Should one be privileged over the other—why or why not?

KEY TAKEAWAYS

- Sustainable development has evolved into a holistic concept encompassing intra- and intergenerational justice.
- Intragenerational justice covers the current generations while intergenerational justice focuses on future generations.
- Current patterns in society show gaps in the status quo of sustainable development regarding intra- and intergenerational justice.
- Sustainable development is a wicked problem as there are often conflicting issues between intra- and intergenerational justice.
- Sustainable development can only be pursued realistically when various actors in society are engaged in achieving the goal.

A.2 Concepts of sustainability and sustainable development

LEARNING GOALS

After reading this chapter you will be able to …

- … define the elements of the IPAT equation.
- … analyze human impact on ecological systems based on the IPAT equation.
- … distinguish weak, strong, and quasi sustainability.
- … explain how the Triple Bottom Line and the Sustainable Development Goals make sustainable development more accessible for companies.
- … distinguish between the terms sustainability management, corporate social responsibility, and corporate citizenship and relate them to each other.

Introduction to Chapter A.2: Screencast
Watch an introduction to the chapter here:

A.2.1 IPAT equation

A widely used approach to reduce complexity and illustrate options to especially improve intergenerational justice is the so-called "IPAT equation" (e.g., Meadows et al., 2004, pp. 124-126). The equation illustrates the human impact on ecological systems through the equation:

Impact = Population x Affluence x Technology

"Impact" refers to the ecological footprint of any population or nation upon the planet (as already discussed with reference to the Earth Overshoot Day in Chapter A.1.2). Changes in any factor on the right side of the equation lead to changes in the ecological footprint we leave on the Earth system.

"Population" includes the number of people influencing the ecological footprint. In 2019, the world's population reached 7.7 billion people (UN, Department of Economic and Social Affairs, Population Division, 2019). By 2050, this figure will likely be between 9.4 and 10.1 billion, and by 2100, between 9.4 and 12.7 billion. Each person leaves an individual ecological footprint through the resources that are necessary to maintain their lifestyle. The population factor in the IPAT equation is determined by fertility and mortality rates around the world which, in turn, are influenced, for example, by wealth, education, national regulations (such as China's former one-child policy), or religious beliefs. Developments in the size of the world's population are relatively stable over time.

"Affluence" is determined by the level of individual consumption, that is, the impact generated by the material, energy, and emissions associated with our lifestyles. The poor population, for example in rural Africa, is often dwelling in huts, has no access to individual transportation (other than maybe bicycles), uses biomass as their main energy source, and lives on a limited vegetarian diet. In contrast, the much wealthier population in Western Europe, on average, is often residing in large apartments or houses, owns one or more cars, travels by plane, and consumes considerable amounts of meat. As a consequence, the wealthiest 10 percent of the world's population are responsible for more than half of the cumulative emissions between 1990 and 2015 (OXFAM, 2020). However, since many of these decisions are based on individual preference, there is some potential to positively influence individual affluence toward a smaller individual ecological impact in the short term.

"Technology" illustrates impact per unit of consumption. It refers to the damage caused by the particular technologies chosen to support our level of affluence, that is, the energy needed to make and deliver material flows, multiplied by the environmental impact per unit of energy. Energy-efficient products or production processes can either allow each individual to consume more without an increasing overall impact or help reduce the impact while maintaining the level of affluence. Other technological advancements, such as energy from renewable sources, can help reduce environmental impacts even more distinctly if they allow for drastic reductions of the ecological footprint. We will shed more light on options to reduce humankind's ecological impact in Chapter A.4.

Task A2-1

Compare two countries with regard to their "impact" on the ecological environment according to the IPAT equation. You could, for example, compare a country from the Global South with a developed country or two seemingly similar countries and carve out their differences. Try to determine how the different factors of "population," "affluence," and "technology" developed over time in these countries and how these changes influenced the "impact." What can be done to reduce the impact in these countries and how feasible are your suggested measures?

Sustainability in society 4: Interdependencies between different factors of the IPAT equation

Let us consider the link between poverty and high population growth rates to illustrate some exemplary interdependencies in the IPAT equation. If all other factors are constant, a growing population puts increasing pressure on the ecological environment. The dilemma here is that it is often an economically rational decision for people living in poverty to have many children, especially in areas where infant mortality is high and family planning is unavailable or culturally unacceptable. Children are often regarded as a "free" workforce and as providers for their parents in old age. Hence, they are a resource to ensure the survival of the whole family. Thus, measures that help reduce the overall level of poverty and create employment opportunities (thereby, often improving affluence) for the extreme and moderate poor of the world may indirectly be beneficial for intergenerational justice if they contribute to a slowdown in population growth in the long term.

A.2.2 Weak, strong, and quasi-sustainability

When will sustainable development be achieved and what would be, for example, an acceptable ecological impact that is compatible with intergenerational justice? Despite providing some general yardsticks for orientation, the Brundtland definition of sustainable development still allows for different interpretations, with some even noting that sustainable development is a journey that will never be finished. For others, sustainable development is easier to achieve. Thus, different interpretations of sustainability may lead to fundamentally different implications for actions and strategies (for further overviews of the different interpretations see, e.g., Ayres, 2007; Neumayer, 2013).

The main goal of "weak sustainability" is to—at the very least—keep the total sum of anthropogenic (i.e., human-made) capital and natural capital constant. According to weak sustainability, natural capital can generally be substituted by anthropogenic capital while still ensuring the continuation of human well-being on Earth. Natural resources such as minerals or biodiversity can possibly be exploited limitlessly if the utility value of the produced goods and services makes up for the loss of natural capital. Strategies to achieve weak sustainability are, thus, mainly focused on technology and trying to increase the utility of every unit of natural capital by, for example, increasing the efficiency of their use (i.e., achieving the same output with less input or more output with the same input) or, ideally, by achieving entirely closed systems that do not require input of new raw materials and that produce no harmful emissions or waste. The drawback of this notion of sustainability is that full substitutability of natural with human-made capital is probably impossible due to technical limitations and laws of nature. Once all nonrenewable resources as well as the Earth's biodiversity and biocapacity are depleted, it is unlikely that humankind will still survive at the same level of prosperity as before, if at all.

The counterpart to weak sustainability is "strong sustainability." The general idea of this perception of sustainability is to live only from the "interest" of natural capital, that is, to use only those natural goods and services that are continuously added without diminishing the natural capital stock. It would, thus, be forbidden to use nonrenewable resources (because they, by definition, do not reproduce in time frames relevant for humankind and hence generate no "interest"), while renewable resources can only be utilized below their regeneration capacity. If followed through, this would mean renouncing any further growth of consumption and production due to the status quo of intergenerational justice as depicted in Chapter A.1.2. To walk this path, society would need to reduce individual levels of consumption (i.e., by asking how much is enough) and improve the efficiency of resource use at the individual and political levels. The drawback of this notion of sustainability is that it has a rather metaphorical character. A complete elimination of any growth does not seem feasible and would also mean that intragenerational justice can only be achieved through a very drastic (thus, probably unrealistic) redistribution of worldwide wealth.

The middle ground between the two extremes is occupied by the idea of "quasi," "critical," or "ecological" sustainability. It builds upon the principle of prudence and on not passing critical levels or critical boundaries (Steffen et al., 2015). An example of such a critical boundary would be the goal of limiting global warming to 1.5°C above pre-industrial times. One rationale for this boundary is that an increase beyond 1.5°C or 2°C of the Earth's temperature will result in various "tipping points" that could push the climate on Earth irreversibly into a completely new state (Lenton et al., 2019). Such thresholds should not be exceeded, and a substitution of natural capital by human-made capital has to be well justified. To achieve this, a mixture of the different sustainability strategies as discussed in Chapter A.4 might be needed despite the uncertainty regarding their technological feasibility and the socio-political enforceability.

A.2.3 The Triple Bottom Line and the Sustainable Development Goals

Regardless of which notion of sustainability one follows, managing sustainability is a task with many potential fields of action, from mitigating climate change or biodiversity losses to human rights protection and implementation of decent working conditions, not all of which are relevant for each and every company in the same way. Thus, to make the elusive concepts of intra- and intergenerational justice within sustainable development more comprehensible and manageable at the company level, they are often broken down into three distinct pillars of action: economic, ecological, and social responsibility, known as the Triple Bottom Line (e.g., Elkington, 1999). It is sometimes also termed the "Three Ps" of people, planet, and profit. In the corporate domain, the economic pillar ("profit") is usually understood as the responsibility of a company to generate profits to be economically sustainable. Furthermore, aspects such as economic prosperity and development are also often mentioned. With regard to the ecological pillar ("planet"), topics such as environmental protection, resource preservation, and corporate actions to achieve these goals are discussed. The social dimension ("people") covers topics such as social justice and equal opportunity and is often connected to the issues of employees and suppliers such as fair compensation, diversity, labor conditions, and work-life-balance.

An even more fine-grained approach to breaking down the concepts of intra- and intergenerational justice into actionable pathways and specific fields of action is illustrated in the UN Sustainable Development Goals (SDGs). In 2015, the UN proposed this set of 17 aspirational goals as depicted in Figure 3. Each goal is further broken down into various targets, 169 in total. The SDGs are intended to influence and guide not only global politics but also businesses and individuals in their actions to serve the idea of sustainable development.

Faces of sustainability 2: John Elkington

John Elkington has shaped the understanding of sustainability in business like few others. Born in 1949 in the United Kingdom, Elkington has been named "a true green business guru," "an evangelist for corporate social and environmental responsibility long before it was fashionable," and "a dean of the corporate responsibility movement" (Evening Standard, 2008). His book "Cannibals with forks" (Elkington, 1999) is one of the most widely cited sustainability books of all times. He coined the phrase "Triple Bottom Line" and introduced the idea of people, planet, and profit to the business world, thus, making the elusive concept of sustainable development more approachable for companies. Actively contributing on many fronts, Elkington is, among other things, an ambassador for the World Wide Fund for Nature (WWF), consultant for sustainability issues, author, speaker, and serial entrepreneur.

Sources: Elkington (n.d.); Makower (2016)

(Photo by JP Renaut, CC BY-SA 3.0, https://upload.wikimedia.org/wikipedia/en/7/7e/John_Elkington_06.JPG)

Figure 3: The 17 UN Sustainable Development Goals (https://www.un.org/sustainabledevelopment/, reproduced with permission. The content of this publication has not been approved by the United Nations and does not reflect the views of the United Nations or its officials or member states.)

Companies nowadays refer to the SGDs to express their commitment to sustainable development and illustrate their own progress and actions. In doing so, many companies first refer to those goals that best fit their business model and activities. However, the 17 SDGs and the 169 targets can also be used as a holistic set of aims and activities to guide future activities and review companies' approaches. Other than the rather vague ideas of intra- and intergenerational justice or the broad approach of the Triple Bottom Line, the SDGs are more fine-grained, which makes it easier for companies to translate them into everyday management. On a country level, there is even a performance ranking which evaluates nation states based on their progress toward achieving the SDGs. However, a closer look at this index also reveals some of the difficulties with such a holistic approach toward sustainability. On top of the list, for example, are mostly wealthy OECD (Organisation for Economic Co-operation and Development) countries. They score high on the index due to their usually good performance in fighting poverty, hunger, illiteracy and due to their good situation in infrastructure, or peace and justice—all of which are outlined in the SDGs. The same countries, however, are usually also the most environmentally unsustainable in the world, and they very often contribute to unsustainability in other countries due to negative socioeconomic and environmental spillovers (J. D. Sachs et al., 2021).

Sustainability in business 1: The Sustainable Development Goals at Henkel

One of the many companies that refer to the SDGs in their sustainability management is the multinational chemical and consumer goods giant Henkel. The company refers to all SDGs and illustrates how its operations relate to the respective goals. It emphasizes that, due to its broad product range and its worldwide presence, it can contribute to almost all of the 17 SDGs. However, Henkel specifically focuses on Goal 4 (quality education, e.g., by offering continuous learning opportunities for their employees), Goal 8 (decent work and inclusive, sustainable economic growth, e.g., by enabling small farmers to certify their crops as sustainable, increase their productivity, and improve their livelihoods), Goal 12 (responsible consumption and production, e.g., by encouraging the responsible use of their products), and Goal 17 (partnerships for sustainable development, e.g., by entering into dialog with all stakeholders, including customers, consumers, suppliers, employees, shareholders, local communities, nongovernmental Organization (NGOs), politicians, and academia).

Source: Henkel AG & Co. KGaA (2020)

A.2.4 Sustainability management, CSR, and corporate citizenship

Let us reconsider some terminological issues and difficulties, especially with regard to sustainable development in the business sphere, that is, to sustainability management. As indicated, sustainability management encompasses a multitude of activities and potential fields of action ranging from ecological issues such as climate change, biodiversity, or animal rights to social issues of (in)equality, health, education, or diversity as well as to economic issues such as the survival of the firm, compliance, risk management, or governance. Many if not all of these issues are also discussed in reference to other terms or concepts such as corporate social responsibility (CSR) or corporate responsibility. The distinction between sustainability management and CSR is, in fact, very blurred. Nowadays, some companies have a CSR department or CSR manager while others have a sustainability board or sustainability manager. Whatever the preferred term is in any given company, the respective departments or actors often undertake similar tasks. Even in academia, these concepts and terms are increasingly used interchangeably (e.g., R. Hahn, 2011).

Sustainability in research 1: Matten and Moon's 2008 article on corporate social responsibility

Why do firms differ in their corporate social responsibility activities across countries? Dirk Matten and Jeremy Moon approach this question in their conceptual article "'Implicit' and 'Explicit' CSR: A conceptual framework for a comparative understanding of corporate social responsibility" published in 2008 in the Academy of Management Review. The authors discuss predictors for geographic differences in CSR efforts with a special emphasis on companies from the United States and the European Union. The authors distinguish between implicit and explicit CSR. The latter comprises explicitly communicated programs, practices, and strategies. Corporations conduct such activities as they voluntarily assume responsibility for the interests of society. In the former (implicit) alternative, CSR practices are incorporated within broader policy arrangements and are thus often codified and mandatory. This form of CSR describes corporations as part of the overall institutions for society's interests and concerns.

The authors build upon institutional theory as a framework to examine the motives of multiple stakeholders within varying institutional, national, and cultural contexts. These motives can affect the CSR efforts of companies. Furthermore, the theory is used to examine cross-national differences in corporate governance practices. Matten and Moon argue that cross-national differences in CSR result from historically grown institutional frameworks that are incorporated within every country and influence the respective national business systems. These frameworks comprise the national political system, the financial system, the education and labor system, and the cultural system. The authors argue that CSR, as an explicit element of corporate policies, can more often be found in liberal market economics such as in the United States. CSR as an implicit element of the institutional framework more likely forms in coordinated market economies such as in the European Union.

The authors then argue that the heterogeneity of institutional environments is decreasing, resulting in standardized practices in organizations across national boundaries. They posit that explicit CSR is spreading globally and explain why companies from the European Union increasingly adopt the U.S.-led explicit CSR model. Matten and Moon argue that the companies' motivation to change stems from the imposed legitimacy. Legitimacy is produced by three processes, namely coercive isomorphisms, mimetic processes, and normative pressure. These processes influence the historically grown institutional frameworks in the long run.

Eventually, the authors propose a framework for comparative CSR that integrates both approaches with their influential factors, which helps to explain historical differences and contemporary trends in global CSR efforts when business responsibility is compared across countries. The article is one of the most influential pieces on business responsibility that has been published in the last decades, and in 2018 it received the paper of the decade award by the publishing journal Academy of Management Review. It will be interesting to observe the further development of CSR in the next decades because, for example, the notion of voluntariness as a central element of explicit CSR seems to have lost some traction in recent years as we will further discuss in Chapter A.3.3.

Source: Matten and Moon (2008)

We already characterized sustainability management earlier as the collective efforts of a company to contribute to sustainable development; companies often refer to the Triple Bottom Line or to the SDGs to make their contribution more accessible. Prominent definitions of CSR characterize it as "the responsibility of enterprises for their impacts on society" (European Commission, 2011, p. 6) or as the "responsibility of an organization for the impacts of its decisions and activities on society and the environment" (International Standardization Organization [ISO], 2010a, p. 3). Such definitions, directly or indirectly, emphasize that organizations are supposed to contribute to different aspects of sustainable development, thus resembling our characterization of sustainability management.

The different terminology can largely be explained by the historical roots of both concepts (Bansal & Song, 2017). The debate around CSR can be traced back to an ethical or social perspective some 100 years ago, which focused largely on employees and on philanthropic activities (for a historical overview, see Carroll, 2008). The idea then gained further popularity in the 1950s starting with Howard R. Bowen's seminal book on the "Social Responsibilities of the Businessman," with another momentum being the introduction of stakeholder thinking advocated by R. Edward Freeman and colleagues in the 1980s. While this included the ecological environment as part of the society at large, up until this time, human resources and socioeconomic aspects were at the center of thinking. Sustainable development and sustainability management, on the other hand, historically began with a clear focus on environmental issues, as illustrated in Chapter A.1.1. With the Brundtland Report in 1987, sustainable development prominently opened its perspective to social issues, for example, when mentioning the overriding priority for the needs of the world's poor. Since then, the boundaries between the concepts of CSR and sustainability management have become increasingly blurred. Lately, in the new millennium, we see a conversion of social, environmental, and economic perspectives in both concepts. The remaining differences between the two concepts are largely academic, with CSR possessing a normative-ethical perspective and sustainability and sustainability management possessing a scientific systems perspective (Bansal & Song, 2017).

Corporate citizenship is another term frequently used to describe corporate efforts in and for society (Matten et al., 2003). Sometimes, corporate citizenship is used synonymously with CSR; this equivalent understanding does not add much value to the debate. The most widespread use of corporate citizenship in practice, however, is that of a limited understanding that only covers voluntary philanthropic activities such as donations. This perspective usually ignores any ethical calls for responsible business conduct, instead taking an instrumental approach of long-term profit maximization through improved social capital. Finally, there is also an extended view of corporate citizenship that examines the role of corporations as citizens of society and their influence on human rights. In sum, corporate citizenship is even more ambiguous than the terms sustainability management or CSR. It is, thus, necessary to clearly identify the intended meaning in any practical or academic debate.

KEY
TAKEAWAYS

- The IPAT equation illustrates the human impact on Earth's ecological systems through the equation: Impact = Population x Affluence x Technology.
- Weak, strong, and quasi-sustainability are different interpretations of the same concept with fundamentally different implications.
- The Triple Bottom Line breaks sustainable development down into an economic, an ecological, and a social pillar.
- The Sustainable Development Goals comprise 17 aspirational goals with 169 targets providing guidance on how to serve the idea of sustainable development.
- Sustainability management, CSR, and corporate citizenship are similar concepts that describe various elements of responsible business conduct, and they are often used synonymously.

A.3 Reasons for sustainable development and sustainability management

LEARNING GOALS

After reading this chapter you will be able to ...

- ... identify various normative-ethical reasons for sustainable development at a societal level.
- ... argue from an ethical and moral perspective why companies should engage in sustainability management.
- ... critically assess the extent of a company's responsibility based on its spheres of influence.
- ... provide arguments for why and when sustainability pays off, thus, arguing for the business case for sustainability.
- ... critically discuss the limits of the business case for sustainability.

Introduction to Chapter A.3: Screencast
Watch an introduction to the chapter here:

A.3.1 Ethical arguments for sustainable development

The idea of sustainable development is widely acknowledged, and for many years, the attention paid to sustainability issues and to sustainability management has been growing in research, business practice, and among the general public. Nevertheless, because sustainable development is sometimes still contested, an argument on why humankind would want to strive for sustainable development is in order.

Sustainable development in general describes the necessary behavior to pursue the ideal of intra- and intergenerational justice. As described in Chapter A.1.1, intergenerational justice focuses on the preservation of resources for successive generations, while intragenerational justice focuses on well-being in existing generations. Thus, the well-being of humankind is of central concern, and sustainable development is a largely anthropocentric ideal. Consequently, whether or not we want to follow the normative idea of sustainable development is largely an ethical decision. In other words, if we (deliberately or not) ignore the basic ideas of sustainable development, it is likely that we will have to face negative consequences such as environmental degradation or social unrest (see again Chapter A.1.2). There is, however, no rule of nature that determines whether or not humankind has to adhere to the principles of sustainable development as long as we are willing to face the consequences.

Faces of sustainability 3: Wangari Maathai

For most of her life, Wangari Maathai, born in 1940 in Kenya, fought for sustainability on all fronts. She was the first black African woman to receive a Nobel Prize and the first woman in Central and East Africa to earn a doctorate degree. Maathai was famous for her environmental activities, being the founder of the Green Belt Movement at the end of the 1970s. The organization planted millions of trees and educated world leaders about conservation and environmental improvement. Furthermore, Maathai was a vocal advocate of social sustainability, fighting for human rights, women's empowerment, and AIDS prevention. The Nobel Committee awarded her the Nobel Peace Prize in 2004 because "she has taken a holistic approach to sustainable development that embraces democracy, human rights and women's rights in particular. She thinks globally and acts locally." From 2002, Wangari Maathai was Assistant Minister for Environment, Natural Resources and Wildlife in Kenya. She died in 2011 in Nairobi.

Sources: Florence (2014); The Norwegian Nobel Committee (2004)

Arguments in favor of sustainable development can be based on some basic ethical concepts. Very often, arguments refer to Immanuel Kant's Categorical Imperative (Kant, 1993, p. 30): "Act only according to that maxim whereby you can at the same time will that it should become a universal law." Similar ideals have been advocated as the so-called "golden rule" in various world religions for centuries (Flew & Priest, 2002). When applied to intergenerational justice, no one should want any other principle to become a universal law because this could lead to a situation in which the current generation could be worse off due to decisions made by others in the past (Matten, 1998). In the same way, future generations are affected by the outcomes of our behavior. In sum, every generation serves as an end for previous generations while being a means for future generations in terms of preserving the ecological basis of human life on Earth. Furthermore, if an excessive impact on nature by a privileged few poses a direct threat for others of the same generation (if, e.g., climate change today leads to droughts, extreme weather events, uninhabitable islands due to rising sea levels, etc.), the principle is also relevant for the idea of intragenerational justice.

Sustainability in society 5: Aspects of sustainability in the UN Universal Declaration of Human Rights

The UN Universal Declaration of Human Rights (UN, 1948) forms the basis of several UN human rights treaties. All UN member states have ratified at least one, and 80 percent have ratified four or more, of these treaties. The following excerpt illustrates some connections of the declaration to sustainable development and to the SDGs.

"Article 2:

Everyone is entitled to all the rights and freedoms set forth in this Declaration, without distinction of any kind, such as race, colour, sex, language, religion, political or other opinion, national or social origin, property, birth or other status. ...

Article 3:

Everyone has the right to life, liberty and security of person. ...

Article 22:

Everyone ... has the right to social security ... of the economic, social and cultural rights indispensable for his dignity and the free development of his personality.

Article 23:

1. Everyone has the right to work, to free choice of employment, to just and favourable conditions of work and to protection against unemployment.
2. Everyone, without any discrimination, has the right to equal pay for equal work.
3. Everyone who works has the right to just and favourable remuneration ensuring for himself and his family an existence worthy of human dignity, and supplemented, if necessary, by other means of social protection.

Article 25:

1. Everyone has the right to a standard of living adequate for the health and well-being of himself and of his family, including food, clothing, housing and medical care and necessary social services, and the right to security in the event of unemployment, sickness, disability, widowhood, old age or other lack of livelihood in circumstances beyond his control. ..."

In addition, John Rawls's Theory of Justice can serve as an ethical reference of intragenerational justice. Rawls's first principle calls for equal freedom for all as "each person is to have an equal right to the most extensive total system of equal basic liberties compatible with a similar system of liberty for all" (Rawls, 1971; p. 302). The second principle allows for a deviation from equal distribution as long as "social and economic inequalities are to be arranged so that they are both: (a) to the greatest benefit of the least advantaged, consistent with the just saving principle, and (b) attached to offices and positions open to all under conditions of fair equality of opportunity" (Rawls, 1971, p. 302). Thus, while fundamental rights are valid for every individual, the second principle claims, in its economic version, the maximization of welfare for the least favored individual, which explicitly adds to intragenerational justice. This seems especially relevant when referring to the overriding prioritization of the needs of the poor as proposed by the Brundtland Report (WCED, 1987; see again Chapter A.1.1). Those, for example, who live in extreme poverty, often cannot even meet their basic needs for survival as they lack access to health care, safe drinking water, or sometimes even basic shelter; they suffer from chronic hunger and they cannot afford education for some or all of their children. Worldwide inequality has been increasing in the last decade, not only in monetary terms (Jahan, 2016) but also with regard to emissions and resource consumption (OXFAM, 2020). These aspects illustrate again that intragenerational justice is still a distant goal, and it underlines the relevance of Rawls's ideas for justifying the ideal of sustainable development. These ethical positions can be assumed to be widespread worldwide as they are mirrored by the UN Universal Declaration on Human Rights (UN, 1948; e.g., Preamble, Articles 1, 2, 3, 22, or 25).

A.3.2 Ethical and moral reasons for sustainability management

Based on this general ethical reasoning for sustainable development, we will now examine the role of companies in the quest for sustainability and ask why companies should be concerned for sustainable development. Let us continue with the Universal Declaration of Human Rights. Historically, national states were viewed not only as the primary players to promote human rights but also as their main threat (Wettstein & Waddock, 2005). Nevertheless, the preamble of the declaration calls on "every individual and every organ of society [...] to promote respect for these rights and freedoms" and, thus, deliberately includes private players. In addition, Article 29 adds that "Everyone has duties to the community in which alone the free and full development [...] is possible." Therefore, companies cannot retreat from the responsibility to uphold these rights. In recent years, this thought has seen increasing recognition not least by the UN itself (e.g., UN, 2011).

Sustainability in business 2: Ignoring human rights in the Global South

An example of an activity that supposedly violated not only legal standards but also human rights was demonstrated by Pfizer in Nigeria in 1996. The company was accused of testing an antibiotic on children during a meningitis epidemic without consent from the children's parents and without governmental authorization. Medical complications and even fatalities occurred. The company claimed that the tests had been a humanitarian relief action. Pfizer was found to have violated internationally agreed upon ethical principles of medical ethics as well as several national and international standards for clinical trials. The company was also accused of exploiting the medical emergency and the financial situation of the families as well as covering up possible malpractice.

Sources: Ahmad (2001); McNeil (2011); Stephens (2006); Stephens (2007)

Why, however, should any company have responsibilities other than making profits? After all, Nobel Memorial Prize laureate and economist Milton Friedman argued in his seminal essay "The Social Responsibility of Business Is to Increase Its Profits" (Friedman, 1970). In an ideal world, "markets" should ensure the efficient allocation of goods and services guided by regulations through governmental actors. In addition, the state should provide social services so that the direct involvement of other actors would not be necessary. Companies would, thus, not have to set standards of appropriate business behavior themselves, because such norms would be determined exogenously and misconduct would be sanctioned. Reality, however, reveals some flaws in these idealized institutions. Completely atomistic companies and free markets are an assumption in economic models so that mere profit maximization does not automatically lead to increased public welfare. Consequently, responsibilities shift, especially in those cases where state authorities do not (or cannot) guarantee responsible management practices (Wettstein & Waddock, 2005).

Multinational corporations in particular can act at least partially beyond the boundaries of single nation states. They, thus, have significant latitude in how they want to conduct their business. The reasons for this freedom are manifold. Rapid advancements in information and communication technology as well as extensive transportation infrastructure allow for transboundary and highly specialized production. The necessary capital is available worldwide and can be transferred easily. Material and immaterial resources are decreasingly location-bound. This flexibility allows many companies to operate in a comparably free manner. Consequently, (multinational) corporations have a significant influence on overall sustainable development. They often employ hundreds of thousands of people, with even more being indirectly dependent as employees of suppliers or as family members of employees. In this way, companies influence the lives of many individuals; Jonas (1979) addresses the special obligations that come with such power. In some extreme cases, the revenue of the largest companies worldwide exceeds the gross national product of entire countries, and technical know-how in genetic engineering, biotechnology, nanotechnology, or other areas is increasingly concentrated in private (company) knowledge. This often triggers the expectation that companies should contribute to solving sustainability-related problems. Consequently, some argue that obligations increase with size (e.g., Oetinger & Reeves, 2007; Wettstein, 2005).

Despite these institutional aspects, it can still be argued that moral responsibility cannot be separated from the human as an individual (Friedman, 1970). Yet the characteristics of legal entities provide further reasons for corporate responsibilities of sustainable development. On an individual level, every employee has a moral responsibility for his or her actions that actively shape the way his or her employer does business. Corporate responsibilities can be assigned to each individual company member. With increasing organizational complexity, however, the perceived individual responsibility might perish in complex company structures. Yet as a member of a larger entity (i.e., a company), individuals usually receive extended credit and resources. Kaufmann (1992) argues that because companies are recipients of collective trust by their customers, employees, suppliers, and so on, they have special obligations even beyond the responsibility of their individual members. Moreover, companies make decisions based on organizational structures, cultures, and targets. Such a collective rationality follows procedures, protocols, and corporate values, which make decisions easier to reconstruct, control, and communicate (Hubbertz, 2006). Consequently, corporations increasingly have to legitimize their actions toward the public and answer to a wider set of stakeholders. This appears to be reasonable since the general public legitimizes (or de-legitimizes) companies' activities. Furthermore, society (usually through governments) also legally provides companies with the necessary rights to conduct business in the first place. Hence, the ethical requirements that apply to individual citizens also apply to corporations (Ulrich, 2002).

While companies nowadays usually accept some form of moral responsibility for their operations and activities (Carroll, 2008), the next question is how far such responsibilities extend. To approach this question, it is helpful to distinguish so-called negative from positive rights. Negative rights such as the right to life and physical integrity, establish passive duties to refrain from certain behavior (i.e., not to harm human rights). These rights have to be obeyed at all times. Everyone (including companies) is duty-bound to respect these rights. Positive rights, in contrast, require collective duties to actively satisfy them (e.g., by providing health care, education, or other social services) instead of merely avoiding harm (Wettstein, 2005). Holistically upholding these rights requires measures that lie beyond the sphere of influence of single actors such as specific companies. The argument for companies to take over responsibilities for positive rights can again be deduced from an individual and organizational perspective. John Rawls argued that "well-ordered peoples have a duty to assist burdened societies" (Rawls, 1999, p. 106) as they benefit from favorable conditions. He further maintained that positive rights need to be improved especially in those societies that "lack the political and cultural traditions, the human capital and knowhow, and, often, the material and technological resources needed to be well-ordered" (Rawls, 1999, p. 106). Similar thoughts were echoed by Margalit (1996) with his concept of "the decent society," arguably the most important work on social justice since Rawls (see R. Hahn, 2011). As of today, burdened societies do not receive adequate assistance from well-ordered societies so the responsibility extends to private actors (Hsieh, 2004, 2009). Therefore, companies might have extended responsibilities, first, directly as members of well-ordered societies and, second, via the individual duties of their owners because the vast majority of shareholders originate from well-ordered (usually industrialized) nations. In sum, we can conclude that companies not only have the responsibility to not cause harm but also are expected to actively promote and disseminate certain human rights and sustainable development.

Task A3-1

Milton Friedman's essay, "The Social Responsibility of Business Is to Increase Its Profits" has long been cited by managers, politicians, and business scholars alike to argue against various forms of social responsibilities of businesses. Engage with Friedman's arguments by reading his famous essay and summarize his main lines of argument:

Why, according to Friedman, should the social responsibility of a business be to increase its profits?

(You can find the essay on the Internet, e.g.: https://www.nytimes.com/1970/09/13/archives/a-friedman-doctrine-the-social-responsibility-of-business-is-to.html)

In the 50 years since its publication, public debate as well as our understanding of society and business has evolved. On the 50th anniversary of Friedman's essay, in Sepember 2020, The New York Times published a piece with a series of responses to Friedman. Engage with these thoughts to collect and systematically arrange arguments:

Why might businesses have other responsibilities than increasing their profits?

(You can find the responses here: https://www.nytimes.com/2020/09/11/business/dealbook/milton-friedman-doctrine-social-responsibility-of-business.html)

A.3.3 Levels of corporate responsibility for sustainable development

In the past (and sometimes even today), practitioners and academics often highlighted the voluntariness of corporate responsibility for societal issues such as sustainable development. Following our previous arguments, however, it makes no sense to characterize any responsibility of companies for aspects related to sustainable development as voluntary. Merely the fact that companies can often not be prosecuted for certain misconducts or for questionable business practices (e.g., due to regulatory loopholes or insufficient governmental controls) or that external effects cannot be internalized is not an adequate argument against corporate responsibilities per se. Instead, it just shows that regulations are often imperfect. Statements that any form of corporate responsibility is voluntary are not only ethically questionable, but also imperil corporate reputation, as such that a perception is hardly a consensus in society. Simultaneously, it is unreasonable to impose an extensive responsibility for virtually all aspects of sustainable development on any single company.

Instead, we should contemplate the question of which aspects fall into the area of corporate responsibility and which are beyond core responsibilities and, thus, indeed voluntary.

Let us reconsider two contemporary characterizations of CSR, which we have introduced earlier and do not emphasize aspects of voluntariness (see again Chapter A.2.4). The European Commission characterizes CSR as "the responsibility of enterprises for their impacts on society" (European Commission, 2011, p. 6) and the international guideline ISO 26000 characterizes the sphere of (organizational) influence as the "range/extent of political, contractual, economic or other relationships through which an organization has the ability to affect the decisions or activities of individuals or organizations" (ISO, 2010a, p. 4). Both imply that there is an organizational sphere of responsibility in those cases where companies' activities have an influence on third parties. Within this sphere of influence, responsibility cannot be voluntary. This applies to not only working conditions in company-owned factories but also to environmental damages caused by a company's own operations. Philanthropic activities such as donations, sponsoring, or corporate volunteering programs are usually not part of a company's core activities and can, thus, be voluntary.

The differentiation is, however, not always clear-cut. For example, does a company shoulder the responsibility for sustainability-related issues with a supplier? How large must the influence of a company on its supplier be to justify a shared responsibility for social or environmental standards? To address these questions, we will try to establish different layers of corporate influence. Figure 4 illustrates how a company's influence on actors and on the results of their activities decreases from the inner to the outer circles. The innermost circle includes only direct relationships within the company itself. The second circle involves external players such as business partners. The number of actors increases toward the outer circles and the power distance while the immediacy of decisions by the company decreases. A company's influence and control are highest in the middle of the model, which reflects the company's responsibility for its actions.

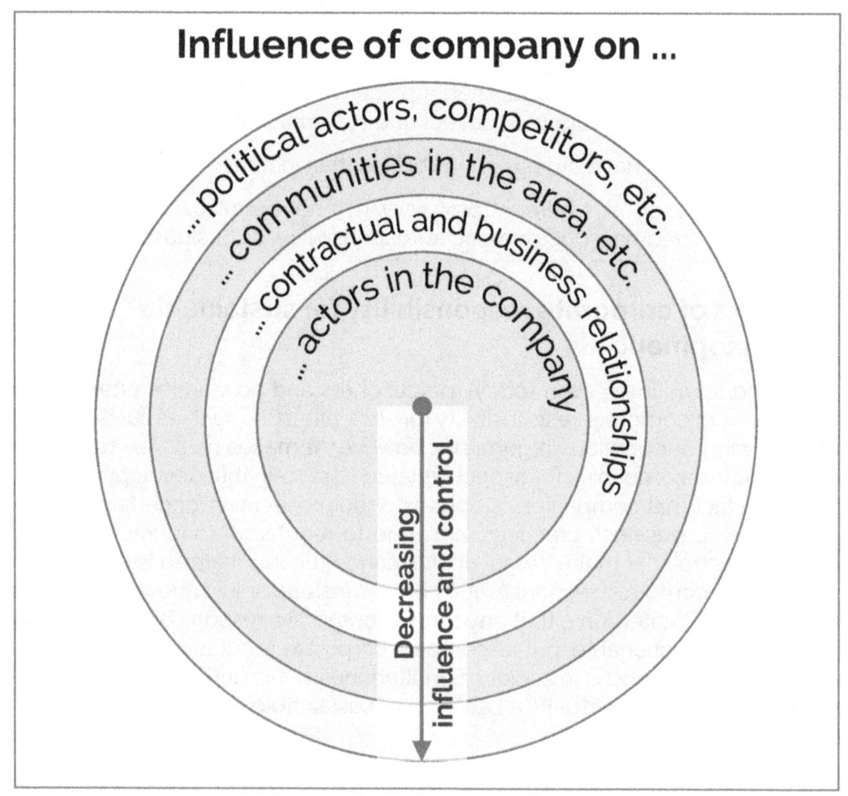

Figure 4: Spheres of corporate influence

In the innermost circle, most decisions within a company (e.g., on working conditions, salaries, or environmental standards) can be made independently and without the influence of actors outside of the company. Although companies have to adhere to certain general requirements such as environmental or social regulations, labor agreements, or industry safety regulations, they have free reign in other decisions. Within its direct sphere of influence, a company can, for example, go beyond legal standards (e.g., paying above minimum wage or exceeding environmental regulations). Following the same logic, companies have to bear immediate responsibility for the negative consequences caused by their business operations.

With increasing external relationships, the influence of companies usually decreases, which also reduces their autonomy to make decisions. In the second circle, decisions cannot be made without considering actors outside of the company who also have an influence on various rights. Think, for example, of suppliers and their influence on their own employees. Even if these suppliers are highly dependent on the company, the ultimate decision to meet or exceed legal standards lies within their immediate sphere of influence. Depending on power structures, however, there might still be a large part of shared responsibility with the purchasing company. In the textile industry nowadays, it is largely a societal (albeit usually not legal) consensus that powerful focal companies—often from developed countries—have, at the very minimum, a shared responsibility for the environmental and social conditions of their suppliers in the Global South.

In the third circle, there are usually no contractual and immediate economic relationships. Corporate influence on aspects of sustainable development is, thus, mostly indirect. A company's influence is usually restricted by a larger number of external relationships and actors. The influence continues to decrease toward the outermost circle where there is usually only an indirect influence, for example, on political actors. Here, companies mostly have no or few possibilities to sanction undesired actions and decisions. However, this picture is not always clear-cut. Sometimes, companies deliberately aim to increase their influence on seemingly distant actors such as politicians through campaign donations and similar measures. Consequently, the relationship with these actors moves further toward the inner circle. Corporate lobbying can also significantly increase political influence to either support or suppress sustainability regulations. In other cases, external actors might generally be weaker, for example, if states rely on private contributions to improve the social situation of their citizens in case of insufficient public finances or weak public institutions.

Task A3-2

This book introduces you to various examples of sustainability and unsustainability in business practice. Fill in the following table with your own specific examples (ideally with company names):

		Dimension of sustainability	
		Social	Ecological
Sphere of influence and responsibility	Sustainable behavior in immediate sphere of influence		
	Sustainable behavior outside core sphere of influence		
	Unsustainable behavior		

Sustainability in business 3: Different spheres of influence at Henkel

The example of the multinational chemical and consumer goods giant, Henkel, and its commitment to the SDGs illustrates not only the variety of activities in sustainability management but also the different spheres of influence. For SDG 3 (Ensure healthy lives and promote well-being for all at all ages), the company defines product safety as well as labor standards and workplace safety as fields of action. These aspects are part of the inner circles involving the company itself and, in part, its suppliers. Thus, they are a core responsibility of the company. The same applies to the company's aim to reduce its water consumption (SDG 6: Ensure availability and sustainable management of water and sanitation for all) or to reduce its CO_2 emissions (SDG 13: Take urgent action to combat climate change and its impacts). Leaning toward a more voluntary responsibility for sustainable development is the company's engagement to procure sustainable palm oil to save the rainforests. The production of palm oil itself is not in the immediate sphere of influence of the company's own operations, because palm oil is purchased as a raw material from external partners. However, the company needs significant amounts of this raw material for many of its products. It, thus, has a comparatively large leverage through its influence on suppliers as well as on the public debate. The company acknowledges this influence by actively advocating for the sustainable production of palm oil through different initiatives. Other engagements for society and for sustainable development are situated in the outer spheres of influence and are of a more voluntary nature. For example, the company's employee volunteering program or its philanthropic activities via various foundations are linked to SDG 1 (End poverty in all its forms everywhere).

Source: Henkel AG & Co. KGaA (n.d.–b); Henkel AG & Co. KGaA (n.d.–a)

A.3.4 The business case for sustainability management

Apart from ethical and moral reasons, one of the most widespread arguments for sustainability management is the so-called business case for sustainability, that is, the assumption that it pays off for a company to be sustainable. If this is the case, advancing sustainability management should be easy, as acting sustainably would then simply be good business practice even without considering the ethical aspects. Indeed, there are plenty of examples of when and why it pays off to be sustainable.

From an overarching risk perspective, the annual Global Risk Report, published by the World Economic Forum, impressively illustrates why companies increasingly consider sustainability an important topic (World Economic Forum, 2021). In its 2021 version, world leaders from business, academia, NGOs, and governments rate four direct sustainability-related issues among the top five risks in terms of their likelihood to occur: extreme weather, climate action failure, human environmental damage, and biodiversity loss. Of those risks with the potentially highest impact, three out of the top five risks are sustainability-related: climate action failure, biodiversity loss, and natural resource crises. Another one of the top five risks in both categories, infectious diseases, is at least indirectly related to sustainability concerns as a loss of natural habitats and biodiversity increases the likelihood of such diseases (e.g., Schmeller et al., 2020). Translated specifically to the business sphere, such risks can be classified into legal and political, physical, reputational, and competitive risks.

Sustainability in research 2: Bansal and Roth's 2000 article on corporate greening

Why do companies go green? Pratima Bansal and Kendall Roth provide answers to this question in their extensive qualitative study from 2000 published in the Academy of Management Journal. Through interviews with 88 managers from the food, oil, automotive, and transport industry, observations, and the analysis of archival material they find that competitiveness, legitimacy, and environmental responsibility particularly motivate companies to implement sustainable initiatives.

The first motivation describes the competitiveness of a company, which is defined as the potential to improve long-term profitability through environmental initiatives such as waste management or source reduction. According to the respondents, an essential competitive advantage could be gained through targeted ecological initiatives. Competitively motivated companies actively use environmentally acceptable processes and products to improve their market position.

Furthermore, legitimacy is considered as a motivating factor for companies. In this context, the legal regulations and the norms of society must be observed to maintain the so-called license to operate. This license denotes the social acceptance of a company. In contrast, environmental responsibility is a motivation based on philanthropic approaches. Respectively motivated companies do not base decisions about environmental initiatives on financial paradigms, but on ethical principles. In such companies, ethical and environmental values are particularly pronounced in top management and the initiatives are usually highly innovative and less imitated.

Bansal and Roth conclude that the following three contextual dimensions determine the motivational characteristics of companies: Issue salience defines the extent of importance attributed to ecological issues. It is influenced by the certainty of ecological impacts, transparency of corporate actions, and emotional issues. Field cohesion determines the intensity of connections between institutions and organizations. Individual concern describes the corporate commitment to environmental responsibility. Companies can show variations in individual motivations and contextual conditions due to different corporate strategies.

The model developed in the study explains when a company adopts which kind of ecologically responsive initiatives according to its individual context and motivational orientation.

Source: Bansal and Roth (2000)

Legal and political risks can stem from uncertainties about potential regulations and governmental interventions. Political actors and regulators might want to mitigate sustainability-related risks that may lead to new regulations as evident, for example, in the worldwide debates around CO2 pricing (see Chapter B.3.2.3). Furthermore, judicial actors could intervene with companies' actions or penalize illegitimate behavior as can be seen from a growing number of climate-related or other sustainability-related lawsuits. Physical risks pose immediate consequences of sustainability-related issues when, for example, extreme weather events have negative implications for certain industries (e.g., agriculture, insurance, or tourism). Reputational risks are often connected to public criticism of companies' seemingly insufficient or illegitimate actions. In recent years, such behavior has increasingly been subject to public outcries, protests, and boycotts (see Chapter B.4.2). Finally, competitive risks surface when companies cannot adequately react to sustainability challenges while competitors have superior products or processes. In this case, outdated products (e.g., high energy-consuming household appliances) may become shelf warmers, energy-intensive processes can lead to cost disadvantages, or potential employees might not be willing to work for an inherently unsustainable company. Thus, in sum, it makes good business sense for companies to have answers on how they deal with such risks.

Sustainability in business 4: Lawsuits against Royal Dutch Shell

In 2021, after a year-long battle in court, environmentalists scored a partial victory when a Dutch court ordered the Nigerian subsidiary of the Dutch oil multinational Royal Dutch Shell to compensate local residents of the Niger Delta. The court ruled that the company is responsible for various oil pipeline leaks in the region. For decades, Shell and other oil multinationals have been accused of insufficient environmental standards in their operation in the fragile ecosystem of the Niger Delta, a region rich in crude oil.

In the same year and also involving Royal Dutch Shell, a Dutch court ordered the company to significantly cut its greenhouse gas emissions by 45 percent until 2030 from 2019 levels. The lawsuit was filed by an environmental NGO and for the first time in history, a court has ordered a company to comply with the Paris Climate Agreement.

Source: Joselow (2021); Peltier and Moses (2021)

However, not only from such a negative and risk-related perspective can sustainability pay off. Any of the mentioned risks can also be regarded as an opportunity if a company is particularly well-suited to deal with these risks and is, thus, ahead of its competition. Many consumers are increasingly willing to consider sustainable alternatives so that sustainability traits can be decisive factors in buying decisions and sometimes even allow for price premiums (C. Wang et al., 2019; see Chapter B.5). Similarly, current and prospective employees often value sustainability and responsibility in companies (see Chapter B.6). Zhao et al. (2022) found, in a meta-analysis of 86 studies, that a positive CSR perception of employees leads to improved organizational trust and identification, which in turn leads to improved organizational commitment, job satisfaction, and turnover intentions. In sum, the business case assumes that a superior sustainability performance has, on the one hand, a positive influence on improving revenues, for example, via better access to markets or product differentiation (Stefan & Paul, 2008); on the other hand, it can reduce costs, for example, of material, energy, or through improved stakeholder relationships and increased labor productivity. It is, thus, not surprising that various meta-analyses confirm that environmental and/or social sustainability performance increases a firm's financial performance in the long run (see Huang, 2021, for an overview).

Despite its prevalence and overall popularity, however, the business case for sustainability is not uncontested (e.g., Barnett, 2019; Crane et al., 2014). Not all sustainability measures pay off in the short term, and sometimes not even in the long term. There are numerous tensions and tradeoffs with which companies have to cope (T. Hahn et al., 2015). Various measures in sustainability management require, for example, substantial upfront investments, which may put pressure on short-term financial objectives. Simultaneously, because benefits of sustainability management are sometimes hard to measure, a (financial) quantification is not always straightforward. On a larger scale, individual organizations usually strive for efficiency and are likely to adopt similar solutions when acting under similar external conditions (e.g., monocultures as efficient means of cultivating agricultural produce). Such a homogenization, however, could lead to a lower resilience of the entire agricultural system due to the loss of diversity. Society is called on to recognize such tradeoffs and tensions and develop solutions to cope with them.

Sustainability in business 5: Cutting the energy bill through green IT – The case of Host Europe

Host Europe is a webhosting company in German-speaking markets. Since energy consumption of modern IT technology is significant and, thus, problematic with regard to issues such as climate change, the company realized several years ago that it has a distinct environmental responsibility. In 2009, it opened a new energy-efficient green data center that consumed significantly less energy compared to other modern data centers at the time. The construction costs were 15 to 20 percent higher than that of comparable data centers due to many energy-saving measures. These measures, however, resulted in 30 percent lower energy consumption. When running at full capacity, the extra costs amortized in about 2.5 years due to reduced energy cost while saving roughly 1,300 tons of CO_2 per year.

Source: R. Hahn (2013)

Furthermore, there are many examples of profitable but concurrently socially harmful, unsustainable, and irresponsible behavior (Wickert & Risi, 2019). In many cases, external costs of economic activities are not internalized (see Chapter B.3.2). It is, thus, advantageous, at least in the short term, for companies to pollute instead of installing costly pollution prevention technologies or relying on less harmful but more expensive processes or materials. In other instances, although corporate wrongdoings might be illegal, corporations are not prosecuted due to weak or missing legal institutions. Finally, many aspects of unsustainability in society cannot be tackled with the sole focus on profitability. Fair wages in many supply chains in the Global South or the highest ecological standards might be desirable from a societal perspective. They are usually not, however, a sensible investment from a purely financial point of view as they often do not offer potential for cost savings or for increased revenues. In its most extreme interpretation, the business case even carries the danger of opportunistic behavior. Sustainable behavior that is reduced to being solely a success factor in business often merely caters to the interest of the most powerful stakeholder, and it might arbitrarily be turned on and off by companies as their financial situation demands.

In sum, sustainability management, building upon the idea of the business case for sustainability, provides important incentives for companies to engage with sustainability and can be an important step toward more sustainable business conduct. However, sustainability management that focuses solely on a narrow interpretation of the business case for sustainability is unlikely to be sufficient to achieve sustainable development, since it reduces sustainability to the purely instrumental perspective of improving the financial performance of a company while largely ignoring any tradeoffs between social or ecological and economic goals. The business case for sustainability cannot prevent the various forms of corporate irresponsibility, such as illegal activities or exploiting weak institutions. Moreover, it does not lead to sustainable behavior in situations when it does not (yet) pay off.

KEY TAKEAWAYS

- Sustainable development is not a law of nature, so it needs normative-ethical reasoning.
- The golden rule and the categorical imperative along with various aspects of justice provide ethical arguments for sustainable development.
- Individual and organizational arguments provide ground for sustainability management of companies.
- Companies often have extensive leeway in their decisions and might have superior resources that elicit an increase in responsibility.
- A company's responsibilities can be differentiated according to its spheres of influence.
- Often, sustainability management pays off, thus, constituting the business case for sustainability management.
- The business case for sustainability management reduces sustainability to a purely instrumental perspective and cannot prevent certain forms of irresponsible behavior.

A.4 Sustainability strategies

LEARNING GOALS

After reading this chapter you will be able to ...

- ... discuss why a decoupling of human development from ecological impact is necessary for sustainable development.
- ... explain the strategy, opportunities, and challenges of eco-efficiency for sustainable development.
- ... explain the strategy, opportunities, and challenges of eco-effectiveness for sustainable development.
- ... explain the strategy, opportunities, and challenges of sufficiency for sustainable development.
- ... explain different types of rebound effects and why they could lead to rising overall impacts despite increased eco-efficiency, eco-effectiveness, or sufficiency.
- ... critically reflect why a combination of all three strategies might be necessary to achieve sustainable development.

Introduction to Chapter A.3: Screencast
Watch an introduction to the chapter here:

A.4.1 Decoupling of human development from ecological impact

As illustrated earlier, the road to sustainability can only be successfully taken if intra- and intergenerational justice are pursued simultaneously. Achieving both these goals, however, has proven to be difficult. In the past, countries that improved their peoples' standard of living simultaneously usually increased their ecological footprint. Almost all countries with a high HDI use significantly more natural resources per capita than countries with a medium or low HDI, and they usually use natural resources beyond their regeneration capacity as illustrated in Chapter A.1.2 and depicted in Figure 5. Thus, their state of development can at best be termed as "sustainable" based on the understanding of weak sustainability (see Chapter A.2.2).

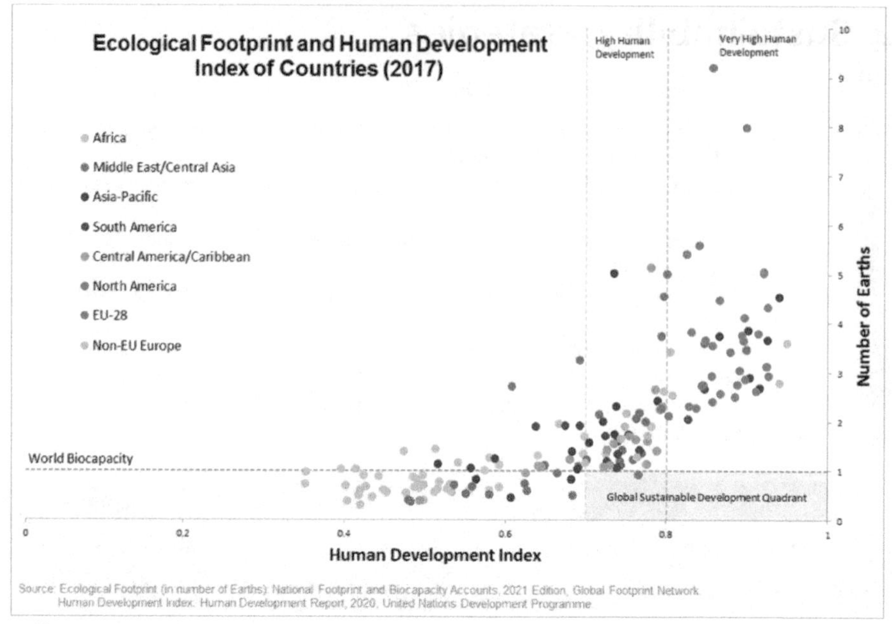

Figure 5: Human development and ecological footprint (Source: Global Footprint Network https://www.footprintnetwork.org/our-work/sustainable-development/, accessed Feb. 26, 2021, reproduced with permission)

This implies that we need to decouple human development from the ecological impact caused and the consumption of resources if we seriously consider all elements of sustainable development in more than just its version of weak sustainability. To achieve such a decoupling, three basic sustainability strategies are often discussed: eco-efficiency, eco-effectiveness, and sufficiency.

Sustainability in society 6: The complex relationship between growth, income, and happiness

The call for a decoupling of human development from ecological impact may have originated in the seemingly everlasting quest for economic growth. From an economic perspective, economic growth helps to increase income at the individual and aggregate levels. In a growing economy, there is less risk of distributional conflict, making it easier for the state to supply public goods. Furthermore, people in richer countries tend to be happier than those in poor countries so that it seems natural to improve wealth through economic growth to achieve greater happiness of the people.

However, the full picture is more complicated. Although people with higher income are happier than those with lower income, raising the income of everybody does not lead to an increase in average life satisfaction—a situation known as the "Easterlin Paradox." An explanation for this paradox is that the perceived life satisfaction or happiness of a person depends on his or her income in proportion to some reference level, for example, to the income of other people or to his or her own income in the past or future. To put it simply, if you earn less than your neighbor, you are less happy no matter how much you earn, and if you earn more today than you did yesterday, you tend to be happier. However, the paradox applies only to wealthy nations; in other words, poor nations profit with a generally higher level of happiness from increased income as people can more easily afford basic needs and live with less economic anxiety.

This begs the question: How and for whom should economic growth be achieved to be sustainable? As former UN Secretary General Ban Ki-Moon paraphrased: "For most of the last century, economic growth was fueled by what seemed to be a certain truth: the abundance of natural resources. We mined our way to growth. We burned our way to prosperity. We believed in consumption without consequences. Those days are gone. ... the old model is more than obsolete. Over time, that model ... is a global suicide pact." (UN Secretary General, 2011)

Sources: Easterlin (2017); Kahneman and Deaton (2010); Weimann et al. (2015)

Sustainability in research 3: Hart's 1995 article on a natural-resource-based view of the firm

The scale of human activities on earth undoubtedly has caused ecological problems. In his 1995 article "A natural resource-based view of the firm", Stuart L. Hart criticizes traditional management approaches for disregarding the limitations imposed by the natural environment and thus calls for a paradigm shift in strategic management. He argues that a resource-based business orientation, which includes the natural environment, can create both competitive advantages and responsible interaction between businesses and the biophysical environment. In his conceptual article, published in the Academy of Management Review, he discusses three strategic capabilities to create corporate resources that are interdependent and can reinforce each other through interference.

The first strategy addresses pollution prevention and includes the reduction of emissions, dirty effluents, and waste. Minimization can be achieved through control mechanisms or general prevention, whereby companies save costs through efficient use of materials. Consequently, this strategy focuses on capabilities in production and operations to optimize supply chains for greater efficiency. It represents a tacit resource, as it refers to process optimizations within the company and is particularly labor intensive. As such, this resource is not obvious to external stakeholders. Without the legitimacy of external stakeholders, however, it is difficult for the company to secure its competitive advantage. Hart therefore argues that it might be necessary to make the internal processes more transparent.

The second strategy addresses product stewardship, in which the entire life cycle of a product should be structured as sustainable as possible. The aim is to reduce the use of nonrenewable materials and to utilize renewable materials only in accordance with their regenerative capacity. This strategy enables companies to conquer new business areas, minimize risks in terms of liability, and create new products. The competitive advantage exists in exclusive rights of use because of revolutionary ideas and political regulation, creating barriers for other companies. It requires complex and intense collaboration within the company as well as the integration of external stakeholders into the development process.

The third strategy addresses sustainable development holistically and involves long-term access to future markets in developing countries. Successful competition depends on the establishment of environmentally friendly technologies through long-term investment and engagement. These investments and activities can result in rare, firm specific resources but it might require broader collaboration in the redesign of systems so that, for example, customers broadly accept new technologies and standards. According to Hart, the strategy of sustainable development deserves specific focus because it paves the way for increased sustainability according to the Brundtland definition and it enables the development of new fields of business. Companies can potentially draw significant sales volumes from such new markets and simultaneously improve their ecological balance. Interestingly, despite referring to sustainable development in general, Hart focuses on ecological aspects and only occasionally touches upon social aspects. In later iterations of the natural-resource-based view of the firm, Hart and his coauthors enriched this perspective to cover aspects of sustainable development more holistically (e.g., Hart & Dowell, 2011).

Source: Hart (1995)

A.4.2 Eco-efficiency

The general eco-efficiency approach aims at relative improvements through the quantitative reduction of resources and emissions in products or processes from "cradle to grave" (i.e., from raw material extraction at the beginning of a product life cycle to the final disposal at the end of the cycle). If successful, less resources are needed or less emissions are generated to produce the same amount of goods and services compared to a previous status quo (thus, easing the environmental burden for a constant level of consumption) or more goods and services can be produced with the same amount of resources and emissions (thus, enabling development without further deteriorating the environment). Eco-efficiency is mainly achieved through technological solutions and innovations either at the product level (e.g., more energy-efficient electrical household consumer devices) or during the production stage (e.g., more resource- or energy-efficient processes), aiming at the "technology" factor of the IPAT equation (see Chapter A.2.1). Possible ways to achieve eco-efficiency include technological and organizational progress, recycling of materials, and avoidance of emissions. There are numerous examples of successful eco-efficiency innovations such as energy-efficient light bulbs, water-efficient dishwashers, or resource-efficient production processes.

Eco-efficiency is often praised for its enormous potential to decouple development from resource consumption. As early as the 1990s, academics described the potential of eco-efficiency measures to improve the efficiency of resource and energy consumption by a factor of 4 (Weizsäcker et al., 1997) and, later, by a factor of 10 or higher (Angrick et al., 2013). The strategy is comparably easy to implement in the corporate domain because companies regularly aim toward the efficient use of various (especially financial) resources and because technological innovations are an established means of progress in many firms.

However, there is widespread criticism regarding the usefulness and relevancy of efficiency measures for sustainable development. For example, improved eco-efficiency, by means of increased output with constant inputs, would not result in any overall decrease in environmental pressures (although global consumption could be increased without further environmental impact). Moreover, products or processes that actually need their eco-efficiency improved tend to be more harmful. In the case of inherently unsustainable systems, such as private fossil fuel-based transport systems, eco-efficiency may stop or at least decelerate the progress of structural changes toward a more sustainable system if the eco-efficient "solutions" are perceived as sustainable. The quest for sustainability through eco-efficiency may well prove to be a conservative measure to preserve capital stock from an imminent change and could be a barrier to more fundamental changes.

Sustainability in business 6: How PUMA's "Clever little bag" failed

Packaging has a significant environmental impact. PUMA, a leader in shoes and sportswear, aimed to improve its environmental footprint and recognized packaging as an important lever. At the beginning of the new millennium, the company partnered with the design firm fuseproject to create the "clever little bag." Ordinary shoe boxes usually have no proposed second use, and disposed boxes contribute to millions of tons of waste each year. The clever little bag combined a reusable bag with a disposable piece of cardboard inside, without any printing or assembly, so that it could be easily recycled. The vision was that the tens of millions of shoes shipped in this bag would lead to 8,500 tons less paper consumed and, with this, large savings in the amounts of consumed electricity, water and fuel oil. While it received numerous innovation and design awards, the clever little bag was only seen on the market for a few years. In 2014, PUMA returned to traditional shoe boxes, now made almost entirely from recycled paper. The company claimed that the main reason for this decision was that retailers and consumers did not fully accept the new packaging concept. The clever little bag was apparently not as easy to stack compared to traditional shoe boxes. Furthermore, customers could not repack the shoes as easily after trying them in stores or at home.

Sources: dpa (2014); fuseproject (2021)

Despite this, eco-efficiency can be an important instrument for sustainable development. Efficiency improvements that decrease the negative impacts of products or processes below the regeneration capacity of the ecological environment would enable more sustainable use of such systems (provided that rebound effects can be prevented, see Chapter A.4.5). Nevertheless, it is hardly imaginable that a truly sustainable use of the Earth's carrying capacity is possible with inherently harmful products and processes or finite resources (e.g., fossil energy). Therefore, the potential of the eco-efficiency approach lies mainly in its relative ease of implementation. The likelihood of success is high because eco-efficiency improvements are based on existing technologies and do not need radical (and often time-consuming) innovations. This leads to immediate improvements via incremental rather than total technological changes (W. Sachs & Santarius, 2007).

A.4.3 Eco-effectiveness

Other than eco-efficiency, eco-effectiveness (or consistency) aims at an absolute instead of a relative decoupling of economic development from environmental burden. The idea is, thus, to not only marginally improve the efficiency of products or processes but also to organize economic processes entirely without environmental impacts, such as waste or emissions. Eco-effectiveness aims for a qualitative change of material flow through fundamental structural change toward closed-loop systems (e.g., Braungart et al., 2007). In such closed-loop systems, each end-product of a consumption or production process serves as a basis for other processes resulting, ideally, in no wastage or emissions. Although the aim is to imitate the eco-effectiveness of natural ecosystems, even if this is not entirely possible, the approach at least means that harmful substances are retained in closed systems or are substituted by less harmful substances. This circular approach is also often referred to as "cradle-to-cradle" and as a counterpart to the linear "cradle-to-grave" thinking.

Faces of sustainability 4: William McDonough and Michael Braungart

The American William McDonough and the German Michael Braungart, co-authored the book "Cradle to Cradle: Remaking the Way We Make Things" (McDonough & Braungart, 2002), one of the most important environmental manifestos of modern times. McDonough and Braungart provide a vivid example of true sustainability benefiting from interdisciplinary cooperation: McDonough is an architect and Braungart is a chemist. The two visionary environmental thinkers argue that industrial systems can be in harmony with the ecological environment if biological and technological nutrients circulate within closed-loop cycles. The two advocates of a circular economy are well known beyond the sustainability sphere as "heroes of the environment."

Sources: Bedford and Morhaim (2002); Lacayo (2007)

Closed-loop systems can emerge in the form of biological or technological loops (Ellen MacArthur Foundation, 2021) as illustrated in Figure 6. In the former, biological materials are produced or farmed and then processed to goods. After being consumed or used, these good finally end up in the biosphere again as biological waste products, which close the loop. Examples are compostable clothing, houses made from organic building materials, etc. In the latter, closing the loop requires technical instead of biological processes. Therefore, recyclability of materials is ideally already included in the design phase of products. This means, for example, allowing easy disassembling or maintenance and refurbishment. After the use phase, products are disassembled. The disassembled parts are then either used again in new products or recycled to be used in entirely new production processes. If it is feasible to develop and implement such kinds of products, they provide the opportunity to fully decouple growth and development from environmental impact by aligning nature with technology.

Sustainability in business 7: Circular economy at Interface

Interface Inc., a company that produces modular carpets largely for commercial but also for residential customers, is one of the pioneers in the circular economy. For 25 years, they have been actively seeking sustainability innovations for their products. They introduced, for example, carpets that did not need to be glued to the surface to enable full recycling, yarn made mainly from bio-based content, and carpets made from discarded fishing nets. Furthermore, they also experimented with service innovations such as leasing instead of selling carpets to clients, and they are pioneers of the Life Cycle Sustainability Assessment method (see Chapter C.6.2) through which the environmental footprint of products and processes along their entire life cycle is analyzed.

Sources: Lampikoski (2012); Stubbs and Cocklin (2008)

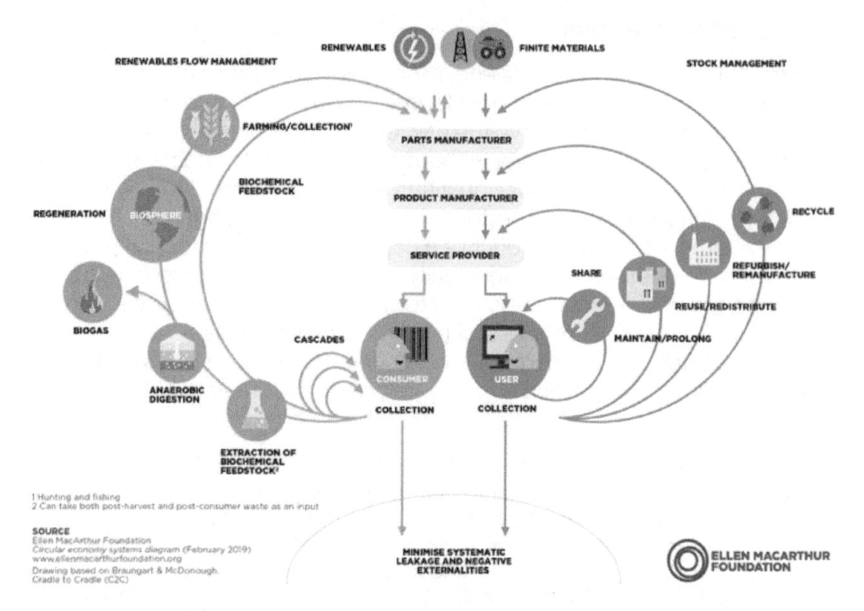

Figure 6: Technical and biological materials in the circular economy (Copyright © Ellen MacArthur Foundation, 2019; https://ellenmacarthurfoundation.org/circular-economy-diagram, accessed Oct. 1, 2021, reproduced with permission)

There are, however, some caveats. The idea of technological loops implicitly suggests that materials can be reused indefinitely. Yet, even supposedly fully recyclable materials such as metal have a limited lifespan due to various unrecoverable losses during the cycle (Helbig et al., 2020). Furthermore, closed biological or technological loops usually require fundamental changes in terms of extensive technological innovations and organizational transformations, usually beyond the boundaries of a single company (Hansen & Schmitt, 2020). Industrial symbiosis networks (e.g., Domenech & Davies, 2011) provide complex examples of (at least partly) closed-loop systems that illuminate the opportunities of such approaches while simultaneously illustrating their often significant technological and organizational complexity. In industrial symbiosis networks, companies in a certain region collaborate by exchanging material and energy. The residual or by-product of one company becomes an input in another company, thereby reducing the intake of virgin raw materials and the output of waste. There are various best practice examples (the Danish Kalundbord Symbiosis, the Finnish Industrial Symbiosis System, or the Circular Basque in Spain) which, however, also illustrate the complexity of the respective networks and the high level of technological and organizational sophistication necessary to sustain such systems. Furthermore, innovations that are often at the center of eco-effectiveness thinking are, by definition, the introduction of something new. Because they always include uncertainties about the future side effects, their ecological, economic, and social impacts cannot be entirely assessed ex ante. If it were possible, however, to develop and implement truly "safe" innovations (i.e., those that can be reversed or adapted, if necessary), eco-efficiency would make an essential contribution to sustainable development.

A.4.4 Sufficiency

Eco-efficiency and eco-effectiveness are mainly driven by technological innovations. Sufficiency, however, is a behavior-based concept and aims for appropriate levels and forms of consumption (e.g., Bocken & Short, 2016). Therefore, sufficiency tries to influence IPAT's "affluence" factor via the aspiration level of consumption. A sustainable lifestyle following this strategy reduces the absolute amount of consumption (i.e., consuming less) and/

or changes the way consumption is performed (i.e., consuming differently), thus, essentially asking: "How much and what forms of consumption are sufficient?" Both approaches should lead to absolute resource savings, as illustrated in Figure 7. Sufficiency, in terms of a quantitative reduction of consumption, requires a downgrading of individual aspiration levels. If performed by large proportions of the population, this would lead to reduced overall resource intensity, especially in developed countries with their resource-intensive lifestyle (see again Chapter A.1.2 and A.2.1). Sufficiency, in terms of a qualitative change of consumption patterns, aims at an adjustment of needs and/or a substitution of unsustainable with sustainable (or at least less harmful) forms of consumption. Examples include longevity of consumer goods, reuse of products, and relying on services instead of owning products (e.g., through new business models in the so-called sharing economy, see Chapter B.6.3), increased regional perspective (e.g., in supply chains or for food products), or moderated mobility (e.g., regional holidays rather than air travel abroad).

Type of change	Quantitative reduction	Qualitative change
Main lever	Level of consumption	Forms of consumption
Aim	Reduced individual and consequently aggregate consumption	Substitution of unsustainable consumption with more sustainable forms

Figure 7: Classification of sufficiency approaches

Problems with the implementation of sufficiency measures arise when unsustainable consumption patterns are deeply anchored in the consumer's mind and also in businesses' mindsets. Ownership of a product itself, for instance, can serve as an elementary way of needs satisfaction (e.g., prestige, autonomy, comfort) and therefore prevent changing the resulting consumer demand. Furthermore, as with eco-efficiency, there is also the problem of dealing with inherently unsustainable goods. A reduced consumption of these goods would only result in incremental savings of products that should be avoided entirely. This raises the question of whether a mere decrease in consumption is enough to achieve sustainable development.

Sufficiency, nevertheless, may make an important contribution to sustainable development. The direct impact of successful sufficiency efforts can relieve environmental pressures in a similar way to the eco-efficiency approach. In contrast to the unpredictable outcomes of technology-based innovations, sufficiency measures can achieve reliable and measurable outcomes. Sufficiency strategies can also play an important role in areas where technological solutions are limited by the effects of overcompensation, because they aim for an immediate reduction of consumption.

Sustainability in business 8: Sufficiency approaches at Patagonia

The outdoor clothing and gear company Patagonia is often praised for its sustainability efforts. The company offers extensive repair services to extend the life of their products. Customers can opt for self-repair with various tutorials, receive extensive product care instructions, or send their gear to Patagonia or visit a company store to have it repaired by professionals. Customers are also encouraged to trade in used clothing and gear if they are not going to use them any longer. Used items are then sold as second-hand items, and the original customer receives credit to be used for new purchases. These efforts culminated in a now famous print advertisement, "Don't buy this jacket" in The New York Times on November, 25, 2011. In the Black Friday ad, Patagonia asked potential customers "to buy less and to reflect before you spend a dime on this jacket or anything else." The ad came with a detailed list of environmental burdens of a new jacket and the company's options to reduce, repair, reuse, and recycle. Thus, Patagonia is a perfect example of employing more sufficient business models.

A.4.5 The rebound effect

Unfortunately, any of the strategies could be subject to the so-called "rebound" (also "boomerang") effect. This effect describes a situation of stagnating or rising overall impacts despite increased efficiency, effectiveness, or sufficiency (Figge et al., 2014). The original and iconic Volkswagen Beetle, which was produced for decades until the end of the last millennium, for example, consumed around seven liters of gasoline per 100 km (or 30 miles per gallon) in the 1950s. Although, generally, much more fuel efficient, the Volkswagen New Beetle, which was produced in the first two decades of the new millennium, consumed roughly the same amount of fuel—a good example of this rebound effect. Instead of reducing the overall fuel consumption, the improved efficiency of the modern engine was used to drive a much more luxurious car with air conditioning, more horse power, increased safety features, etc.

Figure 8 illustrates the different types of such rebound effects. Improved efficiency or effectiveness often lead to cost savings if fewer resources are necessary to produce or operate a given product. These cost savings, in turn, often lead to a disproportionate growth in overall demand for goods and services if the reduced costs are associated with lower prices. Sometimes, old products are used along with new ones as the example of modern information and communication technology has shown. Such innovations have not led to predicted savings in paper use or the overall volume of transport; rather, the reverse has occurred (W. Sachs & Santarius, 2007). However, even if a complete substitution of unsustainable products was possible, the question of how to dispose of these products remains. The resulting ecological burdens have to be subtracted from the sustainability advantages of the new products in order to draw a fair comparison with the older solutions. The same applies to qualitative sufficiency when people save money by relying on shared services instead of owning expensive products such as cars. If the respective savings are spent, say, for future air travel, the net effect for the environment might well be negative.

	Growth effect	**Technological effect**	**Psychological effect**
Exemplified course of action	Cost saving as result of sustainability strategies lead to increasing consumption	Positive contributions of innovations are offset by larger negative effects in areas that have not received attention before	People buy disproportionately greater amounts of a product because it is supposedly environment friendly
Effect	Negative long-term impact > positive initial savings		

Figure 8: Different types of rebound effects

The same pattern might occur in a psychological dimension when improved eco-efficiency, eco-effectiveness, or sufficiency induces people to buy more products or products that they do not need just because they are supposedly eco-friendlier than before. Furthermore, the introduction of a partly sustainable product or process might negatively impact other aspects of sustainability, which have not been considered before, leading to technological rebound effects. The automotive industry, for example, increasingly substitutes metal with lightweight synthetic and composite materials to help improve fuel efficiency. However, such materials might cause difficulties during the production and disposal processes (e.g., if production requires hazardous substances and/or if they are difficult to disassemble for recycling). In sum, because the risk of overcompensation is real in any of the sustainability strategies, true sustainability efforts always need to consider the larger picture of production and consumption.

Sustainability in society 7: Jevons Paradox

One of the first descriptions of the rebound effect in modern times is attributed to William Stanley Jevons in his book "The Coal Question" (Jevons, 1865). Jevons described the fact that in 19th century England, coal was increasingly being used despite the fact that each new generation of coal-powered steam engines was more efficient than the previous one. With the improved efficiency, coal as an energy source became more reasonable and the steam engine itself was introduced in several industries as well as in the transport sector. Overall, the efficiency gains were offset by the increase in consumption. This effect (or paradox) is a logical outcome because a decrease in the cost of a product (here: coal) increases the quantity demanded.

Sources: Alcott (2005); Polimeni et al. (2015)

A.4.6 Strategy combinations and hybrid approaches

Given the different opportunities and obstacles of the three strategies, an isolated pursuit of any one of these approaches seems to offer only limited chances of success. A combination of strategies might be needed depending on the respective products, production and consumption patterns, cultural contexts, and so on. Eco-efficiency serves as a strategy that has enduring importance as these measures tend to be implemented relatively easily and could potentially be successful. Sufficiency (with its focus on individual behavior) and eco-effectiveness (with its innovation approach) could potentially enable an economy in harmony with nature. Therefore, all strategies are essential for the sustainable development of a still growing global population. They affect different aspects of anthropogenic impacts on the environment. Thus, a combination of strategies seems the best option for decoupling human development from ecological impact.

In this regard, the IPAT equation (see Chapter A.2.1) illustrates the different leverages of all approaches. Successful eco-efficiency and eco-effectiveness measures positively contribute to a lower overall impact via a reduction of the "technology" factor. Sufficiency measures may similarly improve the "affluence" factor of human consumption and production. None of the three strategies has a direct impact on the "population" factor. Here, indirect effects might be possible if improved intragenerational justice would lead to poverty alleviation. Reduced levels of extreme poverty in developing countries could positively influence the "population" factor by reducing the need to have many children.

Apart from a parallel pursuit of different strategies for different scenarios, some products or processes provide examples of hybrid approaches that combine different elements of the strategies simultaneously. A handful of companies in the clothing industry, for example, now experiment with renting out or leasing their products (especially long-lasting items such as jeans). These items are designed and produced to last and, once the customers return them, are refurbished and rented out again. This is in line with the idea of making qualitative sufficiency changes in the form of consumption. Companies can simultaneously sell their clothing to customers, while offering to take back the items, once they are worn out, so that they can be recycled by processing and reusing them as raw materials for new products. The latter process contains elements of the technical loop of the eco-effectiveness strategy.

Another example is the cascade use of wood (Vis et al., 2016). Solid wood, as a raw material, can first be used as a building material for houses or furniture. At the end of the product's life cycle, the solid wood waste is used to produce veneers, which, in turn, are further used as chipboards and later as wood fiber panels. This downward cascade of wood improves the utilization of each tree and, thus, enhances resource efficiency. At the end of the product life cycle, the remaining material can be burned to produce energy. The wood ash may then be used as fertilizer, which closes the cycle, resembling the biological loop of eco-effectiveness.

Task A4-1

Find a product or process in the areas of eco-efficiency, eco-effectiveness, and sufficiency, respectively. Explain why these products or processes qualify as an eco-efficient, eco-effective, or sufficient solution. How much does the product or process contribute to sustainable development? Could this product or process be prone to a rebound effect? If so, which type of rebound effect and why?

KEY TAKEAWAYS

- Eco-efficiency aims at relative improvements through quantitative reduction of resources and emissions in products or processes from cradle to grave.
- Eco-effectiveness aims at an absolute decoupling of economic development from environmental burden through closed loops from cradle to cradle.
- Sufficiency is a behavior-based concept that aims for appropriate levels and forms of consumption.
- The rebound effect describes a situation of stagnating or even rising overall impacts despite increased efficiency, effectiveness, or sufficiency.
- A combination of strategies or hybrid approaches might be needed to achieve decoupling depending on the respective products, production and consumption patterns, cultural context, etc.

B. Stakeholder perspectives on sustainability management

Sustainability management potentially has an impact on many different actors in society. For example, on employees through environmental and social standards at work, on customers through the sustainability or unsustainability of product offers, or on civil society organizations through the sustainability projects they conduct in cooperation with companies. Furthermore, various societal actors influence the way companies approach questions of sustainable development and implement sustainability management. Some customers, for example, might be willing to pay a price premium for sustainable product alternatives while others do not care about sustainability. Similarly, some employees might prefer to work for a company who cares about societal issues while others do not, and civil society organizations might put public pressure on companies to enhance their standards and name and shame those who behave irresponsibly. The potential mutual influences between different actors, so-called stakeholders, and companies are thus manifold. Therefore, Part B of this book covers sustainability management from a stakeholder perspective and starts with illuminating the general concepts of stakeholder management. It then delves deeper into the relationships between companies and governmental actors, civil society, investors, consumers, and employees, respectively.

B.1 Stakeholder management

LEARNING GOALS

After reading this chapter you will be able to ...

- ... explain who stakeholders are and explain how different stakeholders can have an impact on companies and vice versa.
- ... distinguish internal from external and primary from secondary stakeholders.
- ... differentiate descriptive, instrumental, normative, and integrative stakeholder theory.
- ... discuss why legitimacy is important for companies and how stakeholders might influence legitimacy.
- ... apply a three-step approach of stakeholder management.
- ... categorize stakeholders according to their power, legitimacy, and urgency.
- ... explain the differences of nine categories of latent, expectant, and definite stakeholders and how companies can manage these.

Introduction to Chapter B.1: Screencast
Watch an introduction to the chapter here:

B.1.1 Introduction to stakeholder management

In his 1984 book "Strategic Management: A Stakeholder Approach," Robert Edward Freeman describes stakeholders as "any group or individual who can affect or is affected by the achievement of the organisation's objectives" (Freeman, 1984, p. 46). This resonates well with the idea of a company's sphere of influence discussed in Chapter A.3.3. Stakeholders can thus be individual persons, formal or informal groups and organizations, institutions, societies, and even more elusive entities such as the natural environment. This already illustrates why stakeholders are of central concern in sustainability management: As we will argue throughout Part B of this book, stakeholders have an impact on whether, how, and why companies engage with sustainability management and how this, in turn, can affect different stakeholders. On the one hand, various stakeholders have an influence on a company's operations. For example, customers can actively seek sustainable product alternatives, employees might want to work for a company with a decent reputation for CSR, and investors increasingly include some form of sustainability performance in their assessments. Stakeholders can pick up environmental or social issues and convey them to companies through public pressure, direct or indirect political power, boycotts, financial pressure, and so on. If, however, stakeholders do not care about sustainable development, companies might feel less inclined to improve their sustainability management. Sometimes companies even refrain from talking about their sustainability initiatives in order not to be perceived as being (too) green or social or to avoid accusations of greenwashing (Carlos & Lewis, 2018; see also Chapter C.1.4). Sometimes, stakeholders can even prevent companies from becoming more sustainable if, for example, certain regulations or incentives hamper progress in sustainability management (e.g., state subsidies for incumbent technologies and companies which might be less sustainable than alternatives).

On the other hand, a company's operations often also have an influence on a variety of stakeholders so that a company might have some moral obligations to respect stakeholder aspirations (see again Chapter A.3.2) or it could experience some external pressure to respect stakeholder expectations. For example, employees expect good salaries and working conditions, suppliers demand fair treatment and prompt payment, or pressure groups advocate for environmental protection and social standards.

Faces of sustainability 5: Robert Edward Freeman

R. Edward Freeman is best known for his work on stakeholder management. His 1984 book on "Strategic Management: A Stakeholder Approach" (reissued in 2010) soon became a classic and has influenced business scholars and practitioners alike. With more than 40,000 citations on Google Scholar, it is one of the most widely cited academic books on any aspect of management. He is an advocate of integrative stakeholder thinking, and his thoughts have redefined our understanding of good management practices and the diverse set of relationships that define management. R. Edward Freeman holds a PhD in philosophy and is currently the Elis and Signe Olsson Professor of Business Administration at the Darden Graduate School of Business Administration, University of Virginia. In 2001, he received the Pioneer Award for Lifetime Achievement by the World Resources Institute and the Aspen Institute.

Sources: Freeman (2014); UVA Darden School of Business (2021)

Any given organization usually has a plethora of different stakeholders whose demands might be in conflict with each other. This is why holistic stakeholder management is a very complex task. Shareholders, for instance, sometimes seek short-term profits and could thus be reluctant to support a company's plans to pay higher wages to staff. Similarly, the decision to outsource production capacities is likely to be viewed differently by employees and (potential) suppliers. Furthermore, satisfying stakeholder needs often requires the use of scarce resources such as time or money so that often not all needs of all stakeholder groups can be met. To be able to manage those different stakeholder interests, it is helpful to distinguish and classify different types of stakeholders. For that reason, stakeholders are often classified into internal versus external and primary versus secondary stakeholders, as illustrated in Figure 9.

- Internal vs. external stakeholders: Just as the name suggests, internal stakeholders are those within a company like owners or shareholders, employees, and managers. External stakeholders are outside of a company such as suppliers, customers, creditors, local communities, or governmental institutions. Depending on the perspective of analysis, the distinction of internal versus external stakeholders is not necessarily bound to a company but can also, for example, be made for projects. In this case, stakeholders can be external to a project but internal to a company (e.g., employees of a company who do not work on a specific project in this company). Thus, internal stakeholders are usually directly involved with the respective entity. That does not mean, however, that external stakeholders are per se less important. On the contrary, most companies or projects cannot succeed without external stakeholders.
- Primary vs. secondary stakeholders: Primary stakeholders are directly affected by a company's operations and thus have a major interest in its activities. Without reasonable support from their primary stakeholders, no company can survive over a longer period of time as they have a direct influence on the business activities. These stakeholders are rather easy to identify as they usually have a clear, often financial connection to a company. Typical examples are employees, customers, shareholders, or suppliers and distributors. All other stakeholders who have no direct interest or formal claim, but some form of reasonable influence, are categorized as secondary stakeholders. Here, competitors, civil society organizations, governmental institutions, trade unions, local communities, or the media are typical examples. These stakeholders are not directly linked to the business activities and are thus usually less important than direct stakeholders. Nevertheless, secondary stakeholders can have a potentially strong influence but they are often less visible due to their indirect connections. Sometimes, primary and secondary stakeholders are also referred to as direct and indirect stakeholders with largely the same reasoning.

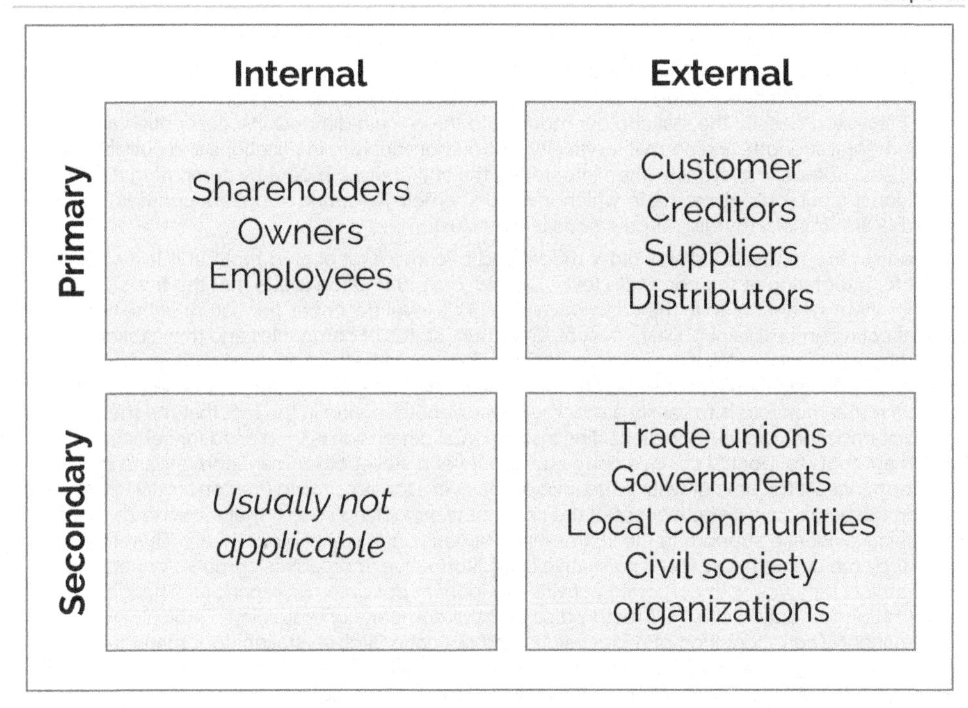

Figure 9: Typical exemplary stakeholder classifications

Apart from asking what stakeholders are and how they can be classified, we can also ask why companies should care about them. The former question is at the core of so-called descriptive and empirical stakeholder theory. This line of stakeholder theory focuses on how companies are managed and on the identification of relevant stakeholders (see Hörisch et al., 2014, or Donaldson & Preston, 1995, for an overview of different streams of stakeholder theory). The latter question (why should companies care?) is at the core of instrumental, normative, and integrative stakeholder theory.

Instrumental stakeholder theory is similar in its assumptions to the business case for sustainability (see Chapter A.3.4) as it puts the company's financial goals in the center of thinking. Stakeholder management in this perspective is a means to achieve these goals and is subject to criticism similar to the business case for sustainability. A self-interested pursuit of profit is not necessarily a responsible conduct (Spitzeck, 2013). Some stakeholders might not have a strong enough voice to express and enforce their claims so that satisfying such needs would not be instrumental for a company's success. Many of such claims, however, might be perfectly appropriate from an ethical point of view, such as upholding human rights in supply chains in countries with weak legal institutions and ensuring decent working conditions and wages. In its extreme interpretation, instrumental stakeholder theory would only consider such claims once they become relevant for a company's profit, for example, through consumer boycotts or intensified regulations.

Normative stakeholder theory instead puts the stakeholders themselves at the center of thinking and asks for the purpose of business in society. It thus brings a moral (instead of instrumental) perspective to stakeholder theory. This approach potentially considers all stakeholder claims in business decision making. Such an inclusion of virtually all stakeholder interests in business operations, however, is practically not feasible as it would require enormous resources and it is not always possible to meet conflicting stakeholder demands.

Sustainability in research 4: Donaldson and Preston's 1995 article on stakeholder theory

In their conceptual article "The stakeholder theory of the corporation: Concepts, evidence, and implications" published in 1995 in the Academy of Management Review, Thomas Donaldson and Lee E. Preston classify the stakeholder model into three main dimensions: descriptive accuracy, instrumental strength, and normative validity. The authors analyze implications and possible complexities a company may face when integrating the stakeholder model by comparing it with the traditional input-output model in which investors, employees, and suppliers contribute inputs which a firm transforms into outputs benefiting its customers.

Already in the 1990s, the stakeholder model had become a respected tool but it lacked a concept for integration at the corporate level. Donaldson and Preston argue that the basis of stakeholder theory is anchored in the descriptive level. This level describes the nature of the company by reflecting and explaining past, present, and future states of companies and their stakeholders. Thereby, a distinct model of the company as an institution with structures and processes emerges. Descriptive justifications for stakeholder theory lie in the fact that managers apparently accept in practice that their role is to satisfy a wider set of stakeholders and in the fact that the theory is an implicit basis for laws and sanctions. The instrumental dimension is then used for selecting management tools to identify positive correlations between stakeholder management and business performance. At the time of writing the article, however, Donaldson and Preston argued that studies on the actual cost-effectiveness of the concept were lacking so that there was no compelling empirical evidence supporting the instrumental dimension of stakeholder theory. Therefore, they saw the core of the theory at the normative level. Normative approaches compare general norms and ethical behavior with corporate activities to identify possible discrepancies. The idea is that implications for action can be structured so that the company operates in an ethically responsible manner. The recognition of moral values and obligations gives stakeholder management its fundamental normative basis. Donaldson and Preston posited that the most thoughtful analyses of why stakeholder management is inevitably linked to corporate performance tend to rely on normative arguments.

The findings of Donaldson and Preston imply that an integration of the stakeholder model into the corporate concept can positively affect both the social and the economic development of a company. The model is highly relevant for sustainability management as it not only aims at long-term economic existence, but also integrates strategies of social development. The authors defined the normative level as the fundamental core of stakeholder theory, implying that future management tools should include ethical and moral implications of action.

Source: Donaldson and Preston (1995)

Integrative stakeholder theory, finally, links the three perspectives of descriptive, instrumental, and normative stakeholder theory and acknowledges that, on the one hand, the purpose of business is beyond merely maximizing short-term shareholder value. On the other hand, it also acknowledges that making a profit is an important element of business activities. Aligning or at least balancing potentially conflicting stakeholder interests is a core challenge and management should take a long-term perspective which complements short-term instrumental approaches.

B.1.2 Companies, stakeholder, and social legitimacy

A prerequisite for companies to operate is that they are perceived as legitimate actors in society. Legitimacy is defined as "a generalized perception or assumption that the actions of an entity are desirable, proper, or appropriate within some socially constructed system of norms, values, beliefs, and definitions" (Suchman, 1995, p. 574). If businesses are socially accepted, rules and regulations generally allow private companies to operate within certain boundaries. If businesses are not socially accepted, rules, regulations, and other boundary conditions such as trust from consumers or civil society in general are likely to be limited, which hinders their business activities. However, not only businesses in general need to be regarded as legitimate actors, but also each individual business so that various stakeholders grant their social license to operate. No company can exist if, for example, primary stakeholders such as customers, employees, or suppliers are unwilling to do business. Furthermore, secondary stakeholders such as governmental actors or neighbors should preferably be at least neutral as they can otherwise cause disruptions or impede operations. All organizations, including businesses, thus "seek to establish congruence between the social values associated with or implied by their activities and the norms of acceptable behavior in the larger social system of which they are a part. Insofar as these two value systems are congruent we can speak of organizational legitimacy" (Dowling & Pfeffer, 1975, p. 122).

These thoughts illustrate two aspects. First, being accepted in and by society is a prerequisite for any business operation. Second, legitimacy and social acceptance is subject to subjective perceptions of stakeholders, which might change over time or differ from country to country and industry to industry. In India, Saudi Arabia, or the Netherlands, for example, general trust in businesses is much higher than in Russia, Japan, or France (see Daniel J. Edelman Holdings Inc., 2021). Trust is also higher on average in the healthcare sector compared to the financial service industry. Furthermore, pressure on businesses to act responsibly and participate in sustainable development seems to generally increase over time. Nowadays, for example, the vast majority of people expect business leaders to publicly speak out about societal challenges. At the same time, important stakeholder groups, such as consumers or employees, are perceived as powerful actors who can potentially force corporations to change in order to keep their legitimacy.

Legitimacy or social acceptance can, of course, not be formally acquired which often makes it difficult for companies to manage, especially if they experience conflicting expectations, for example, from different stakeholder groups. In general, corporate misconduct or irresponsibility facilitate mistrust. This does not only apply to inappropriate behavior of individual companies but sometimes even of entire industries. Especially corporate scandals can have a distinctly negative influence on legitimacy, and even a single negative event can destroy years of work. Consistently responsible business conduct can provide an insurance-like protection against loss of legitimacy and also helps businesses to avoid negative incidents in the first place (Barnett et al., 2018).

Sustainability in business 9: Volkswagen's diesel emissions scandal

In September 2015, the Environmental Protection Agency of the United States found that many VW cars with diesel engines had a software to detect when a car was subject to an emissions test and thereupon change the cars emission performance to improve results. The German carmaker later admitted cheating on emission tests in the United States and elsewhere around the world with millions of its cars. The scandal soon escalated to larger parts of the industry and many well-known brands. The public outcry was massive and the scandal affected almost all relevant stakeholders. Customers were shocked to learn that they might de driving illegal cars and feared a loss in value of their property. Car dealers around the world had to face angry customers and the sales of diesel cars plummeted. Employees saw a slump in bonus payments and were often embarrassed by the irresponsible behavior of their employer. Shareholders saw a plunge in stock prices immediately after the scandal became public. Over the next couple of years, Volkswagen faced several lawsuits and payed billions of dollars in compensations. Finally, the scandal was also a massive blow for the company's sustainability endeavors. It was, for example, expelled from the Dow Jones Sustainability Index (see also Chapter B.5.3) and from the UN Global Compact initiative (see also Chapter C.7.1.1) and not readmitted to the Global Compact until the year 2021. In sum, the legitimacy of the company was severely and negatively influenced in the eyes of different stakeholders.

Sources: Jung and Park (2017); Mansouri (2016)

Task B1-1

Find a specific negative example of a company which, from your perspective, behaved very unsustainably with regard to its products or its operations.

What happened and how did this affect the legitimacy of the company? Who are the relevant internal and external stakeholders that could change the company's behavior? And why do you think the company did not engage sufficiently with sustainability management before?

Now think of a specific positive example of a company which, from your perspective, behaves comparably sustainable with regard to its products or its operations.

What is different with this company and the environment it is operating in? Why and how is this company able to be more sustainable than the company you discussed/thought of before?

In sum, legitimacy and social acceptance can be regarded as scarce resources that need to be managed. Sustainability management (or stakeholder management more generally) can be an instrument to recognize this scarcity, to assess the influence of companies in society and of society on companies, and to secure legitimacy in the long run. This also resonates well with the original meaning of the term "responsibility" which deviates from the Latin word "respondere," (=to answer). Companies need to have good answers for all question on their activities in particular, and on their role in society in general. Sustainability management can help provide these answers by doing the right things and communicating them to the relevant stakeholders or, in other words, "walking" the path of responsible business conduct and "talking" about this path (Schoeneborn et al., 2020).

B.1.3 Concepts of stakeholder management

Once we acknowledge that stakeholders are relevant for a company's success and, vice versa, that a company can have substantial influence on a wide variety of stakeholders, a number of practical questions usually follows: Who are the relevant stakeholders? How can their interests be balanced and served? How many resources should be allotted to serve these interests? Practical concepts of stakeholder management can help companies answer these questions by following the three steps of identifying, prioritizing, and eventually dealing with stakeholders.

In a first step (identification of stakeholders), companies are advised to identify all stakeholders and their respective interests. It is important not to miss any stakeholders as they might be relevant at later stages of stakeholder management. To compile a comprehensive list, companies can start with the general characterization of stakeholders as those who can affect or are affected by the company's activities. The resulting questions are, thus, who might be affected by the company's operations either negatively or positively and who might have an influence on the company's decisions. This can be accompanied by various sub-questions such as who has some form of physical contact with the company's activities, to whom does the company have legal obligations, or who speaks about the company. Often it might also be helpful to use the stakeholder classification illustrated in Figure 9. All identified stakeholders have their own interests in an organization and these interests can either be positively (harmony of interests) or negatively (conflict of interests) related or they may have no impact on each other (neutrality of interests). It is thus important to not only identify all stakeholders but also to have a clear idea of their interests with regard to the company. Owners, for example, often strive for increased profits while employees or suppliers want to increase their payments and have secure contracts and relationships with the company.

In most cases, the list of potential and actual stakeholders of any given company or project is long and heterogeneous. Furthermore, it is unlikely that all stakeholder interests can be met at the same time. This can be due to conflicts of interest between the different stakeholders' objectives or between the objectives of stakeholders and the company or due to limited resources available to fulfill stakeholder interests. Thus, stakeholder management in a second step (prioritization of stakeholders) tries to assess each stakeholder or stakeholder group by applying certain criteria which help to prioritize the field to make it more approachable for actual interaction and management. Mitchell et al. (1997), in their seminal paper provide a structured model to assess stakeholders based on three dimensions as illustrated in Figure 10: legitimacy, power, and urgency.

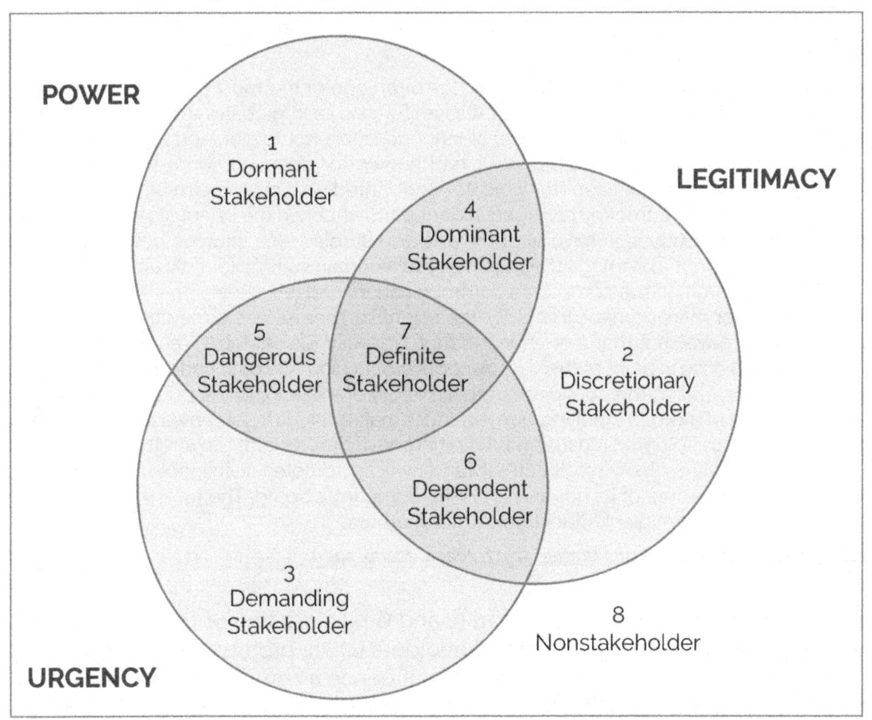

Figure 10: Stakeholder typology according to Mitchell et al. (1997, p. 874), reproduced with permission

Power is the degree to which a stakeholder can get a company to do something that it would not have otherwise done. Such power can originate from coercion based on physical resources (e.g., force, violence, restraint), utilitarian considerations based on material or financial resources, or normative considerations based on symbolic resources (e.g., prestige, acceptance). Legitimacy, as discussed above, is the idea that something is socially accepted in a shared perception in society. Urgency asks whether or not a stakeholder claim calls for immediate attention. Immediate attention, in turn, is necessitated by two conditions: time sensitivity (i.e., managerial delay would be unacceptable for the stakeholder) and criticality (i.e., the claim is important to the stakeholder).

Latent stakeholders in the classes 1, 2, and 3, according to Figure 10, meet only one of the three attributes and are thus of low salience, that is, they receive a lower priority by a company's management. Managers usually only invest little or no resources in these stakeholders and sometimes do not even recognize their existence. Dormant stakeholders (1) are powerful but they have no immediate interest or legitimate relationship with a company. Former employees, for example, may have insider knowledge they can use against a company but their claims may be unwarranted and they may have no urgent impetus to act against their former employer if they, for example, received a significant payoff. Since urgency and legitimacy can potentially change, it is nevertheless advisable to observe those stakeholders. Discretionary stakeholders (2) have legitimate claims without any power or urgency. A nonprofit organization receiving donations from corporate philanthropy programs would be a classical example. Demanding stakeholders (3) have urgent claims but they have neither power nor are they perceived to be legitimate. Mitchell et al. (1997) describe them as "irksome but not dangerous, bothersome but not warranting more than passing management attention" (p. 875). Examples would be lone protestors against certain otherwise accepted business practices. Here again, it is advisable to pay some attention as the legitimacy or power of these stakeholders might change over time.

Sustainability in business 10: ExxonMobil's stakeholder mismanagement through misleading climate change communication

The multinational oil corporation ExxonMobil has been one of the most prominent targets of climate change activists and it faces severe criticism for its role in global warming. For many years, ExxonMobile and other oil companies tried to influence stakeholders and public opinion by shedding doubt on climate science, although it had known for decades about the facts of global warming, as internal company reports indicate. Confronted with overwhelming evidence of their miscommunication, the company engaged in denial and attacked the scientists who analyzed the company's communications in several peer-reviewed studies (see sources below). This can be regarded as an attempt to damage the legitimacy of a certain stakeholder group (in this case, scientists doing research on the company's communication) and it is clearly an element of misconceived stakeholder management. Ironically, the scientists themselves turned the stick, assessing that ExxonMobil "have shot themselves in the foot. Because ExxonMobil's reaction to our work is nothing short of a case in point of the very deceptive behaviour we described in our study. ExxonMobil are now misleading the public about their history of misleading the public. And therein lies the greatest irony of all. It's a smoking gun reminder that, behind the greenwash, the tiger has yet to change its stripes." (Supran, 2020) An interesting new chapter of the overall play was opened in May 2021, when a relatively small activist fund, which promotes sustainable investments, was successful in setting three of its nominees on the company's board. The fund was backed in this voting by investment firm giant, BlackRock, among others.

Sources: Phillips (2021); Supran and Oreskes (2017; 2020a; 2020b; 2021)

Expectant stakeholders in the classes 4, 5, and 6 possess two of the attributes and are thus of moderate salience. Dominant stakeholders (4) are prototypical stakeholders most visible in companies. They have the power to influence a company's operations, and their claims are perceived as legitimate. Managers usually actively engage with such stakeholders, trying to maintain a positive relationship. Companies, for example, often have investor relations departments, and seats on their board of directors are generally available for dominant stakeholders such as representatives of owners. Dangerous stakeholders (5) lack legitimacy. Since they have power and an impetus of urgency to use this power, however, they can exert significant influence on a company, such as terrorist groups or criminal organizations in some part of the world. These stakeholders are often coercive and sometimes even violent, which makes them dangerous, for example, when they engage in sabotage or defamation. Therefore, companies usually want to be prepared despite choosing not to acknowledging these stakeholders as legitimate. Dependent stakeholders (6) only lack power to directly enforce their claims. They are sometimes ignored by managers assuming that these stakeholders cannot influence a company's operations. This is dangerous, however, as other stakeholders sometimes assist and provide power which changes the dynamics of the situation. Environmental advocacy groups or the media, for example, can provide normative power to otherwise ignored stakeholders (such as the ecological environment) which might be threatened by company activities.

Definite stakeholders in group 7 have the highest priority as they possess all three attributes together. Companies and managers should give highest priority to such stakeholders and their claims. Important investors, for example, have the legitimate expectation that their investment is treated with care and that it is not devaluated. In case of a looming sharp decline of stock prices, exactly this could happen so that a degree of urgency develops, leading to a situation in which these stakeholders might exercise their power against the management. Finally, any individual or group who has no power over a company and no legitimate or urgent claims is a nonstakeholder (8) and will thus not be included in stakeholder management.

How a stakeholder is classified on any of the three dimensions is not an objective fact but rather a matter of perception so that it is advisable to involve multiple people and to constantly challenge their assumptions to arrive at a robust assessment. Furthermore, any of the three dimensions is a variable which can change at any time and with it the classification of specific stakeholders in the typology. Thus, priorities can change over time so that it is advisable to repeat not only the first but also the second step in stakeholder management every once in a while, depending on the dynamics of the business and its stakeholder relations.

After compiling a list of all (potential) stakeholders and prioritizing them in a first and second step of stakeholder management, the third step (dealing with stakeholders) would be to derive and implement suitable strategies to interact with the different stakeholder and their claims. The range of options is vast: simply doing nothing, observing stakeholders' positions, complying with expectations, changing perceptions, and so on. The suitability of any of these and other approaches is highly context specific so that it is difficult to provide concrete suggestions on how to proceed in this regard.

Task B1-2

Companies from the extractive industry usually have a significant social and environmental impact. Imagine you are a senior manager of a company from this industry and your company plans operations in a newly identified natural deposit. This deposit is near an important national park in a developing country. Several villages of indigenous people are in the respective area. The new operation would bring significant change to the region, which could be positive or negative.

Now conduct a stakeholder analysis as discussed in this chapter.

1. Who are the current stakeholders of the company and the potential stakeholders of the project? What are their (potential) claims and objectives?
2. Evaluate each stakeholder according to the framework by Mitchell et al. (1997). How do they score with regards to the three attributes of power, legitimacy, and urgency – and why?
3. Now compare your assessment with that of some of your fellow students – do you differ in some of your evaluations and if so: why? Come up with a joint assessment.
4. Now imagine your company decides to go on with the project. When would the claims and assessment of various stakeholders change and why? Which strategies do you propose to deal with stakeholder claims in the process of establishing the new operation?

Finally, and as partly already mentioned above, the relevance of different types of stakeholders can and has changed significantly over time for certain firms, industries, regions, or in society in general. Assembly line workers in supply chains in China, for example, used to be in an underprivileged position with very little influence or power in low skill jobs in which they used to work very long hours for a very low wage. Today, the working environment often looks very different with many higher skilled jobs. On average, employees in China are now in a much better position as their relevance as stakeholders has changed. Another example of changing relevance over time relates to the ecological environment. Some aspects of environmental protection have long been on the agenda of advocate groups, governments, and companies. Nevertheless, the awareness for issues such as anthropogenic climate change has further increased significantly over the last years and decades. Interestingly, the ecological environment as such is often not regarded as a stakeholder itself despite the fact that it can be affected by a firm's activities and it can, in turn, influence a firm's objectives, for example, when looking at the effects of climate change on worldwide supply chains or certain business models (e.g., in the insurance industry). Therefore, some scholars have long argued for a more immediate inclusion of the ecological environment in stakeholder thinking (e.g., Haigh & Griffiths, 2009; Starik, 1995). Whether or not the ecological environment is directly regarded as a stakeholder itself or indirectly via other stakeholders who act as its advocates, firms increasingly include it into their decision-making processes. This is either done for normative reasons (i.e., because they think it is the right thing to do) or for instrumental reasons (i.e., because they otherwise risk ignoring important developments and demands which can negatively affect their business) or both.

Sustainability in business 11: Strategic stakeholder management at Shell Philippines

In 2002, the Malampaya Deep Water Gas-to-Power Project of Shell Philippines Exploration (SPEX), Chevron Texaco, and the Philippine National Oil Company began its operation. The plans to extract natural gas off the coast of Palawan Island had an impact on local fishermen and pearl divers and part of the local population had to be relocated. SPEX was responsible for bringing the project to completion and for its subsequent operation. In 1996, two years ahead of construction, SPEX engaged with the affected local stakeholders and integrated them throughout the project also after its completion. The company organized consultations, public events, and met with opinion leaders of the various interest groups. The local population was included in planning the environmental management of the facility, and together with SPEX they developed a pipeline route with the least possible impact on the natural environment. Those parts of the population that had to be relocated or had suffered from loss of business were compensated. The company also tried to establish perspectives for the population by offering microcredits or by educating and training locals so that they could engage in the development of the project. Furthermore, the training aimed at offering job perspectives once the facility started operating.

The entire project was a USD 4.5 billion joint venture. The various activities to consult and engage with the local stakeholder groups cost about USD 6 million. However, the company calculated that the benefits far outweigh the costs as it resulted in cost savings of USD 50 to 72 million due to avoided penalties, avoided delays, and the construction being finished even ahead of schedule.

This example shows how an integrated stakeholder approach cannot only satisfy ethical and moral obligations but also results in economic benefits such as increased reputation and reduced costs. Nevertheless, the entire operation of the Malampaya Project still aimed at the extraction of natural raw materials which contribute to global warming, despite the fact that natural gas is regarded as potentially less harmful compared to crude oil. Furthermore, Shell itself remained under critique for various other activities.

Source: Herz et al. (2007)

KEY TAKEAWAYS

- Stakeholders are important for sustainability management as they influence companies and are influenced by companies.
- Stakeholders and their interests can be very heterogeneous, which makes stakeholder management a complex task.
- There are different instrumental and normative reasons why companies should engage in stakeholder management.
- Legitimacy and social acceptance are scarce resources that need to be managed and sustainability management can help to secure legitimacy in the long run.
- Stakeholder management is an ongoing task that follows three ideal steps: stakeholder identification, stakeholder prioritization, and strategy development.
- Stakeholders can be categorized along three dimensions (power, legitimacy, and urgency) into latent, expectant, and definite stakeholder groups.

B.2 Employees

LEARNING GOALS

After reading this chapter you will be able to ...

- ... explain the effects of sustainability management and CSR on employees.
- ... explain how these effects on employees have a positive effect on a company's overall operations.
- ... distinguish different categories of sustainable employee behavior and provide examples.
- ... illustrate various drivers for sustainable employee behavior.
- ... explain the special influence of top management on sustainability management.
- ... illustrate how personality traits and top management characteristics influence sustainability management and CSR.

Introduction to Chapter B.2: Screencast
Watch an introduction to the chapter here:

B.2.1 Effects of sustainability management on employees

Numerous empirical studies underline the beneficial relationship of sustainability management and various direct and indirect outcomes on the employee level. In most studies, sustainability management is usually measured in the form of a positive and subjective perception of CSR.

Task B2-1

Is sustainability and CSR a decision criterion for you when seeking a new employer? Why or why not? Does it make a difference what kind of job you are seeking (internship, summer job, first, second, or third job after graduation, etc.)? How would you try to judge the level of sustainability and CSR of your prospective employer? Elaborate!

In their meta-analyses of empirical studies, Y. Wang et al. (2020) and Zhao et al. (2022) summarize a number of these effects. First, perceived CSR is connected with higher perceived organizational justice, that is, employee's perception of whether they and potentially other stakeholders are treated fairly by their employer. Apparently, CSR or sustainability is used as a heuristic for fair treatment. Second, perceived CSR usually positively correlates with organizational identification, that is, the feeling of employees that they belong to an organization. Reasons might be that CSR signals a positive image which, in turn, can enhance employee's self-esteem and pride in working for the company. Third, CSR and sustainability can have a positive influence on organizational trust as it, for example, signals moral values. Furthermore, CSR and sustainability management regularly provide benefits to various stakeholders (see Chapter C.2.2) who are then urged to reciprocate. Consequently, Zhao et al. (2022) found that CSR practices targeting employees have a stronger effect on organizational trust compared to sustainability measures for the environment.

While all these effects are noteworthy, they do not constitute immediate positive effects for a company's operations. However, researchers also have found extensive evidence for positive effects on aspects that are of even more direct relevance for most companies—usually as an indirect outcome through the above-mentioned effects (see again Y. Wang et al., 2020; Zhao et al., 2022). Accordingly, perceived CSR is positively related to organizational commitment, job satisfaction and even work engagement, creativity and, eventually, job performance. Moreover, there is also a negative correlation with, from an employer's point of view, undesirable outcomes such as turnover intentions (i.e., employees have fewer intentions to leave the organization), organizational cynicism (i.e., employees do not develop a negative attitude toward the organization), and organizational deviation (i.e., employees exhibit fewer negative behaviors such as stealing, neglecting duties, or delaying work).

Sustainability in research 5: Turban and Greening's 1997 article on social performance and organizational attractiveness

The relationship between sustainability or CSR and firm attractiveness is one of the most long-standing research topics in the realm of sustainability and employees. In their widely cited study published in 1997 in the Academy of Management Journal, Daniel B. Turban and Daniel W. Greening assess the influence of corporate social performance (CSP) on organizational attractiveness to prospective employees. The authors used an external rating of CSP which measures various elements of CSR including responsibility toward the environment and other stakeholders. They hypothesized that companies with a higher CSP score are perceived as more attractive employers than companies with lower CSP scored.

They derived their hypothesis from social identity theory and signaling theory. Social identity theory posits that people are influenced in their self-concept by the affiliation in social groups. The authors argued that CSP influences the attractiveness of belonging to a company, as applicants expect a positive impact on their self-concept. Signaling theory addresses the fact that a good CSP communicates certain values to applicants. Overall, Turban and Greening argued that CSR and initiatives can create competitive advantages by attracting a higher quantity and quality of human resources through improved corporate reputation.

For their quantitative analysis, the authors used CSP scores from the "Kinder, Lydenberg, Domini & Co." database for more than 150 companies for which they also obtained attractiveness ratings scored from students as potential applicants while controlling for company size and profitability. Using an independent CSP score from this database is an interesting methodological feature of the article, as most other studies usually directly asked survey participants to what extent they have a good or bad perception of a company's sustainability and CSR activities. The results demonstrated that companies with a higher CSP level indeed enjoy a more positive reputation than companies with lower CSP ratings. The authors inferred that this results in a competitive advantage because prospective applicants are more attracted to companies with a more positive reputation. In terms of today's sustainability management, the article illustrates that companies might want to raise awareness for their achievements and thus create an atmosphere of social values for applicants.

Source: Turban and Greening (1997)

These aspects generally provide strong arguments for the business case of sustainability when looking at the stakeholder group of employees. However, most researchers examine employees' perceptions of CSR and sustainability management, which is not necessarily identical with real sustainability performance. This implies, on the one hand, that a positive perception should—from a sustainability point of view—be the result of actual sustainable practices and a good sustainability performance, and Part C of this book provides ample instruments for how companies can act (more) sustainably. On the other hand, these aspects also show that sustainability management and a good sustainability performance should be communicated properly so that they can translate into a good perception of a company's CSR and sustainability management.

B.2.2 Influence of employees on sustainability management

Technically, organizations themselves do not decide about resource consumption, working conditions, or other sustainability-related issues. Instead, respective decisions are made by individuals within the company—albeit usually on behalf of the company (see Chapter A.3.2 for related ethical thoughts). Thus, employees have a strong influence on sustainability management and, eventually, on the sustainability performance of their employer. Many scholars specifically focus on pro-environmental or green behavior at work. Research on environmental psychology which tries to explain such behavior, however, also uses concepts of prosocial and moral behavior thus covering the broader area of sustainability (Lülfs & Hahn, 2014). Ones et al. (2015) summarize several categories of respective green behavior, which can be extended to sustainable behavior in general:

- Avoiding harm or conserving aims at reducing impact, preserving resources, and mitigating damages. This includes preventing pollution or social harm, for example, in the form of environmental pollution, work accidents, or unfair treatment of co-workers or subordinates. Simple actions such as switching off lights when leaving the office can already improve a company's environmental footprint. Accordingly, monitoring and being aware of one's own individual social or environmental footprint is an important element of avoiding harm so that it ultimately results in reducing use, reusing, and recycling.
- Beyond this negative perspective of avoiding harm, the category of transforming describes a more proactive and positive approach. Respective activities involve an active adaptation and change to be more sustainable. To achieve transformation, employees engage in creating innovative solutions, "such as changing how work is done to be more sustainable and creating new sustainable products and processes, as well as adopting innovations made by others, such as choosing responsible alternatives (e.g., green products, renewable energy, durable materials) and embracing technologies that are better for the environment" (Ones et al., 2015, p. 84) or society.
- In the category of influencing others, employees look beyond their own behavior and aim at changing the behavior of co-workers and other employees. This includes social support and encouragement for other individuals' sustainable behavior as well as education and training or incentives and motivations to behave more sustainably. Such trainings and incentives can also be part of organizational programs to support individual sustainable behavior at the workplace.
- When taking initiative, employees take a larger step toward sustainable behavior in their company, which may even include a certain level of personal risk. Employees can, for example, engage in activism or lobbying to advance sustainability in their company or they can initiate new programs and activities.

Sustainability in business 12: Social Intrapreneurs as change makers for sustainability

Although many companies have recognized that there is more to the purpose of business than just making profits, as we discuss throughout this book, the bandwidth of corporate sustainability management is vast. Some companies merely pretend to be sustainable and try to get along with a bare minimum. Others, however, have truly embraced the topic. In these latter companies, the development toward sustainability is sometimes driven by the owners (e.g., for ethical or religious reasons) and sometimes it also comes from deeper down the company ranks. An interesting topic in this regard is that of social intrapreneurs. The Yunus Social Business initiative describes social intrapreneurs as "an entrepreneurial employee who develops a profitable new product, service or business model that creates value for society and her company" (Yunus Social Business, 2020, p. 4). These change makers try to harness the resources of larger companies to tackle sustainability challenges. A reputed example of such a change maker is Gib Bulloch. Bulloch worked as management consultant for Accenture for several years before turning into a social intrapreneur in the company. Following his ideas, the company offered consultancy services to NGOs and donor organizations on a sustainable basis. The services were made accessible by foregoing margins, keeping overheads and expenses low, encouraging consultants to waive parts of their salary, and charging fees to clients on a cost recovery basis. The initiative broadened the consultants' skills, and it helped the company in recruiting new talents. However, taking the road as social intrapreneur also incorporates several challenges, which Bulloch described in his book "The Intrapreneur-Confessions of a corporate insurgent" (Bulloch, 2018).

Sources: Bulloch (2018); Grayson et al. (2014); Yunus Social Business (2020)

Since employee behavior has a significant influence on sustainability management and sustainability performance, it is important to know what drives it. In their research overviews, Gond et al. (2017), Lülfs and Hahn (2014), and Ones et al. (2015) discuss such drivers. An initial prerequisite for acting sustainably, regardless of whether it is in the working sphere or in private life, is a general awareness of need to act sustainably and an awareness of the consequences of individual behavior. To develop such awareness, knowledge and skills seem to be necessary but not yet sufficient for sustainable behavior at work. Awareness can then lead to the development of personal norms about the need to behave sustainably. Such personal norms are rooted in the individual in the form of values, assumptions, or beliefs about what is right or wrong with regard to her or his personal behavior in the firm and of the firm's overall sustainability stance. Accordingly, moral or prosocial motives and a sustainable value orientation can be important drivers of employees' sustainable behavior.

Personal norms and values are accompanied by social norms. Social norms are general perceptions of acceptable behavior in and by peer groups. Such norms are an important force which have an influence on the employees' need for external recognition. Acting sustainably is then a response to the desire to conform with the expectations of others, for example, of co-workers or supervisors. If such group norms in a company favor sustainable over unsustainable forms of behavior, they can be an important driver for sustainable behavior at work. Together, awareness, personal norms, and social norms can lead to positive sustainability attitudes. Individuals who are committed to sustainability likely act in ways that support their attitudes. Finally, while personal and social norms are often rather stable constructs, other aspects might be more easily influenced from the outside. Awareness, for example, can be influenced through education and training. Furthermore, employees often also act in their own personal interest to some extent, which places the individual benefit of sustainable behavior at work at the center of thinking. If sustainability engagement is driven by the personal goals of employees, it can be influenced through (economic) incentives to act sustainably (for further interventions, see Chapter C.2.1).

B.2.3 Influence of (top)management on sustainability management

In general, managers and even a company's top management are just another type of employees in a firm. Accordingly, the drivers for sustainable behavior at work we discussed above also apply to managers. Notably, with increasing rank in a company, the influence on a company's policies, strategies, and activities also usually increases. Managers and especially the top management can thus be expected to have a significant influence on sustainability management. Without the support of top management, many sustainability activities are doomed to fail, as they often require initial or ongoing resources or they need approval from the top management to commence.

Accordingly, numerous empirical studies show that (top) managers have a strong influence on organizational sustainability decisions and measures (e.g., Dai et al., 2014; Reimer et al., 2018). CEOs alone explain about 30 percent of the total variance in CSR (Wernicke et al., 2021). Companies can try to actively signal such top management support for sustainability. Having a chief sustainability officer, for example, was found to increase socially responsible activities and reduce socially irresponsible ones (Fu et al., 2020). Furthermore, and not surprisingly, the managerial and personal background characteristics of top managers or of top management teams have an influence on their actions and decisions.

When looking specifically at the person of the CEO, having a company leader with environmental expertise, for example, is beneficial for reducing corporate environmental impact (Walls & Berrone, 2017), while her or his reflexive capacity in general relates positively to a company's sustainability performance (Jia et al., 2021). Interestingly, personality traits with negative connotations can sometimes be beneficial for corporate sustainability. CEO narcissism, that is, a high level of vanity and self-admiration by the company leader, has a distinctly positive influence on corporate sustainability and CSR, probably because it helps the manager to gain attention and a positive image (Al-Shammari et al., 2019; Petrenko et al., 2016). There seems to be a fine line, however, as CEO hubris as well as greed are negatively related to a company's CSR or sustainability activities (Sajko et al., 2021; Tang et al., 2015).

Sustainability in business 13: The role of former Danone CEO Emmanuel Faber on the food giant's sustainability profile

In March 2021, Emmanuel Faber had to step down from his position as CEO of the French food giant Danone after two activist investment companies explicitly asked the board to find a replacement. One of the investment companies is being cited with its critique that the company under Faber's leadership "did not manage to strike the right balance between shareholder value creation and sustainability" (Bris, 2021). The public outcry following his forced resignation was immense, because Faber was regarded by many as the driving force behind the multinational corporation's numerous sustainability initiatives. Under his leadership, the company even became a certified "B Corporation" (see Chapter C.9.2), which signals that the company meets high standards of verified social and environmental performance and balances profit and purpose. As one result, the NGO CDP recognized Danone as a global environmental leader in 2020. Therefore, the story of Emmanuel Faber as CEO of Danone is often used to exemplify the influence of top management on a company's sustainability efforts. However, and as often in the realm of sustainability management, the picture is not as clear cut as it might initially seem. While the company certainly pursued many sustainability initiatives and integrated sustainability-thinking comparably deep in its processes, it still remained relatively depended on its bottled water business, which was highly contested for its social and ecological consequences. Furthermore, in 2020 the company announced its decision to cut 2,000 jobs to improve its financial performance. In sum, this episode shows how difficult it is for a large multinational company to holistically embrace sustainability despite having a CEO who was applauded for his green agenda.

Sources: Bris (2021); Hanke (2021); van Gansbeke (2021)

Beyond the individual person of a CEO, the entire top management team of a company matters for a company's stance toward sustainability and thus, ultimately, for its sustainability performance. Integrative and open-minded as well as functionally diverse top management teams, for example, yield higher sustainability performance (L. A. Henry et al., 2019; Wong et al., 2011). Moreover, ethical leadership and the leaders' own pro-environmental behaviors have been found to improve employees' proenvironmental behaviors and reduce unethical behavior (Paterson & Huang, 2019; Resick et al., 2013; Robertson & Barling, 2013). Thus, management influence on sustainability and CSR seems to be not only through direct power in an organization but also through being a role model.

KEY TAKEAWAYS

- Perceived CSR is connected with an increasing perceived organizational justice, organizational identification, and organizational trust.
- Perceived CSR is positively related to organizational commitment, job satisfaction, work engagement, creativity, and job performance.
- Perceived CSR is negatively correlated with turnover intentions, organizational cynicism, and organizational deviation.
- Sustainability behavior at work can take the form of avoiding harm or conserving, transforming, influencing others, and taking initiative.
- Drivers for sustainability behavior at work are awareness of need and consequences, personal norms, and social norms.
- Top management has a significant influence on sustainability management.
- Various personality traits and characteristics of top managers and top management teams influence CSR and sustainability performance.

B.3 Governmental actors

LEARNING GOALS

After reading this chapter you will be able to ...

- ... explain the idea of market failures and governmental failures.
- ... distinguish indirect from direct political actors.
- ... explain negative externalities and why they are relevant for sustainable development.
- ... explain how command-and-control instruments work, discuss their advantages and disadvantages, and provide examples.
- ... explain how different types of information requirements and governmental support work, discuss their advantages and disadvantages, and provide examples.
- ... explain how different types of market-based instruments work, discuss their advantages and disadvantages, and provide examples.
- ... discuss how different external factors and regulatory regimes influence the effectiveness of different sustainability policy instruments.

Introduction to Chapter A.3: Screencast
Watch an introduction to the chapter here:

B.3.1 Actors in legislation and regulation

Societies around the world have embraced the idea of sustainable development as can be seen from the broad acceptance of the SDGs (see Chapter A.2.3), the widely accepted insight that climate change is largely human-made and should be stopped, and many other issues of sustainability-relevance. However, the status quo in most societies worldwide shows a picture of unsustainability (see Chapter A.1.2). Thus, normatively speaking, something is going wrong. Two explanations for this development are market failures and government failures (e.g., Andrew, 2008; Stiglitz, 2009).

Basic economic theory assumes that markets are efficient in such a way that they lead to an optimal allocation of goods and services that is overall welfare enhancing. However, this is often not the case in reality, as can be seen from the many sustainability issues ranging from climate change to aspects of global injustice. While market systems often did improve overall welfare over time, the overall efficiency is not optimal or we would not have a situation in which, for example, ongoing climate change threatens humankind's long-term prosperity. Market failures thus describe situations of inefficient distribution of goods and services in the free market. Reasons for market failure are manifold and often connected to basic assumptions of elemental economic theories. Often, for example, market actors can make profits at the expense of others if they have better information or more power. In other instances, there are negative externalities, which means that the party who caused damages or negative effects does not have to pay for these in full—as is often the case with pollution. Furthermore, certain public goods (such as the natural environment) are often overused as they are seemingly free for all which encourages free-riders to extensively use these goods.

Due to market failures, governments are often assumed to step in to regulate markets and ensure a desired outcome of economic activities. This chapter discusses potential governmental interventions. However, similar to market failures, government failures are also often discussed. Governments, like markets, often cannot act efficiently or ensure an optimal outcome, for example, if they do not possess the necessary information or if they look at short-term solutions considering only the next election cycle. Furthermore, political actors sometimes act in their self-interest instead of public interest or they are influenced by others (e.g., pressure groups or lobbyists). Finally, governments around the world often have to compete with each other. Consequently, they fear that implementing stricter sustainability-related regulations would lead to higher direct and short-term costs for the economy, thereby becoming less attractive to companies and individuals alike.

Thus, both markets and governments are not perfect. What is uncontested is the fact that various actors have an influence on legislation and regulations which, in turn, have an influence on how companies act in society. These actors can be distinguished as direct and indirect. Direct actors are all institutions that have a direct influence on legislation and regulations. This usually includes national and regional parliaments, governmental administrations (cabinet, ministers, etc.), supranational institutions such as the European Union and other international organizations as well as courts. Indirect actors are those that cannot directly put forward legislation and regulation but who can influence direct actors in their decisions. This could be NGOs, the media, consumer associations, trade associations, unions, churches, and so on.

These indirect actors have different means to enforce their interests. They can formally intervene, for example, in hearings of legislative processes or they can create public pressure through public relations activities or threats. Informal influence through lobbying or campaign contributions as well as personal connections can also be used to influence regulations and legislation. Many trade associations, large individual companies, unions, or influential NGOs have representatives or lobby offices in political centers such as national capitals. Some also have their own think tanks which publish studies or information material to support their views or they support respective initiatives or institutions. Any of these actors can try to influence political actors in favor of or against sustainability initiatives, and their interests are often very heterogeneous.

Sustainability in society 8: Corporate advocates for and against combating climate change in the United States

The fight against climate change and the stance of the industry in the United States is a vivid example of the heterogeneity of indirect actors even from seemingly homogeneous parts of society. On the one hand, for example, there are actors such as the Competitive Enterprise Institute (CEI). The CEI is a nonprofit libertarian think tank which, over the years, received significant donations from many big industry players not least from the oil extracting industry. In 2006, they launched a campaign with the tagline "Carbon dioxide: They call it pollution. We call it life." The campaign aimed at shedding doubt on scientific evidence on human-made climate change. On the other hand, organizations and initiatives, such as the "Coalition for Environmentally Responsible Economies" (CERES) or "We are still in," who are also supported by businesses throughout the United States, advocate for combating climate change and sometimes support even stricter regulations.

Sources: Baumeister (2018); MacKay and Munro (2012)

B.3.2 Sustainability policy instruments

Policy instruments are used when states or state-like actors want to achieve certain outcomes or encourage or restrict certain behaviors of others. For sustainable development this could be the achievement of certain environmental or social goals by, for example, setting standards, restricting the use of certain harmful substances or otherwise unsustainable behavior, and encouraging actors to act more sustainably. Here again, the normative quality of sustainable development itself comes to the fore (see again Chapter A.3.1), as governmental actors do not necessarily have to support the quest for sustainable development, but it is a political (or societal) decision to apply sustainability policy instruments or not.

Applying sustainability policy instruments and thus regulating firm or individual behavior is especially relevant in cases of negative externalities. An externality in general is something (either a cost or benefit) that an individual has to incur even though they did not agree to it. Such externalities are usually perceived as a sign of market failure, because the overall social cost originating from production or consumption is not included in market prices. The idea of such externalities was devised by Arthur Cecile Pigou in the early 20th century (Pigou, 2017), and it is relevant for many sustainability-related issues. One of the most widely used examples for negative externalities is environmental pollution. Often, the production or use of goods goes along with, for example, greenhouse gas emissions, air pollution, or water pollution. Without any regulation, producers or consumers would not have to bear these costs as the natural environment is usually a common good. As a consequence, the natural environment is overused due to such negative externalities. Such an overuse, however, is harmful for society as a whole which cannot benefit from an intact natural environment any longer. A similar argument can be made for issues of social sustainability. For example, forced labor, modern slavery, or poor working conditions in many supply chains around the world have manifold negative impacts, apart from being morally objectionable. They usually lead to lower productivity, a lack of investment in human capital, and most obviously, severe poverty which harms entire communities and society as a whole. However, these negative impacts are usually not incurred by the producers or consumers of the products which caused them.

Various sustainability policy instruments are used to tackle such problems. These instruments come in three general categories: command-and-control instruments (also referred to as regulatory instruments), information requirements and governmental support, and market-based instrument (also referred to as economic policy instruments or economic incentives)—for in-depth overviews see, for example, Harrington and Morgenstern (2007), Stavins (2003), or Stiglitz (2009). In reality, many regulations combine elements of more than one of these categories. For the sake of clarity, however, we will separately discuss how these instruments work as well as their benefits and drawbacks. As we will see, there is no one-size-fits-all approach. Many determinants have to be considered when deciding which instruments are most suitable in a given situation, for example, a country's governmental infrastructure, regulatory capacities as well as the nature of the problem which is to be regulated.

B.3.2.1 Command-and-control instruments

Command-and-control instruments prescribe certain outcomes. Thus, as the name already indicates, they directly influence the behavior of individuals or firms. This can be done in the form of mandates (i.e., things firms must do) or proscriptions (i.e., things firms may not do) by setting standards for certain technologies (e.g., what technologies to use or not and how), processes (i.e., how to do something), emissions (e.g., allowed maximum of certain substances), or performance (e.g., energy efficiency of products or processes). Emission limits, for example, can dictate how much of a substance a company is allowed to emit in absolute or relative terms while certain substances, products, or practices (e.g., the dumping of waste or the use of child labor) might be banned entirely. Such standards thus set the limits within which businesses must operate and thereby try to achieve certain control targets or levels of pollution. A special form of such command-and-control instruments are planning instruments such as land utilization plans which regulate the use of land under governmental jurisdiction. Overall, proscriptions are the most direct sustainability policy instruments, as they ban actors from doing something. Mandates take the opposite approach and dictate certain must-dos. In some countries, for example, companies are required to provide certain social benefits or minimum wages to their employees, they have to ensure various forms of employee participation, or they are obliged to use a certain amount of renewable energy.

Command-and-control instruments, on the one hand, are relatively easy to implement at first as they are not very complex themselves. Furthermore, as they only require the respective actions or behavior to be prescribed (i.e., mandated or denied), they can be implemented relatively fast. The issues that are regulated through command-and-control instruments are usually clear and comprehensible (i.e., "do that" or "don't do that") so that they are relatively predictable for the involved parties without much uncertainty. In sum, these types of instruments are comparably feasible in achieving a desired outcome.

On the other hand, respective instruments usually come with comparably high monitoring costs due to often high complexity of the regulated topics. Various industries and their countless processes and products require detailed and complex regulations catering to the different situations. Regulators then need to set up and maintain inspection and enforcement procedures for all parts of the respective policies. To be able to monitor compliance, the administrators require information that needs to be obtained and processed. Furthermore, the economy, technology, and our knowledge and expectations about sustainability issues are constantly evolving. Keeping up-to-date with regulations is thus a never-ending task. The cost argument also applies to the other side, that is, to those entities that are subject to the regulation. Command-and-control instruments allow for little flexibility, and they force each regulated entity (e.g., a firm) to apply the same standards regardless of the cost. Therefore, they typically result in relatively high overall costs of all actors combined. Those who could reduce, for example, pollution to levels beyond a required standard have little incentive to do so while those who cannot cost-effectively meet the standard are nevertheless forced to hold them. Therefore, command-and-control instruments are relatively static and do not generate much innovation drive. If standards prescribe the use of a certain technology, other options are off the table despite the fact that the same technology may not be appropriate and cost-effective in all situations.

Task B3-1

Find different examples of sustainability-related command-and-control instruments from your country and from a neighboring country and try to think of social and environmental issues. To what extent did they achieve a desired outcome, and how could that outcome have been achieved otherwise?

B.3.2.2 Information requirements and governmental support

Information requirements or offers and governmental support aim at changing the priorities that actors assign to sustainability issues. They are also referred to as suasive instruments because they aim at changing behavior toward sustainability through incentives and information. These instruments function in a more indirect way compared to direct command-and-control instruments. Examples for such instruments are diverse: Governments often foster sustainable development by supporting companies with a better sustainability performance or with more sustainable products. They can, for example, provide financial support through loans or subsidies. In many countries, public development banks have dedicated credit programs for sustainability-related issues. Another form of such governmental support can come in the form of public procurement when, for example, governmental institutions include sustainability issues in tender offers. Instead of offering such incentives, some instruments rather try to discourage certain behaviors. Take-back obligations, for example, commit companies to take back products after their end-of-life to discourage the use of hazardous and difficult-to-recycle substances.

Regarding information, governmental actors and regulators can, for example, launch campaigns, publish manuals or studies, or offer trainings on sustainability-related issues, thus influencing the supply of information. The idea is to create awareness among actors (e.g., consumers) for sustainability and thus influence their behavior. Moreover, governmental actors can also impact the supply of information by others. In this case, public authorities do not disseminate the actual information themselves. Instead, they require certain information to be published by companies or other actors. The basic idea is that markets cannot function well with imperfect information so that information requirements are sometimes necessary to improve resource allocation.

The variety of options for such information requirements is vast. Companies, for example, often have to disclose sustainability information on the corporate level in their annual reporting (see also Chapter C.8) or when implementing an environmental management system (see also Chapter C.7.2), or they have to provide certain information about sustainability aspects of their products (e.g., CO_2 emissions of cars). Sustainability-labeling programs are also product related. While they are widely known as eco-labels, such labels can provide information on a wide range of sustainability issues including social aspects. The idea is to make sustainability information more easily available to consumers to influence their purchase decisions. Such labels can be voluntary or mandatory. Voluntary labels can be used by companies to differentiate their products by promoting certain sustainability traits of their products. Well-known examples for voluntary eco-labels are the "Canada's Environmental Choice," the Nordic Swan in Scandinavian countries, the German "Blue Angel," or the Green Seal in the United States. Labels for social aspects of sustainability are less widespread and often do not yet have a long history. The "Green Button," for example, was introduced in Germany in 2019. It is a governmental label which can be used by companies from the textile industry in Germany to signal responsibility on environmental and social issues. Mandatory labels sometimes warn consumers about possible hazards or display otherwise relevant information. In contrast to voluntary labels, companies cannot opt to display the required information. In some countries, such labels cover entire industries or product ranges. Well-known examples are energy labels which provide information on the energy efficiency of electronic appliances. They are prevalent around the world, for example, the China Energy Label, the Indian BEE star rating, the energy rating label in Australia and New Zealand, the European Union Energy Label, or the EnergyGuide or EnerGuide in the United States and Canada, respectively.

Any of these instruments is usually regarded as less invasive than the command-and-control instruments discussed above. Furthermore, they are relatively flexible in their application and are usually well accepted by companies because they do not intervene drastically with existing operations. Overall, they are often said to be of high practicability as they are relatively easy to implement by policy actors because they create little resistance compared to other instruments. However, their downside is that their effectiveness in promoting sustainable development is also often relatively low and that they usually do not induce long-term behavioral changes. The economic incentives for actors to behave more sustainably are usually rather subtle. Some consumers, for example, adjust their buying behavior and include considerations about energy efficiency in their purchase decisions when seeing an energy label. Others are less interested or put only low weight on such issues, especially when they do not influence their own financial bottom line as is the case for many sustainability issues (e.g., working conditions in supply chains or higher standards in animal husbandry) as will be further illustrated in Chapter B.6.

Task B3-2

Find different examples of sustainability-related information requirements from your country and from a neighboring country. What is their purpose and which stakeholders are addressed with the required information? Under which circumstances can these information requirements lead to a more sustainable business performance?

B.3.2.3 Market-based instruments

Market-based instruments, also referred to as economic sustainability policy instruments, do not issue explicit directives such as command-or-control instruments but they aim at encouraging more sustainable behavior through market signals usually in form of price signals. Thus, they try to improve information of actors in the same way as information requirements. This improved information, however, is directly related to market transactions so that they ideally encourage market actors to undertake sustainability efforts that are in their own interests, which in the end leads to collectively meeting policy goals. In a nutshell, the idea is to internalize negative externalities so that they are given a price in the production and consumption of goods and services. This change in prices should then lead to a change in behavior. The way in which certain sustainability goals are reached is not prescribed so that economic actors can, for example, decide for themselves which technologies they want to apply. Market-based instruments come in two prototypical forms: fees or taxes and tradable permits.

Fees or taxes are directly applied to the amount of pollution generated by a certain source (e.g., a factory or a company). Carbon taxes, for example, are tariffs on the emission of greenhouse gases. With an (increasing) market price for the emission of greenhouse gases, it is reasonable for companies to reduce their emissions. Policymakers thus can use carbon taxes to reach the overarching goals of preventing climate change by reducing greenhouse gas emissions. This example can also be used to illustrate how different forms of taxes can potentially lead to the same outcome but with different implications. A tax on greenhouse gas emissions directly tackles the root causes of climate change, that is, human greenhouse gas emissions. A difficulty of such a tax might be, however, that greenhouse gas emissions indeed need to be calculated, measured, and controlled to be able to tax emitters. It might be easier to tax energy consumption, a strategy that is easily implemented because energy is generally sold in certain measured amounts. A reduced energy consumption can thus also be used to lower greenhouse gas emissions. In this case, however, it might be necessary to differentiate the tax by energy source, because energy produced from lignite or crude oil creates more emissions than energy produced from natural gas or from wind or solar facilities. A special case of such fees or taxes are deposit-refund systems. Users of certain products (e.g., certain types of packaging) pay a surcharge for potentially harmful products for which they receive a refund upon returning the product. The surcharge is thus only permanent when the user does not return the respective item. The idea of such systems is thus to allow for adequate reuse, recycling, or disposal, which would not take place if the user would simply discard the respective product.

Tradable permits (sometimes also referred as cap-and-trade) are similar to fees and taxes in that they try to achieve a cost-efficient reduction of burdens. While fees and taxes directly intervene with the price, tradable permits instead regulate the amount of pollution. With a tradable permit system, regulators set a maximum level of pollution and allocate this level to polluters in the form of tradable permits. Polluters that keep their emission levels low can then sell any of their surplus permits to other polluters. The main differences between these two systems of market-based instruments is thus that in the one case (tradable permits), regulators set a quantity and let the price adjust while in the other case (fees and taxes), regulators set a certain price which then leads to an unknown quantity of burdens. Both systems can also be combined (for more details see, e.g., Stavins, 2003, or Stiglitz, 2009).

Sustainability in society 9: The European Emissions Trading System (EU ETS)

The EU ETS is a well-known example of a market for tradable permits. The system defines a cap for the total volume of greenhouse gas emissions in the European Union from different sources and allows trading of the allocated emission allowances among market actors. With the EU ETS, the European Union aims at meeting emission reduction targets over time as it gradually reduces the amount of emission permits over time. Especially in the beginning, the system was heavily criticized for various aspects in its implementation (e.g., a large number of permits were allocated), which led to a low price of only about EUR 5 per ton of greenhouse gas emissions. Recently, however, the price increased significantly to above EUR 80 per ton in 2021. It is expected to increase further in the next phase of the EU ETS during which the maximum number of permits will be reduced further to reach the emission reduction targets of the European Union. According to a report by the International Monetary Fund, the price per ton of greenhouse gas emissions needs to increase from USD 50 to 100 to be consistent with the 2°C goal. Interestingly, parts of the recent price increase are attributed to hedge funds acting on the market and speculating with tradable permits. Furthermore, organizations such as "Compensators" (www.compensators.org) entered the scene to buy emission allowances with donations from civil society. These allowances are then no longer available and thus ideally reduce emissions as per the market system. Further emissions trading systems exist worldwide.

Sources: Ellerman et al. (2016); International Monetary Fund (2019); Nissen et al. (2020); Schulz (2021)

One of the most important arguments for market-based instruments is that they are supposedly efficient in achieving a desired outcome. Because they directly influence market prices and aim at internalizing negative effects, these instruments provide incentives for the greatest reduction of burdens by those actors who can achieve these reductions most cheaply. In theory, command-and-control instruments could achieve similar cost-effective outcomes if different standards would be set for each source of social or environmental burden. In practice, however, this is not possible because regulators do not know the different compliance costs of the various actors so that they cannot individually adjust the standards. For market-based instruments, instead, regulators do not need this kind of information as the markets themselves provide incentives to the different actors to engage in a cost-effective allocation of reducing burdens. Thus, market-based instruments are also relatively light in terms of their administrative efforts as they do not require the same amount of inspection, enforcement, and compliance procedures compared to command-and-control instruments. Another often made argument in favor of marked-based instruments is that they are dynamic and allow for a high degree of innovation. Prices for burdens such as greenhouse gas emissions can be easily increased over time or the quantity of tradable permits can be reduced. The way in which companies deal with these parameters is not prescribed so that such instruments permit flexibility in achieving certain targets without, for example, prescribing the use of certain technologies or denying certain procedures.

On the downside, agreeing upon and then implementing market-based instruments on a sufficiently large to tackle global sustainability is a challenging task, to say the least. Take the example of combating climate change. Setting-up market-based instruments only in some isolated markets will likely not limit climate change resulting from human activities as actors could then simply move their activities to unregulated markets. International negotiations, however, are extremely complex and need to consider very diverse claims. Free-riding on the expense of others as well as various forms of the prisoner's dilemma, a situation in which it is in the best interest of actors not to cooperate, make it difficult to arrive at a satisfactory consensus (e.g., Clémençon, 2016). Furthermore, market-based instruments are often rather complex to implement in the first place. Taxes and fees need to be defined. For such a definition it is necessary to at least roughly estimate their effects on the desired outcome to be effective in achieving, for example, emission reduction targets. While this might be plausible for large emitters, such as industrial plants, it seems rather difficult for smaller operations, households, or even specific appliances and devices. Without such information, however, the outcome of a tax is uncertain. This could lead to taxes and fees that are either too high (which could harm economic activities) or too low (which would not lead to sufficient behavioral change). Tradable permits are equally complex as they require the implementation and operation of permit markets. This includes the definition and allocation of permits as well as enforcement procedures such as antitrust authorities to ensure open and competitive markets. After all, Stiglitz (2009) points to well-known market imperfections when assessing that "the very conditions (such as imperfect and asymmetric information) … imply that markets by themselves do not in general lead to (constrained) Pareto efficient outcomes" (p. 23). In sum, we can thus characterize market-based policy instruments as an efficient way to address negative externalities, but their effectiveness is uncertain and has to be observed in each case to achieve the desired outcomes.

B.3.3 Differences in regulatory regimes and welfare states

In general, sustainability policy instruments have seen a significant spread worldwide since the 1960s (see, e.g., Tews et al., 2003, for environmental policy instruments) with market-based instruments becoming more popular since the late 1980s (e.g., Stavins, 2003). Despite this trend, the aforementioned overview already illustrated that there is no ideal way to approach all sustainability issues from a policy perspective. Instead, determining which instrument is most appropriate in any given situation likely depends on the nature of the problem or challenge as well as on various institutional factors. This is even more relevant as these institutional factors differ quite significantly all over the world.

Regulatory policies and capacities exhibit vast differences among regulatory actors in different countries and national regimes. In some countries, strict regulations sometimes accompanied by extensive welfare policies display a comparably strongly regulated economy with an active governmental sector while in other countries, social policies are less extensive and regulatory systems might not be as well equipped (see, e.g., Arts & Gelissen, 2010, for a comparison of models of the welfare state). Some countries lack formal, market-enabling institutions and are therefore subject to so-called institutional voids. Khanna and Palepu (2006) characterize institutional voids as "the absence of specialized intermediaries, regulatory systems and contract-enforcing mechanisms" (p. 62) that prohibit the efficient functioning of markets. Such situations can especially be found in developing markets. Here, sustainability-related policies are sometimes either less prevalent or they are not strictly enforced so that they lose impact. In such cases, regulators from other countries sometimes come to the fore and implement regulations which extend their sphere of influence toward such countries (e.g., in the case of the UK Bribery Act or the Foreign Corrupt Practices Act in the United states which both allow prosecution of violations conducted in other countries). This can be the case, for example, when companies from a developed country can be sued in their home country for sustainability-related incidents in a host country (see also Chapter C.3.4). In other cases, transnational rules and regulations try to provide a level playing field. This, however, is not yet foreseeable for the entire world economy but rather for confined areas such as the European Union.

Therefore, different forms of soft law and private governance are sometimes implemented as a substitute for worldwide regulations. Soft law in this regard refers to quasi-legal instruments which do not have any legally binding force such as resolutions by the UN. Private governance is a substitute or supplement to national regulations as it reflects "voluntary, collective CSR initiatives with which companies engage to fulfil their social and/or environmental obligations" (Leitheiser, 2021, p. 1287). The variety of respective instruments is vast, with very different implications for sustainability management and sustainable development. Some of these instruments will be discussed later in this book (see Chapter C.7.1).

Faces of sustainability 6: Kate Raworth

Kate Raworth is a British economist and radical thinker for a new way of economic theory which aligns economic performance with sustainable development. In her book "Doughnut Economics: Seven Ways to Think Like a 21st-Century Economist" she visualizes a doughnut-shaped framework for sustainable economic development which reframes economic problems based on social and ecological goals. According to this framework, 12 social foundations (e.g., peace & justice, education, health etc.) have to be met without overshooting nine ecological boundaries (e.g., biodiversity loss, climate change etc., largely following the work by Steffen et al., 2015) in order for an economy to be prosperous according to the general idea of sustainable development. Raworth's idea has been praised, among others, as "a breakthrough alternative to growth economics" (Monbiot, 2017) but it also received some heavy criticism (Nugent, 2021)—both of which will likely shape the economic debate of the coming century.

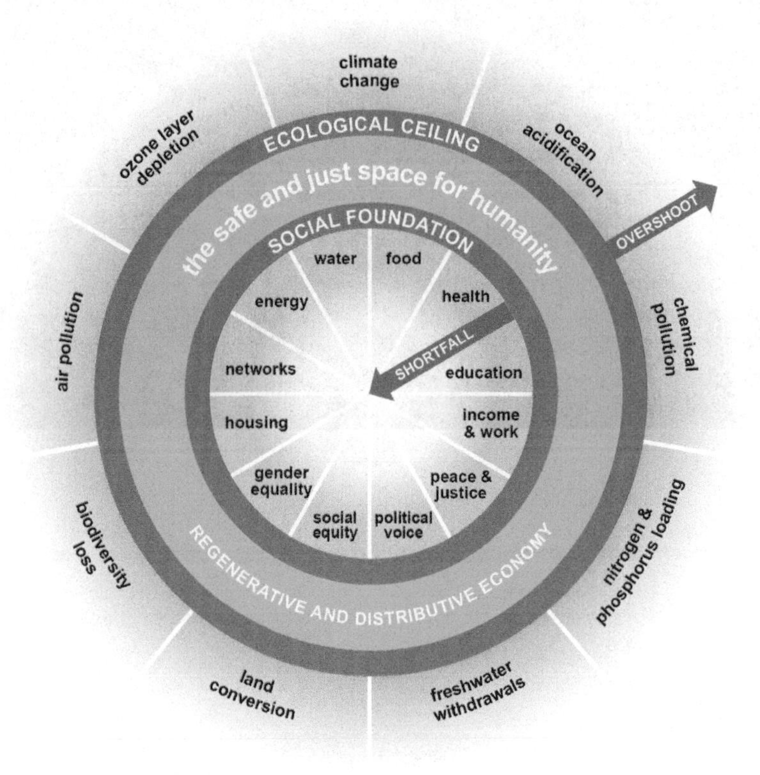

(Model of the doughnut economy, CC BY 4.0, https://commons.wikimedia.org/wiki/File:Doughnut_(economic_model).jpg)

Source: Raworth (2017)

KEY
TAKEAWAYS

- Due to market failures, governments are often assumed to regulate markets and ensure a desired outcome of economic activities but government failure sometimes impedes this endeavor.
- Direct actors have a direct influence on legislation and regulations while indirect actors cannot directly put forward legislation and regulation.
- Indirect actors have different means to enforce their interests.
- With negative externalities the overall social cost originating from production or consumption are not included in market prices.
- Command-and-control instruments prescribe certain outcomes through mandates or proscriptions.
- Information requirements and governmental support aim at changing behavior toward sustainability through incentives and information.
- Market-based instruments aim at encouraging more sustainable behavior through market signals, usually in the form of price signals.
- Market-based instruments are usually distinguished into taxes and fees and tradable permits.
- It depends on the nature of the problem or challenge as well as on various institutional factors, which combination of instrument is most appropriate in any given situation.
- Regulatory policies and capacities exhibit vast differences among regulatory actors in different countries and national regimes.

B.4 Civil society

LEARNING GOALS

After reading this chapter you will be able to ...

- ... explain the role of civil society as "third sector" and give examples of actors in all three sectors as well as potential hybrid forms.
- ... characterize NGOs and distinguish different types along the two dimensions of beneficiaries and activities.
- ... give examples for different NGO activities and tactics.
- ... name various firm-specific risk factors that increase the likelihood of confrontation.
- ... explain potential benefits as well as risks and challenges of cross-sector partnerships for NGOs and for companies.
- ... explain various factors companies should consider when selecting partner organizations.
- ... explain best practices for partnership management.
- ... differentiate different types of partnerships depending on the scope and intensity.

Introduction to Chapter B.4: Screencast
Watch an introduction to the chapter here:

B.4.1 Introduction into civil society and nongovernmental organizations

Next to the state and markets, the civil society is another significant sector in modern societies. It is often referred to as the "third sector" and includes a broad variety of actors that can neither be subsumed as market actors nor as governmental actors. Basically, every one of us of us is part of this third sector when we are not directly acting as customers, as entrepreneurs, as employees, or as politicians. However, individuals are usually not regarded as central stakeholders alone which is why especially more organized elements of civil society are deemed relevant, for example, in sustainability management. Nevertheless, individual actors can be the roots and faces of civil society movements. Greta Thunberg, for example, was the sole origin of what then became the Fridays for Future movement—nowadays a more or less decentrally organized civil society movement (see again Chapter A.1.2). Figure 11 illustrates the position of the civil society as the third sector. It also shows that there are sometimes hybrid forms of organizations that can be positioned on the overlap of two sectors. State-owned companies or public–private partnerships (i.e., collaborations between a private company and a government agency), for example, can be positioned as hybrids between the market and the state sector. Social enterprises (see also Chapter C.9.2), commercial branches or activities of some NGOs, and various partnerships between businesses and NGOs are located between the market and the civil society sector. Finally, NGOs, which are in large parts funded through governmental subsidies, are expressions of hybrids between the state and the civil society sector.

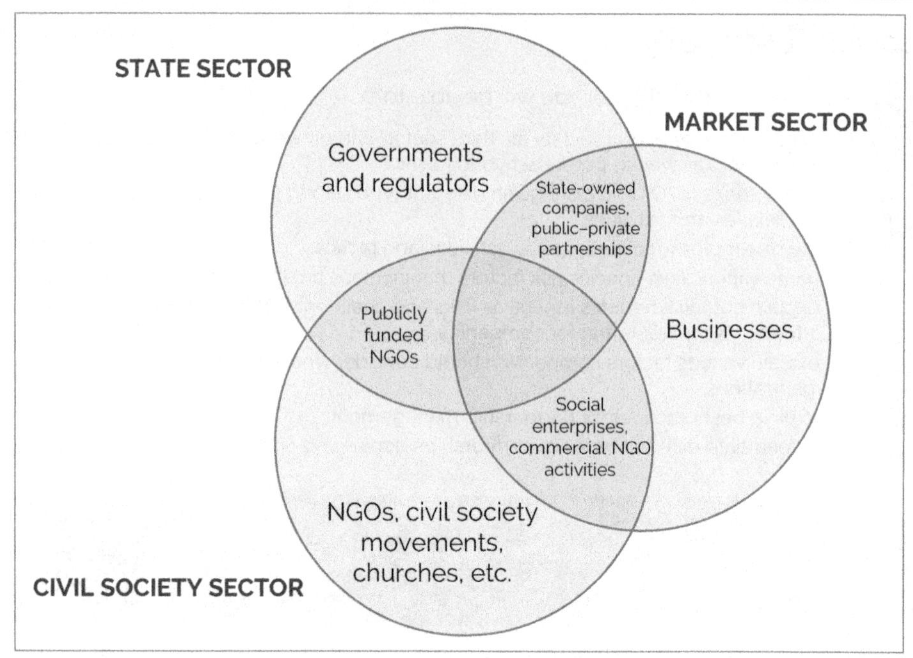

Figure 11: Civil society as third sector

Civil society organizations usually form around a common cause, interest, or idea. This can be, for example, religious groups or loosely organized movements such as the Fridays for Future movement, especially in its early stages. Arguably, the most prevailing type of civil society organization in many instances are NGOs. According to Yaziji and Doh (2009), the UN characterizes an NGO as "any nonprofit, voluntary citizens' group which is organized on a local, national or international level. Task-oriented and driven by people with a common interest, NGOs perform a variety of services and humanitarian functions, bring citizens' concerns to governments, monitor policies and encourage political participation at the community level. They provide analysis and expertise, serve as early warning mechanisms, and help monitor and implement international agreements. Some are organized around specific issues, such as human rights, the environment or health." (p. 4) Market and governmental failures (see again Chapter B.3.1) have led to voids in different areas and NGOs increasingly seek to fill these voids. Especially in the new millennium, the number of NGOs has increased significantly (Jahan, 2016). In the United States, for example, there are now more than 1.5 million NGOs and in India even more than 3 million (Anand, 2015; Bureau of Democracy, Human Rights, and Labor, 2021). They have become an important voice in modern society by their sheer number, their accumulated knowledge, and their often high legitimacy in society.

The influence on companies of civil society in general and of NGOs in particular is already by definition indirect. Since NGOs and the civil society at large are nongovernmental, they cannot influence private business actors via laws or regulations. Furthermore, they are also not part of the market sector and thus have usually no direct financial or contractual leverage over companies compared to more direct stakeholders from the market sector such as customers or suppliers. This does not mean, however, that they are powerless. Instead of direct influence, NGOs revert to indirect pressure. They use, for example, consumers, employees, regulators, or actors from jurisprudence to exert power over companies. Furthermore, NGOs often also leverage other actors which also have an indirect influence as multiplicators, for example, the media or analysts. They gain their relevance and power from several factors (Yaziji & Doh, 2009), such as a high legitimacy in the eyes of society, their status as underdogs which often brings them sympathy, or their capabilities to build and leverage networks that are often extensive.

Faces of sustainability 7: Naomi Klein

Naomi Klein is a strong voice in civil society. The Canadian journalist and bestselling author is a well-known criticist of globalization and capitalism. In her book "No Logo" she vividly attacks today's consumer culture and criticizes many large corporations for their unethical practices especially in their value chains in the Global South. Later, she also attacks market fundamentalism as blocking reforms to protect our climate and the environment in general. Her books and documentaries are translated in many languages and have received numerous prizes. Usually, companies do not treat single persons as relevant stakeholder groups (after all, individuals are not groups). In some cases, however, even single actors in civil society can become powerful voices. In the case of Naomi Klein, for example, her role as journalist and author makes her an important multiplier. Thus, she is being heard by many, which makes her a powerful, yet contested voice for many aspects of sustainable development. In "No Logo", for example, she criticized the multinational apparel giant Nike for poor working conditions in its supply chains so that the company even published an extensive response to her accusations. Some food for thought: What do you think—how would the company have assessed Naomi Klein according to the stakeholder typology introduced in Chapter B.1.3?

(Photo by Ben Powless, CC BY 2.0, https://www.flickr.com/photos/peoplessocialforum/14996438642/)

Sources: Ekhardt (2015); Klein (1999); Klein (2014); Nike (2020)

Sustainability in society 10: Targeting companies using their own weapons – Activists hijacking of HSBC climate advertising

In November 2020, the management of HSBC, the British multinational investment bank, was caught by surprise by a billboard campaign in the United Kingdom mimicking the banks own recent ads. In its own campaign titled "We are not an island," the bank pictured itself as a responsible company announcing, among others, that it aimed to reduce carbon emissions from its investment portfolio to zero by 2050. Various civil society groups criticized HSBC for a lack of short-term targets and its continuous investments in fossil fuels as well as numerous other issues related to socially or environmentally unsustainable investment activities. Activists from the group Brandalism used more than 250 billboards, bus stops, and other advertising spaces across 10 cities in the United Kingdom to display spoof HSBC adverts. The ads accuse the bank of "climate colonialism" and broach the issues of the financing of climate destruction, fossil fuels, and immigration detention centers. In 2021, the group repeated its efforts with similar campaigns targeting Barclays and Standard Chartered, which were all picked up by large media outlets and received significant attention.

(Photo by Matt Bonner, reproduced with permission, www.brandalism.ch)

Sources: Ferrer (2021); Mistlin (2021); Westwater (2020)

While this may sound as if NGOs or other civil society organizations are a homogeneous group, they are in fact not. Instead, the definition above already implies that the variety of NGOs is large as they cover a vast array of issues ranging from human rights, to the environment, health, anti-corruption, animal rights, and so forth. To sort this variety, Yaziji and Doh (2009) cluster NGOs along two dimensions: (1) the beneficiaries of the NGO and (2) the activities of NGOs. The first dimension distinguishes between self-benefiting NGOs and other-benefiting NGOs. The former NGOs are designed to provide a benefit to their own members such as automobile associations, unions, community groups, or amateur sports clubs. In the latter types of NGOs, those who contribute to the cause of the organization usually do not benefit themselves from their efforts. Here, many environmental or social advocacy groups such as Greenpeace, the WWF, the Red Cross or Red Crescent Movement, or the animal rights organization PETA can serve as examples. The second dimension distinguishes advocacy NGOs from service NGOs. The former NGOs use a variety of activities such as informing the public, monitoring activities of others (usually businesses or governments), lobbying, or organizing boycotts to promote their social or environmental causes. Moreover, advocacy NGOs themselves can come in different flavors. Social movement NGOs advocate for rather radical changes. Watchdog NGOs instead usually try to ensure that others do not act against the rules and thus rather support the existing system. Service NGOs provide concrete goods and services to beneficiaries who cannot meet their needs themselves. Thus, they try to fill existing voids where especially the state sector is unable or unwilling to provide for basic needs. Finally, many NGOs cannot easily be categorized along the two dimensions as they conduct multiple activities from both dimensions or they change their approaches over time.

In general, NGOs try to further their cause by influencing others. For instance, they can influence actors from the market or the state sector or civil society at large. With regard to the regulators and governmental actors from the state sector, especially larger NGOs can engage in lobbying activities. Furthermore, just like companies, NGOs can use public relations activities for opinion making. Many NGOs also engage in knowledge transfer and use their knowledge and expertise in specific fields to publish studies related to their issues or they engage in awareness raising. Some NGOs see themselves as think tanks or facilitators for different issues. The World Resources Institute with its vision to support the elimination of poverty and the sustaining of the natural environment for all people, for example, provides guidance to governments, businesses, and communities on energy, climate, food, or water issues, and so on. Other well-known NGOs publish studies and reports on environmental issues (e.g., the WWF or Greenpeace) or on social issues (e.g., OXFAM). When acting vis-à-vis the market sector and, thus, companies, NGOs have a broad variety of strategies at their disposal, which range from positive engagement to hostile activities as summarized in Figure 12. In the following, we will first discuss confrontative strategies before turning to collaboration and partnerships between NGOs and businesses.

General attitude	Positive	Sympathetic	Moderate	Suspicious	Hostile
	←				→
Exemplary activities	Dialogue strategies, Persuasion	Claims for codes of conduct	Claims for legal rules	Lawsuits	Calls for boycott

Figure 12: Overview of NGO activities vis-à-vis companies

Task B4-1

Identify different NGOs with different approaches. What is their leverage to improve sustainability, what are the disadvantages? Can you identify an organization that simultaneously pursues a confrontative and a cooperative approach?

B.4.2 Confrontative strategies of nongovernmental organizations

Many NGOs are known for their confrontative strategies and campaigns against companies and their activities. Such campaigns can have a significant, negative influence on a company's operations as they are a potential threat to company legitimacy in the eyes of different stakeholders. Thus, they can negatively influence the perception of a company in the eyes of current and potential employees, customers, investors, governmental actors, and others. Some companies seem to be more prone for confrontations with NGOs than others. According to Yaziji and Doh (2009), these companies are characterized by a number of firm-specific risk factors such as ...

- ... offering life-saving, life-threatening or "socially sensitive" products (e.g., pharmaceuticals, health care, weapons, and tobacco).

- ... confronting changing social values (e.g., fashion, media, alcohol, pornography, gambling).
- ... generating large externalities (e.g., pollution, use of "commons" resources).
- ... having high power in a supply chain or market.
- ... having high brand awareness (e.g., retail, clothing, food and beverage, automotive, media, finance).
- ... using new technologies (e.g., genetic engineering, stem-cell-based research, personal-data collection).
- ... doing business in different regions with differing ethical or social expectations (e.g., virtually every multinational company, particularly those operating in both developed and developing countries).
- ... being a representative of controversial institutions (e.g., capitalism, globalization, American culture).

Task B4-2

Identify a few specific companies from different industries—preferably some with direct connections to end consumers and some in the business-to-business segment. How do they differ in terms of the above-mentioned risk factors? Explain why!

Depending on the basic stance of an NGO against companies or society at large, NGOs have different tactics against companies at their disposal (Yaziji & Doh, 2009). Ideologically mainstream NGOs generally engage constructively with existing institutions. They can, for example, engage in cross-sector partnerships to further their cause through dialogue and mutual activities or they can build on so-called "watchdog campaigns." The aim is then usually to persuade or force the targeted company to change their behavior so that it acts in accordance with existing standards and expectations. Activities in such campaigns can come from a broader portfolio of activities as outlined in Figure 12 above, for example, by exerting public pressure through (social) media, via lawsuits, or by influencing or supporting governmental institutions and regulators. Moderate NGOs often target a company with their campaigns in a kind of "proxy war." In such cases, the NGOs not only try to achieve a change in the specific activities of the company in the spotlight but, moreover, aim at general changes beyond the specific case (e.g., in terms of how businesses or governments act with regard to certain social or environmental issues). Greenpeace's campaign against Shell's disposal of the oil platform Brent Spar in 1995 is a classic example of such a case. Not only did Greenpeace try to inhibit the deep-sea sinking of the oil platform by Shell, but it also tried to influence governments to change common regulations toward more environmentally friendly regulations in general (see box "Sustainability in business" in this Chapter). The most extreme form of confrontation, finally, lies in barely institutional or even contra institutional tactics such as disruption, violence, or destruction of property. Organizations engaging in such tactics are usually ideologically radical and promote fundamental institutional change.

Sustainability in business 14: Shell and the public outcry on the Brent Spar

The year 1995 is regarded by many as a turning point in the relationship between the market sector and the civil society sector. In this year, the worldwide environmental NGO Greenpeace brought the multinational oil corporation Shell to its knees over a dispute on the sinking of an abandoned oil platform in the European North Sea.

The Brent Spar was an oil storage platform in the North Sea off the coast of Scotland. It was jointly owned by the two oil multinationals, Shell and Esso, and wholly operated by Shell. In 1991, the company decided to sink the platform as it was of no longer of use. The company announced the planned sinking of the Brent Spar in early 1995 after the British government approved the procedure and all neighboring states agreed. Only shortly later, Greenpeace activists occupied the platform to protest against the disposal and to demand an environmentally friendly onshore dismantling. This would avoid dumping several tons of oil mud and weakly radioactive residues into the ocean. Overall and beyond the specific case, the NGO was lobbying for a comprehensive ban on ocean dumping. Shell as operating company, however, insisted on the governmental permission and attempted to force the activists from the platform. At that point in time, the entire matter became a global media event with public outcries, boycotts, protests, and even threats of attack on Shell facilities. Shell suffered significant loss of revenues in several European countries and took a heavy punch on its reputation and public legitimacy. On June 20, 1995, the company eventually gave up and the Brent Spar was later dismantled in Norway.

Interesting in this case is not only the example of a confrontative NGO campaign but also the fact that it showed the power of civil society organizations even toward large multinational corporations. Furthermore, it illustrates how legitimate (or not), different claims might be perceived in society. More than 30 studies performed by consultancies and universities confirmed that the deep-sea disposal would be the preferred option for the environment as well as for the health and safety of the involved people. Scientists later argued that "the addition of extra dumped metal would probably act as nutrient to the local ecosystem" (Nisbet & Fowler, 1995, p. 715) and that "the bacteria of the ocean floor would have greeted the arrival of Brent Spar as if all their Christmases had come at once" (n.a., 1995, p. 708). In September 1995, Greenpeace even apologized to Shell for miscalculating an alleged 5,500 tons of oil residues on the Brent Spar, while it was in fact less than 100 tons as previously reported by Shell. Nevertheless, the public largely believed and supported Greenpeace in its claims and goals throughout the process, which illustrates the potential influence of civil society on sustainable development—and on stakeholder management. As an end to this episode, a 1997 report of Det Norske Veritas, a Norwegian accredited certification body, reassessed that no form of disposal was per se superior and that the onshore option indeed has some ecological advantages over a sinking in the deep-sea.

Sources: Grolin (1998); Jordan (2001); Koch et al. (2005); Lofstedt and Renn (1997)

B.4.3 Partnerships between companies and nongovernmental organizations

While many people instantly think of confrontation and campaign when talking about businesses and NGOs, collaboration and so-called cross-sector partnerships, that is, initiatives "in which a firm and at least one partner from the nonprofit sector work together to pursue at least one noneconomic, sustainability-related objective" (Feilhauer & Hahn, 2021b, p. 685), have become a common tool in sustainability management. Both partners, NGO and companies, have a lot to gain from such relationships (e.g., B. Gray & Stites, 2013; R. Hahn & Gold, 2014; Yaziji & Doh, 2009). NGOs often lack financial, human, or other resources to pursue their mission. Partnerships with companies can provide them with such resources as well as with operational know-how in areas where the NGO might not be as experienced. The same applies the other way around, as NGOs often bring specific skills, competencies, as well as specialized knowledge in their field of expertise to the partnerships. An NGO dedicated to conservation of biodiversity in a specific region, for example, is likely to have detailed information about the local ecological environment that can be useful for sustainability management projects. An NGO with a mission to end modern slavery probably has in-depth knowledge about the conditions in local supply chains in the Global South. Both might be experienced in interacting with local communities. NGOs also often have distinct networks that provide them with access to further information and resources. Due to their mission they are usually aware of pressing social and environmental issues as well as of larger social forces and sentiments. Finally, as illustrated above, many NGOs have a high legitimacy and reputation, which can be beneficial for mutual projects and increase the credibility of the company partners.

However, cross-sector partnerships with NGOs frequently come with some distinct risks and challenges as well (e.g., Berger et al., 2004; Rondinelli & London, 2003). The relationship between companies and NGOs can be complicated as they operate from very different backgrounds and frequently there is initial scepticism or even mistrust. Accordingly, there is often a rather long learning curve and both partners need to adjust their expectations and accept the different values of their counterpart. Before such learning occurs, there is an increased possibility of misunderstandings which can also lead to misallocations of resources. Finally, as with any other partnership, both partners provide each other with information that is often sensitive that could potentially be misused.

Rather than broadening their networks with new partnerships, companies prefer to reinforce existing partnerships with NGOs (Feilhauer & Hahn, 2021a). This is, however, not necessarily the most effective way to establish new partnerships. Instead, there are several aspects to consider when selecting new partners (Berger et al., 2004; B. Gray & Stites, 2013). First, partners should be relevant for the given issue that is to be tackled. Thus, there should be a fit of mission (i.e., the issue at hand should be at the core of the NGO's mission) and the goals of the company partner and the NGO partner should be reasonably aligned. Second, partner resources should be adequate. That means that resources of both partners should complement each other and also the credibility of both partners should be high so that one partner does not harm the other in the relationship. Furthermore, the gap in power balance between both partners should not be too large so that the risk of manipulation is lower. Third, the partners' approach should be fitting. In general, suspicious or hostile NGOs are unlikely to partner with businesses in the first place. However, also not all NGOs with a moderate to positive stance toward businesses might be suitable for any kind of partnership. Service NGOs, for example, might be especially adept at providing social services to specific types of beneficiaries while advocacy NGOs often have extensive experience in lobbying or information policies. Furthermore, some cultural fit between partner organizations is desirable. This applies to issues of national or regional culture as well as to issues of organizational culture. NGOs, for example, usually have a different mindset (roughly: mission driven) than many businesses (roughly: profit driven) so that both partners need to be aware of such differences to avoid a cultural clash. In this regard, previous experience with respective partnerships on both sides can be beneficial.

Once a partnership has been established, B. Gray and Stites (2013) suggest a few best practices for managing partnerships. First, they recommend to be inclusive which involves sharing power, finding consensus, and clarifying decision-making authorities. Second, they advise setting expectations for the partnership. This includes agreeing on norms and management processes in terms of rules that guide conversations, protect confidentiality and, if applicable, property rights. Furthermore, and as in any partnership, conflicts can surface at some point in time also in cross-sector collaborations. Conflicts are more likely if the partners are distinctly different, for example, with regard to their goals and management procedures, therefore, clear rules for managing conflicts should be defined. Evaluation of the success of a partnership can help in the process as it also enables continuous improvements. Third, partners should build understanding for each other by exploring their differences and finding a shared vision for their partnership. In this regard, it can be helpful to understand the partnerships as a process of continuous learning and to be patient as it likely takes time to build a mutual understanding and to work together on often highly complex issues of sustainable development.

Argenti (2004, pp. 110–113) summarizes these recommendations in seven best practices:

- Realize that socially responsible companies are likely targets but also attractive candidates for collaboration.
- Don't wait for a crisis to collaborate.
- Think strategically about relationships with NGOs.
- Recognize that collaboration involves some compromise.

- Appreciate the value of the NGOs' independence.
- Understand that building relationships with NGOs takes time and effort.
- Think more like an NGO by using communication strategically.

Sustainability in society 11: The foundation of the Marine Stewardship Council by WWF and Unilever

The Marine Stewardship Council (MSC) is an international NGO devoted to protecting oceans and promoting fishing in line with intergenerational justice so that seafood supplies are safe for future generations. Its main instrument is a fishery certification program with its own ecolabel that can be found on many seafood products of various brands in grocery stores around the world. The idea behind the label is to increase consumer awareness for sustainable fishing practices and, eventually, to arrive at a seafood market with a sustainable basis. It was initially founded in 1996 as a partnership between the WWF, as a well-known international conservation NGO, and Unilever, the multinational fast-moving consumer goods giant. In the beginning, the MSC was thus a hybrid organization between the civil society and the market sector. Already in 1997, however, the MSC was registered as an independent organization, and its 2019-2020 annual report described that 17.4 percent of all wild marine catch was engaged with the MSC with 18,735 different MSC labeled products worldwide.

The MSC fills a void as it provides private governance through voluntary certification for the global issue of overfishing and sustainable fishery, which is discussed controversially in global politics and overall receives very limited regulatory guidance. The sheer numbers illustrate that the MSC's approach is relatively successful in promoting sustainable fishery. However, the MSC has also been regularly criticized for weak standards and being too lenient with third-party certifiers. In this regard, some interesting hypothetical thoughts are salient: Would higher standards have led to the same success with regard to the diffusion of MSC certificates? If not, is approaching the industry with, from the industry's point of view, attractive standards a promising approach to promoting sustainable fishery and to induce gradual change? Or does it maybe even cement only seemingly sustainable practices by offering the industry the opportunity to promote itself as sustainable in the eyes of the consumer? Would a radical opposition of current fishing practices lead to a faster change toward a truly sustainable fishing industry?

Sources: Christian et al. (2013); Le Manach et al. (2020); Marine Stewardship Council (2020); Wijen and Chiroleu-Assouline (2019)

If the procedure of partner choice and partnership management are successful, they can lead to different types of partnerships depending on the scope and intensity (Austin, 2000; B. Gray & Stites, 2013). Reactive or philanthropic partnerships are usually rather limited in their scope, and they do not involve an extensive sharing of responsibilities. They can be used to work on short-term problems or very specific issues (e.g., an environmental impact assessment). Through philanthropic engagement, a company provides financial contributions to an NGO without much further engagement. Transactional partnerships move a step further with regard to their scope and shared responsibilities. They often aim at improving profit or market share, for example, through eco-labeling supported by NGOs or a project-based partnership to improve the sustainability performance in supply chains. Integrative or transformative partnerships are broadest in scope and shared responsibilities. They try to align financial with social and ecological considerations and often combine values, missions, and strategies of both partners. Examples are joint sustainability standards or partnerships to include income-poor parts of the population in value chains.

KEY TAKEAWAYS

- The power exerted by civil society actors is important and should be considered in sustainability management.
- NGOs can be very heterogeneous. They can be categorized in self-benefiting and other-benefiting NGOs as well as in advocacy and service NGOs.
- NGOs try to further their cause by influencing others, e.g. companies. Their activities can range from being positive to being hostile.
- Some companies seem to be more prone for confrontations with NGOs than others, e.g., when they generate large externalities or due to other factors.
- Companies and NGOs can benefit in numerous ways from cross-sector partnerships (e.g., gaining expertise or specific resources) but relationships can be complicated due to the different background.
- Partners should be relevant for the given issue that is to be tackled, partner resources should be adequate, the partners' approach should be fitting, and there should be some cultural fit between partner organizations.
- Partners should be willing to share power, find consensus, and clarify decision-making, they should set expectations for the partnership, and they should build understanding for each other.
- There are different forms of cross-sector partnerships ranging from reactive or philanthropic partnerships to transactional partnerships to integrative or transformative partnerships.

B.5 Investors

LEARNING GOALS

After reading this chapter you will be able to ...

- ... explain the general idea of sustainable investments.
- ... describe the development and current relevance of sustainable investment.
- ... explain the differences between active and passive approaches and their different forms.
- ... explain how sustainability ratings complement financial ratings.
- ... describe how sustainability ratings are conducted and critically discuss their opportunities and limitations.
- ... critically discuss how different forms of sustainable investment might have an impact on sustainable development.

Introduction to Chapter B.5: Screencast
Watch an introduction to the chapter here:

B.5.1 Background and recent developments of sustainable investments

The idea of sustainable finance and sustainable investments is to additionally consider sustainability criteria when making investment decisions. An emphasis here lies not only on "sustainability" but also on "additionally," as the basic premise is that we are still talking about investments and financial decisions. Thus, financial returns are still of central importance as are, depending on the type of investment (e.g., stocks, bonds, ...), the risk and the liquidity of the investment. The different goals of this magic triangle of investment (i.e., the interplay of returns, risk, and availability) are usually competing. There is no investment which can offer high yields, low risks, and high liquidity at the same time. In sustainable finance, the situation becomes even more complex, as the triangle becomes a square by adding the fourth dimension of sustainability, that is, the sustainability performance of the issuer, for example, of a stock or a bond. Accordingly, sustainable investments are not restricted to a specific asset class but can include stocks, corporate and government bonds, loans, or even crowdfunding.

Task B5-1

You are the Vice President of Asset Management at a small private bank. Your institution plans to launch a new sustainability-focused investment fund. The CEO asks you to come up with a set of criteria that seem suitable for your bank, under consideration of the magic triangle of investment. Prepare your ideas!

The added dimension of sustainability is often also referred to as the "ESG" dimension or criteria. ESG stands for "environmental, social, and (corporate) governance". These three factors are widely used to measure the sustainability performance or impact of an investment object. However, just as there is no absolute conceptual clarity and some widely used synonyms and related terms for sustainability management (see again Chapter A.2), there are also many terms frequently used when talking about sustainability-related issues in finance and investment. You often find terms such as "sustainable investment," "ethical investment," "socially responsible investment," or "green investment" (Sandberg et al., 2009). While some may carry nuanced differences with regard to their orientation (e.g., green investments usually focus on the "E" of ESG while ethical investments often highlight the "S" or "G"), others are virtually identical in practice (e.g., sustainable investments and socially responsible investments can focus on any of the three aspects of ESG). The underlying premise of any of these ideas is that they complement regular investment criteria (risk, return, liquidity) with further sustainability-related considerations.

The overall market for sustainable investments has seen staggering growth rates worldwide over the last years. In 2020, global investments considering some sort of sustainability criteria have reached USD 35.3 trillion or 35.9 percent of total assets under management (Global Sustainable Investment Alliance, 2021). That is an increase of 55 percent in just four years. While this is impressive, the proportion of sustainable investments relative to other managed assets is highly uneven around the world. In Canada, a staggering 61.8 percent of total assets under management follow some sort of sustainability criteria while Japan reaches only 24.3 percent. Furthermore, what classifies as sustainable investment is not clearly defined so there might be differences in estimates of the total market share and size when looking at different sources. In any case and no matter where you are located in the world, it should be relatively easy to find some sort of sustainable investment opportunity, because almost any financial service provider nowadays offers respective products.

Sustainability in society 12: The UN Principles for Responsible Investment

The UN Principles for Responsible Investment (PRI) is a high-profile initiative under the roof of the UN with more than 3,000 signatories and almost USD 120 trillion in assets under management in 2020. It addresses investors around the world and encourages them to sign six aspirational principles (UN PRI, 2020, p. 6):

"1. We will incorporate ESG issues into investment analysis and decision-making processes.

2. We will be active owners and incorporate ESG issues into our ownership policies and practices.

3. We will seek appropriate disclosure on ESG issues by the entities in which we invest.

4. We will promote acceptance and implementation of the Principles within the investment industry.

5. We will work together to enhance our effectiveness in implementing the Principles.

6. We will each report on our activities and progress towards implementing the Principles."

The PRI works with investors around the globe providing support, for example, through frameworks for action, trainings, events, and collaboration platforms. As such, it is not a regulatory body and it has no significant checks and balances. Becoming a signatory thus does not necessarily mean that the respective investor automatically has a solid approach or superior performance in sustainable investments (Eccles, 2020).

This comes as no surprise, because not only does society seem to be moving toward sustainability thinking at a different pace around the world (as we have argued throughout this book) but also regulations around the world push the topic higher up on the agenda. The European Union, for example, recently developed a sustainable finance taxonomy (14970/19 ADD 1, 2019). According to this taxonomy, business activities will be classified according to sustainability aspects. The taxonomy provides definitions on which economic activities can be considered sustainable and thus enables investors and policymakers to make decisions based on these definitions—including a controversial debate on the question of whether energy from natural gas and nuclear activities should be label as sustainable in the taxonomy or not (Rankin, 2022). Initially, the taxonomy is focusing on climate change aspects with a planned extension to include social and environmental issues. The idea is to shift financial flows toward supporting green business activities. Initially, capital-market oriented companies with more than 500 employees as well as banks and insurance companies have to disclose the extent to which their activities are in line with the taxonomy to allow for a better comparison of their sustainability efforts. Similar and other regulatory efforts are also under way not only in major financial markets such as the United States but also in many emerging country markets (International Finance Corporation, 2019; Macbeth et al., 2020).

B.5.2 Sustainable investment approaches

As we already illustrated above, sustainable investment means different things to different people. A common differentiation is between passive and active approaches (Eurosif, 2018; Global Sustainable Investment Alliance, 2021; US SIF Foundation, 2020). The central question in this regard is whether or not the investor actively engages with the investment object to influence the sustainability behavior of the investee.

As you might have guessed, in the active approach (also called investor advocacy or engagement), providers of capital engage with the investee to drive social and ecological topics and standards. This can be done by exercising voting rights as a shareholder of a company or by initiating a dialogue with the management of the company. The former is restricted to specific occasions—usually the annual meeting. Here, shareholders are asked to vote on various company related issues, often with relevance to various sustainability topics or they can file shareholder resolutions. As voting rights are specific to shareholders, this form of active engagement is also restricted to investments in company stocks. Another form of active engagement is a dialogue with the management of a company. Large investors often meet with the top management of their investment objects in investor calls or at investor conferences or roadshows. Here, they can actively advocate for sustainability issues and consult with, for example, the board of a company on how to improve sustainability performance. One idea of this approach is to not only invest in front runner companies but also in those companies that improve or have the ability to improve in sustainability matters to support companies and promote transition processes toward sustainability. However, such an active engagement with a company's management is not restricted to a positive influence toward sustainability but can also be pursued by investors with rather the opposite stance, that is, with a sole focus on short-term profits or shareholder value maximization. As such a form of active engagement is not regulated, it is not restricted to equity investors but it can also be used by debt providers. It is usually restricted only to important financers while retail investors cannot directly interact with the management of a company outside of annual meetings. However, retail investors can of course look for active approaches, for example, in sustainable investment funds.

In passive approaches, investors by definition do not actively engage with the investment object. Instead, they consider various sustainability-related criteria before making an investment decision. This can be done via negative and positive criteria, which take previous performance or activities into account. When applying negative criteria (or negative screening), certain investment options are excluded from the investment universe (i.e., from all generally available investment options) based on ESG criteria. This can either be done via value-based screening or via norm-based screening. When applying value-based screening, investments are excluded based on personal or religious values. Norm-based screening instead relies on an external perspective and considers investment objects when they are in accordance with certain international standards and norms such as, for example, the UN Global Compact (see also Chapter C.7.1.3), the OECD guidelines for multinational enterprises, or core norms of the International Labour Organization. Widely applied negative criteria for exclusions are, for example, the production of weapons, tobacco products, nuclear energy, or pornographic material and gambling (the latter two often due to religious reasons) as well as companies using child labor. Applying negative criteria is arguably the most basic form of sustainable investment as it excludes only relatively small areas from the investment universe. It is relatively easy to carry out negative screenings so that this is a very widespread type of sustainable investments.

Other than negative criteria, using positive criteria (or positive screening) aims at choosing investments that achieve certain minimum standards or are characterized by certain ESG criteria or a (relatively) positive performance in these areas. Most well-known, with many retail investors, are the so-called sustainability themed investments. This means that investors specifically seek to invest in certain areas they connect with sustainability such as the production of renewable energy or investments related to water management or sustainable transportation. Compared to negative exclusion criteria, this approach lies on the other end of the spectrum when looking at the restriction of the investment universe, because such themed investments specifically single out certain areas in which investments are then made. Another option of positive screening is the best-in-class approach. It looks at investing in those investment objects that are relatively sustainable compared with their peers. Typically, a performance evaluation based on certain ESG criteria needs to be conducted (see Chapter B.5.3) which rates different investment objects to allow for a comparison among comparable investment objects usually of the same industry. Only investment objects that are above a certain relative threshold enter the potential investment universe. Finally, usually the smallest niche in the sustainable investment market is the field of impact investing. Impact investments can be defined as "investments made with the intention to generate positive, measurable social and environmental impact alongside a financial return" (Hand et al., 2020, p. 74). Thus, investors not only consider certain ESG criteria as additional criteria but they make investments with the explicit intention to generate a positive and measurable sustainability impact, for example, by improving human rights, working conditions, environmental protection, etc. Investments are then made into sustainable innovations, projects, or companies to support solving societal problems, for instance, via sustainability themed crowdfunding (Bento et al., 2019). Figure 13 provides an overview of all approaches and how they restrict investment options in the investment universe.

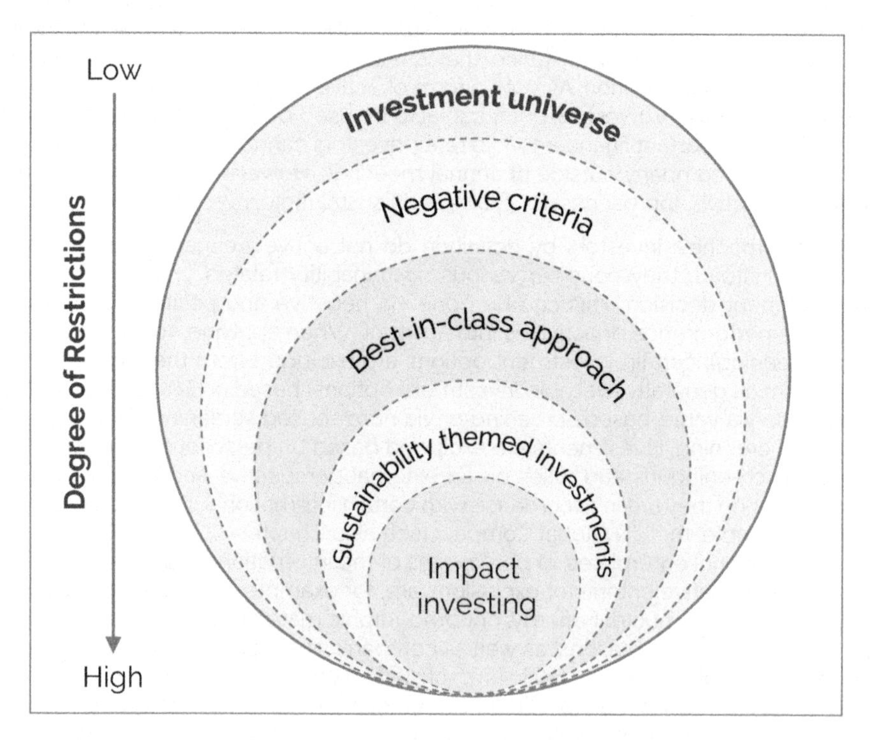

Figure 13: Overview of sustainable investment approaches in the investment universe

Finally, negative and positive criteria can of course be used in combination and also passive and active approaches can be used simultaneously. An important note at the end: Active and passive approaches in sustainable investment are not to be confused with actively managed investment funds (i.e., a selection of investments made and managed by a fund manager) versus passive exchange-traded funds (ETFs, i.e., an index fund that passively mirrors a certain stock or bond market index). Many actively managed sustainability investments funds, for example, follow a passive approach when the fund manager picks stocks based on the best-in-class-idea while an ETF can at least potentially also follow an active approach by engaging with the companies included in its portfolio.

Task B5-2

Have a look at the portfolio of your bank (or any other bank in your country): What kind of sustainable investment products to they offer for retail investors? Have a closer look at the background information of some of these products (e.g., investment funds) and assess which sustainable investment approaches they follow. Do you see differences and which approach does best fit your own understanding of sustainability?

Sustainability in business 15: Sustainability-linked bonds by Henkel

Sustainable finance can of course not only be interesting from an investors perspective but it can also be used as an element corporate financing strategy. In 2021, for example, the German consumer goods company Henkel issued bonds with a volume of more than EUR 700 million that are linked to the achievement of certain sustainability targets defined by the company. If the targets are not met, the interest rate is adjusted. The respective performance indicators cover reduced CO2 emissions and an increased proportion of recycled plastic used in plastic packaging.

Source: Henkel AG & Co. KGaA (2021)

Task B5-3

You are (again) the Vice President of Asset Management at a small private bank. Your institution plans to launch a new sustainability-focused investment fund. The CEO asks you to brief her on the pros and cons of the different approaches for sustainable investments based on the following criteria: (1) efforts needed to identify suitable investment objects, (2) certainty to contribute to sustainable development, and (3) general financial risks (and opportunities).

B.5.3 Sustainability-related ratings

Sophistically and holistically including sustainability aspects into investment decisions is a challenging task, because sustainability management in itself is highly complex with many different issues and areas of activities as outlined throughout this book. Assessing sustainability performance by evaluating goals, strategies, or performance indicators is thus a resource intensive task (see also Chapter C.6), which has resulted in its own market for sustainability ratings that investors can use to either completely outsource or complement their own internal research activities.

Sustainability ratings assess the sustainability performance of companies or entire countries. Their main purpose in sustainable investments is to be used as a basis for the sustainability aspects of investment decisions. Thus, they complement regular financial ratings in which rating agencies (e.g., the well-known "Big Three," i.e., S&P Global Ratings, Moody's, and the Fitch Group) assess, from a financial perspective, the likelihood with which a debtor will pay back its debt. The idea is that by assessing ESG aspects, an investor receives a more holistic picture of the risks and opportunities of an investment object. Furthermore, such ratings can be used to include normative and nonfinancial values in investments.

In theory, such ratings can either be initiated by the entity that seeks a rating for itself (e.g., the company that wants to obtain a rating to signal its sustainability performance), by the entity that wants to use the information from the rating (e.g., the investor that wants to include rating data into its decision processes), or by the entity that wants to sell the information from the rating (i.e., the rating agency itself who offers their services to investors). In practice, however, ratings initiated by the entity that seeks a rating for itself (e.g., a company) are extremely rare due to obvious credibility issues. Since sustainability is not a clear-cut and easily defined issue, the rating agencies must first decide how to evaluate sustainability. That is, they need to decide what areas to cover, what indicators to assess (or not), whether they want to include strategies and goals or only past performance, how to translate qualitative information into a rating score, etc. Very often, the rating agencies themselves revert to external norms and standards as a basis for their rating concepts. Such norms can be, for example, environmental standards (e.g., ISO 14000 or EMAS, see Chapter C.7.2.2), social standards (e.g., by the International Labour Organization or SA8000, see Chapter C.7.2.3), or overarching standards (e.g., by the Global Reporting Initiative, see Chapter C.8.2). Thus, in the end, the rating agencies might have very different "recipes" when it comes to assessing sustainability, and the results of such rating might differ significantly even for the same investment object (Chatterji et al., 2016; LaBella et al., 2019).

Sustainability in society 13: Sustainability ratings for countries

When people think of ratings, they most often have company performance in mind. Countries, however, can also be evaluated for their financial or sustainability performance and policies. Candriam, a subsidiary of the insurance company New York Life, compiles its sovereign analysis which ranks the countries of the world according to their scores on natural, human, and social capital. It also applies negative screening criteria and excludes countries that do not meet certain democracy and freedom characteristics. On average, developed economies are ranked much higher than emerging economies. While this might not be surprising for many aspects of human and social capital, it also applies for natural capital. Switzerland, for example, is marked as a leading country while Zambia is one of the laggards. This is noteworthy, as the ecological footprint in Switzerland is more than three times higher than in Zambia (see also Chapters A.1.2 and A.4.1). The reason for this discrepancy lies in the methodology. The rating not only includes emissions and carbon footprint data but also evaluates aspects such as environmental regulation and preservation or energy transition.

Sources: Global Footprint Network (2021); Sourov and van Hyfte (2020)

The result of such ratings is usually an absolute rating of the sustainability performance of a company, for example, either on a score from 0 to 100 or on a scale from D- to A+ or other formats in which the rating agency wants to express the result. These absolute ratings are then often put into perspective with the rating of, for example, industry peers (e.g., as an absolute position in the industry or as quantile or decile rank) to enable an investor to make best-in-class decisions. The rating agency might also choose to provide fine-grained results for the different areas it assesses (e.g., for the environmental, social, or governance sub-performance) as well as information on how the aggregate overall score was calculated (e.g., how much weight was put on the environmental, social, or governance sub-performance as well as the information that was obtained to calculate the scores). Furthermore, many rating agencies use negative criteria to flag companies, for example, if they are involved in corruption scandals or in the production of controversial weapons. Usually, such companies then cannot obtain a positive rating, which is why you likely will not find a rating of something like "the most sustainable producer of biological and chemical weapons." Finally, full-blown ratings include a dedicated analyst opinion to provide perspective on or detailed evaluations of various aspects that are not solely expressed in the overall numerical or alphabetical grading scale rating.

To gather data for their ratings, respective agencies usually rely on various sources for input. This can be primary data from the investment object (e.g., the company) itself such as annual reports, nonfinancial reports, or questionnaires sent to the company as well as secondary data from media screenings, etc. Furthermore, they can include interviews with external experts from civil society, academia, and so on. This directly points to some shortcomings and problems with regard to compiling data for such ratings. Some companies are reluctant to disclose information, for example, in sustainability reports, or they only have limited resources for extensive disclosure so that firm size can have a positive influence on rating scores (Drempetic et al., 2020). Moreover, NGOs usually only concentrate on hot topics and multinational corporations, which influences media coverage of (mainly) negative events. Finally, in some cases, it is one person's word against another's (e.g. the company contact vs. an NGO contact). Thus, in many cases, ESG information cannot easily be compared with financial data due to differences in the availability and reliability of the information.

In sum, sustainability ratings are a useful tool especially for investors with limited resources or lack of internal knowledge on sustainability. They often provide in-depth information which, however, may suggest exactness whereas the process on how a rating was achieved is more akin to a "black box."

Sustainability in business 16: The Dow Jones Sustainability Indices (DJSI)

The DJSI are a family of stock indices with different regional breakdowns (e.g., world, emerging markets, Europe, Chile, and others). The DJSI World index includes global sustainability leaders based on the research conducted by the sustainability rating specialist SAM which is, like the DJSI, part of S&P Global. SAM annually calculates an ESG score for companies. The 2,500 largest companies from the S&P Global Broad Market Index are invited to complete the questionnaire. The assessment consists of three dimensions (environmental, social, and economic) with 20 key themes and a total of 80 to 100 industry-specific questions. Companies with a score that is less than 45 percent of the highest scoring company are excluded from the eligible universe. Furthermore, companies may be excluded based on results from a media and stakeholder analysis or if the index committee "determines that a company is no longer behaving in a matter that is consistent with the Corporate Governance Compliance." (S&P Dow Jones Indices, 2021a, p. 7). In addition, a series of negative screening criteria is applied. Some of these criteria are used irrespective of company size or revenues (e.g., excluding companies that are active in the production of alcoholic beverages, nuclear power, or gambling operations) and some are applied if the respective business activities exceed a certain revenue threshold (e.g., when business activities of manufacturing and selling assault weapons to civilian customers exceed 5 percent of revenues). The remaining companies from potential industries are then chosen based on a best-in-class approach.

Sources: S&P Dow Jones Indices (2021b); S&P Dow Jones Indices (2021a); SAM (2020)

B.5.4 Impact of sustainable finance

From a financial standpoint, one of the most frequently asked question is "does it pay to invest sustainably?" and there is a plethora of empirical studies focusing on this question (see meta analyses by Friede et al., 2015; Wallis & Klein, 2015). One assumption is that sustainable investments underperform conventional investments because sustainability criteria limit investors' allocation options which, in turn, leads to increased costs and risks and thus to a negative impact on performance. However, only few studies provide evidence for this hypothesis. The opposing hypotheses are that sustainable portfolios either outperform conventional portfolios because negative news (in terms of poor sustainability performance) leads to the underperformance of conventional portfolios or that there is an equal performance because sustainability is not priced in the market. Indeed, the vast majority of studies finds a nonnegative relation between sustainability performance, with most results indicating a positive impact, at least in the past (Friede et al., 2015; Wallis & Klein, 2015).

Sustainability in business 17: Sustainable finance at BlackRock - How serious is the world's largest asset manager?

BlackRock is the world's largest asset management firm with roughly USD 9 trillion in assets under management as of April 15, 2021, thus arguably one of the most, if not the most influential financial service companies on Earth. For a couple of years now, BlackRock CEO Larry Fink addresses the CEOs of the world's leading companies in an annual letter in which he regularly and prominently addresses sustainability topics.

He argued that "generating sustainable returns over time requires a sharper focus not only on governance, but also on environmental and social factors facing companies today. These issues offer both risks and opportunities, but for too long, companies have not considered them core to their business" (Turner & Fink, 2016) and that "society is demanding that companies, both public and private, serve a social purpose. To prosper over time, every company must not only deliver financial performance, but also show how it makes a positive contribution to society." (Fink, 2018). Recently, he specifically turned to the issue of climate change, positing that "climate change is almost invariably the top issue that clients around the world raise with BlackRock. From Europe to Australia, South America to China, Florida to Oregon, investors are asking how they should modify their portfolios" (Fink, 2020). The words of Larry Fink have weight in the financial community and beyond. Not surprisingly, one of the main arguments for an increased sustainability orientation is that "the more your company can show its purpose in delivering value to its customers, its employees, and its communities, the better able you will be to compete and deliver long-term, durable profits for shareholders" (Fink, 2021).

In his 2018 letter, Larry Fink prominently promised that "BlackRock recognizes and embraces our responsibility to help drive this change. Over the past several years, we have undertaken a concentrated effort to evolve our approach … towards an approach based on engagement with companies" (Fink, 2018). With this claim, he directly addresses an active approach of sustainable investments which surely could have significant impact when looking at the enormous leverage of several trillion USD of assets under management. At the same time, BlackRock is sometimes criticized for not living up to the claims of its CEO. In 2020, the charitable initiative ShareAction assessed that BlackRock was one of the laggards in the financial service industry when it comes to support for shareholder resolutions on climate and social issues, and it is still heavily invested in coal producing companies. Thus, while big money can potentially have a big influence on the sustainable development of economies, it remains to be seen whether and how this influence is used to make a change.

Further sources: BlackRock, Inc. (2021); Cuvelier and Pinson (2021); ShareAction (2020)

The question of impact can also be asked differently in terms of "when and how do sustainable investments have an impact on sustainability (performance)?" thus asking whether it makes sense to include sustainability considerations in investment decisions not only to have a good conscience but also to really foster sustainable development (Busch et al., 2021). This question has, however, only been answered preliminary in empirical studies and the answer likely depends on the chosen approach for sustainability investments (Kölbel et al., 2020). Merely applying negative aspects might, for example, discourage respective activities but will likely not have a strong effect on overall sustainable development. Positive criteria such as the best-in-class approach might encourage superior sustainability performance. However, the respective evaluations on which investments are based are usually looking backward at past performance. The effect on future sustainability efforts is thus unclear. Furthermore, it is questionable, whether buying stocks or bonds of companies with a superior sustainability performance directly leads to positive effects on sustainability. Indirectly, positive effects might materialize when companies react to an increasing sustainability-focus of investors and rating agencies with increasing efforts to satisfy these stakeholders. Other aspects such as sustainability-themed funds or impact investments might offer opportunities especially if they channel investments toward more sustainable use and when these investments are additional to what would otherwise have gone into these areas. An active engagement with companies can push them to become more sustainable but it is, as discussed, most feasible only for large-scale investors or well-organized groups of smaller investors. Finally, some new approaches such as sustainability-linked bonds can also be interesting elements of sustainability management and sustainable finance assuming that the respective targets linked to the interest rates are reasonably ambitious for the company. Overall, the question of how exactly sustainable finance and sustainable investments influence sustainability performance will likely be subject of scientific debates and studies in the next couple of years.

Sustainability in business 18: Sustainable crowd investments

With crowdfunding, ventures or specific projects are funded through funded through a large number of small (or smaller) contributions, nowadays typically via specialized Internet platforms. Investors can either lend money, invest in companies on an equity basis, provide funds for some form of rewards (often in form of pre-purchased products), or engage philanthropically via donations. Crowdfunding is not per se related to sustainability issues. However, a multitude of specialized platforms such as Bettervest (Germany), chuffed (Australia), Energy4Impact (United Kingdom), Fueladream (India), Oneplanetcrown (Netherlands), trine (Sweden), or others focus on sustainability-related projects. On these platforms, one can monetarily support projects on clean energy, community led activities, education, and so on in the form of equity, loans, or donations depending on the respective platform and project.

Sources: Maehle et al. (2020); Shneor et al. (2020)

KEY TAKEAWAYS

- Compared to philanthropy, sustainable investments are investments that include a financial return.
- Sustainable investments are on the rise and already a major element in financial markets.
- Exercising voting rights and engagement with management are the major active approaches.
- Negative and positive criteria are the major elements of passive approaches.
- Sustainability ratings complement financial ratings by assessing the sustainability performance of companies or entire countries.
- There is no uniform approach of how sustainability ratings are conducted.
- The impact of sustainable investments on sustainable development is ambiguous and contingent on the different approaches.

B.6 Consumers

LEARNING GOALS

After reading this chapter you will be able to …

- … characterize and provide examples for different types of sustainable consumption.
- … explain sustainable and unsustainable consumer behavior by referring to the SHIFT framework.
- … use the green (or sustainable) purchase perception matrix to explain why individuals might (not) purchase sustainably.
- … characterize collaborative consumption and the sharing economy.
- … illustrate different systems of collaborative consumption.
- … distinguish collaborative consumption from the perspectives of business to consumer (B2C), peer to peer or consumer to consumer (P2P/C2C), and business to business (B2B).
- … discuss the potential and limitations of collaborative consumption for sustainable development.

Introduction to Chapter B.6: Screencast
Watch an introduction to the chapter here:

B.6.1 Introduction to (un)sustainable consumption

Consumers have a significant impact on companies as their consumption processes are often regarded as the ultimate end of all business activities. Thus, consumers can influence companies' sustainability efforts via their buying behavior. They can, for example, deliberately purchase and thus ultimately promote certain goods associated with a sustainable lifestyle (e.g., regional products, vegan food, products made from recycled materials) or they can choose to consume more or less of a certain product and use others more or less intensively. However, many consumers are still unaware of the sustainability aspects of many products or simply do not care. One fundamental question at the beginning of a chapter on consumers and sustainability is: What is sustainable consumption and what sets it apart from less sustainable or unsustainable consumption? In 1994, the Oslo Symposium on Sustainable Consumption characterized sustainable consumption as "the use of goods and services that respond to basic needs and bring a better quality of life, while minimising the use of natural resources, toxic materials and emissions of waste and pollutants over the life cycle, so as not to jeopardise the needs of future generations" (UNEP, 2010, p. 12). This definition closely relates to the broad Brundtland definition of sustainable development itself, and responsible consumption is also included in the SDG 12 (see Chapters A.1.1 and A.2.3).

Task B6-1

Search for "footprint calculator" online and you will find a number of calculators which help you identify your impact on the environment. Choose one and calculate your own ecological footprint. How does your lifestyle influence your footprint? How could you change your footprint and how difficult or easy would this be for you?

Compare your own footprint with those of your friends and family. Do you see any differences? You can also try different calculators and see whether the results differ and if so, try to find out why!

In many footprint calculators you can calculate individual footprints for people living in different countries. Find one of these calculators and calculate the footprint for someone from another country with a standard of living that is similar to your own. Compare this footprint with your own! Do you see any differences despite the mostly identical lifestyle? If so: Why would you see any differences?

For further insights on how to measure sustainability performance see also Chapter C.6.

Sustainable consumption can mean many things and it is connected to almost every part of daily life. Most prominently, people often associate aspects such as buying products with sustainability-characteristics (e.g., Fairtrade coffee, organic fruits, or renewable energy) or following a more sustainable behavior (e.g., conserving energy and water or living a vegan lifestyle) with (more) sustainable consumption. Sometimes, it is merely about changing little things such as abstaining from using extra packaging or consciously trying to avoid food waste, sometimes it is about more profound changes such as changing to a meat-free diet or completely renouncing the ownership of a car and instead relying on shared mobility and commuting by bike instead of by car. In general, however, there is not one solution or approach for sustainable consumption. Rather, it is about looking at the individual circumstances and trying to improve your own ecological footprint in general while avoiding harm for others through one's own consumption. This, however, is not always straightforward as sustainable consumption is usually also about long-term benefits for others or for the environment instead of merely about immediate benefits for oneself. Furthermore, there might be tradeoffs (see again Chapter A.1.3). For example, is it more sustainable to buy regionally grown food rather than organic food which had to be shipped from its origin to the consumers' location?

The awareness for sustainability in general and for sustainable consumption specifically is growing in most countries around the world. In a recent survey of more than 25,000 people worldwide, 98 percent stated that they know the term "sustainability" and 50 percent were even aware of the much more specific idea of the SDGs (Frank & Cort, 2020). With this awareness, the markets for different sustainability-related products develop as well. The market for organic food, for example, has seen significant growth in many countries worldwide and is expected to grow further in double digit numbers over the next few of years in all world regions (Research Dive, 2020). Fairtrade products followed a similar growth path in recent years (Fairtrade International, 2020). Initially, Fairtrade products were restricted to only a few specialized retailers in many countries around the world. Over time, many larger retail chains began to list Fairtrade products, initially often restricted to coffee or bananas. Nowadays, we find a multi-billion-dollar market with a wide range of Fairtrade products from tea to flowers and from cocoa to sports balls.

Sustainability in business 19: Fairtrade or not? The banana fiasco at discounter Lidl in Germany

In 2019, the retail discounter Lidl made a move to switch entirely to Fairtrade bananas in its German, Swiss, and Belgium stores. This would have been a significant step, as Lidl is one of the largest retailers in Germany and one of the largest discounters worldwide. The company already pushed this change in 40 percent of its German stores when it suddenly renounced its plans. The company mentioned an insufficient willingness of its customer to pay for the Fairtrade product. Apparently, a price premium of 10 to 20 cents per kilo compared to conventional bananas led to a significant decline in sales. As a consequence, the company started offering conventional bananas again alongside their Fairtrade counterparts.

Source: Joyce (2019); Knowles (2019)

B.6.2 Factors influencing (un)sustainable consumer behavior

Along with the growing interest in sustainability issues, consumers all over the world regularly report an increasing willingness to behave and purchase sustainably, and even to pay a premium for more sustainable products (Kumar et al., 2021; TNS Opinion & Social, 2014). This is encouraging from a sustainability perspective, especially since the general awareness for sustainability has increased over the last decades. However, despite consumers reported favorable attitude, this does not always translate into actual behavior. The discrepancy between what people say and do is generally known as the attitude-behavior gap or intention-behavior gap and it is often relevant in a sustainability context (Auger & Devinney, 2007; Park & Lin, 2020). Thus, it is important to understand what drives as well as hinders people to behave sustainably or unsustainably.

Based on an extensive review of research, White et al. (2019) developed their SHIFT framework to explain sustainable consumer behavior. The framework includes social influence (S), habit formation (H), the individual self (I), feelings and cognition (F), and tangibility (T) as explanatory factors. White et al. (2019) describe these factors as follows:

- Social influence: People not only follow their own expectations and wishes. They also consciously or unconsciously consider the expectations and behavior of others when, for example, making consumption decisions. Depending on your social environment you might chose to buy or not buy certain products (e.g., green energy or organic food) or you behave in a certain way (conserve energy or water and recycle) because of what you think is expected of you in different contexts. This can be the result of general social norms which informally describe what is accepted (e.g., "littering is inappropriate"); or it can be because of your social identity, that is, your (formal or informal) membership to a certain group such as a local community ("I am part of a group committed to sustainability"); or it can be the results of social desirability when you want to make an impression on others (e.g., conveying a social status by early adopters of electric cars or buying Fairtrade coffee to positively impress guests).
- Habit formation: Habits are a form of usually subconscious and routinely performed behavior and they can support and also hinder sustainable consumption and behavior. Often habits rather cement unsustainable forms of behavior when, for example, you are used to always buying or consuming the same products without questioning their sustainability aspects. Once more sustainable forms of behavior become a habit (e.g., always switching off lights when leaving the office or regularly buying organic, Fairtrade coffee), they are more easily performed. Thus, habits can also offer a chance for sustainable consumption. Unsustainable habits might be broken through external changes (e.g., a product is not sold anymore and one has to find an alternative), penalties or incentives, supportive messages, feedback, and generally making sustainable behavior as easy as possible (e.g., encouraging recycling by providing nearby bins).
- Individual self: Personal norms can be important for sustainable consumption as well. People may be generally concerned for the environment or for social aspects which supports sustainable consumption. Furthermore, people tend to be self-consistent. Individuals, for example, who think of themselves as being concerned for sustainability usually try to live up to these self-expectations. However, research also found inconsistency effects related, for example, to psychological rebound effects (i.e., consuming more of an environmentally friendly product), which we discussed in Chapter A.4.5. In addition, people tend to discard information that collides with their personal opinion or that can harm their self-perception. This can inhibit sustainable behavior (i.e., by downplaying the negative effects of flights on climate change) as people want to view themselves positively. Furthermore, individuals may of course also be driven by self-interest so that sustainable consumption might be hindered if sustainable products are viewed as costlier, less functional, etc. (i.e., if their perceived costs are high). It can, however, also be supported by highlighting the personal benefits (e.g., potential health benefits of organic food) of sustainable consumption when, in sum, the perceived benefits outweigh the perceived costs. Finally, it helps if people know or think that their behavior actually makes a difference.

- Feelings and cognition: Negative and positive emotions have an impact on sustainability-related behavior. Feeling guilty or responsible can influence sustainable behavior as can fear if it is neither too intense nor too distant. Positive feeling such as pride or joy can reinforce sustainable behavior but also unsustainable behavior, if the latter also elicits the mentioned positive feelings. On the cognitive side, knowledge (e.g., about the effects of climate change or the potential of recycling) and information (e.g., about a product's sustainability traits) can be important.
- Tangibility: One inherent trait of most forms of sustainable consumption and behavior is that the benefits are distant and not immediately visible and thus not tangible for the individual (e.g., how taking the train instead of a plane helps to combat climate change or how buying fair trade chocolate helps farmers in the Global South). Sustainability marketing is thus confronted with the task to make the impacts and benefits more tangible to consumers (see Chapter C.1.4)

A useful tool to explain and predict when and why consumers might generally be willing to purchase sustainable products specifically with regards to elements of the individual self (i.e., the "I" in "SHIFT") is the green purchase perception matrix proposed by Ken Peattie (Peattie, 2001) as illustrated in Figure 14. While Peattie originally focused on "green" purchases, the matrix can easily be applied to all sorts of sustainable products because not only are environmental (i.e., "green") products and product traits subject to the two illustrated dimensions but also, for example, social aspects and claims: The degree of compromise and the degree of confidence. The degree of compromise posits that the purchase or usage of sustainable products might involve some form of compromise for the individual such as a higher price or a lower performance compared to the purchase or usage of unsustainable products. Especially product designers have to deal with this aspect to ideally minimize the necessary compromises associated with a sustainable product alternative (see Chapter C.1.2). Furthermore, some individuals may be more willing to compromise on different aspects of a product than others. The degree of confidence illustrates how convinced an individual is of the sustainability benefits offered by the product and of their impact on aspects of sustainable development. "Win-win-purchases" only require few or no compromises on the user side while the buyer or user can be rather certain that the sustainability claims are true and relevant. Such products should be easier to position on the market than the other extreme, that is, the "why bother purchases." The latter requires a rather high degree of compromise while the sustainability benefits are small or their impact is uncertain. The middle ground, "feelgood purchases" or "why not purchases" are marked by either a high degree of confidence or a low degree of compromise and thus require different efforts in sustainability marketing, either increasing the degree of confidence or decreasing the degree of compromise. The ultimate aim for any sustainability-related product should thus be to move as far to the upper-right quadrant in the matrix as possible.

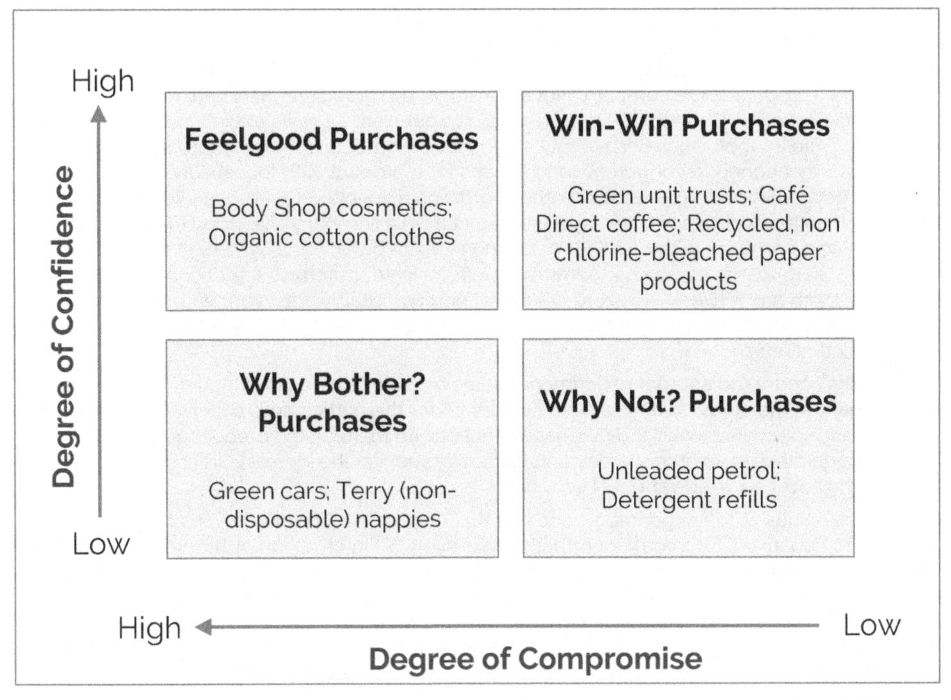

Figure 14: The green purchase perception matrix according to Peattie (2001, p. 139), reproduced with permission

Task B6-2

Ken Peattie's green purchase perception matrix has been around for more than 20 years, and some of the products he used as examples might be outdated from today's point of view. Which of these products might have moved into a different quadrant over time and why? Which of his examples might nowadays not be applicable at all? What could be new examples for the different quadrants and why? Furthermore, identify examples beyond green purchases which cover other aspects of sustainability to arrive at a "sustainable purchase perception matrix"!

Let us end our thoughts here on an encouraging note: Sustainability-related behavior has been consistently found to be positively associated with personal wellbeing with regard to pro-environmental (Zawadzki et al., 2020) and prosocial behavior (Aknin et al., 2019). And since this is a textbook: To what element of the SHIFT framework does this information relate?

Sustainability in research 6: Sen and Bhattacharya's 2001 article on consumer reactions to corporate social responsibility

Does doing good for society always lead to doing better for the company? Sankar Sen and C. B. Bhattacharya examine this question with regard to consumer responses to CSR initiatives in their article in the Journal of Marketing Research published in 2001. The answer was, as often in sustainability-related matters: it depends. In two experimental studies, the authors found that company-specific factors as well as individual-specific factors have an influence on consumers' responses.

In the first experiment, participants were presented with a company profile indicating either a good or a bad CSR performance (and a control group with no CSR information) as well as either a low or high product quality. In the scenario with good CSR performance, the company was evaluated significantly better than in the scenario with bad CSR performance. This result was even more pronounced for participants who generally supported the idea of CSR. Furthermore, participants were not only asked to generally rate the company but also to indicate their purchase intention for a product of the company. Not surprisingly, the product quality had a strong influence on purchase intention. Overall, CSR performance did not have a significant influence on purchase intentions. A closer look, however, reveals some interesting details. Participants with low interest in CSR even mentioned lower purchase intentions for a product with low quality when the company had good CSR performance (or in other words: participants on average indicated that it was less likely that they would buy a low-quality product from a company with good CSR performance compared to a company with bad CSR performance). For participants with high support for CSR in general, there was a somewhat contrasting effect. Here, purchase intentions were lower for companies with a positive CSR record when the product quality was high. With these results in mind, Sen and Bhattacharya then further asked: When are CSR efforts likely to increase product purchase intentions?

The authors conducted another experiment and now also included whether the CSR activities of the company in the study were relevant or irrelevant for the participants. CSR initiatives in a relevant domain indeed increased the purchase intentions no matter if the product quality was low or high and regardless of whether participants generally support the idea of CSR or not. This was not the case, however, for irrelevant CSR activities.

Overall, the results of the experiments showed that consumers' company evaluations were more sensitive to negative CSR information than to positive CSR information at the time of the study. Only those individuals who were supportive of CSR in general reacted positively to positive CSR information. The authors conclude that managers should be aware of the hazards of being perceived as socially irresponsible. Furthermore, they posit that companies should ask themselves what is relevant in terms of their CSR activities in the eye of the consumers if they want to create a positive relation between their CSR activities and consumers' purchase intentions.

Source: Sen and Bhattacharya (2001)

B.6.3 Collaborative consumption and the sharing economy

When we think of consumption, we mostly think about buying things in the form of acquiring property. Once we own the products, we either consume them more or less right away, in the case of expendable goods (e.g., food), or we use them over time and sell or discard them once they are no longer needed in the case of durable products (e.g., a bicycle). However, we of course also consume not only physical products but also services (e.g., getting a haircut). Collaborative consumption now brings a service element to physical and durable products so that these can be used without exclusive ownership. Accordingly, Roos and Hahn (2019) define collaborative consumption as "acquiring or providing resources from or to others for collaborative, shared use among consumers or peers as opposed to acquiring or providing new resources for private use" (p. 681). Such forms of consumption are often proposed as a potentially more sustainable form of consumption compared to conventional consumption patterns.

Main characteristics of collaborative consumption are that ...

- ... the use of resources is shared between consumers or peers: passive consumers become collaborators or even producers themselves,
- ... ownership of resources is usually replaced by access to resources and physical products are often turned into services,
- ... "needs" and "haves" are often matched through technology,
- ... the exchange of shared resources depends on reputation and trust between the different parties involved in sharing.

Of course, the sharing of resources and collaborative use of products is not a new thing, and respective forms of behavior have always existed, for example, in families, neighborhoods, communities, or cooperatives. However, the rise of modern and especially mobile technology as well as social networks has boosted respective forms of consumption in the last few years. If you like, you could live without owning many durable products and still access all the amenities of modern life. Not only can you use carsharing services or carpooling communities instead of owning your own car, you can also borrow tools in local sharing communities, offer your couch to travelers from all over the world, and even share your skills and workforce in exchange for help from others. Most of these activities are conducted in some sort of sharing economy, in which the exchange and rental of resources is at the center of thinking (Schor & Cansoy, 2019). The consulting giant PwC refers to this as "one of the most important global trends" (PwC, 2015, p. 5) and estimates the value of the global sharing economy at more than USD 300 billion by 2025 (Statista, Inc., 2021).

In their widely cited book "What's mine is yours", Botsman and Rogers (2011) describe three different systems of collaborative consumption:

- Product service systems combine a physical good with an intangible service. They allow consumers or peers to pay for the benefit of using physical products or tangible assets without needing to own them outright. Thus, they provide value to consumers as they offer relevant services which substitute individual purchases for ownership. Product service systems are usually what many people have in mind when they hear about collaborative consumption or the sharing economy and there are numerous commercial examples of these such as carsharing or bike sharing. For a more fine-grained overview of different forms of product service systems see Chapter C.1.2.
- Communal economies allow the exchange of less tangible assets such as time, skills, money, experience, or space among peers or they allow the exchange of unused or only sporadically used physical items of owners. While the former type of exchange is often done through forms of give and take or quid pro quo (e.g., one hour of lawn mowing in exchange for 30 minutes of piano lessons), the latter is often rather a form of lending (e.g., offering the use of a drilling machine in the local community). Finally, some forms of communal economies such as coworking spaces or couchsurfing show elements of collaborative lifestyles.
- Redistribution markets allow consumers or peers to redistribute products or tangible assets from where they are not needed to someone or somewhere they are needed. Such markets facilitate swapping, reusing, bartering, or donating. This means that physical products are still owned by individuals. Instead of sharing products in a specific period of time like the other two systems, redistribution markets redirect the focus on extending product life by sharing its use over time and by allowing for an easier exchange of used items. Examples of this are electronically facilitated second hand markets or traditional local flea markets.

Another typical categorization of collaborative consumption separates business to consumer (B2C) from peer to peer or consumer to consumer (P2P/C2C) and business to business (B2B) activities. In B2C models, companies offer their sharing services to individual, private customers. Here you find many of the well-known players of the sharing economy such as Share Now (worldwide carsharing), as well as many local companies (e.g., offering bikesharing services in countless cities around the globe). In P2P networks, platforms facilitate the sharing of resources by individuals who own the respective resources. The exchange itself then occurs between the consumers themselves. This applies for communal economies such as carpooling (the sharing of car journeys so that more than one person travels in a vehicle) as well as for redistribution markets (e.g., specialized markets for used clothes in many countries or more general channels such as Craigslist in the United States and beyond). Any of these models can in general be commercial or non-commercial. Many local sharing communities and neighborhood platforms, for example, operate on a nonprofit basis. Beyond the individual consumer in B2C and P2P, thus leaving the "traditional" perspective of sustainable private consumption, models of collaborative and shared consumption also enter the business to business (B2B) area. Companies can, for example, use B2B sharing services to improve the utilized capacity of trucks through pooling and on-demand planning, rent out available store space to popup stores, share work spaces, storage areas, or even workshop capacities, or improve the utilization of their fleet through sharing among employees.

Sustainability in business 20: Vinted – Second-hand clothing all over Europe

Clothes are a major object of consumption and especially fast fashion has significant negative impact on people and the environment. Working conditions in value chains mostly in the Global South are often poor: Suppliers sometimes pay only starvation wages, environmental standards are low, and the overall resource-use for clothing that is worn only once or twice is high. As a consequence, a countermovement has emerged over the last couple of years and the sharing economy plays an important role. According to its own testimony, Vinted is Europe's largest online-platform for used clothing. "Vinted is open to everyone who believes that good clothes should live long" (Vinted, 2021). Founded in 2008, it grew to almost 40 million members in 2021. Users can list items for free using the Vinted app, and deals are made directly between users through the platform. In addition to selling items to each other, they can also swap them, thus catering to the ideal of the sharing economy. Consequently, Vinted can be regarded as a redistribution market. The use of the platform is free but users can opt for additional payed services such as buyer protection, or increased visibility for sellers.

Sources: Gerstmeyer (2020); Vinted (2021)

These last examples illustrate the potential of collaborative consumption for sustainable development as they allow physical resources to be used more intensively and thus efficiently throughout the product life. A typical European car outside of the sharing economy, for example, is parked 92 percent of time (Ellen MacArthur Foundation & McKinsey Center for Business and Environment, 2015). Nevertheless, collaborative consumption is not—per se and in any case—a more sustainable form of consumption compared to regular product ownership as summarized by Leismann et al. (2013). The authors categorize various potentially positive and negative effects on the environment both directly and indirectly.

- Negative direct effects: Products might be overused if they are shared among users. They could experience, for example, greater wear and tear. Additional resources might be needed to extend their useful life and durability and also if the products have to be transported to and from different users depending on the product category. Furthermore, commercial operators of sharing services might, on the one hand, be inclined to use inefficient appliances for a long time, which could result in a net negative effect on the environment or they could, on the other hand, withdraw rental products from service earlier than necessary if, for example, consumers expect to use only the newest products on the market.
- Negative indirect effects: Collaborative consumption can mean that it is easier for some consumers to use products due to the absence of purchase costs. This could be especially relevant for expensive durable goods. If using goods collaboratively leads to savings in income, this could furthermore lead to increased demand in other areas (see again the rebound effect in Chapter A.4.5).
- Positive direct effects: Using goods collaboratively can extend their useful life and

maximize their utilization. Both effects can lead to a more efficient use of resources per product. Furthermore, providers of product service systems in the B2C segment, for example, are incentivized to consider ecological progress in the form of energy- or resource efficiency if this leads to a lower operating cost and they might be willing to specifically watch out for recyclability if this simplifies processes at the end of product life.

- Positive indirect effects: Collaborative consumption can lead to the avoidance or postponement of purchases if shared access and usage indeed substitutes ownership. It also potentially helps to reduce overall demand if the increased cost transparency, for example of product service systems, helps in conveying the true cost of product usage which not only includes a purchase prize but also use and post-use cost (see also Chapter C.1.3).

Task B6-3

Did you already use products or services from the sharing economy sphere? What negative or positive direct or indirect effects have you experienced?

KEY TAKEAWAYS

- Sustainable consumption has many forms, and different aspects of sustainable consumption have become mainstream for different types of products in many markets.
- Different factors from the areas of social influence, habit formation, the individual self, feelings and cognition, and tangibility can explain sustainable consumption.
- Sustainable products might be prone to a certain degree of compromise and/or confidence—both factors influence consumer purchase intentions.
- Collaborative consumption is a special form of consumption in which ownership is usually replaced by access to resources.
- Product service systems, communal economies, and redistribution markets are different forms of collaborative consumption.
- Collaborative consumption can come in the form of business to consumer (B2C), peer to peer or consumer to consumer (P2P/C2C), and business to business (B2B) activities.
- Collaborative consumption is not per se sustainable—it has various potential direct and indirect, negative and positive ecological effects.

C. Instruments and functional perspectives of sustainability management

Companies have a wide range of instruments at their disposal to improve their sustainability performance, to deal with various stakeholder expectations and, potentially, to influence different stakeholders to behave more sustainable. Part C of this book will introduce many of these instruments and approaches. To achieve this, the different chapters focus on various functional perspectives (e.g., marketing, human resource management, production, accounting) and their related instruments. Not all instruments are relevant for all companies. Instead, the usefulness and general applicability of these instruments might be dependent on specific company characteristics (e.g., industry or size) or other circumstances (e.g., country of operation). Furthermore, successful sustainability management is always interdisciplinary and requires efforts throughout a company and potentially even beyond so that none of these instruments should be viewed in isolation.

C.1 Sustainability marketing

LEARNING GOALS

After reading this chapter you will be able to ...

- ... characterize sustainability marketing.
- ... describe various forms of product service systems and how they can help to improve sustainability.
- ... distinguish different elements of total customer cost and describe to what extent they are relevant for sustainability marketing.
- ... illustrate some ethical issues in pricing policy.
- ... describe problems of unsustainable promotion policy.
- ... distinguish different types of product level and firm level greenwashing.
- ... explain how labels can help to increase trustworthiness and discuss limitations of labels.
- ... discuss difficulties of product placement for sustainable products.

Introduction to Chapter C.1: Screencast
Watch an introduction to the chapter here:

C.1.1 Characterizing sustainability marketing

The American Marketing Association defines marketing as "the activity, set of institutions, and processes for creating, communicating, delivering, and exchanging offerings that have value for customers, clients, partners, and society at large" (American Marketing Association, 2017). Marketing as such is instrumental for the success of businesses, as the value created for the various stakeholders is appreciated by market actors which, in turn, influence the financial bottom line of a company. Other than widespread assumptions, the definition shows that marketing is nowadays not solely focused on the customer but includes other stakeholders as well. Nevertheless, in reality the focus of conventional marketing is still largely on consumer benefits and on the act of selling and buying products. Already in 1960, Levitt argued in one of the most influential marketing articles of all times, that companies are often too focused on producing and selling products without actually asking what the consumer wants (Levitt, 1960). He criticized this "marketing myopia" largely because of its inherent risks to the companies themselves, because it would eventually lead to ignoring customer needs. Nowadays, we can extend these thoughts by including a sustainability perspective as well. A sole focus on selling products instead of fulfilling customer (and other stakeholder's) needs is not only potentially unsustainable, as we will illustrate throughout this chapter, but it also risks corporate competitiveness, if companies are unable to adapt to the increasing demands for sustainability.

To overcome this myopia, sustainability marketing deliberately includes socioecological aspects and thus considers the collective consequences of marketing activities. In their award-winning textbook on the topic, Belz and Peattie (2012) refer to sustainability marketing as the "planning, organizing, implementing and controlling [of] marketing resources and programmes to satisfy consumers' wants and needs, while considering social and environmental criteria and meeting corporate objectives" (p. 29). A related concept is marketing for sustainability, which aims at developing marketing strategies and measures to promote sustainability-related activities or institutions usually in a noncommercial setting, such as campaigns for sustainability NGOs, campaigns against littering, or to promote recycling in a local community. We will now discuss certain peculiarities of sustainability marketing along the classic "4Ps" of the regular marketing mix: product, price, promotion, and place.

Sustainability in research 7: Brown and Dacin's 1997 article on corporate associations and consumer product responses

As consumers, we often have a more or less clear perception and knowledge of specific companies. How do such associations influence our evaluation of the respective company's products? Tom J. Brown and Peter A. Dacin explored this question in their report of three studies that were published in 1997 in the Journal of Marketing. They specifically distinguished two types of corporate associations: associations related to corporate ability, that is, a company's competence to produce and deliver products, and associations related to CSR.

For the first study, the authors conducted a laboratory experiment with university students using descriptions of a company. In this experiment, the authors manipulated the relative CSR performance of the fictive companies, indicating either good or poor performance. The results provided preliminary evidence that CSR associations influenced product evaluations predominantly by changing the consumer's overall evaluation of the company. The perception of positive CSR activity thus had an indirect indirect influence on product evaluation.

The second study aimed to replicate the first study using information on real companies again with a sample of university students. This time, the authors did not actively manipulate the information on CSR performance but instead they measured the respondents' CSR associations and then asked for an evaluation of a fictitious new product. The results again showed a positive effect of CSR associations on the consumer's overall evaluation of the company, that is, companies which were perceived as superior regarding their CSR performance also received better overall evaluations by the participants. This time, however, there was a negative relationship between company evaluation and product evaluation, or in other words, companies with a better corporate evaluation received lower product evaluations.

Since this finding seems counterintuitive at first glance, the authors explored it in more detail in a third study. For this purpose, an experiment was conducted with 229 respondents in shopping malls to acquire a nonstudent sample. The participants were asked about their opinion of a high-tech product from a fictitious company. The results showed that the negative relationship between company evaluation and product evaluation in the second study was not driven by the participants' CSR associations of a company but instead by associations related to corporate ability. When CSR associations formed the corporate context, positive corporate associations enhanced product evaluations and negative corporate associations deflated product evaluations.

In sum, consumers use corporate associations to draw conclusions about the product even if these associations tend to be less relevant to the product, such as CSR associations.

Source: Brown and Dacin (1997)

C.1.2 Sustainable product policy

A central question in marketing, and even more so in sustainability marketing, is what kind of product with what kind of (sustainability) traits is offered to a customer. This is often referred to as product policy. Here, marketing has direct connections to sustainable supply chain management or sustainable production and logistics. A more sustainable product2 with a smaller social or environmental footprint throughout its life cycle is, for obvious reasons, more easily compatible with sustainability marketing than a more unsustainable alternative. Approaches to achieve a better sustainability performance in supply chain management, production, and logistics are covered in depth in Chapters C.3 and C.4.

Theoretically, circular economy and eco-effective products would allow for a continuation of ownership-oriented product policies, that is, of selling products to consumers. However, the discussion of the hurdles and limitations of eco-effectiveness approaches in Chapter A.4.3 has illustrated that alternative approaches might be needed as well. A concept that has been discussed for some time in this regard are product service systems (see Tukker, 2004). Product-service systems consist of physical goods that are combined with intangible services to fulfill customer needs. They can be depicted as a continuum that ranges from products with a pure focus on physical goods, on the one hand, to pure

2 *In this book, product is used as the generic term for physical goods as well as services. In case a further differentiation is necessary, we refer to goods or physical/tangible products on the one hand, and services, on the other.*

services, on the other. A physical product (e.g., a car) that is being sold to a customer is initially not connected to any service. At the same time, the user is usually the owner of the product (apart from when she or he lends the good to someone else). A pure service, as the other extreme, is not connected to a physical product at all (e.g., a massage). In between pure physical goods and pure services are three forms of product service systems which combine tangible goods and intangible services to different degrees as illustrated in Figure 15.

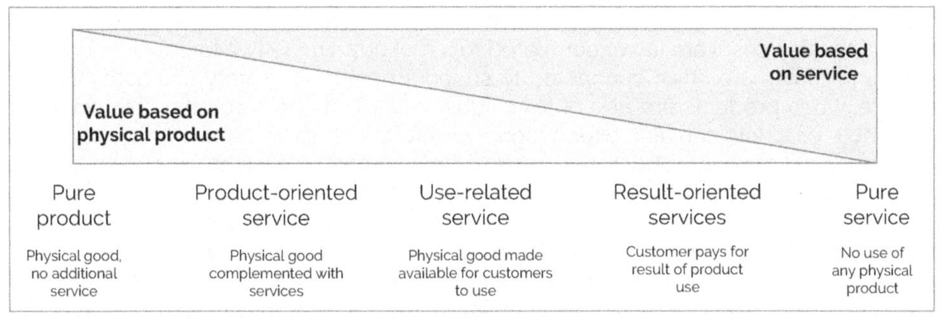

Figure 15: Overview of product service systems

Product-oriented services, the first form, build upon the same basic model as physical goods (i.e., a tangible good is sold to a customer) but subsequently provide additional value through supplementary services. This can be achieved through product-related services (e.g., maintenance contracts or financing schemes) or advice and consultancy (e.g., on how to best use a product). This can be sustainability enhancing, especially if the respective services allow for a more sustainable use of the product, for example, when maintenance contracts extend the product life or when consultancy services provide advice on efficient product use. In use-related services, as the second form of product service systems, the focus of the business model is not on selling physical goods. Instead, the ownership stays with the provider who makes the good available for customers to use. A widely known form would be leasing (e.g., leasing a car) but also product renting (e.g., renting a car) or sharing (e.g., carsharing as discussed in Chapter B.6.3) are widespread nowadays. In such systems, customer needs are fulfilled through using rather than owning the product. Use-related services can potentially be implemented for almost all physical goods apart from very short-lived products or products that are meant to be consumed (e.g., food or soap). However, in cases where the ownership of a product is connected to prestige or increased self-esteem, such systems are bound to fail. The third form of product service systems are result-oriented services where the customer neither owns nor uses the physical product. Instead, the customer pays for a result which, in turn, requires someone else to use a product. This can be done via outsourcing (e.g., of catering services or office cleaning), as pay-per-service unit when a customer pays for the output of a certain product (e.g., pay-per-print schemes of office copiers), or as functional result (e.g., cleaning clothes at a laundry). For most result-oriented services, the specific type of the tangible product being used is not even predetermined (e.g., it is not important what type of car a taxi is as long as it gets you from point A to point B).

Product-service systems try to overcome the prevalent marketing myopia by asking how customer needs can be fulfilled without necessarily selling physical goods. This can be beneficial for sustainability, if the respective schemes lead to fewer resources or emissions being used while not causing any negative effects for social sustainability (e.g., paying only famine wages for service providers). Product-service systems can potentially even help to enforce eco-effectiveness as they more easily allow closing the loop at the end of a product life cycle. This would be the case if the respective product did not change ownership to the end consumer but instead had been used as part of a product-service system. Often, companies which offer the service or product-service combination can more easily implement recycling, refurbishing, or repairing processes compared to end consumers who usually need extensive and decentralized collection systems or will otherwise often simply discard a product so that it is lost for recycling.

Sustainable or more sustainable products, whether they come in the form of product service systems or as regular goods and services, can offer some inherent benefits for consumers. Using carsharing instead of owning a car can lead to lower total cost of ownerships. Often, even a higher purchase price of, for example, an efficient electric car can pay off if the use costs are lower compared to a fuel guzzling SUV. Moreover, (more) sustainable products are often connected to superior health and safety characteristics, for example, when products are free of toxic substances. Depending on the product, many sustainable products can also offer a higher comfort such as when a longer working life or an increased product robustness leads to time savings, for example, due to avoided search costs for a new product or absent repairs. Finally, some sustainable products can even become status symbols or an expression of lifestyle if sustainability in general is perceived as trendy. For marketers it can be important to increase the consumer confidence in the functionality and sustainability of their products and reduce the degree of compromise to also reach those customers for whom sustainability is not a major purchase criterion (see again Chapter B.6.2).

Task C1-1

Which product service systems do you know? Discuss which type they belong to and how the business model adds value with regard to sustainability.

C.1.3 Sustainable price policy

When talking about price policy, most customers instinctively think about the purchase price of a product, and this is usually indeed the main element of price a company has to consider for its products. For the customer, however, the purchase price is only one element of the total customer cost as elaborated by Belz and Peattie (2012, pp. 233-235). Apart from the price itself, customers also have to bear other (often nonmonetary) purchase or transaction costs. Furthermore, the use of most goods is connected to certain use costs (e.g., energy or maintenance cost), and even the post-use phase is usually not free but generates cost for collecting, storing, or disposing a product. In product service systems many of these other types of costs have to be included by the provider and charged to the customer to allow the provider to operate profitably. The further such an offer deviates from "just" selling a tangible product, the more of these other costs usually accumulate at the provider so that they eventually are included in the price the company asks from the customer for their service or product service system. In many ways, therefore, product service systems provide a more honest picture of the total customer cost compared to the selling of tangible goods. Let us look at the different elements of total customer cost in more detail.

The price is what the customer directly pays for a tangible product or service, either in one sum or in several payment rates, for example, when financing the purchase. Contrary to the other types of customer costs, the price is usually transparent and known to customers in advance—usually in form of a price tag. From a producer's perspective, the price that is asked for a product is often the only source of revenue when the company has no other related revenue streams, for example, from maintenance or product-oriented services. When judging the price of a product, customers often tend to minimize the immediate costs (i.e., the price) but do not consider any future costs (e.g., use cost).

While higher prices can signal higher quality, a lower price is often an important decision criterion for choosing between two products that are otherwise perceived as equal. Especially in cases where other elements of the total consumer cost are not transparent and difficult to judge for the consumer, they rely heavily on the price as a decision criterion. Therefore, more sustainable products sometimes have a difficult stance because they might have a higher price. A higher price might be caused, for example, by a better build quality or because they possess other qualities that are not directly transparent such as the improved environmental or social properties of organic or Fairtrade food. In some cases, more sustainable products might even be less costly when looking at the total customer cost although they have a higher price, for example, very energy-efficient household appliances. In such cases, sustainability marketing is tasked with communicating superior product qualities or overall cost advantages so that customers take all cost of a product into consideration when making their purchase decision

Other than price, transaction costs are usually nonmonetary. Only if you pay for added services such as brokerage fees you get a better idea of the true monetary value of transaction costs which can include, among others, search and information costs (e.g., finding out where to buy a product or which features and qualities are relevant). Sustainable products often incur higher transaction costs compared to conventional products, and this becomes obvious when looking at the three different types of product attributes usually distinguished in information economics and marketing (e.g., Mitra et al., 1999): search, experience, and credence attributes. Search attributes can be evaluated prior to purchase, for example, through physical product inspection or any other information search activities (e.g., you can see whether or not a banana is ripe). Experience attributes can only be fully assessed after the purchase when the product is being used or consumed (e.g., you do not know in advance if the banana is tasty but you will know after consumption). Credence qualities, finally, usually cannot be fully judged at all because the consumer does not have the necessary knowledge or information to make such a judgment (e.g., you cannot see or taste whether the banana was grown organically or not). If sustainability attributes are considered in addition to other product attributes when buying a product or service, this usually requires further search activities. Furthermore, many sustainability characteristics are not even search attributes but experience or credence attributes. These attributes, however, induce even higher search and information costs. Customers have to find and evaluate, for example, the experience of others who previously bought and used the product, they have to rely on third-party information (e.g., independent tests), or they have to gather information that is not always readily available (e.g., on environmental or social aspects in a company's supply chain). Furthermore, because sustainability is such a vast, complex, and often wicked problem, many consumers simply do not feel qualified to judge sustainability issues so that informing themselves about sustainability in general (not even about specific products) already increases transaction costs. This problem is especially pronounced for initial purchases of a product or when first acquiring information on sustainability aspects of an entire product category.

As the name suggests, use costs occur when using a product, for example, for electricity or fuel to drive a car, or for product maintenance or repairs. They are especially relevant for long-lasting products and often negligible for nondurable consumer goods. However, even some nondurable consumer goods can have implications for use costs. Detergents that allow washing at colder temperatures without compromising on the outcome can help to significantly reduce costs in the process of washing clothes or dishes. Many sustainable products, when they are designed to be more efficient in the use phase, have the advantage of lower use costs compared to regular products, for example, by using less energy. However, consumers often underestimate use costs and instead focus on the price, which can be problematic for providers of sustainable products. Also, some sustainable products require changes in consumer behavior. Highly insulated houses, for example, require less heating but might also need to be kept shady (in terms of using window blinds more often) because they conserve heat better by design compared to many older houses. Even more pronounced, using shared services by engaging in collaborative consumption requires entirely new usage patterns compared to driving one's own car. Respective changes incur switching costs which are also part of the use cost.

The final element of total consumer cost are post-use costs for collecting, storing, and disposing or recycling products at the end of their life cycle. Here again, sustainable products can have an advantage depending on their design (see Chapter C.4.3). Consumers, however, are often not aware of the total post-use costs. Often, waste management systems are in place based on public infrastructure and these are mostly financed through taxes and are thus not connected to the single product to be disposed of or recycled. If that is not the case at all or when consumers are incentivized to produce less garbage, for example, when they have to pay for the amount of waste they produce, post-use costs have to be (partly) covered by the consumer who could then reap the benefits of more sustainable products (e.g., less packaging) or behavior (e.g., using certain appliances for a longer time). Alternatively, post-use costs have to be covered by the general public and are thus a form of negative externalities (see again Chapter B.3.1), for example, when people use unregulated dump sites. In sum, price policy in sustainability marketing needs to consider all these types of cost and the specific challenges attached to sustainable products and how they relate to customer decisions. In combination with the other elements of the marketing mix, strategies and measures need to be developed to successfully market sustainable products.

Furthermore, some ethical issues might arise when thinking about price policy as part of sustainability marketing and management. Crane et al. (2019, pp. 347-349) classify these issues into four types of pricing practices: excessive pricing, price fixing, predatory pricing, and deceptive pricing. Excessive pricing builds on the idea that a fair price has been exceeded. While it is difficult to clearly judge what a fair price would be, we can certainly think of examples in which excessive pricing might occur. People in need of life-saving medical services or drugs, for example, might be charged excessive prices by unethical individuals or companies that try to take advantage of such emergency situations or of systematically lower bargaining power. Price fixing occurs when two or more otherwise competing market actors collude to fix prices above the market rate. Predatory pricing, in contrast, goes in the opposite direction and describes a situation when a company charges prices significantly below the market rate. The aim of such practices is usually to force competitors out of the market so that in the end, higher prices or otherwise favorable market conditions can be exploited. Deceptive pricing, finally, describes practices which deliberately try to obscure the true cost of a product, for example, by charging dubious fees on top of the advertised prices or by offering the actually advertised price to only a very small number of customers. Such practices can be deemed irresponsible and also unsustainable especially when they impede the quest for intra- or intergenerational justice or undermine the SGDs.

C.1.4 Sustainable promotion policy

Promotion policy and sustainability do not seem to go well together—or at least they have a difficult start. The general aim of promotion policy is to inform customers and then to eventually convince them to purchase a product. While the former is generally neutral, the latter is prone to unsustainable activities. In fact, advertising as a core element of promotion policy is often regarded as exactly the opposite of sustainability as summarized by Crane et al. (2019, pp. 345-346). It can create artificial demand if it makes us want and eventually buy things we do not need. Furthermore, we are often urged to constantly buy new things so that we are often only satisfied with the newest fashion or technological gadget. All this can eventually lead to a pervasive consumerism and materialism with the overall negative consequences for sustainability as illustrated in Chapter A.1.2, especially if the promotion policy does not build on a sustainable product policy. More on the social side of sustainability is the problem of perpetuated, undesirable social stereotypes. Often, advertising is criticized as discriminatory (e.g., against women or minorities) or demeaning.

However, sustainable promotion policy can also play an important role in sustainability management. Any sustainable solution has to be known to customers or it cannot succeed. Think back to the example of Patagonia, which was illustrated in Chapter A.4.4. The company once advertised its brand, a certain product, and especially its sustainability efforts in a print advertisement with the slogan "Don't buy this jacket." On the one hand, this advertisement created much positive attention for the company and its sustainability approach. If, on the other hand, all customers would not have followed the call and instead did indeed buy the jacket, this would have caused additional consumption at least in the short term. Without such promotion efforts, however, it would be difficult for the company to communicate its mission. Furthermore, a general sense for sustainability on the end of the customers is a prerequisite for the success of many sustainable products and for sustainable consumption in general—and a suitable sustainable promotion policy can foster such awareness. Apart from this awareness, sustainable consumption and sustainable purchase decisions often require specific knowledge to be able to distinguish more sustainable from less sustainable products and to appreciate them. It is important for consumers to know the relationship between consumption, production, and sustainable development in all its dimensions to be able to act (and potentially buy) sustainably. While sustainable promotion policy usually cannot replace general sustainability education, it can nevertheless supplement it with regard to specific behaviors or products. To achieve this, that is, to inform customers about sustainability and a product's sustainability characteristics, sustainable promotion policy generally has a similar portfolio at hand as regular promotion policy. As it would be far beyond the scope of this book to engage with promotion policy in all its facets, we will now instead highlight some peculiarities of sustainable promotion policy.

Faces of sustainability 8: Anita Roddick

Anita Roddick was a pioneer in sustainability and sustainability marketing. The British entrepreneur is most known as founder of The Body Shop, a company selling cosmetic and skin care products which is recognized for its sustainability approach. With the idea of selling ethical products which were not tested on animals and directly sourced from producers, Roddick founded her first The Body Shop store already in 1976. Over the years, the company expanded massively and went public in 1984. Roddick always stayed true to her course. She was a known social activist and outspoken supporter of various environmental and social NGOs. Roddick also believed in the responsibility of businesses to give something back to society. Company franchisees therefore had to agree to support community or environmental projects while employees were encouraged to volunteer in community projects. Anita Roddick was made a Dame of the British Empire in 2003, and she died in 2007 at the age of 64.

Sources: Horwell (2007); Lyall (2007)

As sustainability aspects have increasingly become a purchase criterion for many consumers (see again Chapter B.6.1), signaling positive sustainability characteristics of their products or the entire organization becomes increasingly attractive for companies. A downside of the increasing popularity of sustainability is that many companies merely claim to be sustainable while they are in fact not, which is often referred to as greenwashing. Delmas and Burbano (2011) define greenwashing as "the act of misleading consumers regarding the environmental practices of a company (firm level greenwashing) or the environmental benefits of a product or service (product level greenwashing)" (p. 66). However, greenwashing can extend beyond the ecological sphere and also involve further misleading claims of sustainability, for example, on social issues. Less often, respective practices are also referred to as social washing (e.g., Rizzi et al., 2020) or bluewashing (e.g., Berliner

& Prakash, 2015), a term that originated from the idea that companies use the blue logo of the UN to falsely signal their solidarity with sustainability issues through a membership in the UN Global Compact (see Chapter C.7.1). Greenwashing is especially problematic if customers cannot assess the credibility of respective claims. Delmas and Burbano (2011) explain several drivers of greenwashing. A lax and uncertain regulatory environment, for example, reduces a company's risks associated with greenwashing, while a rising demand of various stakeholders (customers, investors, etc.) for companies to become more sustainable increases the incentives to engage in it. Furthermore, certain organizational-level characteristics also influence greenwashing tendencies. Some industries and firms are, for example, more prone to greenwashing as they can potentially reap greater benefits from appearing more sustainable than they are (e.g., consumer goods firms). Others might see greater risks and costs of being caught, which can also be related to industry or firm characteristics. Such companies are, for example, more likely to be the target of NGO campaigns and media monitoring than others (again, e.g., consumer goods firms are often highlighted in this regard). Furthermore, some companies have a more pronounced ethical climate than others which would counter greenwashing intentions.

Freitas Netto et al. (2020) summarize various forms of product level and firm level greenwashing. On the product level, the most commonly used differentiation is that of the marketing firm Terra Choice that described the following seven sins of greenwashing:

- Hidden trade-off: Advertising a product as sustainable based on a narrow set of attributes while ignoring other sustainability-related issues. For example, organic fruits that are grown sustainably but at the same time have a large carbon footprint because they are imported from other continents.
- No proof: Making unsubstantiated sustainability claims. For example, referring to the high energy efficiency of a product without providing supporting data or claiming that a product improves the livelihood of workers in the supply chain without evidence.
- Vagueness: Referring to broad and poorly defined claims that are prone to misunderstanding. For example, referring to a product as being overall sustainable, made of "all-natural" ingredients, or using recyclable material.
- Worshipping false labels: Misleadingly using certification-like images or even fake certification labels or wordings. For example, using jargon such as "eco-safe" or creating company own sustainability labels without true content.
- Irrelevance: Making a sustainability claim that is not useful as a characteristic of a more sustainable product. For example, referring to something as a positive and seemingly voluntary sustainability characteristic although the respective practice is already in general predetermined by regulations and laws.
- Lesser of two evils: Claiming to be more sustainable than a competitor's products although the entire product category itself is inherently unsustainable. For example, additive-free cigarettes.
- Fibbing: Making sustainability claims that are plain false. For example, falsely claiming that a product was produced without child labor or selling a conventional cucumber as organic.

Sustainability in business 21: Plastic or paper – How unclear communication can lead to accusations of greenwashing

What is better, plastic or paper packaging? And what about bioplastic? Most people would say paper is better than plastic and bioplastic is a good alternative. Not surprisingly, companies focus on paper and bioplastic to present themselves as sustainable which, however, has led to some interesting cases of greenwashing accusations. In 2021, the South Korean cosmetics brand Innisfree presented a new bottle with the claim "Hello, I'm a Paper Bottle" that was highlighted not only in promotional materials but also very prominently on the bottle itself. The bottle was released as part of a company initiative to reduce the use of plastic packaging. Customers were not amused, however, when they discovered that the bottle was actually a plastic bottle wrapped in an outer paper shell. While the new bottle reduced the amount of plastics by more than 50 percent and the product itself contained instruction on how to separately recycle the plastic and the paper parts, customers nevertheless felt fooled by the bold statement. In this case, a potentially well-intentioned move to reduce plastic by the company actually backfired due to the exaggerated claims. Furthermore, many customers are unfortunately too lazy to separately recycle such combined packaging, which then hinders proper recycling.

In a related case, in 2011 French consumer goods giant Danone sold yogurt on the German market in cups consisting of bioplastics made from cornstarch. The stumbling block of greenwashing accusation in this case was the claim on the product that advertised the cups as environmentally friendly. While bioplastic made from cornstarch generates less carbon emissions and does not use fossil fuels, the overall life cycle sustainability assessment provided no clear-cut results. In most dimensions, there was no definite better or worse and, in some categories, such as the stress on soil and water, the new material underperformed. Similarly, the material was difficult to recycle in industrial recycling processes and, most often, respective cups were thus incinerated instead of recycled, which put a further strain on the eco balance.

These two examples show that it is important not to overstate sustainability claims and instead engage in open and honest communication. Possibly, both companies had good intentions when innovating their product packaging but as often the case in sustainability management, the results were not perfect (which they hardly can be as the road to sustainability is long) and came with some trade-offs. Advertising and marketing efforts in both cases, however, went all in and ignored the complex reality, which led to the accusations of greenwashing. With regard to the question "plastic or paper" and "bioplastic or regular plastic," by the way, there is until today no definite answer as it usually depends on the circumstances. As a general rule of thumb, it is currently an accepted best practice in many cases to use recycled (not merely recyclable) material to close the loop and avoid the intake of further virgin material or, if possible, to not use any packaging at all.

Sources: bbc.com (2021); Deutsche Umwelthilfe (2011); Elsner et al. (2021); n-tv.de (2011); Tan (2021)

On the firm level, Freitas Netto et al. (2020) describe five further sins of greenwashing.

- Dirty business: A firm with an inherently unsustainable business or from an unsustainable industry promotes its sustainable practices or products.
- Ad bluster: A company uses advertising to aggregate certain sustainability achievements to divert attention from other more pressing sustainability issues and sometimes even spending more on the campaign than on the actual sustainability initiatives.
- Political spin: A company communicating sustainability commitments while lobbying against sustainability-related laws and regulations. For example, the automotive industry was long known for their political lobbying activities against stricter environmental regulations while at the same time communicating their sustainability achievements.
- It's the law, stupid!: Corresponding to the sin of irrelevance on the product level, a company communicates sustainability achievements or commitments that are required by laws or regulations anyways.
- Fuzzy reporting: A company uses often unregulated or only loosely regulated sustainability reporting as a one-way communication channel to put itself in a positive light.

While greenwashing can be beneficial for a company if customers do not recognize the false or misleading claims, it comes with certain risks as well. If, for example, an independent third party such as an NGO uncovers and publicly condemns greenwashing activities, this can have a negative impact on the respective company's reputation (see again Chapter B.4.1). Furthermore, extensive greenwashing in some industries or for some product groups can even negatively influence the credibility of truthful firms if it leads to a general skepticism toward all sustainability claims. In some countries, there are even some guidelines and regulations in place nowadays to prevent certain forms of greenwashing. In the United Kingdom, for example, regulatory bodies can sanction companies for breaching certain consumer laws based on the "green claims code." According to this code, companies must, among other things, "not omit or hide relevant information" and they "must consider the full lifecycle of the product" (Competition & Markets Authority, 2021). Overall, for companies having an honest ambition to be sustainable it is therefore advisable to be consistent in their claims to increase credibility.

Task C1-2

Find further examples of greenwashing that have been discussed in the (social) media, by NGOs, or otherwise. In which category do they fall? What do you think—why did the respective companies engage in such greenwashing? Do you think it was worth the risk? How could greenwashing be avoided in the future?

An important task of sustainable promotion policy is to signal the trustworthiness of sustainability traits to customers. Labels are a specific tool in this regard to increase creditability and signal trustworthiness. They can reduce complexity and increase confidence for customers (Asioli et al., 2020; Prieto-Sandoval et al., 2016). Instead of informing themselves in detail about sustainability aspects of a certain product or product category, customers can refer to labels to obtain certain otherwise complex and opaque information. The content and procedures of sustainability labels are probably as diverse as the topic of sustainability itself. Some labels focus on single issues such as the energy efficiency of certain products (e.g., various energy-star labels around the world) or human rights aspects (e.g., various labels for child labor free products). Others include multiple sustainability aspects from the social and ecological dimension. Most often, sustainability labels are either positively framed (e.g., labels for organic food or Fairtrade) or they provide information from a neutral perspective (e.g., relative energy efficiency of a household appliance on a certain scale). Much less prevalent are labels with negatively connoted information that communicate product characteristics a consumer might want to avoid (e.g., air freight fruits). Another important characteristic of different labels is their origin. Some labels are initiated and monitored by governmental institutions, others by NGOs, and some have their roots in the private sector, which can have different implications for their credibility and reach. An important caveat of sustainability labels is their seemingly ever increasing quantity. The general prevalence of labels in some areas makes it increasingly difficult for consumers to distinguish stronger from weaker labels and to evaluate the trustworthiness of the labels themselves. Label initiatives themselves thus have to make sure that they convey credibility or otherwise they will not be able to increase customers' degree of confidence in sustainable products.

When planning communication messages in sustainability marketing, these messages can be framed positively (e.g., "this product is 30 percent more energy efficient") or negatively (e.g., "If you do not purchase this T-shirt, you miss out on the opportunity to sponsor 1-year of education for a child in Bangladesh"). Generally, negative frames tend to be "stickier" than positive frames, and consumers care more about future losses than about future gains (for an overview, see White et al., 2019). Sustainability marketers and product developers thus might want to focus on comparing future costs and how to avoid them (e.g., energy cost over a product's life time). When combined with concrete information on how to engage in more sustainable behavior (e.g., information on how to recycle), such messages have been shown to be especially effective in spurring sustainable behavior. However, since framing can have different effects on different customer segments, there is no universal and straightforward way on how to best design sustainability marketing messages. Overall, such messages can focus on rational, emotional, and moral appeals (Belz & Peattie, 2012). Rational appeals focus on the self-interest of the customer. Organic food, for example, can be advertised by highlighting health aspects. Similarly, the cost-saving opportunities of energy-efficient household appliances can be highlighted. Next to the individual benefits, also from an overarching perspective, supporting sustainability can be framed as rational because it is in the best interest of all stakeholders to preserve the planet. Emotional appeals try to reach the targeted individual by establishing an emotional connection. Organizations seeking donations, for example, to support children in the Global South, endangered animals, or the environment in general often use emotional appeals (e.g., think of the pictures of seabirds or fish being caught in plastic waste). Moral appeals, finally, aim at triggering people's sense of right and wrong. In the case of sustainability, this can start with highlighting a duty to protect the environment or to improve the rights of the world's poor, as discussed in Chapter A.3.1.

Task C1-3

Identify different sustainability labels from the same industry (e.g., food, textiles, raw materials)! Now compare them with regard to different characteristics: What kind of organization(s) initiated and manage(s) the label? What sustainability criteria do products have to fulfill to obtain the label? How are these criteria controlled (e.g., by whom, in which intervals, based on what kind of data)? Finally, discuss: Of the labels you assessed, are any "better" or "worse" than others? Are the criteria and processes better than having no label at all? Are they sufficient for sustainability?

C.1.5 Sustainable product placement

In the regular marketing mix, the element of place is about how a good or service is brought to the customer. Even if consumers are willing to consume (more) sustainably, and assuming they are aware of what more sustainable consumption looks like, there might still be hurdles which prevent them from doing so. As we have discussed in Chapter B.6.2, a general awareness for sustainability does not necessarily lead to sustainable behavior. Awareness can only translate into actual behavior when there is the opportunity. Important aspects in this regard are missing opportunities to actually consume more sustainably, and often factors hindering sustainable consumption are outside the sphere of influence of individual consumers. For example, while many sharing services (e.g., carsharing or bike sharing) are readily available in many cities around the world, such business models are usually not viable in more rural or less densely populated suburban areas. Moreover, whether or not somebody thinks that there are opportunities to behave sustainably can differ significantly when looking at different customer segments. In many cases, for example, options to consume more sustainably are generally available but they might require more effort (see again the sustainable purchase perception matrix in Chapter B.6.2). For example, buying sustainable clothing might require going to specialized retailers, which are not yet widespread in most shopping malls. For people of conviction who are truly into sustainability, such efforts are usually not an obstacle. Others, however, might generally be interested in sustainability but not willing to invest further efforts. For those people, more easily available, low-threshold options would increase the chances of acting sustainably. Product placement can thus be an important lever to improve sustainable consumption on a larger scale.

Many sustainable products often come from innovative niche players, startups, or smaller brands. Especially these types of companies, however, encounter difficulties reaching customers due to limited resources and access to markets and distribution channels. Supermarkets have limited shelf space for which there is often significant competition, so that the retailers are an important gatekeeper. Overall, an increasing trend toward sustainability in society has led to an improved availability of a variety of products in many countries that were formerly only available via specialized channels. Organic fruits and vegetables, vegan or Fairtrade products, for example, used to be available mostly via specialized supermarkets, health food stores, or directly from producers. Today, however, they have become widely available in regular grocery stores or supermarkets in many regions of the world. Another opportunity for smaller or new players can be the increasing trend of online retailing which, for obvious reasons, has fewer limitations, for example, with regard to shelf space. Furthermore, the trend toward sustainability in many regions around the world has led to the sprouting of specialized retailers, such as organic food store chains (e.g., Whole Foods in the United States or the United Kingdom), which try to cater to a growing number of people interested in sustainability. Other players try to foster the availability of sustainable products and sustainable consumption through increased access to used goods or product service systems as illustrated above and in Chapter B.6.3.

Sustainability in business 22: Zero waste and package free shops

An interesting trend in many regions around the world are specialized supermarkets selling unpackaged food and other items. In these stores, customers bring their own boxes, flasks, or other containers to buy everyday items such as pasta, cereals, dried fruits, nuts, sweets, detergents, and all kinds of products that can be purchased in bulk for package-free retailing. Interestingly, this can be regarded as a "back to the roots" trend, as especially food was sold unpackaged for centuries until the times of industrialization. A challenge for such stores is often the fact that they primarily sell unbranded products because the brand recognition is usually connected to the product packaging. Because brands are an important signal (e.g., of quality) for many customers, such zero waste or package free shops often only cater to a small niche of sustainability enthusiasts. In some cases, regular supermarkets also nowadays offer a "package free" corner with a limited range of unpackaged goods, and some producers, for example, of laundry detergent experiment with refill stations in drug stores to reduce packaging.

(Illustration by Obsidian19, CC BY-SA 4.0, caption translated to English by the author https://commons.wikimedia.org/wiki/File:Unverpackt_-_Wie_funktioniert_das.jpg)

KEY TAKEAWAYS

- Sustainability marketing tries to overcome marketing myopia by deliberately including socioecological aspects and considering the collective consequences of marketing activities.
- There are product-oriented services, use-oriented services, and result-oriented services which can potentially improve eco-efficiency as well as eco-effectiveness and lead to lower resource use or emissions while at the same time offering consumer benefits.
- Total consumer costs are composed of the purchase price, transaction costs, use costs, and post-use costs. Sustainability marketing should focus on all costs as there might be specific advantages and drawbacks associated with sustainable products.
- Ethical problems are often connected with excessive pricing, price fixing, predatory pricing, and deceptive pricing.
- Promotion can create artificial demand, lead to pervasive consumerism and materialism, perpetuate undesirable social stereotypes, and be discriminatory or demeaning.
- Greenwashing is described as the act of misleading consumers regarding sustainable practices, and it is often classified into seven products related and five firm level sins.
- Labels can act as a signal to illustrate otherwise complex and opaque facts, but it is often difficult to distinguish stronger from weaker labels.
- Product placement can be difficult due to competition for shelf space. Different channels specialize on sustainable products.

C.2 Sustainable human resource management

LEARNING GOALS

After reading this chapter you will be able to ...

- ... distinguish employees as a means and as an end of sustainable human resource management.
- ... illustrate different interventions to increase the likelihood of employees to act sustainably.
- ... explain how structural measures can be used to implement sustainability throughout a company.
- ... illustrate what companies can do for their employees through sustainable human resource management.

Introduction to Chapter C.2: Screencast
Watch an introduction to the chapter here:

Sustainable human resource management covers two perspectives. On the one hand, companies aiming at improving their sustainability performance need the support or at least basic cooperation of their employees to reach their sustainability goals. This part of sustainable human resource management focuses on fostering employees' sustainable behavior at work and regards employees as a means to improve a company's sustainability performance. On the other hand, sustainable human resource management is also about what companies can, could, or should do for their employees. In this perspective, employees are an end of sustainable human resource management. Both aspects will be illustrated in this chapter.

C.2.1 Fostering employees' sustainable behavior at work

In Chapter B.2.2, we discussed the influence of employees on sustainability management and how awareness for sustainability as well as personal and social norms may influence employee behavior. In an ideal sustainability-focused world, employees would naturally act sustainably and refrain from unsustainable behavior. In current reality, however, employees often do not care for sustainability, they might lack necessary knowledge, they might think it is too difficult or uncomfortable to act sustainably, or they might feel that their own actions are not meaningful, and so on. Companies can therefore implement interventions to increase the likelihood of employees to behave sustainably at work. In their reviews, Ones et al. (2015), Renwick et al. (2013), and Yuriev et al. (2018) categorize and discuss interventions and activities employers can use (outlined in the following).

The most far-reaching intervention probably lies in recruiting processes that aim at choosing sustainability-conscious employees. As illustrated in Chapter B.2.2, personal norms are an important driver of employees' sustainability behavior. Personal norms are, however, usually deeply rooted in individual value systems and exist for a long time. Therefore, the influence companies can exert on these norms is limited. Consequently, choosing people with personal norms that are compatible with the idea of sustainability as adopted by the company is a way to influence their behavior at work early on. To achieve the goal of choosing sustainability-conscious employees, companies can, for example, emphasize respective topics in job advertisements or probe applicants about their sustainability orientation. Given that sustainable companies are often attractive for job seekers (see Chapter B.2.1), such measures can also be regarded as an element of employer branding. However, making such choices is not always easy or possible and, in some cases, having employees with strong sustainability-related personal norms might not be sufficient to holistically elicit sustainable behavior at work. Therefore, further interventions might be necessary.

Interventions for improving attention to and reducing barriers for sustainable behavior at work aim at the individual employees' motivation and at making respective behavior easier for the individual employee. Such interventions can consist of (infra-)structural measures such as placing waste separation systems in offices, compost bins in cafeterias, or providing e-bikes for employees' business and personal use instead of offering managers a company car. Furthermore, soft measures such as providing prompts (e.g., "switch off your computer when leaving the office") or voluntary campaigns (e.g., employee volunteering or a voluntary vegan day per week) can support such infrastructural activities. However, many types of behavior are habitual and thus relatively resistant to short-term variations. Interventions that focus on persuasion or social influence are less effective in changing habitual behaviors. If habits are barriers for more sustainable behavior at work, situational changes might be necessary to break these habits and help employees to establish new patterns of behavior. Examples of such changes are requiring employees to use public transport for business trips instead of providing company cars, or mandatory assignments for management trainees to subsidiaries in the Global South to provide them with first-hand experience with the local social reality. While respective measures can indeed help to break habits, they can also be unpopular and lead to discontent.

Another set of interventions aims at improving employees' knowledge and skills to perform sustainable behaviors. The rationale of such interventions is that information about sustainability aspects can improve awareness of sustainability problems and consequences thus strengthening the intention to behave sustainably. This requires that sustainability is generally already part of the employees' personal norms and that an improvement of knowledge and skills can then help to activate these norms. Information campaigns or an emphasis on sustainability in onboarding programs, for example, can illustrate why employees should act sustainably. Furthermore, regular sustainability-oriented training is widely regarded as a key instrument in improving knowledge and skills. Respective education and instructions illustrating how employees can act sustainably might increase the employees' knowledge of sustainability issues, of the company's impact, and of the individual's influence on this impact. Such instruments are relatively common in many organizations. Nevertheless, they do not always result in behavioral changes, which is why they should be accompanied by further interventions.

Interventions involving feedback, rewards, and recognition aim at developing a sustainability-related climate in a company through tangible and intangible measures. Tracking individual sustainability performance allows the company to provide penalties or incentives. Such punishments (e.g., suspensions, criticisms, or warnings) and rewards are regarded as feasible instruments for providing behavior reinforcement. Especially penalties, however, might be problematic if they lead, for example, to employees covering up sustainability problems for reasons of self-protection. Positive incentives can come in a tangible form—either monetarized (e.g., financial rewards, gift certificates) or nonmonetarized (e.g., time off).

Furthermore, incentives can also be intangible, for example, by providing social rewards that are institutionalized (e.g., sustainable employee of the month or greenest team of the factory) or collegial (e.g., praise or expression of gratitude). Monetary reward systems are increasingly common, especially for senior managers, when the achievement of certain sustainability targets is linked to bonus payments. They are less widespread at lower levels of a company hierarchy, because setting targets and measuring sustainability performance is often more difficult to account to single employees. Regardless of the hierarchy level, incentives can be institutionalized in sustainability-related suggestion schemes, for attending a certain amount of sustainability training courses, and so on.

Sustainability in business 23: Sustainability aspects in top management compensation

Various companies nowadays include sustainability goals in their compensation plans. One example is Bayer, the German multinational pharmaceutical and life sciences company that is famous, among other things, for the painkiller Aspirin and the controversial merger with agrochemical and agricultural biotechnology corporation Monsanto in 2018. In 2021, the compensation of Bayer's board members comprises a base compensation of roughly 30 percent of the overall compensation, supplemented by roughly 30 percent short-term variable compensation and 40 percent long-term variable compensation. The short-term variable cash compensation depends on the company's success in the respective year, and it includes nonfinancial factors based on the individual performance of each board member in that year. In 2020, targets for individual performance for different board members included, for example, the launch or implementation of the sustainability strategy. Some team targets also covered sustainability issues such as to "integrate sustainability into divisional strategic plans and evaluate sustainability objectives."

In 2021, Bayer furthermore introduced sustainability as a criterion for the long-term compensation, with a weighting of 20 percent (the remaining 80 percent were relative capital market performance and return on investment). The long-term compensation is based on performance goals in a four-year period. At the start of each four-year period, a minimum value and a maximum value are set. The sustainability goals are supposed to be measurable and they will be disclosed in the compensation report as part of the 2021 annual report published in 2022. So go ahead and have a look at how Bayer integrated sustainability in its board compensation plans!

Source: Bayer AG (2021)

Interventions to improve self-commitment and social support can include asking employees to make commitments and set their own sustainability-related goals or persuasion via role models. Asking for self-commitments can help to match individual sustainability values with behavior. In this context, codes of conduct or corporate sustainability statements can support the self-commitment of employees. Furthermore, supervisors seem to be an important factor of social support as they are often seen as role models. Role models in general can motivate sustainability-related behavior, for example, through leading by example or through motivational appeals via e-mail or newsletters as a low-cost means of encouragement.

Commitment and social support can also be increased by structural measures, which aim to anchor sustainability as a topic in organizational routines and processes. To achieve this, sustainability should be included in an organization's mission and values to underscore its relevance for the company. Sustainability advocates can then drive the topic and integrate it into strategic and operational considerations. Top management support is usually regarded as important to improve the sustainability orientation of a company. Hence, an executive level advocate can be essential to underline seriousness as such a person can, for example, secure resources for the interventions described above. Nowadays, sustainability is thus increasingly linked to board members, and in many companies the position of a Chief Sustainability Officer has been installed high in the company hierarchy. Apart from such top-level strategic considerations, for a company not to be engaged in window dressing and greenwashing, sustainability aspects also have to be implemented into the daily business routines. A dedicated sustainability department can be suitable as a central location providing expertise to the entire company and to act as a facilitator. Again, however, merely having a central sustainability department is usually not sufficient to achieve a broad dissemination of the topic in a company. Therefore, responsibilities for sustainability should be determined in the various functional departments and at the different (physical) locations throughout a company. This can be achieved by installing "sustainability ambassadors," "green teams," and "sustainability councils" as advocates of sustainability who develop suggestions, improve awareness, and thus anchor the topic in organizations'' processes.

Overall, the various types of interventions should not be used in isolation but instead be regarded as a comprehensive toolbox to foster employees' sustainable behavior at work. Ideally, the combined use of various measures strengthens a supportive overall culture for sustainability and thus integrates the topic into the everyday thinking and actions of all employees.

Task C2-1

Have another look at the different elements of sustainable behavior at work as introduced in Chapter B.2.2: "Avoiding harm or conserving," "transforming," "influencing others," and "taking initiative." Now come up with a list of measures to improve sustainable behavior at work. To what extent do your proposed activities influence these different elements of behavior? Under which circumstances are these activities and measures (not) effective and to what extent do they (not) influence employees' sustainability-related awareness, knowledge, and personal norms as well as social norms? What might hinder companies to implement your proposed activities and measures?

C.2.2 Sustainable human resource management for employees

Apart from asking how companies can foster sustainable behavior among their employees to improve the corporate sustainability performance, sustainable human resource management also encompasses what companies can, could, or should do for their employees. Various guidelines, such as ISO 26000 on social responsibility (International Standardization Organization [ISO], 2010; see Chapter C.7.1.3) or the standards of the Global Reporting Initiative (GRI; see Chapter C.8.2), provide insights into corporate responsibilities for their employees.

Being employed and having a secure job is a very important element in most people's lives. A fundamental issue of responsibility in employer–employee relationships for a company is thus to provide secure employment and adequate working conditions to its employees to enable a decent and possibly even continuously improving standard of living. Companies should thus avoid relying on work performed on a causal or temporal basis, such as short term or seasonal contracts, wherever possible. Labor intermediaries can be a means to increase flexibility but they should be legally recognized and also adhere to the various elements of sustainable human resource management. Through active workforce planning, layoffs should be minimized and, if unavoidable, consider social criteria while at the same time eliminating arbitrary or discriminatory dismissal practices. Another fundamental topic of employer responsibility is to allow employees to engage in collective bargaining and facilitate social dialogue through work councils or other consultation mechanisms. When outsourcing work to external partners, companies should make sure that they do not benefit from their suppliers' exploitative or abusive labor practices (see Chapter C.3), and they should not exploit weak legislations, for example, in countries that restrict the right to collective bargaining. Furthermore, companies working internationally can be expected to make use of local workforces and contract local enterprises to increase employment in the respective host country.

Next to having a job, the most important issue for employees is usually to stay healthy and safe on that job, which of course also has positive implications for the employing company. Companies thus should care about occupational health and safety, implementing measures to uphold the physical and mental well-being of employees and prevent harm caused by the respective working conditions. Companies can therefore be expected to have and promote a health and safety policy. This usually covers obvious issues such as providing adequate personal protective equipment and analyzing health and safety risks associated with a job. Furthermore, employees should receive training on all relevant matters. Requirements and procedures for safe working practices should be clearly communicated, and workplaces should be designed with employee safety and health in mind. This can include ergonomic working conditions to avoid long-term damages. Depending on the type of work, measures could include ergonomic desks and desk chairs for office workers, shock absorbing mats for assembly line workers, noise insulation, and so on. Furthermore, companies can strive to reduce psychological hazards that can lead to chronic stress and stress-related illnesses, for example, by setting realistic targets or avoiding piecework. While many measures in the area of occupational health and safety are universally applicable to all employees, some issues are more person specific or applicable to certain groups of employees (e.g., pregnant women, workers with disabilities, older employees, or inexperienced workers) so that the relevant circumstances need to be considered. Because occupational health and safety is an important matter (topic, subject) for any kind of company and a core element of sustainable human resource management, dedicated management systems standards (e.g., ISO 45001) exist that help companies to manage and continuously improve this issue (see also Chapter C.7.2).

Apart from health issues, other conditions of work as well as social protection can also be regarded as important in sustainable human resource management, as they influence the quality of life of employees and their families. Most obviously, this applies to wages, working hours, holidays, and weekly days off. The International Labour Organization provides some general benchmark for minimum requirements in this regard and, wherever possible, national customs and religious traditions should be respected. Wages should be paid directly to employees in accordance with the respective laws and regulations and at the same time be adequate for the needs of the employees and their families, considering the cost of living as well as general wage levels and living standards in a certain country or region. Overtime work should be compensated adequately and at the same time remain voluntary. Working hours within the limits of laws and collective agreements should provide employees with weekly rest and paid holidays. All these aspects cater to a decent work–life balance which can, however, be subject to the different personal influences of each individual employee. Employees with children or who care for sick relatives, for example, might have different needs than other employees. Sustainable human resource management aims at catering to such needs, for example, by offering parental leave, childcare facilities, or other support to improve work–life balance and provide employees with the opportunity to combine work with family responsibilities. Company canteens, access to medical services, or sanitation facilities can also improve working conditions and thus be regarded as part of sustainable human resource management, where applicable. Social protection, finally, refers to measures which mitigate risks—especially income risk—stemming, for example, from parenthood, work injuries, unemployment, etc.

Sustainability in society 14: Negative health effects of long working hours

A recent study based on worldwide data from the World Health Organization and the International Labour Organization clearly highlighted the negative effects of certain forms of unsustainable or irresponsible company behavior: excessive working hours. The authors found that people working long hours (≥55 hours/week) face a significantly higher risk of potentially lethal cardiovascular diseases. They estimated that around 750,000 deaths were attributable to the exposure to long working hours. Responsible employee-related sustainability management thus requires interventions to reduce such long working hours to protect employee health.

Source: Pega et al. (2021)

Closely connected to the issue of work–life balance is the topic of flexibility. In sustainable human resource management, flexibility is mainly considered from the employee perspective and not from a company perspective. It aims at reconciling the individual needs of employees with the overall work requirements of the company. In many jobs, for example, there might not be the need for strict working hours so that employees can benefit from certain flexibility with regard to when to start and end their work. Similarly, offering options for remote work can help employees in harmonizing their private and working lives. Such measures ideally benefit employees and employers at the same time, if they, for example, increase employee satisfaction, loyalty, and motivation. Often, however, such measures come with challenges, as flexible work arrangements might be more difficult to plan, they might lead to reduced team spirit, and they might even have negative effects on the individual employee as working from home has been shown to be related to reduced promotion rates (Bloom et al., 2015). Moreover, such measures of flexibility might not even be appreciated by those employees who favor traditional work arrangements.

Employment not only helps individuals to generate income and provide for their families. It can also be regarded as an option to improve skills and capabilities. Sustainable human resource management thus also aims to improve employability. It aims not only at developing skills and capacities that are currently relevant but also at skills and capacities that are likely to be needed in the future. Potential measures include, for example, on-the-job training to improve specialized skills and professional capabilities through direct experience, off-the-job training to develop new skills, or apprenticeships. Such measures can again be beneficial for the company itself to improve the quality of its workforce, especially in volatile environments, or to improve a company's attractiveness on the job market. When necessary, employees who have been made redundant should receive assistance such as training or counsel to seek a new job. Respective measures should be offered to employees on an equal and nondiscriminatory basis.

Additional considerations of nondiscrimination, fairness, equality, and diversity complement the field of sustainable human resource management. Diversity usually refers to employee's sociodemographic traits such as gender, ethnicity, or age but it can potentially also include less visible aspects such as attitudes, beliefs, and values. On a minimum level, companies should ensure nondiscrimination, for example, with regard to promotions or wages. This can be measured as ratios of wages of women to men or between different ethnic groups. However, sustainable human resource management can also go one step further to actively promote, for example, diversity in the workforce at different hierarchy levels or provide training opportunities focusing on diversity and nondiscrimination.

Task C2-2

The demographic change in many countries around the world is leading to an aging population. Companies in those countries therefore face an aging workforce. What are the potential risks and changes of an aging workforce for companies? What is the task of sustainable human resource management with regard to an aging workforce? Develop measures in the areas of health and safety, social protection, flexibility, and employability to minimize risks and maximize benefits of an aging workforce.

Sustainability in society 15: Diversity in reality – Gender pay gaps and ethnicity pay gaps

A frequently discussed topic in diversity are so-called pay gaps, that is, differences in average wages between different groups. Such pay gaps are often mentioned as indicators of inequality in access to higher paid jobs, promotions, or rewards. Numerous studies show, for example, that although continuously declining, gender pay gaps still exist across most industries worldwide. In the European Union, the adjusted pay gap that compares women and men with similar characteristics was 9.4 percent in the years 2010 to 2014.

Reasons for this gap can be manifold. Women are, for example, usually overrepresented in industries with lower pay levels (e.g., nursing or child care) or they work more often in part-time or flexible jobs due to family-related leaves, as compared to men, which also means that they are only able to pay less money into pension funds and other financial security arrangements. Thus, the gap does not necessarily have to be the result of open discrimination. Beyond this issue, diversity is of course not restricted to gender issues. In the United Kingdom, for example, only one percent of university professors are black compared to three percent in the total population, and only six out of more than 800 partners at the five largest law firms are black. While there are some explanations for such differences and gaps, discrimination might also occur and companies should be aware of such issues to actively avoid them.

Concepts such as the glass ceiling or leaky pipelines point to the disadvantages of women or minorities on the labor market. Glass ceiling describes artificial barriers that prevent women (or other qualified individuals) from moving up the hierarchical ladder in a company. This ceiling often hinders women to acquire well-paid positions, and it cannot be explained by a (lack of) job competencies or related factors. The concept of leaky pipelines describes the phenomenon that women often "leak out" before reaching management positions, for example, due to family-related leaves. Sustainable human resource management can try to remedy such disadvantages and problems with respective measures.

Such measures usually start with collecting adequate information on gender, ethnicity, and disabilities on the various hierarchy levels and company functions to gain an understanding of the situation—supported by an internal information campaign on the why and how of such data collection. Such information, including general pay reviews, can then be transparently reported to the workforce and beyond to increase awareness and subsequently develop measures to avoid discrimination in recruitment or annual review processes. Furthermore, accompanying measures can aim at minimizing structural disadvantages of certain groups (e.g., by offering flexible childcare programs or supporting paternal leave) or at supporting employees with certain characteristics (e.g., offering leadership workshops for employees from an ethnic minority). Processes such as recruitment or promotions can be monitored, for example, by observing the percentage of qualified applicants with certain characteristics.

Sources: L. Adams et al. (2018); Bishu and Alkadry (2017); Boll and Lagemann (2018); Sikka (2021)

Task C2-3

Think of the different aspects of CSR and sustainability management for employees introduced above. Are all of them relevant to the same extent in all industries and around the world or would you see a different emphasis depending on the circumstances in which a company operates? Which aspects might be universally relevant and which not—and why? Discuss these questions based on examples of specific industries and countries.

KEY
TAKEAWAYS

- Sustainable human resource management covers two perspectives that ask (1) how to foster employees' sustainable behavior at work to improve a company's sustainability performance and (2) what a company can, could, or should do for its employees.
- Companies can recruit sustainability-conscious employees, improve attention, and reduce barriers for sustainable behavior at work, improve employees' knowledge and skills to perform sustainable behaviors, use feedback, rewards, or recognition to develop a sustainability-related company culture, and encourage employees' self-commitment and social support.
- Structural measures such as establishing a designated chief sustainability manager or sustainability management teams aim at anchoring sustainability as a topic in organizational routines and processes.
- Companies have responsibilities to provide secure employment, to care about occupational health and safety, to provide decent conditions of work as well as social protection, to allow reasonable flexibility, to improve employability, and to ensure nondiscrimination, fairness, equality, and diversity.

C.3 Sustainable supply chain management

LEARNING GOALS

After reading this chapter you will be able to ...

- ... characterize sustainable supply chain management.
- ... discuss the relevance of sustainable supply chain management for sustainability management.
- ... illustrate challenges of sustainable supply chain management.
- ... explain supplier management for risks and performance as a rather reactive strategy.
- ... explain the steps of commitment, evaluation, control, and development in this strategy.
- ... explain supply chain management for sustainable products as a rather proactive strategy.
- ... explain the idea of decommoditization along with its opportunities and challenges.
- ... discuss how regulation can be a driver for sustainable supply chain management.

Introduction to Chapter C.3: Screencast
Watch an introduction to the chapter here:

C.3.1 Introduction to (sustainable) supply chain management

"A supply chain consists of all parts involved ... in fulfilling a customer request ... the manufacturer and suppliers, but also transporters, warehouses, retailers" (Chopra, 2019, p. 15). Supply chain management, thus, involves managing the relationships along the supply chain to gain competitive advantages and increase the surplus of the entire chain. While supply chain management is about all stages and organizations in a supply chain, the most important nucleus is often the focal firm. In each supply chain, there is usually one central company which shapes large parts of the supply chain through its decisions—that is, focal firm. This company ultimately selects suppliers and distributors and is thus the key in managing supply chains. The focal firm is in direct contact with the end consumers and it designs the main aspects of the product and, thereby, determines its characteristics and also sustainability impacts. Importantly, while a focal firm might be a company that actually manufactures or assembles a product, the actual production is not a necessary condition. In the textile industry, for example, most of the well-known brands do not have their own production facilities. Instead, they usually outsource production to suppliers. Nevertheless, these companies are the focal firms of their respective supply chains because they fulfill the above-mentioned attributes.

Now, what makes supply chains sustainable or unsustainable and what exactly is sustainable supply chain management? Let us start with the latter aspect. According to two well-cited definitions, sustainable supply chain management is "the strategic, transparent integration and achievement of an organization's social, environmental, and economic goals in the systemic coordination of key interorganizational business processes for improving the long-term economic performance of the individual company and its supply chains" (Carter & Rogers, 2008, p. 368) or "the management of material, information and capital flows as well as cooperation among companies along the supply chain while taking goals from all three dimensions of sustainable development, i.e., economic, environmental and social, into account which are derived from customer and stakeholder requirements." (Seuring & Müller, 2008, p. 1700).

Considering sustainability in supply chain management offers significant levers to improving the sustainability performance of products and companies. For example, companies report that greenhouse gas emissions in their supply chains are on average more than 11 times higher than their own operational emissions (CDP, 2021a). Consequently, sustainable supply chain practices that consider not only the environmental performance of one company but instead take a holistic approach toward reducing environmental burdens in the entire supply chain have indeed been found to significantly contribute to improved environmental performance (Eggert & Hartmann, 2021). Moreover, social issues are also highly relevant in modern supply chains. A central reason underlying why many supply chains moved large parts of their production to the Global South over the last decades was the aim to decrease the cost of labor and other direct costs associated with the production of goods, for example, due to lower wages and weaker regulations with regard to various environmental and social issues. While offshoring has created some income opportunities in and technology transfer to poor countries, it has also led to precarious employment situations for millions of people around the world. While many companies nowadays have made commitments to pay living wages within their supply chains due to increasing pressure from unions, consumers, and civil society, there is often little progress toward achieving these commitments (LeBaron et al., 2021).

Sustainability in society 16: Modern slavery in global supply chains

Modern slavery, that is, "situations of exploitation that a person cannot refuse or leave because of threats, violence, coercion, deception, and/or abuse of power" (International Labour Organization, 2017, p. 9), is prevalent in many supply chains around the world. The International Labour Organization estimates that in 2016, around 25 million people were in forced labor, which can include, among other things, forms of child labor, illegal harvest helpers, or even forced prostitution. The largest share of adults who were in forced labor were domestic workers. Forced labor is also an issue in supply chains of typical consumer products as it is widely found, for example, in manufacturing or agriculture. The means to force people involuntarily into work are diverse, ranging from withholding wages or confiscating passports to (threats of) physical violence to the workers or their families. Modern slavery is very often a hidden issue unknown to many consumers. The website (and app) http://slaveryfootprint.org offers a calculator to estimate the number of slaves working for any individual around the world and sheds light on this ugly aspect in many supply chains. So why don't you go and find out: How many slaves work for you?

Sources: International Labour Organization (2017)

Sustainable supply chain management offers the opportunity to improve the sustainability performance of products and companies, and there are numerous approaches and best-practice examples, as we will discuss throughout this chapter as well as in other parts of this book. However, there are also vast challenges which need to be dealt with. Most modern supply chains have not only one or two tiers of suppliers and subsuppliers but sometimes four, five, or more and companies often have thousands of suppliers spread over dozens of countries worldwide. Every new tier level of suppliers makes it more complex to exchange information and ensure transparency. Often focal firms have several hundreds or even thousands of suppliers with hundreds of thousands of workers in facilities around the world. Furthermore, the increasing sophistication of modern technology has led to a significantly growing breadth in the spectrum of used materials, such as rare-earth metals and others, which also increased the complexity of products and, eventually, supply chains. Finally, many supply chains are dynamic in the sense that the network of potential and actual suppliers is constantly evolving when new partners enter and old ties are dissolved.

While the challenges for sustainable supply chain management are significant, so is the impetus to move toward improved sustainability. As often the case, various actors provide incentives or exercise pressure on companies (see the entire Part B of this book). Governmental actors can implement regulations, customers increasingly voice their preference for sustainable products, or NGOs exercise public pressure on companies to improve sustainability standards throughout their supply chains. However, often there is a lack of enforcement of regulations, customers are unwilling to pay a price premium, and many NGO campaigns find no resonance in the broader public so that the overall situation is complicated.

Sustainability in business 24: How an NGO brought Starbucks to sourcing Fairtrade coffee

In early 2000, the U.S.-based NGO Global Exchange that focused on human rights issues launched a campaign targeting the coffee company Starbucks for not buying Fairtrade coffee. The NGO organized an Internet campaign as well as rallies at Starbucks stores. Even before the campaign, the company engaged in talks with a Fairtrade organization in the United States, but the NGO pressure quickly sped things up. In October 2000, Starbucks announced that it would introduce Fairtrade coffee in all of its stores and became the country's largest roaster and retailer of certified Fairtrade coffee.

Source: Argenti (2004)

Seuring and Müller (2008) illustrate two strategies companies can pursue to become more sustainable in their supply chains: (1) supplier management for risks and performance and (2) supply chain management for sustainable products. While the former is a more reactive strategy to avoid risks, the latter is a more proactive approach to holistically implement sustainability in supply chains. Whereas we will subsequently discuss both strategies separately, the two approaches are not mutually exclusive and can also be used simultaneously.

Task C3-1

Palm oil is a very versatile ingredient which increases the shelf-life of many products. The colorless and odorless oil is used for a variety of products, ranging from food to toiletries or even animal feed. However, palm oil production is a major driver for deforestation in Africa and Southeast Asia and therefore responsible for greenhouse gas emissions and biodiversity losses. Furthermore, accusations of child labor and exploitation of workers on the palm oil farms are being raised every now and then. Against this background, the Roundtable on Sustainable Palm Oil (RSPO), a not-for-profit organization founded by NGOs, palm oil processors, palm oil producers, and other actors, aims at fostering a sustainable production of palm oil by means of a certification system. Nevertheless, the RSPO is not undisputed.

Do some research: What do critics of the RSPO say? And what are the arguments of its advocates (in industry but also from the NGO sector)? How has the RSPO evolved over time? Are there any alternative products (i.e., substitutes), and how do they compare with regard to different sustainability aspects? Imagine you are the chairperson of the RSPO and you really want your organization to have a positive impact on sustainability—what would you do to promote sustainability standards and get large parts of the industry on board? What makes your job difficult?

Sustainability in research 8: Seuring and Müller's 2008 article on sustainable supply chain management

The pressure on companies for socially, ecologically, and economically sustainable supply chains has increased significantly in recent years, forcing firms to rethink value chains in response to external pressures. In their article "From a literature review to a conceptual framework for sustainable supply chain management" from 2008, Stefan Seuring and Martin Müller seek to understand the drivers and strategies for sustainable supply chains by analyzing 191 articles published between 1994 to 2007. The authors identify triggers and barriers to sustainable supply chain management, and they derive two corporate strategies that we also illustrate in-depth in this chapter.

According to Seuring and Müller, the most important external triggers of corporate sustainable development stems from customers and public authorities. Generally, a company cannot ensure its long-term existence without the legitimacy of its customers. In addition, government authorities can inhibit or support development through norms and laws. To satisfy external stakeholders, companies are forced to increasingly control their ties with suppliers and to verify the environmental and social performance of production at all stages. Based on these drivers, Seuring and Müller first address the strategy of supply chain management for risks and performance. Companies with potential reputational losses due to environmentally damaging action can evaluate their suppliers according to additional environmental and social standards, adding sustainability criteria to their portfolio. Management systems standards such as ISO 14001 for environmental management systems or SA8000 for social management systems provide selected indicators for evaluation and facilitate the selection process. However, the authors find that social criteria are rather sparsely addressed in the literature. Such criteria can reduce the potential risks for companies procuring in global supply chains, even though this often involves higher costs. The second strategy addresses the supply chain in relation to sustainable products and requires holistic life cycle-based standards which consider the environmental and social performance of the product. Companies and suppliers accept close cooperation to ensure optimal performance of operational processes. Often, new products require a high level of investment and learning efforts for establishing an optimal supply chain. Notably, a socially and environmentally sustainable supply chain management requires high levels of coordination, collaboration, and investment.

Source: Seuring and Müller (2008)

C.3.2 Supplier management for risks and performance

Supplier management for risks and performance, in its core, aims at evaluating and eventually choosing suppliers based on an extended set of criteria that not only cover economic aspects (such as price, quality, or reliability) but also sustainability aspects. For these sustainability aspects, usually certain minimum criteria and standards are defined by the company which have to be met by its suppliers. The main aim of this strategy is to mitigate the most severe environmental or social risks, not least to avoid economic harm for the focal company, for example, due to negative media coverage or NGO activities. Furthermore, the strategy is used to ensure the long-term overall performance of the supply chain, assuming that sustainability-related risks can translate into economic risks. In this regard, there is often an assumed win-win situation when higher sustainability standards lead to lower economic risks or an improved economic performance, for example, due to satisfied customers, employees, or other stakeholders. However, improving sustainability in the supply chain can also lead to trade-offs, especially because many sustainability measures increase costs at least in the short term. Overall, considering sustainability aspects in supply chain decisions, for example in supplier selection, is increasingly relevant. A recent survey by the CDP, for example, revealed that 73 percent of the survey participants expect to deselect suppliers based on inadequate environmental performance (CDP, 2021a). Such measures are especially relevant for focal firms, because consumers usually do not make a difference as to where sustainability issues arise in the supply chain. Instead, they blame the focal firm for the unsustainable practices of their suppliers (Hartmann & Moeller, 2014). To mitigate such risks, supplier management for risk and performances can follow the four basic steps of committing, evaluating, auditing, and developing suppliers as illustrated in Figure 16 and described in the following.

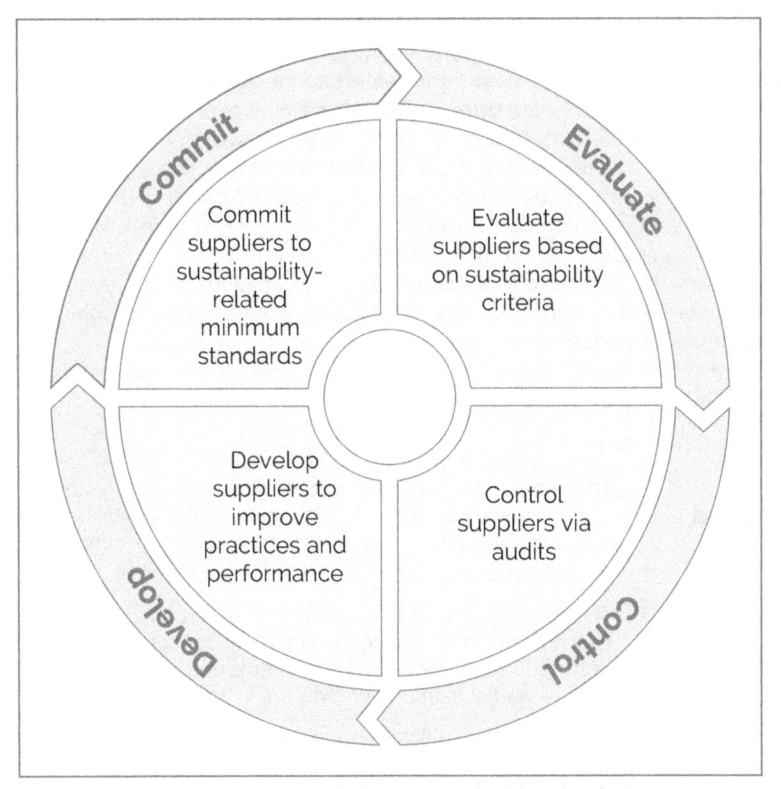

Figure 16: Core steps in supplier management for risk and performances

In the first step, companies commit their suppliers to uphold a certain sustainability-related minimum standard. Such standards can be company internal commitments, based, for example, on a company code of conduct (see Chapter C.6.2). Such codes of conduct can provide recommendations for the behavior of suppliers or employees of suppliers, suggested courses of action, or certain measures which should be taken. The content, form, and implementation of such codes of conduct is not regulated so that they are a form of voluntary commitment. Moreover, companies can also rely on external codes of conduct in form of industry initiatives or overarching initiatives such as the UN Global Compact, which is a voluntary initiative providing 10 general commitments in the areas of human rights, labor issues, environment, and anti-corruption. Furthermore, companies can commit suppliers to present certificates, for example, for certain sustainability-related management system standards (see Chapter C.6.3) or they can provide incentives such as price premiums for suppliers with such systems and standards. This is very common for quality management systems (the most widespread standard worldwide for quality management is ISO 9001) but also environmental management systems standards such as ISO 14001 are prevalent worldwide. For social issues, however, respective standards such as SA8000 are far less widespread.

In a second step, companies collect sustainability-related information from their suppliers and evaluate them based on certain sustainability criteria as part of their risk management. A common form of such evaluations are self-assessments, that is, suppliers are asked to supply certain information, usually through one-time or periodic questionnaires (e.g., Fraser et al., 2020). Such self-assessments are relatively inexpensive for a company to assess its suppliers so they can be used even when financial or human resources are limited. They can provide indications for areas where it might be necessary to conduct audits (see the next step) or to improve the supplier's performance through supplier development measures. A company should put most of its emphasis and efforts on those suppliers whose self-assessment revealed an increased likelihood of sustainability-related risks or severe impacts through such risks. However, self-assessments can be prone to social desirability bias, that is, suppliers might answer questions in a way that will be viewed favorably by their customers. Figure 17 provides some examples for supplier evaluation criteria based on self-assessments. Companies can use these evaluations to decide on how to proceed with their suppliers. They can, for example, choose to work only with suppliers who reach a certain threshold or pay premiums or provide preferred contracts to suppliers which receive top evaluation. They can also use the evaluation to identify those suppliers with whom the company should work to improve their sustainability processes and performance.

Assessment	Indicators
Very good	• The company conducts a holistic analysis of weaknesses • The company has an environmental management system • The company goes beyond regulatory minimum standards for environmental issues (e.g., emissions or use of resources) • Remaining weaknesses are communicated openly
Average	• The company shows basic interest for environmental issues • First concepts (e.g., waste management concepts) are pending • Descriptions of processes and systems do not exist • Further verifiable improvements are in the pipeline

Figure 17: Exemplary criteria for an ecological supplier evaluation

As self-assessments and supplier evaluations through questionnaires are nowadays a widespread and low-threshold method in sustainable supply chain management, suppliers are increasingly confronted with filling out such questionnaires for a large number of customer firms. This can be quite a time-consuming task, and evaluation fatigue is increasing among suppliers. To reduce efforts and costs, industry-wide efforts for common standards have evolved in some industries. Furthermore, specialized service providers offer software solutions and platforms for supplier assessments so that a supplier can store its information in the platform and this can then be accessed by various (potential) customers, thus reducing transaction costs for both sides.

Another element of evaluation is the screening and monitoring of issues and risks. Companies can monitor, for example, (social) media for sustainability-related incidents in their supply chain, at their suppliers, or for general issues and risks. Ecological risks can be associated with emissions of harmful substances or with the extraction or farming of raw materials. Social risks are often in the areas of child labor, forced labor, or corruption. Monitoring of such risks should, if possible, take place in all tiers of the supply chain, from the sourcing of raw materials up to the disposal of products at the end of their product life. Sustainability-related risks, however, are often more difficult to grasp compared to financial risks. There is usually no uniform definition for these risks. How "risky" is, for example, child labor in the supply chain with regard to its potential impact on sustainable development and for the focal company? How do you measure child labor when even one case would be enough to cause a public outcry? Furthermore, many sustainability-related risks are often qualitative in nature (such as, again, child labor), and they are based on subjective evaluations.

It is thus reasonable to structure sustainability-related risks to make them more easily accessible for monitoring. A common distinction is between external and internal risks. External risks refer to risks outside of the supply chain itself, for example, country risks. A well-known example of this kind of risks lies in corruption, which is very unevenly prevalent around the world and can thus impact supply chains very differently, depending on their location. The corruption perceptions index (Transparency International, 2021) published by the NGO Transparency International provides some first insights on where and why supply chains might be affected by or prone to corruption. The index measures the level of corruption in the public sector based on the perceptions of business people and country experts. Bangladesh, for example, an important center of the worldwide garment industry, ranked number 146 out of 180 countries with a score of 26 out of 100 (from 0 – highly corrupt to 100 – very clean). Companies with supply chain partners in countries with a high risk of corruption thus might want to exercise increased caution when it comes to compliance issues. Internal risks are inherent to the supply chain and relate to its specific processes and products. Some materials or substances, for example, are known for their environmental or health-related risks. Companies might want to exercise specific caution and ask their suppliers who deal with such substances to provide specific evidence of their ability to handle them without negative effects on employees, customers, or the environment. Another option would be to increase monitoring and audits at the respective suppliers or try to avoid problematic materials already when designing products (see also Chapter C.4.3). Various national or industry-specific databases provide first insights into potential effects of and necessary precautions when dealing with different substances.

In the third step, audits are used to control suppliers. In regular supply chain management, such audits usually cover quality issues. With the increasing relevance of sustainable supply chain management, environmental and social audits also become a standard tool. Respective audits can cover products or processes (i.e., looking at on-site working conditions) or they verify the existence and operational capability of environmental or social management system standards (see Chapter C.7.2). Audits can come in different forms and are usually distinguished in first-, second-, and third-party audits. A first-party audit is an internal audit that is conducted by people who work at the audited organization itself (i.e., employees) or who are paid by the company to conduct the audit (e.g., consultants). Such kinds of self-assessment are often used to uncover weaknesses and blind spots. They can be genuine, in-depth audits if the company has the motive to truly improve itself. Ideally, to avoid governance issues, the persons or teams that conduct the audit should not have any personal interest in the results of the audit. Both second- and third-party audits are external audits. In second-party audits, a company directly conducts an audit at its suppliers, that means, it sends auditors (either its own employees or it hires external auditors) itself. Such audits tend to be more formal compared to first-party audits, because the results may have an impact on the relationship between the company and their suppliers. Third-party audits, finally, are conducted by an auditing organization independent of any specific customer–supplier relationship. Usually, the company which is to be audited (here: a supplier company) initiates and pays for the audit. The auditing company then checks whether the company that commissioned the audit complies with certain requirements such as those of an environmental or social management system standard. If all requirements are met, the auditing company issues a certificate which can be used by the suppliers to signal compliance with the respective standard to its (potential) customers.

The fourth and final step is the development of suppliers. The idea is to set up an action plan—ideally together with the suppliers—that provides specific measures on how the suppliers can improve their practices and performance and how the focal company can assist them on the way. Progress should be tracked to allow further measures to be taken (e.g., rewards and incentives but also penalties and eventually the termination of the relationship, if necessary). Measures on such an action plan can either be corrective actions or improvements or they can be precautionary measures. The former is especially used to eliminate errors or undesired behavior and to avoid recurrence. Therefore, corrective actions are usually reactive in trying to fight the causes of trouble. Precautionary measures, instead, try to proactively avoid undesired situations or behavior.

C.3.3 Supply chain management for sustainable products

While supplier management for risks and performance is often marked as a rather reactive strategy, supply chain management for sustainable products instead tries to proactively influence supply chains to deliver sustainable products to the customer. The distribution of deliberately (more) sustainable products is thus also the decisive characteristic which sets this strategy apart from the strategy of supplier management for risks and performance. Whether or not a product indeed is more sustainable than alternative products should ideally be determined with tools such as life cycle sustainability assessment (LCSA; see C.6.2). LCSA can be used to determine the environmental (and social) impact of products and processes along their entire life cycle and can thus be used to provide guidance early during product design, for example, by comparing different materials or production techniques.

Sustainability in society 17: Increasing the supply of more sustainable cotton – The Better Cotton Initiative (BCI)

Sustainably sourced cotton was long a scarce commodity in the textile industry and even producers who wanted to move toward more sustainable input material had difficulties in sourcing sufficient amounts at adequate prices. Therefore, the WWF, supported by several major companies, founded the BCI in 2009 with the aim to bring more sustainable practices to the textile supply chain. The initiative provides training on more sustainable farming practices to ensure the supply of this resource. Members of the BCI span the entire cotton supply chain from farmer organizations through to retailers and brands. Farmers grow cotton based on seven principles that cover ecological and social sustainability aspects such as water stewardship, biodiversity, or decent working conditions. While more sustainable alternatives to conventional cotton were a scarce commodity for many years, by 2019 cotton produced by BCI farmers already accounted for more than 20 percent of global cotton production. However, the BCI has also been criticized for applying rather loose standards, which could undermine the success of more stringent schemes such as the Global Organic Textile Standard (GOTS).

Source: BCI (2019); BCI (2020); Changing Markets Foundation (2018); Riisgaard et al. (2020)

The development and distribution of sustainable products usually requires close and strategic cooperation between the different tiers in the supply chain. This includes setting up a system for sustainable supply chain controlling to be able to track all elements of a product along the supply chain and determine its environmental and potentially also its social footprint through the entire product life cycle. Such a controlling system includes information and communication systems that link all actors throughout the chain. Furthermore, new technologies such as blockchain can also facilitate a reliable flow of information even in complex and fragmented supply chains (see Chapter C.10.2). The idea is to allow extensive information flows, which not only cover price and quality (as in most supply chains), but also sustainability aspects such as data on the environmental effects of substances. Such systems can usually only work and are economically feasible when the composition of the supply chain is relatively stable. Changing suppliers would mean integrating new partners in such systems, which is challenging not only from a technological point of view but even more so from an organizational perspective (e.g., aligning different organizational cultures, building trust).

Against this background, proponents of sustainable supply chain management often highlight the necessity to decommoditize products and suppliers, that is, "explicitly treating a supplier and/or entire chain that provides a commodity (lots of substitutes/competition mainly on price) as if it supplied a rare/strategic input." (Pagell et al., 2010, p. 64) This can be achieved, for example, through long-term contracts to avoid frequent changes in the supply chain and by paying above market prices to ensure the economic survival of suppliers. With such long(er) term perspectives of cooperation, investments in supplier development, that is cooperating with suppliers to improve their performance, becomes increasingly viable. Such a development is often helpful to build specialized knowledge about sustainable production techniques, an adequate handling of substances in production processes, and more. Increasingly, supplier development and an adequate supply of sustainable or sustainably sourced material is part of entire industry initiatives.

Sustainability in business 25: Tony Chocolonely and fairafric – Efforts for sustainable chocolate supply chains

The supply chain of cocoa for chocolate production has many sustainability challenges. Most of the cocoa is produced in Africa. However, only a tiny fraction of the raw material is actually processed in Africa so that the value creation and—with it—most of the profits are made somewhere else. Furthermore, the cocoa supply chain is notorious for being nontransparent, with often poor working conditions and prevalent conditions of modern slavery. In this challenging environment, some companies actively try to develop (more) sustainable supply chains and products.

Fairafric, a German-Ghanaian social enterprise, for example, processes raw materials locally in Africa to transfer the added value as much as possible to Africa and thereby also creates local employment opportunities. Furthermore, the company only processes organic cocoa, uses its own solar energy, and relies on innovative packaging made from wood pulp and so on.

Another pioneer is Tony's Chocolonely, a Dutch producer of chocolate. The company's mission is to make chocolate slave-free. The chocolate producer developed an initiative to advise other chocolate brands to follow their path: Tony's Open Chain consists of five sourcing principles to achieve slave-free cocoa (paying a higher price for farmers, having traceable cocoa beans, developing strong farmers, having a long-term perspective, and improving the quality and productivity of the cocoa production).

At Tony's Chocolonely, there apparently is a great deal of supplier management for risks and performance that tackles the most severe risks of child labor and other pressing supply chain issues. Furthermore, the rather holistic approach of transparency and decommoditization illustrates one way to produce truly (more) sustainable chocolate, and it sets the company apart from many other chocolate producers. A challenge for the industry as a whole, but also for these role model companies, is the scaling of such approaches to arrive at a generally (more) sustainable sourcing of chocolate worldwide. In 2021, for example, Tony's Chocolonely was criticized for its commercial ties with a manufacturer that has admitted that its own supply chain was not free of child labor and exploitation.

Sources: fairafric (2021); Kenber (2021); Tenner and Hörisch (2020); Tony's Chocoloney (2020)

One measure of decommoditization, as discussed above, is often to pay above market prices to ensure the economic survival of suppliers. This opens up the interesting question of what the levers for decent living wages in many supply chains are, especially in the Global South. Let us engage in a brief thought experiment: Assume you are working as a manager in sourcing for a focal company in the textile industry and your main supplier is based in Bangladesh. At the end of 2018, the minimum monthly wage in Bangladesh was significantly increased to 8,000 taka, which is less than USD 100 (Ahonen, 2018). You buy T-shirts from your supplier for USD 3 per piece, which your company sells for USD 9.99. The factory of your supplier produces 50 million pieces per year and employs 10,000 workers. If your company paid just 10 cents more per piece, this would result in additional revenues for the supplier of USD 5 million. If the supplier passed this entire surplus to its workers, each worker would earn roughly USD 40 more per month—which equals an increase of their salary of more than 40 percent compared to the minimum wage. If your company passed on the price increase completely to your customer, the price for a T-Shirt would increase by merely 1 percent to USD 10.09. While it is literally a matter of cents to significantly improve the conditions for the workers, there are some significant hurdles which illustrate the complexity of sustainable supply chain management. While many customers are nowadays considering sustainability issues in their purchase decisions, many others still do not really care (see Chapter B.6). Moving from USD 9.99 to 10.09

would pass an important price threshold and would thus likely lead to sales decreases for the focal company. Furthermore, albeit being significantly above the minimum wage, paying USD 140 per month for supply chain workers would likely not be a good advertising argument to win sustainability-conscious customers. If your company bore the additional cost itself, this would reduce its margin—at least in the short term. Especially for publicly traded companies this could be challenging as it might increase pressure from shareholders. Finally, when looking at the supplier itself, an important assumption of our thought experiment is that the entire surplus is passed on to the workers. Ensuring that this would indeed be the case, however, might prove difficult as it would require significant efforts by the focal company to truly observe this issue.

Sustainability in business 26: Fairtrade certification as an example of sustainable supply chain management

Producers in the Global South are among the most marginalized actors in global supply chains with very little influence. The Fairtrade movement tries to make a difference in empowering producers and achieving more sustainable trade relationships. At the core of the Fairtrade system is the idea to pay a certain minimum price for agricultural produce even when the market price is lower to secure a decent and predictable income for farmers. The Fairtrade system aims at strengthening smallholder farmers and cooperatives, promoting decent working conditions, and banishing child labor or discrimination. Furthermore, Fairtrade nowadays can also cover some environmental standards such as prohibiting certain pesticides or offering a surplus for organic produce. Fairtrade products are visible for the end consumer through a label, which can be found, for example, on coffee, cocoa, sugar, fruits, or flowers.

This label is a central element of Fairtrade as it provides transparency for standards at the beginning of the supply chain to customers at the end of the supply chain. The entire certification process is managed and controlled by standard-setting organizations that provide the Fairtrade guidelines, certification organizations that conduct audits of producers, and trading organizations throughout the supply chain to ensure that the guidelines and standards are met. As you probably already have noticed, Fairtrade combines elements of both strategies we discussed until now: supplier management for risks and performance, and supply chain management for sustainable products. With regard to the latter, Fairtrade aims at providing transparency and enhanced sustainability standards throughout the supply chain to arrive at more sustainable products. Moreover, audits as evaluation are also part of the former strategy to avoid sustainability-related risks in the supply chain. Both strategies complement each other in this case, as companies that want to offer sustainable products to their customers should evaluate the social and environmental performance of their suppliers. Furthermore, a company that starts with a risk avoidance strategy can eventually also extend this strategy to offer truly sustainable products.

Sources: Fairtrade International (2019); Rocha et al. (2021)

This does not mean, of course, that sustainable supply chain management is doomed to fail, and there are likely as many stakeholders who can promote sustainability in supply chains as there are stakeholder who can hinder it. NGOs increasingly expose malpractices and sustainability shortcomings in supply chains and bring formerly hidden topics to the fore. Many customers are interested in sustainability and watch out for labels and standards. Investors nowadays often consider ESG criteria in their investment decisions (see Chapter B.5). Many companies also increase the pressure on their peers by providing best practice examples and proof of concepts. Until a few years ago, for example, focal companies usually considered the names of their suppliers to be company secrets. Today, many large players have increased transparency and provide lists of suppliers and their factories on their websites, which potentially increases the pressure to uphold at least minimum standards of sustainability. Finally, governments around the world recognized that many sustainability topics may require some regulatory pressure to be taken seriously on a broad scale as we will discuss in the following section.

C.3.4 Regulation and sustainable supply chain management

An often-made assumption is that regulation in global supply chains is difficult precisely due to their cross-border nature. Regulators in Country A might have difficulties in enforcing their high sustainability standards on a focal company from their own country, if the suppliers of this company have their facilities in Country B with less strict standards. Furthermore, if companies always follow the lowest or least enforced global sustainability standards (e.g., environmental standards or health and safety standards), building on the assumption that stricter standards equal higher costs, there might even be a "race to the bottom" in which governments might be willing to reduce standards further and further to attract businesses.

However, in recent years, an increasing number of national and transnational regulations aim at influencing sustainability issues in global supply chains. On a transnational level, various quasi-legal instruments for sustainability are in place that do not have a directly binding force. The UN Guiding Principles on Business and Human Rights (UNGP), for example, is a set of 31 guidelines to prevent, address, and remedy human rights abuses committed in business operations (UN, 2011). Since 2015, there is also an accompanying reporting framework which provides guidance for companies to report on human rights issues (Shift Project Ltd. & Mazars LLP, 2015). Although not legally binding per se, the UNGPs proclaim the duty of nation states to protect human rights—usually through national regulations. Indeed, many national laws have been implemented in recent years in the realm of human rights issues in global supply chains, and here are some examples:

Since 2014, publicly listed companies in the United States must disclose their practices related to conflict minerals (Dalla Via & Perego, 2018). A similar regulation came into effect in the European Union in 2021 that established due diligence requirements for companies importing certain minerals (i.e., tin, tantalum, tungsten, and gold) over predefined thresholds ((EU) 2017/821, 2017). The regulation requires these companies to identify and control smelters and refiners in the supply chain and, in the end, to source the minerals responsibly. In Great Britain, the Modern Slavery Act of 2015 requires large companies to annually publish steps taken to ensure that slavery and human trafficking are not taking place in their supply chains (Voss et al., 2019). In France, a Law on the Corporate Duty of Vigilance was enacted in 2017 (Savourey & Brabant, 2021) and in the Netherlands, the Dutch Child Labour Due Diligence Law comes into effect in 2022 (Hoff, 2019). A little later, the German Supply Chain Law requires companies with more than 1,000 employees from 2024 onwards to ensure that human rights are respected in the entire supply chain, and it lays out requirements for corporate due diligence (Depping & Walden, 2021). In sum, there is increasing pressure from governments and regulators to take sustainable supply chain management seriously.

KEY TAKEAWAYS

- Sustainable supply chain management integrates social, environmental, and economic goals in all stages of a supply chain.
- Sustainability in supply chain management offers significant levers to improving the sustainability performance of products and companies.
- The complexity of modern supply chains is a challenge for achieving sustainability.
- Supplier management for risks and performance aims at evaluating and eventually choosing suppliers based also on sustainability criteria.
- Supplier management for risks and performance consists of the steps commit, evaluate, control, and develop.
- Supply chain management for sustainable products tries to deliberately distribute (more) sustainable products.
- This strategy usually requires close and strategic cooperation between the different tiers in the supply chain.
- An increasing number of national and transnational regulations aim at influencing sustainability issues in global supply chains.

C.4 Sustainable production and logistics

LEARNING GOALS

After reading this chapter you will be able to ...

- ... explain the waste hierarchy of "reduce, reuse, and recycle."
- ... discuss the relevance of product development for sustainable product use.
- ... illustrate examples of eco-design.
- ... distinguish four reduction-oriented product use concepts.
- ... apply the 4R framework at the end of a product life cycle.
- ... explain options of material-oriented approaches at the end of a product life cycle.
- ... illustrate options of reducing the environmental impact of logistics by referring to the strategies of eco-efficiency, eco-effectiveness, and sufficiency.

Introduction to Chapter C.4: Screencast
Watch an introduction to the chapter here:

C.4.1 Introduction to sustainability in production and logistics

The basic idea of any production system is to transform different sorts of inputs into outputs. Considering sustainability can be relevant in any of these three elements of production: input, transformation, and output. For the input side, a sustainability-related aim could be, for example, to reduce the amount of necessary input to save natural raw materials, to substitute virgin material with recycled input or to reduce the amount of harmful or toxic substances. For the transformation of input into output (often also referred to as "throughput"), becoming more sustainable can mean to reduce the amount of energy or consumables per unit of output or to ensure health, safety, and decent working conditions and so on. Achieving sustainability at the output side can be related, among others, with generating less waste, producing energy-efficient products, reducing the amount of unplanned and unused by-products, or extending the product life to achieve longevity. Usually, environmental aspects are especially prominent and relevant with regard to input and output while social aspects of sustainability are more pronounced for the transformation and the input of the production system.

Options to achieve a more sustainable production can be manifold. Let us take a closer look at by-products as an example. By-products are secondary products which come with the production of a primary product. Examples for by-products would be sawdust, which occurs with the production of wood panels, or industrial waste heat, which occurs in many transformation processes. In general, by-products can either be useful for the producing company or other organizations or they have to be considered as waste. If the latter is the case, a suitable strategy would be to improve the efficiency of transformation processes and reduce the amount of sawdust or waste heat. An alternative could be, however, to aim for a more eco-effective approach and turn previously unused by-products into input for the same company or other organizations (for the strategies of eco-efficiency and eco-effectiveness, see again Chapter A.4). Waste heat could, for example, be used to produce energy or as district heating while sawdust might be used to produce oriented strand boards.

A well-known classification of options for dealing with by-products and waste is that of "reduce, reuse, and recycle (and sometimes recover)"—which is often also referred to as "waste hierarchy" (Gharfalkar et al., 2015; Kirchherr et al., 2017) as illustrated in Figure 18. At the top of this hierarchy, thus receiving the highest priority, is the aim to induce fewer or ideally no environmental damages by reducing waste or harmful substances as much as possible. This can ideally be achieved by bringing only such goods to the consumer that are actually needed. Reducing is regarded as the first-best option because it requires no further processes in later stages of a product life cycle. Products that are not produced in the first place do not require raw materials, manufacturing processes, or subsequent distribution and, eventually, disposal. In production process itself, reduction can be achieved, for example, by cutting down the absolute amount of input (e.g., by reducing offcuts or leakages or using thinner material) or by changing the type of input (e.g., avoiding harmful substances by substituting them with other substances). The second-best option according to the hierarchy is reuse. Reusing means giving products a second life without any significant changes other than some refurbishing. While reusing is a commonplace activity for many households (e.g., when buying used products), it is less prevalent in production processes. Some elements, modules, or devices in various products, however, might also be reused as parts in new products or when repairing damaged goods. The third option is recycling, which means that waste materials are reprocessed into new products, materials, or substances either for the original purpose or to be used in some other products and processes. Such recycling can be done mechanically (e.g., plastic is crushed, melted, and then used as plastic granulate), chemically (e.g., plastic is converted into basic chemicals through chemical processes), or biologically (e.g., compostable plastic is converted into biomass by using living organisms). Depending on the type of recycling and the material that is being recycled, these processes come with different costs and benefits. At the bottom of the waste hierarchy, finally, comes the recovery (i.e., incineration to recover the energy from the original material) and disposal. At the bottom of the hierarchy, materials are disposed. This least preferred option should only be taken if all other alternatives are not applicable. Furthermore, disposal should be conducted in an orderly way, for example, limiting the amount of waste water discharged into rivers to avoid negative ecological consequences. Uncontrolled dumping at sea or illegal landfills usually come with severe negative sustainability consequences.

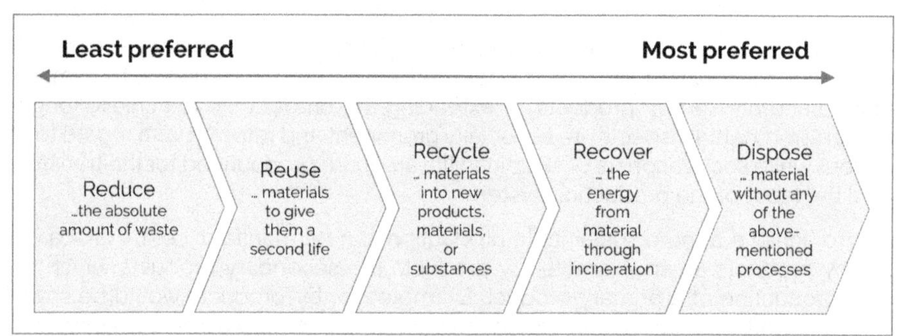

Figure 18: Waste hierarchy

Sustainability in society 18: Electronic waste in the Global South

A very large portion of old electronic devices from developed countries end up in landfills in the Global South. A center of this procedure is the African country of Ghana, especially Agbogbloshie, a suburb of Ghana's capital, Accra. While there is a thriving second-hand market for discarded electronic devices ranging from televisions to laptops and microwaves, there is also a gigantic and heavily polluted electronic waste dumpsite in Agbogbloshie. Over time, the area has become a symbol of the unsustainability of end of life processes of electronic products. Workers, including many children, work under horrible circumstances to extract recyclable materials from the electronic waste. Often the fastest and cheapest ways, for example, to recycle copper from insulated wire is to burn them. A typical burning material is old automobile tires and the fires made from these produce dioxin, heavy metals, and other hazardous substances. A holistic design for sustainability thinking can consider these impacts and aim at mitigating or avoiding them by using alternative materials or a modular design that is easy to disassemble. Furthermore, regulations for and enforcement of mandatory recycling in the country of origin could slow respective waste flows.

Sources: Kuper and Hojsik (2008); Minter (2016); Ottaviani (2016); Yeung (2019)

Turning to logistics as a process to transport materials and goods through the supply chain, most people first think about the last mile delivery of products to their doorstep or to retailers. Indeed, this last part of logistics, that is, the final distribution of products at the end of the supply chain, bears significant sustainability effects such as emissions of transportation or the working conditions of truck drivers or parcel service employees. However, the last mile delivery is usually only a fraction of the logistics involved in most modern supply chains so that the logistics processes during the transformation phase or from input to transformation are often even more important with regard to their sustainability impacts, despite often being less visible for the end consumer.

Many sustainability-related aspects in production and logistics are already specified through norms and regulations. In many countries, for example, some social aspects are partly regulated via certain minimum wages or through regulations for occupational health and safety. For environmental aspects, regulations often prohibit the use of certain input materials or they dictate certain output limits for various substances and emissions. Such output thresholds (e.g., Dyckhoff & Souren, 2008, p. 199) generally limit the quantity of by-products and, thus, they restrict production volumes or the use of production techniques. They can come in form of absolute limits (e.g., x kg of an output allowed per y hours of operation) or of relative limits (e.g., x kg of an output allowed per y kg of product output or per y kg of emitted air or water, etc.).

Sustainability in research 9: Kleindorfer, Singhal, and Van Wassenhove's 2005 article on sustainable operations management

How has research on sustainability in production and operations management developed over time? Paul R. Kleindorfer, Kalyan Singhal, and Luk N. Van Wassenhove answer this question in their 2005 article by analyzing the first 50 issues of the academic journal "Production and Operations Managements" from 1992 onwards. With this, they provide an in-depth historic account of the development of an entire discipline. The authors highlight the overarching importance of operations management in establishing corporate sustainability along the triple bottom line. They define sustainable operations management as "the set of skills and concepts that allow a company to structure and manage its business processes to obtain competitive returns on its capital assets without sacrificing the legitimate needs of internal and external stakeholders and with due regard for the impact of its operations on people and the environment" (p. 489).

In the article, operational management is divided into internal and external strategies. Internal strategies include the continuous improvement of processes, for example, through improved employee involvement or the redesign of products with a focus on lower material and energy consumption. External strategies can consist of improved analysis of existing supply chains and, in the long-term, the development of core competencies and strategies to ensure sustainability.

The authors argue that the shift toward a more holistic interpretation and consideration of operations management, which considers the three Ps of profit, people, and planet, is particularly evident in three areas. First, green process and product development aims is to identify innovation potential through economic analyses and sustainable process design. The idea is to optimize the entire supply chain through green products with modular design which enable reuse. Second, green and lean operations management is concerned with the inclusion of environmental, health, and safety parameters in evaluating business processes, for example, to improve image, reduce overall risk, or comply with public regulations. Third, remanufacturing and closed-loop supply chains can potentially revolutionize a business model. Here, companies are confronted with adopting a multidisciplinary perspective and coordinating forward and reverse flows in the supply chain under increased effort, costs, and uncertainties.

Several capabilities favor the implementation of sustainable operations management. These include cross-disciplinary and cross-functional cooperation, measuring and modeling the relationship between outcome and action, execution of strategies, and operational and conceptual integration of the various activities. The authors conclude that there are still research gaps, for example, with regard to the people component in the triple bottom line and that there is a need to rethink traditional operation management models. Nevertheless, assuming companies are both willing and receptive toward embracing sustainability, operations management can be a powerful tool for driving and implementing the triple bottom line.

Source: Kleindorfer et al. (2005)

C.4.2 Product development for sustainable product use

From a sustainability perspective, product development is of paramount importance in focal companies because product specifications determine the sustainability impacts of products along their entire life cycle from raw material extraction to disposal. In general, the early product design phases are usually most important as they determine the overall requirements a product has to fulfill which, in turn, has significant impact on the way a product will be designed, its functionalities, the materials and production processes to be used, and so on. Therefore, this phase should not only include market research in terms of customer needs but also an assessment of a product's various (potential) impacts along the entire product life cycle. The results of this early design stage determine the boundary conditions for the technical product development. In this later stage, product designers and engineers can then try to further improve the sustainability performance of a product by applying elements from the three basic sustainability strategies (see again Chapter A.4) of eco-efficiency (e.g., using lightweight materials or energy-efficient components), eco-effectiveness (e.g., by using nontoxic materials that are easy to disassemble and reuse), or sufficiency (e.g., by building durable products that can more easily be shared). We will now illustrate the impact of production and product development on sustainable product use before turning to the post-use phase in the next section.

When following the waste hierarchy introduced above, an ideal scenario of product development would be to introduce products to the market that generate less impact along their entire life cycle. Apparently, the bulk of sustainability impacts of many products lies in the product use phase and not in the production itself. For decades, for example, nonrenewable fuels were the only thinkable source of energy for cars, and most of the energy pumped into the tank was actually lost due to inefficiencies (Ellen MacArthur Foundation & McKinsey Center for Business and Environment, 2015), so that, in the end, the environmental impact of the use phase was much higher than that of the production phase. The same applies to many other products: Laundry detergents which enable the same performance by washing at lower temperatures can significantly reduce the energy usage in the use phase, energy-efficient household appliances can help to reduce environmental impacts of private households, and heat pumps that run on renewable energy can cut emissions of buildings significantly. It thus makes sense to already consider the entire product life cycle (see Chapter C.6.2) when designing a product to minimize its sustainability impacts. However, such aspects of design for the environment have long been neglected in product development because they usually do not result in immediate savings of energy or material (and thus often costs) at the producing company itself. Therefore, efficiency gains in the production phase itself as illustrated in the previous section were often the first starting point of sustainability considerations in production, while the use phase was often ignored despite its promising potential for sustainability. To move beyond such a narrow perspective of sustainability in production, the approaches of design for the environment, eco-design, or design for sustainability (Fiksel, 2011; Spangenberg et al., 2010) aim at reducing the overall impact of a product (i.e., physical good or service) on human health and the environment across the entire life cycle.

Examples for product design that consider a more sustainable use are manifold. Lighter materials in vehicles can lead to reduced energy needs, better insulation reduces the need to heat or cool things, durable materials or a modular design can extend the product life in general thus reducing the need for new products, and so on. Importantly, such proactive considerations of sustainability impact along the product life cycle do not have to be limited to environmental aspects. The question of what kind of raw materials and ingredients go into a product, for example, immediately, also determines many social impacts. Certain materials, for example, are connected to health issues for consumers when using or consuming the products, for workers when extracting raw materials, or for workers during the production phase. However, as often the case in sustainability management, trade-offs might surface here as well when positive effects in one stage of the product life cycle can lead to negative effects in other stages. While electric vehicles, for example, can significantly reduce carbon emissions compared to vehicles powered by combustion engines during the use phase, there are currently still significant environmental and social challenges in the production and recycling of batteries (Dolega et al., 2020; Peters et al., 2017).

A general approach to identifying opportunities for reducing negative impacts goes even further and fundamentally asks how to generally avoid (more) goods being produced. This question can be contented by considering the two parameters of usage intensity and useful life, which leads us to four potential scenarios as depicted in Figure 19 (Dyckhoff & Souren, 2008). If one assumes that the overall levels of consumption are stable, these scenarios can lead to a reduced impact because overall less goods are necessary. Less goods being produced then equals less material and energy for production processes in the first place.

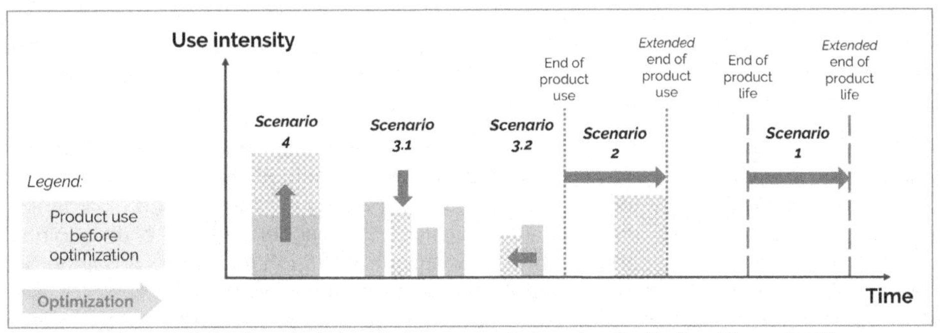

Figure 19: Reduction-oriented product use concepts, based on Dyckhoff and Souren (2008)

In the first scenario, the potential useful product life is extended by delaying mechanical wear. This can be achieved, for example, by using more durable materials, allowing for a gentler use of the product, or by nudging the consumer into appropriately using the product. Such concepts fail to achieve the intended goal, however, if customers do not use products for a longer time even though they would still be functional (e.g., some consumers buy a new smartphone every year). Against this background, the second scenario asks how the actual product use can be extended especially when products are not used until the end of their technically possible product life. Exemplary strategies could be timeless designs to avoid products being dumped before their technical product life has ended, modular designs which allow for technical updates (e.g., new processor or battery for laptops), or extended software updates for smartphones. The third scenario looks at the product utilization by asking how the usage of products can be intensified across their life time. It can be more ecologically efficient, for example, to constantly run a production line instead of regularly shutting it down and starting it up again after a short idle time (Scenario 3.1). The more obvious alternative for an intensified product utilization is, however, to create additional use intervals for the same product (Scenario 3.2). The average private car, for example, is parked 92 percent of its lifetime (Ellen MacArthur Foundation & McKinsey Center for Business and Environment, 2015). With carsharing, rental cars, or transport services (see again Chapter B.6.3), the product utilization of vehicles could be increased significantly. This can be ecologically beneficial if a vehicle (or any other product) that is used more often during its lifetime provides benefits to generally more people so that overall fewer products have to be produced. The fourth and final scenario looks at how use intensity can be increased not only across a product's lifetime but at any given point in time when the product is actually in use. An example would be an increase of the capacity of public local transport (e.g., double-decker busses or trains) or carpooling. Another regularly used practice comes from the (inherently eco-unfriendly) air travel industry. Airlines regularly overbook their flights to compensate for late cancellations and no shows to increase the utilization of their capacities. While this is mainly done for economic reasons, a full plane is also ecologically more efficient due to the lower emissions per passenger.

Task C4-1

How can the production of further goods be avoided? Identify real-life examples (other than those mentioned in the text) for all four scenarios and explain why the respective examples fit to each scenario!

C.4.3 Sustainable reduction and recycling

Sustainable reduction and recycling are concerned with the question of what happens with goods after their useful life. When it comes to the question of what to do with a product after its useful life, several alternatives are discussed, which further specify the above-mentioned stages of reuse and recycle from the 4R framework as illustrated in Figure 20 (see, e.g., Hansen et al., 2021; Kirchherr et al., 2017).

The first option is to keep the original product and extend its product life (similar to Scenarios 1 and 2 discussed above). This can be done through actually reusing a product, that is, a product which is still in good condition can be used by another person or organization in its original function. Furthermore, if a product has reached the end of its originally intended purpose, this end can possibly be postponed through repair (i.e., repairing and maintaining a defective product so that it can be used with its original function) or even refurbishing (i.e., restoring an old product and bringing it up to date). The second option is not using the product in its original state and potentially not even for its original purpose. Instead parts of the product are used in another product either in their old function (e.g., using parts from a discarded product to replace broken parts in another product) or in a new function. The former is usually referred to as remanufacturing while the latter is sometimes termed repurposing (e.g., using the battery from a discarded electric vehicle as stationary energy storage in a family home).

The third option, finally, is described by the omnipresent concept of recycling. Recycling takes place at the level of materials, that is, the product is broken down into its parts to gain materials which are then to be used again. Ideally, such recycling closes the loop in a sense that high-quality recyclates replace virgin material in production processes. Often, however, the value of the original material can only partly be restored due to quality losses. In this case, the recycling processes result in lower grade materials, which is also referred to as downcycling (e.g., when high-quality plastic from bottles is turned into lower quality plastic to be used for single-use plastic bags). Eventually, with downcycling, the material loops are not perfectly closed as some form of virgin material needs to be added somewhere ("open-loop-recycling"). A special form of material use at the end of the life cycle is the recovery of energy, that is, the original material is incinerated and used for energy production. In this case, however, the original material is ultimately lost apart from its energy content so that this is not recycling in the usual sense, which is why recover as an option is separated in Figure 20.

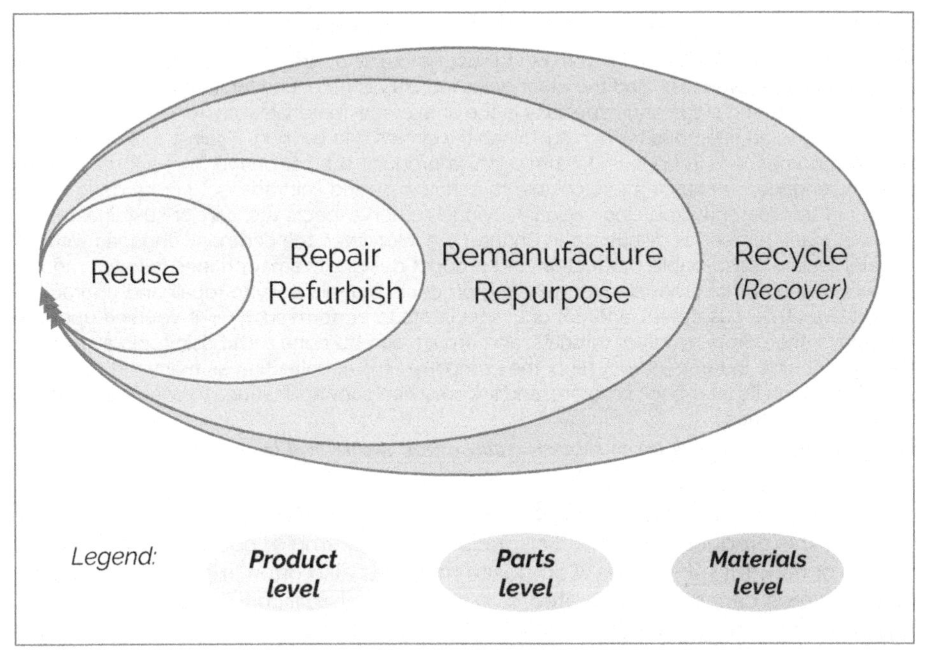

Figure 20: Approaches to achieve closed loops and enable a circular economy

A special concept which does not quite fit into the categorization described above is upcycling. Upcycling can be regarded as counterpart to downcycling as it refers to "a process of converting materials into new materials of higher quality and increased functionality" (Ellen MacArthur Foundation, 2013, p. 25). While the term suggests that it is part of recycling processes at the materials level (e.g., when using biological and chemical processes to upcycle plastic waste; Sohn et al., 2020), upcycling can also be found at the product or parts level. The Swiss company Freitag, for example, manufactures backpacks, messenger bags, and other accessories from used truck tarps, discarded bicycle inner tubes, and car seat belts. More precisely, however, such a use of parts from waste products for new products is already covered by the concept of repurposing described above. Furthermore, the term upcycling is not always used identically. The circular economy pioneers, Michael Braungart and William McDonough, for example, refer to the upcycling when materials maintain their status as resources of highest possible value, that is, instead of achieving a higher value, upcycling can also be understood as not losing value and thus similar to recycling in general (Braungart et al., 2007).

The answer to the question of what can be done at the end of the product life cycle is often already determined during the early product development. There are various approaches to enable more sustainable solutions at the end of the product life cycle that can generally be classified as process oriented and material oriented (see Dyckhoff & Souren, 2008). Process-oriented approaches aim at enabling an easy disassembly at the end of the product life. Designers and engineers can use manufacturing techniques that use screws or snap-fit connections instead of gluing or riveting pieces together. Alternatively, the industry nowadays offers specialized dissolvents for certain adhesives in the business to business segment, for example, in the automotive industry to enable disassembly. Furthermore, disassembly and repairability can also be improved by designing modular products. Some seemingly simple design steps, such as improving accessibility for tools, can also significantly improve respective processes at the end of product life.

Sustainability in business 27: Fairphone - Modular smartphone design

Most modern smartphones are far from being sustainable. They are often used only for one or two years, sometimes even less, and the electronics industry is notorious for its human rights issues in the manufacturing stage and especially in the area of raw materials with, for example, "conflict minerals" being an infamous term in sustainability circles and beyond. Against this background, the Dutch company Fairphone is on a mission to produce a fairer phone. To walk the talk, the company engages in sourcing responsible materials by using Fairtrade gold or by decommoditizing and transparently sourcing cobalt. Obviously, such aspects are part of sustainable supply chain management as discussed in Chapter C.3. Moreover, the company engages with various elements of sustainable production and product design. Its smartphones follow a modular design with the aim of producing long-lasting products that are easy to repair and upgrade. To support even their customers, and not only specialists to perform such do-it-yourself upgrades and repairs, the company offers tutorials, and repairs can be done with basic tools available in most households. In terms of recycling, the company aims at collecting as many old phones as possible through its take-back program, and it works with partners in Africa to enable sustainable recycling of batteries.

Sources: Closing the Loop et al. (2020); Mestre and Cooper (2017); Reuter et al. (2018)

Material-oriented approaches are another way to enable more sustainable solutions at the end of the product life cycle. This includes, for example, not using nonrecyclable materials or harmful substances. Composite materials also often impede recyclability as they sometimes cannot be separated or a separation is difficult or costly so that recycling is not economically feasible. To facilitate recycling in commercial processes and for complex (technological) products, detailed information in dismantling manuals or recycling passports can be helpful to inform actors at the end of the value chain of how to adequately process products for repair, remanufacture, or recycle. Alternatively, many innovative companies instead nowadays rely on recyclable, sometimes renewable raw materials even in unusual settings. The Ghanaian company Boomers, for example, manufactures bicycle frames made from local bamboo instead of metal (see https://www.boomers.com). The stylish bikes, made in Ghana, are sold in Europe and North America. Often, however, such measures have to be regulated through governmental authorities and laws because customers usually do not voice demand and companies usually see only few opportunities to develop unique selling propositions or customer benefits from process-oriented and material-oriented approaches. To boost awareness in this regard, France introduced a "repairability index" in 2021 requiring manufacturers of smartphones and laptops to inform consumers of how repairable their products are (Stone, 2021).

From an organizational perspective, Hansen and Revellio (2020) showed, in an extensive case study, that reuse, repair, and remanufacturing seems to require higher degrees of vertical integration (i.e., companies pursue the required steps at the end of the product life themselves instead of partnering with other companies) compared to recycling. Apparently, the respective activities require more specific assets and are of greater strategic relevance than recycling activities. Furthermore, higher degrees of vertical integration better enable closed-loop systems and also improve feedback into process design, which illustrates the general organizational complexity and hurdles of the eco-effectiveness strategy (see again Chapter A.4.3). Here again, decommoditization (see again Chapter C.3.3) might be necessary to improve the options of sustainable reduction and recycling.

C.4.4 Sustainability in logistics

Logistics refers to the process of how resources are stored and transported from tier to tier in a supply chain until they finally reach the consumer. These processes have various sustainability-related impacts. Most prominently, transport processes require resources that are largely based on fossil fuels and, thus, emit significant greenhouse gases but also other substances such as fine dust particles and nitrogen oxides. As of 2015, the

CO_2 emissions from international freight alone accounted for seven percent of global CO_2 emissions and the absolute amount is estimated to grow even more in the upcoming decades (International Transport Forum, 2015). When looking at the entire transport sector (including private vehicles), it is the largest emitter of CO_2 in the United States with almost 30 percent of total emissions in 2019 (United States Environmental Protection Agency, 2021). Furthermore, logistic processes require land (for roads, railroads, etc.), they emit noise, and in many countries around the world the logistics sector is notorious for poor working conditions.

To illustrate the various options for reducing the environmental impact of logistics, we will refer to the three strategies of eco-efficiency, eco-effectiveness, and sufficiency as introduced in Chapter A.4. Sufficiency measures in transportation aim at reducing the overall volume of transport. This can be done either by reducing the transport amount or by reducing the transport distance or both. In reality, however, the globalization of the last decades has led to a considerable increase of both factors. Nevertheless, companies can aim, for example, at introducing more regional products or supply chains on an individual basis to tackle their emissions. Elements of eco-effectiveness are rarely discussed in relation to logistics processes, because closed-looped approaches are difficult to achieve for a generally linear activity such as transporting something from point A to point B. Electro mobility might be a step toward eco-effectiveness in logistics if vehicles are indeed powered by entirely renewable energy resources. Furthermore, linear transport structures can sometimes at least partially be closed if the delivery of products is linked to the collection of waste products or deposit.

By far the most widespread decoupling strategy in logistics is that of eco-efficiency. Here, strategic as well as operational measures aim at reducing the average transport distance, at improving the capacity utilization of transports, or at using more environmentally friendly means of transport (see Dyckhoff & Souren, 2008). When trying to reduce the average transport distance, this is not to be confused with sufficiency approaches. Sufficiency strategies try to reduce the necessary transport distance by aiming at more regional or local supply chains. The respective efficiency strategies, however, do not necessarily look for regional or local approaches but instead try to optimize the overall logistics system so that the same supply chains can be sustained while still reducing the average environmental impact. Measures aiming at reducing the average transport distance and measures aiming at improving capacity utilization of transports are often in a tradeoff with one another.

Two important strategic levers for these two aspects of distance and capacity utilization are the number of stages in distribution networks and the (de-)centralization of storage facilities. With regard to the number of stages of a distribution network, fewer stages (e.g., direct delivery to customers from the production facility instead of via wholesalers and retailers) usually require less land consumption (due to fewer facilities) and a shorter transport distance per individual delivery process (because each product can go directly to the customer instead of taking a detour via wholesalers, retailers, etc.). However, the average number of transport processes increases (as customers usually do not order entire truckloads of goods but only single items) and thus transport efficiency per transport unit usually decreases as transport bundling is much more difficult. If that is the case, the cumulative transport distance might be high due to a very large number of (individually shorter) logistics activities. Therefore, direct delivery is ecologically and also economically only feasible for larger and continuous quantities.

Sustainability in society 19: E-commerce – boon or bane for sustainability?

E-commerce and online shopping are booming, and not only since the beginning of the COVID-19 pandemic. However, is this good or bad for sustainability? Is e-commerce more or less sustainable than traditional retail? As so often with sustainability, the answer is not clear-cut. When looking at environmental effects, many people think that e-commerce is worse than traditional retailing, and they highlight the countless delivery trips needed to bring all the online orders to the right customers. This ignores, however, that you also need to go to your local retailer for buying shoes, electronics, groceries, etc. Last-mile delivery, for example, of specialized parcel services is often very efficient as there is the opportunity to bundle trips and plan routes efficiently. Furthermore, online shopping requires less space for the physical shops and respective infrastructure such as parking lots. Various studies, therefore, highlight that e-commerce can, in fact, be more environmentally friendly than traditional retail.

This result, however, is not generally applicable and it depends on the circumstances. On the one hand, a high percentage of return shipments increases the environmental footprint of e-commerce (especially if returned products are not sold again) while driving by bike to the local retailer takes a big chunk out of the CO_2 footprint of regular shopping trips. On the other hand, efficient last mile deliveries (using, for example, electric vehicles), a green IT infrastructure, an abandonment of secondary packaging and other measures can help greening e-commerce further. Furthermore, e-commerce might especially be a chance for smaller sustainable labels, for example, in the apparel industry but also in other areas due to the significant hurdles of gaining retail space. Finally, social aspects need to be considered as well to holistically evaluate sustainability impacts. In many countries around the world, the logistics industry is notorious for its problematic working conditions with sometimes low salaries, long working hours, and high stress for employees. Again, however, it is not possible to generalize these aspects as they might be very different from region to region and even from company to company.

Sources: Fernández Briseño et al. (2020); van Loon et al. (2014); Zimmermann et al. (2020)

Regarding the (de-)centralization of facilities, decentralized storage (i.e., smaller regional or local instead of larger centralized national warehouses) enables an easier bundling of inbound transport (i.e., the transport leading into the warehouses or retail stores) and thus also a higher degree of capacity utilization. For the outbound transport (i.e., from the facilities to the customers), there is usually also a positive effect as the final transport distance to the customer decreases. However, more warehouses and other storage facilities lead to higher land use and usually also to more inventory being stored in the supply chain, as each warehouse requires its own inventory including safety stock. Another question is whether or not to use transport service providers. Such service providers usually have better options to utilize transport capacities because they can bundle orders from different clients. Therefore, they can also often avoid empty trips. Another strategic decision with an influence on environmental impact is whether or not to rely on just-in-time-delivery. Just-in-time-systems align material orders from suppliers with a manufacturer's production schedules. The aim is to increase efficiency and decrease waste by receiving goods exactly as needed for production processes. Well-designed just-in-time-systems require fewer warehouses but they require sophisticated logistics processes. From an ecological and economic point of view, they are usually only favorable for larger and continuous product volumes.

Task C4-2

Do some research: What are the main sustainability impacts in e-commerce? How can online retailers make their business more sustainable? Develop measures!

At the more operational level, various measures can be used to improve capacity utilization. Combined transportation, for example, can bring economic and ecological improvements if several tours can be combined. The benefit usually lies in an overall reduced travel distance compared to several individual transport processes. Furthermore, there might also be potential for optimization also within a transport unit through an intelligent cargo loading via computer aided systems or space saving packaging. Especially these latter optimization measures can also be implemented at a rather strategic level when the actual product design is involved (e.g., by designing products and packaging in a way that uses less space). Finally, different modes of transportation are known for their different sustainability impacts. In general, transport via air produces the highest emissions per distance followed by road transport. By far the most efficient means of transport in this regard are rail- and waterways as well as pipelines (R. Sims et al., 2014). However, it is not always possible to simply switch to rail, ship, or pipelines simply due to structural reasons (unavailable infrastructure or unsuitable freight). Furthermore, other issues such as time or flexibility also play an important role. Often, combined modes of transportation are necessary to fulfill all needs but there might even be different alternatives within one mode of transportation (e.g., using gasoline powered vehicles vs. electric vehicles). In many cities around the world, there are now even entirely different options in use which were unthinkable a few years ago, such as electric cargo bikes bikes as a replacement for small trucks for last mile deliveries.

Sustainability in business 28: Wecyclers reverse logistics services in Nigeria

Reverse logistics "refers to the sequence of activities required to collect the used product from the customers for the purpose of either reuse or repair or re-manufacture or recycle or dispose of it" (Agrawal et al., 2015, p. 76). To allow for proper disposal and recycling, and thus eventually for closing the loop, reverse logistics is obviously essential. However, in many regions around the world there are no sophisticated reverse logistics systems in place, for example, due to lack of public resources. Instead, potentially valuable material is littered with negative consequences for the environment. A very prominent example of such negative consequences is the Great Pacific Garbage Patch, an enormous collection of marine debris in the North Pacific Ocean, but of course uncontrolled littering also has very visible consequences at the local level.

In some regions, private companies try to address these issues and provide solutions. Wecyclers in the Nigerian capital of Lagos is one of these companies. In the city, the bulk of waste was previously not collected and recycling companies could not operate properly due to lack of waste supplies. Wecyclers operates locally in the neighborhoods of the megacity and collects recyclable waste from households. Collectors are often formerly unemployed young people who can generate an income from collecting waste. Households receive points for recycled waste, which is transported to various hubs around the city using locally assembled cargo bikes. The waste is eventually sold as valuable recyclable material to again enter the life cycle of new products.

(Photo by King Baudouin Foundation (KBF) - Africa program; Nyancho Nwanri/Arete, CC BY 2.0, https://commons.wikimedia.org/wiki/File:Wecyclers_win_the_King_Baudouin_International_Development_Prize_(46504739825).jpg)

The topic in general, however, also offers some insights into potential trade-offs between different aspects of sustainability. Collecting waste can, on the one hand, be regarded as a job opportunity for previously unemployed people. On the other hand, in some cultures such forms of informal recycling are sometimes carried out specifically by marginalized groups. If societies do not accept respective employments, waste collection could bring people closer to the edge of society rather than fostering integration. Furthermore, while respective jobs provide some income to poor people, it is sometimes "only practicable from a business point of view if it is connected with very low wages so that it is financially advantageous for the entire RL [reverse logistics] chain" (Brix-Asala et al., 2016, p. 421).

Sources: Adebiyi-Abiola et al. (2019); Brix-Asala et al. (2016); Godfrey et al. (2018); Lebreton et al. (2018)

KEY
TAKEAWAYS

- Product designers and engineers can improve the sustainability performance of a product by applying elements from eco-efficiency, eco-effectiveness, or sufficiency.
- Eco-design aims at improving sustainability of a product across the entire life cycle.
- Options for reduction-oriented product use concepts are (1) the extension of potential useful product life, (2) the extension of effective product use, (3) an intensified product utilization over the product life time, and (4) an intensified product utilization during its use time.
- The waste hierarchy consists of reduce, reuse, recycle, and disposal.
- Reuse and recycle are further specified in the 4R framework which covers reuse, repair (and refurbish), remanufacture (and repurpose), and recycle.
- Material-oriented approaches at the end of the product life cycle include not using nonrecyclable materials or harmful substances as well as dismantling manuals or recycling passports.
- Sufficiency measures reduce the overall volume of transport, eco-effectiveness is difficult to pursue for a generally linear activity such as transporting something from point A to point B, and eco-efficiency covers strategic as well as operational measures to reduce the average transport distance, improve the capacity utilization of transports, or introduce more environmentally friendly means of transport.

C.5 Sustainable innovation management

LEARNING GOALS

After reading this chapter you will be able to ...

- ... distinguish inventions, innovation, and diffusion.
- ... describe what sustainability-oriented innovation is.
- ... explain push and pull determinants of sustainability-oriented innovation, provide examples, and discuss their interdependence.
- ... explain how directional certainty can be achieved.
- ... explain organizational optimization, organizational transformation, and systems building as approaches of sustainability-oriented innovations and provide examples.
- ... explain the basic idea of business at the base of the pyramid.
- ... distinguish BoP 1.0, 2.0, and 3.0 approaches and discuss their potential opportunities and limitations.

Introduction to Chapter C.5: Screencast
Watch an introduction to the chapter here:

C.5.1 Introduction to sustainability-oriented innovation

Before we can discuss sustainability-oriented innovation, we must first clarify what innovation in general is, as there is often some confusion about terms and concepts (see Dosi & Nelson, 2010). The beginning of any innovation process is usually an invention, that is, a novel and original idea or discovery that can potentially lead to novel products or processes. Innovations are based on such inventions as they cover the actual introduction and initial economic exploitation of the respective novel ideas or discoveries. To be successful in the long run, the respective innovations then need to be diffused, that is, they need to be disseminated more broadly and even potentially imitated. Thus, an invention is usually the relevant starting point but not the end of a process and it only leads to broader change if the respective invention is incorporated into (mostly economically exploitable) products and processes by means of innovation and diffusion.

In an early attempt of definition, Rennings (2000) describes eco-innovations as "all measures of relevant actors (firms, politicians, unions, associations, churches, private households) which develop new ideas, behavior, products and processes, apply or introduce them and which contribute to a reduction of environmental burdens or to ecologically specified sustainability targets" (p. 322). However, based on our understanding of sustainability and sustainable development, eco-innovations cover only a part of all sustainability-oriented innovations. R. Adams et al. (2016) extend this understanding and posit that sustainability-oriented innovation "involves making intentional changes to an organization's philosophy and values, as well as to its products, processes or practices, to serve the specific purpose of creating and realizing social and environmental value in addition to economic returns" (p. 181). What we can take from both definitions together is that sustainability innovation potentially involves various actors and thus requires cooperation. This seems reasonable given that sustainable development is an overarching societal concept which is inherently complex, as we have seen repeatedly throughout this book. Furthermore, sustainability-oriented innovation is not limited solely to technological issues but may also encompass organizational, social, or institutional innovations such as changing behaviors or new kinds of business models (see also Chapter C.9.1) as we will discuss throughout this chapter.

Determinants for sustainability-oriented innovation are diverse depending on the respective industry, area of society, sustainability topic, and so on. In general, the literature distinguishes between various push and pull factors (e.g., Clausen et al., 2011; Rennings, 2000; Fichter & Arnold, 2003). On the push side, we distinguish between regulatory push, technology push, civil society push, and cost push. A regulatory push describes situations in which sustainability-related specifications from governmental and supra-governmental institutions, via laws, decrees, and other forms of regulations, require companies to change their approaches and behaviors. Sometimes, such a push is already initiated by the mere political debate about potential regulations. Examples of regulatory pushes toward sustainability-oriented innovation are CO2 emission performance standards for cars, tightened guidelines regarding supply chain transparency, or the ban of certain types of disposable packaging in various countries and regions around the world. Technology push is a factor that arises when new technologies open avenues for new business models, products, and processes which potentially disrupt industries and render certain products or processes obsolete. Mobile technologies, for example, enabled a breakthrough of many business models in the sharing economy, and increasingly sophisticated battery solutions as well as renewable energy supply will render most technologies from combustion engineering unattractive for most private customers. The push from civil society increased with the growing relevance of many actors from civil society (see again Chapter B.4). Environmental and human rights activist groups and also scientists together with the media can induce a normative pressure on other actors to act more sustainably by providing evidence, scandalizing issues, and so on. Finally, cost pressure, for example regarding raw materials, can also induce a push toward innovation. Planetary boundaries and the finiteness of many raw materials but also increasing regulations or the increasing internalization of external effects have led to a price increase for many input factors so that companies seek ways to optimize their resource usage or substitute certain materials by relying on innovation.

On the pull side, again regulatory factors can play an important role. Other than regulatory push factors, they do not require companies to act in a certain way but instead they provide incentives to voluntarily act in a certain way. Regulations for diligent environment and health processes at the workplace, for example, do not necessarily prohibit the use of certain toxic materials. However, increased obligations on how to handle such substances may nevertheless incentivize companies to substitute them. Even more direct incentives for sustainability-oriented innovation are governmental support programs or research funding. A visionary pull describes pull factors usually from within the market sector. Certain companies or even industry associations might have a strong vision and normative impetus toward sustainability, for example, visionary company leaders or industry codes of conduct, but also national roadmaps and agendas for sustainability can guide the way to sustainability-oriented innovations. Finally, a market pull describes changes in demand which incentivize companies to innovate sustainably. Increasingly, sustainability becomes a purchase criterion for many customers and companies often try to improve their image with more sustainable products and processes. Usually, the respective push and pull factors are at least partly interdependent and cannot be viewed in isolation. For example, a regulatory push and pull toward alternative forms of transport other than gasoline powered automobiles influenced an increasing market pull while regulations itself were influenced by civil society demands for increasing climate protection. All these factors together at some point of time induced a technology push when new renewable forms of transportation overtook previously prevalent technologies in their efficiency and effectiveness.

Task C5-1

Think of one recent innovation with relevance for sustainability. Through which specific push- and pull determinants did it emerge? Can you foresee potential unintended negative consequences or side effects in the future?

An important caveat of any innovation is that their effects are, by definition, uncertain because innovations are inevitably something new. Thus, whether a seemingly sustainability-oriented innovation indeed is sustainable in its economic, ecological, and social dimension or whether it instead induces, for example, unintended negative consequences or side effects, is something only time can tell. At the time of its discovery, for instance, it was not yet clear what drastic consequences nuclear power could have if it is not contained properly. Against the background of such inherent uncertainties of innovations, Paech (2007) summarizes different elements of directional certainty which could help deal with the respective uncertainties and allow innovations to be developed and implemented without compromising future sustainability. To achieve directional certainty, innovations have to be economically reversible and they have to avoid extreme effects so that they are also ecologically reversible. Economic reversibility means that innovations generally can be taken back from an economic perspective. Economic reversibility can be improved, on the one hand, by avoiding supply-side lock-ins, that is, irreversible capital in terms of immobile and product-specific investments should be avoided as much as possible. On the other hand, demand-side lock-ins should also be avoided, that is, customers should not be restricted to specific technical solutions and standards, and alternative means for the fulfillment of needs should be available. Ecological reversibility is achieved when innovations do not induce irreversible damages such as loss of biodiversity or accumulated emissions. This also includes avoiding innovations with potentially extreme effects that could negatively impact entire generations. In sum, the idea is thus to allow for sufficient leeway for errors as it is likely that not all sustainability-oriented innovations turn out to be holistically sustainable in the long run. Figure 21 summarizes all these determining factors for sustainability-oriented innovations.

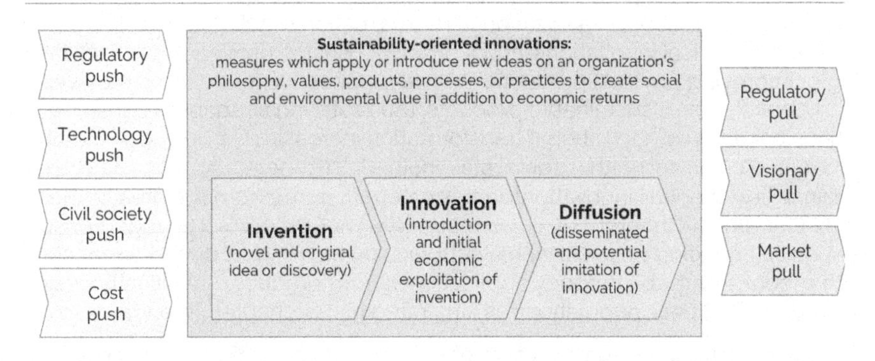

Figure 21: Characterization of and determining factors for sustainability-oriented innovations

C.5.2 Approaches of sustainability-oriented innovation

Innovation itself takes place through different approaches. Based on a systematic literature review, R. Adams et al. (2016) clustered innovations into three levels. These three levels start from an insular and mainly technology-focused perspective of organizational optimization and move via the second approach of organizational transformation to the third approach of systems building, which is rather integrated, systemic, and people-oriented.

The most frequently mentioned and widespread approach is that of operational optimization. Respective sustainability-oriented innovations build upon a given set of needs and try to satisfy them more (eco-)efficiently than before (see Chapter A.4.2). Such innovations are usually reactive, incremental, and internal. That is, they are typically incremental innovations addressing a single sustainability issue at a time. With this, respective innovations aim at reducing current negative environmental and social impacts without fundamental changes to the business model. Instead, they tend to focus on new technologies but without drastic changes and by relying on company internal resources to innovate. Typical examples of this type of sustainability-oriented innovations at the product level are product miniaturization, a redesigning of packaging, reducing hazardous materials or energy consumption, and further elements of eco-design (see Chapter C.4.2). At the organizational level, companies implement more resource-efficient processes, improve their waste management, engage in pollution control measures, and so on.

Sustainability in business 29: Xerox Solid Ink as potential example of operational optimization

Countless best-practice examples of "doing the same things better" (R. Adams et al., 2016) exist, in which innovations reduce harm through eco-efficiency, and some of these are also illustrated throughout this book. However, even such seemingly simple, incremental improvements are not always successful. In contrast to typical printer cartridges, solid ink printers use nontoxic crayon-like ink sticks and thus come in a cartridge-free design. Hence, printing can be more efficient as it generates 90 percent less waste and, consequently, reduces the environmental impacts of manufacturing and transportation. Despite these apparent efficiency benefits, the product was not a market success for office or home printers, as the idea also involves some significant disadvantages. For example, because the solid ink first has to be turned into a liquid state before printing, it often takes some time before the first page is printed. Furthermore, the ink must be heated, which results in a comparably high energy need especially in stand-by mode. This example illustrates the complexity of even seemingly simple innovations, which always have to be evaluated holistically before any conclusions on their possible sustainability impacts can be made.

***Sources:** Weiler (2017); Xerox Corporation (2016)*

The next evolutionary step of sustainability-oriented innovations lies in organizational transformation. Respective activities aim at providing novel goods, services, and business models, thus moving toward a fundamental shift in an organization's mindset. Unlike organizational optimization, organizational transformation regularly combines technological and socio-technical innovations, and it often focuses on delivering services instead of creating or improving physical products. This way, respective innovations may even serve new markets with novel, sustainable products, thus catering to adapted consumer needs. Innovations based on organizational transformation increasingly build upon collaboration along the value chain and with external stakeholders to generate holistic value. Examples for sustainability-oriented innovations in this category come from the area of the sharing economy (see again Chapter B.5.3), from services that otherwise change consumption habits such as replacing physical with electronic services (e.g., reduced paper consumption with e-books or mobile money applications), from products specifically designed to cater to the need of poor populations as illustrated in this chapter below, and so on.

The most far-reaching approach is that of systems building. So far, only few organizations or industries occupy this realm. Respective innovations require a rather radical shift in the sense that they require thinking beyond the boundaries of a single organization to include partners in previously unrelated areas or industries. Cooperation and the creation of sustainable value in networks is thus key in this approach, in which economic activity is regarded as being part of society, not distinct from it. The results are novel products or even entirely new business models and business thinking that drive institutional change. Examples of systems building are still rather rare due to the often radically new perspective of such approaches. Industrial symbiosis networks, as introduced in Chapter A.4.3, can be regarded as systems building. In such networks, companies in a certain region collaborate by exchanging material and energy to achieve a circular economy. Industrial symbiosis networks illustrate why systems building is often a rather radical shift as these networks are usually highly complex and require a high level of technological and organizational sophistication and exchange.

Sustainability in business 30: The Kalundborg symbiosis as innovative approach of systems building

Kalundborg is a small city in Denmark, which is known worldwide for its extensive industrial ecosystem. The basic idea of this ecosystem, which has developed over the last 50 years and is also known as the Kalundborg symbiosis, is that the by-products or waste of one company are used as a resource by other companies to achieve a circular system. The various companies in the ecosystem exchange material, water, and energy, which leads to environmental and economic benefits. The industrial symbiosis in Kalundborg includes, among others, a power plant, a refinery, a plaster board company, local farmers, fish factories, and recycling facilities as well as other actors and companies. Innovation is a key component in the ecosystem, which requires close cooperation among the different actors. Not only innovative new processes and products help to facilitate circularity (e.g., algae production facilities or bio-ethanol production) but also new forms of cooperation, improved logistics, and increased knowledge transfer. The symbiosis in Kalundborg has developed into a resilient system. However, the sheer amount of time it took to establish and refine the system indicates the challenges that come with such system building innovations.

Sources: Domenech and Davies (2011); Ehrenfeld and Gertler (1997); Valentine (2016)

Other examples of systems building can be found in extensive cross-sector partnerships between companies and civil society organizations, if the respective projects go beyond a narrow business mindset and focus on sustainable value creation. Such partnerships have been discussed in Chapter B.4.3. Finally, many social enterprises indeed seem to have embraced the idea of systems building through cooperation (see Chapter C.9.2). Social enterprises "pursue a social mission while engaging in commercial activities that sustain their operations" (Battilana & Lee, 2014, p. 399). Sustainability is often in the genes of such businesses as they "proactively engage sustainability as part of their business models" (R. Hahn & Ince, 2016, p. 33). Interestingly, social enterprises have often been found to be driven by the quest to support a transformation of society toward sustainability by co-creating values with a diverse set of partners (R. Hahn & Ince, 2016; Ostertag et al., 2021).

Task C5-2

Identify further examples for the three approaches of sustainability-oriented innovation! To what extent do you think they can contribute to sustainable development? What are the benefits and drawbacks of the three approaches in general?

C.5.3 Innovations and the "Base of the Pyramid"

A specific setting for innovations is that of the base (or bottom) of the pyramid (BoP), which has received significant attention in academia and business practice over the last years. Initially conceived by Prahalad and Hart (2002) and Prahalad and Hammond (2002), the BoP refers to the bottom tier of the world income pyramid. It thus encompasses the large share of people living in poverty, and it is also often described as those people living on less than USD 2.5 (sometimes also USD 5 or USD 10) measured in purchasing power parities. As such, the BoP describes a large segment of the world's population, that is, individuals whose standards of living are generally low or very low. Beyond this descriptive aspect, the idea of the BoP is that exactly this segment of the world is often not included in formal markets so that there are potential business opportunities as well as chances for poverty alleviation through sustainable development and sustainability-oriented innovations (R. Hahn, 2009).

Faces of sustainability 9: Coimbatore Krishnarao Prahalad

Coimbatore Krishnarao Prahalad, popularly known as CK, was a management professor at the Ross School of Business of the University of Michigan. Born in India in 1941, he became one of the most influential business thinkers of his time, and together with co-authors he coined the idea of alleviating poverty through profitably engaging in innovative business models with the poor. In his bestselling book "The Fortune at the Bottom of the Pyramid" (Prahalad, 2004), CK Prahalad extensively laid out his idea to stop thinking of the poor as victims and instead seeing them as important actors in value chains. With his ideas, he advised businesses around the world, which also provided him with the opportunity to showcase numerous case studies of successful BoP innovations. Prahalad, who received numerous awards and recognitions for his various ideas and activities, died in 2010 at the age of 68.

Sources: Bajaj (2010); Rajghatta (2010)

(Photo by Eric Miller, CC BY 2.0, https://commons.wikimedia.org/wiki/File:CK_Prahalad_WEForum_2009.jpg)

In their literature review, Dembek et al. (2020) provide a historic overview of how the BoP idea evolved over time as illustrated in the following. The different approaches all show that innovations at the BoP can come in many different forms and are (again) not restricted to technological innovations. The first evolution of BoP business models (BoP 1.0) focused largely on viewing the poor as an underserved customer group with the aim of selling to them. This idea was born from the paradoxical observation that people living at the BoP often have to pay significantly higher prices ("poverty penalties") for comparable goods and services compared to people living at the top of the pyramid. Reasons for this can be inefficient infrastructure and distribution channels, a price-inflating role of local intermediaries, or a prosperous informal economy. Successful BoP 1.0 business models could reduce these disparities, which would set free purchasing power to be used to alleviate poverty. Typical examples of respective innovations often focused on adapted products for poor customers and sometimes harsh BoP environments or on adapted product sizes, redesigned packaging (e.g., selling goods such as shampoo or detergents in affordable single servings sachets), or an extended distribution system. While the core idea of poverty alleviation through mutual value creation for companies as well as for local BoP communities does sound tempting, the idea of BoP 1.0 also received some fierce criticisms. For example, luring customers into spending parts of their already meager income for items that they do not necessarily need (e.g., hard liquor being sold in sachet packages specifically to the poor population) was seen as a problem as well as imposing Western business practices on an environment with an entirely different trajectory and background. Potential downsides for ecological sustainability were also brought up, for example, when BoP 1.0 products build upon inherently unsustainable approaches (e.g., throwaway plastic sachet packages in areas without proper waste management structures).

Sustainability in business 31: Hindustan Unilever Limited's "Shakti project"

One of the most frequently mentioned examples for a BoP 1.0 approach comes from Hindustan Unilever Limited, the Indian subsidiary of the Dutch consumer goods company Unilever. With its project "Shakti,", the company reaches out to the BoP with an extensive rural distribution network by engaging women from the BoP as local dealers. The Shakti dealers are self-employed female entrepreneurs who receive training on distribution management from the company. They sell products such as soaps, detergents, and sanitizers to small retail outlets in their immediate surroundings and also directly to households. By 2020, the Shakti network covered roughly half of the villages in rural India and is thus a cornerstone of the company's sales. The project and the sales activities are flanked by various measures to cater to the BoP. It uses, for example, single-serve sachet packaging, affordable pricing, and customized advertising through word-of-mouth, local self-help groups, and on-the-ground information campaigns.

Sources: Garg and Ramachandran (2019); Rangan and Rajan (2007); Singh (2021)

The BoP concept soon evolved further into BoP 2.0 approaches, which shifted toward an integrative perspective instead of merely seeing the BoP as a potential customer base. The main idea of BoP 2.0 is to access the BoP as a resource for adapted business models and thus integrate them into value co-creation. BoP businesses thus should be embedded into local communities to understand local demand and also create opportunities to generate income. While usually still being connected to larger corporations, the idea of BoP 2.0 allows for more local approaches that are somehow free of traditional corporate structures, metrics, and routines. While they tackle many of the issues criticized with BoP 1.0 thinking, innovative BoP 2.0 approaches also receive significant criticism. For example, portraying the poor at the BoP as resilient entrepreneurs, which only have to be included in value-generating activities to solve some of the direct consequences of poverty, was criticized for being naïve and could result "in too little emphasis on legal, regulatory and social mechanisms to protect the poor" (Karnani, 2008, p. 49). Furthermore, BoP 2.0 business models may encourage unsustainable consumption behaviors in the same way as BoP 1.0 approaches have done.

The most recent iteration of BoP approaches, BoP 3.0, now puts a greater emphasis on integrating a triple bottom line perspective and on seeing poverty more realistically as a complex and multidimensional issue instead of solely focusing on monetary income. It builds upon the BoP 2.0 idea of integrating the poor into value-creating activities, but it aims more consequently at encouraging self-management, capacity building, and sharing of skills and knowledge. Furthermore, complex entrepreneurial and social ecosystems are being considered and engaged through cross-sector partnerships to achieve greater well-being in bottom-up processes instead of imposing ideas merely from a corporate (and potentially Western) perspective.

Finding innovative approaches to cater to a segment of the world population that has long been ignored by many companies is a challenging endeavor. The UNDP (2008) illustrate a series of constraints. Especially Western companies but often also local companies, which previously acted only at the top of the pyramid, regularly have little knowledge about consumer preferences, local capabilities, and so on. There is, thus, only limited market information available especially since the BoP is not a homogenous segment but instead characterized by high geographic and also cultural diversity. The regulatory environment is often ineffective and, for example, rules and contracts might be difficult to enforce. In many cases, the physical infrastructure (such as roads, electricity grids, or access to telecommunication) is inadequate, especially in rural areas. Finally, the access to financial products and services might be restricted so that poor customers but also producers at the BoP are not able to finance larger investments. Apart from these external constraints, many companies also face internal hurdles such as cognitive barriers or dysfunctional management structures (Halme et al., 2012; Reficco & Gutiérrez, 2016). Against this background, as potential success factors, Gold et al. (2013) identified a proactive top management, committed employees, cooperation with and learning from partners (e.g., NGOs), and localized, innovative approaches to integrate the BoP into supply chains.

Sustainability in business 32: Grameen Danone Foods Ltd - Producing and selling at the BoP

Grameen Danone Foods Ltd is a joint venture by the French food multinational Danone and the Grameen Bank of Bangladesh. The company produces a yoghurt enriched with various micronutrients to fulfill the nutritional needs of children in Bangladesh, where malnutrition is prevalent. The company operates locally by sourcing the milk from surrounding villages. It employs the local population in its plant and relies on female micro entrepreneurs to sell the product door-to-door. The aim of the company is thus to integrate as many people as possible into productive processes and to serve fortified yoghurt to people in Bangladesh to improve the health situation. The company's factory near the town of Bogra was supposed to be a prototype for many more to come. However, the company struggled with its growth plans and faced difficulties when prices for raw materials increased. While the company eventually succeeded through a mixture of changes of its recipe, the price, and the serving size, the ambitious growth plans had to be postponed.

Sources: John (2011); Rangan and Lee (2016); Reiner et al. (2015)

Task C5-3

Do some research and find further innovations at the base of the pyramid! Classify them as 1.0, 2.0, or 3.0 approaches and think of how these approaches can contribute to sustainable development. Can you see any drawbacks of these approaches with regard to sustainability? What do you think: Will they be successful in the future? Why or why not?

Sustainability in research 10: Prahalad and Hart's 2002 article on the fortune at the bottom of the pyramid

The 2002 article, "The fortune at the bottom of the pyramid" by C.K. Prahalad and Stuart L. Hart is widely regarded as the accelerator of the idea of business for and with the poor. In their thought-provoking piece, the authors analyze the market potential of the population segment of the world's poor, and they encourage companies to develop these markets economically and sustainably. They argue that the lowest level of the world economic pyramid (Tier 4) represents about 4 billion people, while the population of the richest segment at the top of the pyramid (Tier 1) consists of merely 100 million people. Although Tier 4 markets lack wealth, education, or attractive infrastructure, they evidently have a large growth potential and should no longer be disregarded by companies.

The authors discuss four factors to advance the respective markets in developing countries. First, they argue that it is necessary to create relevant purchasing power, especially through credit access, enabling Tier 4 consumers to systematically build up their equity. Second, Prahalad and Hart envision that companies shape aspirations of how people live around the world through sustainable product innovation initiated at the bottom of the pyramid. They argue that the large Tier 4 markets can create sufficient market pull for disruptive technologies, which could eventually replace unsustainable products also in developed markets. Third, they call for improved access of often isolated communities at the bottom of the pyramid. Here, improving distribution and communication networks is essential to reduce the dependency of the poor on isolated local products and services. Fourth and finally, companies need to tailor local solutions. So far, usually only high-income markets were considered to be relevant in companies. This has resulted in inefficient product portfolios for the Tier 4 markets that did not meet their specific demands. Prahalad and

Hart argue that it is important for companies to combine local skills and market knowledge with global best practices so that business models do not disrupt the cultures and lifestyles of local people.

Overall, the four factors discussed in the article supposedly have the potential to create a lucrative market position and competitive advantage while requiring significant investments of time and money. In the next couple of years following its publication, the article and its main idea received much praise but also fierce criticism, and the entire idea of business for and with the poor has developed significantly not least thanks to the initial impetus by Prahalad and Hart.

Source: Prahalad and Hart (2002)

A specific type of innovation that is often connected with the BoP are frugal innovations. Such innovations are sometimes also referred to as resource-constraint innovations or good-enough innovations (see Zeschky et al., 2014, for an overview), and they are described as "good-enough, affordable products that meet the needs of resource-constrained consumers" (Zeschky et al., 2011, p. 38). Simula et al. (2015) further specify that the result is "a product, service or a solution that emerges despite financial, human, technological and other resource constraints, and where the final outcome is less pricey than competitive offerings (if available) and which meets the needs of those customers who otherwise remain unserved" (p. 1568). On the input side, frugal innovations build upon little resources and low costs with the output of a rather cheap but still highly effective and outcome-oriented solution. Bhatti et al. (2018) as well as Zeschky et al. (2014) describe several typical traits of frugal innovations:

- Cost-effective raw materials and low operation cost.
- Local sourcing and production, that is, the innovation should enhance local value creation and reduce imports.
- Limitation to core features and less automation, that is, the innovation should build on minimalist features and intuitive functionality.
- High ease of use, that is, the innovation should be based on an intuitive design that require little to no prior knowledge or training to utilize.
- Tailored for BoP environments, that is, the innovation should be capable of coping with harsh physical environments and poor infrastructure.

Sustainability in business 33: M-PESA – The mobile money pioneer in Kenya

Mobile money allows consumers to access financial services through their mobile phone even when they do not have a bank account. Despite popular assumptions especially in the developed countries, mobile money does not need sophisticated technologies. A simple mobile phone offering short-message-service functionality is sufficient to use most services. Mobile money has been shown to have various positive effects on poverty alleviation especially at the BoP where it can help to mitigate negative income shocks, empower women by improving their financial agency, and to facilitate the operations of small businesses.

While not being the world's first mobile money service, M-PESA in Kenya is certainly one of the most well-known and successful ones today. It was introduced in 2007 as a joint venture between the Kenyan Safaricom and the British Vodafone and it has reached penetration rates in excess of 80 percent. The innovation successfully exploited the fact that most Kenyans had no access whatsoever to formal financial services. It provides a solution which allowed, for example, people living in the cities to easily and cheaply transfer money to their families in rural areas. To do so, users load their mobile account with money and transfer cash via a regular text message to another user who can convert it back to cash via a local agent who sells air-time.

Sources: Kabengele and Hahn (2021); Onsongo (2019); Suri and Jack (2016)

KEY TAKEAWAYS

- An invention is a novel idea or discovery that can potentially lead to new products or processes. Innovations cover the actual introduction and initial economic exploitation of novel ideas or discoveries. Diffusion is the broader disseminated and potential imitation of innovations.
- Sustainability-oriented innovation potentially involves various actors, requires cooperation, and is not limited solely to technological issues but may also encompass organizational, social, or institutional innovations.
- Push determinants for sustainability-orientation are regulatory push, technology push, push from civil society, and cost pressure push. Pull determinants consist of regulatory pull, visionary pull, and market pull.
- To achieve directional certainty, innovations have to be economically and ecologically reversible.
- Operational optimization builds upon a given set of needs and tries to satisfy them more (eco-)efficiently than before; organizational transformation requires a fundamental shift in an organization's mindset to provide novel goods, services, and business models; systems building requires thinking beyond the boundaries of any single organization to include partners in previously unrelated areas or industries.
- The BoP refers to the bottom tier of the world income pyramid and illustrates the idea that there are potential business opportunities as well as chances for poverty alleviation through business activities.
- BoP 1.0 focuses on the poor as an underserved customer group; BoP 2.0 aims at accessing the BoP as a resource for adapted business models and integrating them into value co-creation; BoP 3.0 puts a greater emphasis on integrating a triple bottom line perspective and on seeing poverty as a complex and multidimensional issue.

C.6 Sustainability accounting

LEARNING GOALS

After reading this chapter you will be able to ...

- ... explain the different elements of life cycle sustainability assessment (LCSA) and their areas of application.
- ... describe the general approach and different steps of an environmental life cycle analysis (ELCA) and subsequently ...
- ... explain the differences of conducting an ELCA compared to life cycle costing (LCC) and social life cycle assessment (SLCA).
- ... differentiate scope 1, 2, and 3 emissions and explain the relevance of this differentiation.
- ... critically analyze different types of carbon emissions reduction targets.
- ... explain the potential and limitations of carbon offsetting and criteria for high-quality schemes.

Introduction to Chapter C.6: Screencast
Watch an introduction to the chapter here:

C.6.1 Introduction to sustainability accounting, management control, and reporting

In the next chapters, we will navigate through the interrelated topics of sustainability management control, sustainability accounting, and sustainability reporting step-by-step as illustrated in Figure 22. Sustainability accounting is the gathering of sustainability-related information for transparency and decision-making purposes. Without adequate information, sustainability management would resemble flying blind in the fog as it would be impossible, for example, to evaluate the success or failure of certain activities. Sustainability management control covers the use of management tools to influence sustainability-related organizational behavior. It thus aims at integrating sustainability information into management decision making to foster more sustainable behavior. Furthermore, sustainability-related information needs to reach the relevant decision makers within and outside of the organization. Here, sustainability reporting is defined as the disclosure of sustainability-related information to internal and external stakeholders. Ideally, the outcome of this continuous process of accountability is an improved sustainability performance over time. The distinction into sustainability accounting and sustainability management control in this book is mainly drawn for didactical reasons. Often, both aspects are combined as part of the concept of sustainability management accounting and control, because the distinction into information gathering and information usage might not always be clear-cut and many tools combine elements of both.

Figure 22: Overview of sustainability accounting, sustainability management control, and sustainability reporting

Sustainability accounting is relevant on various levels. For example, sustainability-related information on the product level (e.g., the energy intensity of products) can help to inform customers about (more) sustainable choices, foster sustainable consumer behavior, or help product designers in improving sustainability performance. Sustainability-related information on the process level (e.g., work accidents or the use of certain materials) can help companies include sustainability considerations into their daily business. Sustainability-related information on the organizational level (e.g., emissions, data on diversity) can support sustainability management at the company level and beyond (e.g., by informing investor decisions, B2B relationships, or regulations). Many elements of sustainability management depend on reliable information. Without adequate information, human resource management cannot include sustainability in remuneration systems, marketing cannot inform customers, supply chain management cannot improve suppliers, innovation management cannot develop more sustainable products and processes, communication cannot inform stakeholders, sustainability management systems would basically be useless, and so on. Sustainability accounting is thus a vast topic, and we will concentrate in this chapter on exemplary tools (i.e., different forms of life cycle assessment) and areas of application (i.e., carbon accounting).

C.6.2 Life cycle sustainability assessment

One tool for information gathering in sustainability accounting is a life cycle sustainability assessment (LCSA), which aims at assessing the sustainability impacts of products along their entire life cycle (e.g., Kühnen & Hahn, 2019). A product life cycle describes all stages through which a product passes. This often starts with the mining and extraction of raw materials and then continues with the design and production processes, the shipping and transportation in general, the use process until the end of the product life and the corresponding disposal or the reuse or recycling of the products or materials. This physical life cycle of the product is not to be confused with product life cycle thinking from the marketing domain, which describes the process of developing, introducing, and selling new products. Instead, LCSA is about collecting and assessing information about environmental, economic, and social resources used during the life span of a product.

The purpose of a LCSA is to gain a holistic understanding of the entire system of supply, production, consumption, and end of life of products with regard to the various sustainability impacts. Such information allows companies to recognize and model trade-offs across the different dimensions of sustainability (economic, social, and environmental) and across different steps of the life cycle. Trade-offs can occur, for example, when improvements in one phase have consequences in other parts of the life cycle. Using lightweight composite materials, for instance, might reduce the energy consumption of vehicles during the use phase but it might lead to challenges at the end-of-life stage if these materials are not recyclable (see also the concept of rebound effects in Chapter A.4.5). Furthermore, LCSA also helps to assess the true cost of a product, which not only includes production costs but also externalities in form of environmental and social costs (see again Chapter B.3.1). Despite being a powerful tool as we will outline throughout this chapter, LCSA usually cannot fully address all impacts in the life cycle of a product as most systems and products are far too complex to be modeled with the respective data in their entirety. Therefore, identifying "hot spots," that is, those areas that likely have the most severe or relevant impact on sustainability performance, can help companies to get an idea of where to start with improving their sustainability efforts. Apart from serving as a basis for management decisions, results from LCSA can potentially also be used to communicate with different stakeholders, for example, via reports, press releases, or through labels on the respective products.

To illustrate the potential complexity of product life cycles and their sustainability assessments, take the example of a simple red cotton t-shirt. An adequate LCSA needs to cover data on sustainability impacts for the full life cycles of all relevant materials that are used in the production of the T-shirt. This includes, as one of the most obvious aspects, the impacts from the procurement of raw materials. This material then has to be shipped to a textile company where it is refined into a fabric to be sewn into T-shirts. The T-shirt itself also has to be sent to the point of sale and there might be impacts when using and disposing it. However, it is not as easy as that. The dying of the fabric as well as the stitching, potential prints, and also little things such as the neck labels inside the T-shirts have to be factored in. Dyes, fabrics, threads, and all the other parts have their own intricate life cycles full of their own specific inputs. Furthermore, the complexity does not end with the different elements and steps of the product itself. It is also important to decide which elements of sustainability impact should be evaluated in a LCSA. Different life cycle steps cause different sustainability impacts. Various environmental impacts occur ranging from, for example, high water consumption when growing cotton to greenhouse gas emissions in various steps of the value chain or environmental hazard when using potentially toxic chemicals for coloring or bleaching. Social impacts can be as diverse as ranging from poor working conditions, cases of child labor, or health and safety issues in the various steps of the production process. Usually, the scope of an LCSA is quite large, and it is nearly impossible to truly assess the entire life cycle of a product. If the life cycle of a simple T-shirt is already so extensive, imagine how complex it becomes for more technological products. Often, such a study thus only covers a fraction of those issues due to the inherent complexity.

The example already illustrated that a full blown LCSA covers different areas of sustainability which are usually separated into three subelements. These elements can be used in combination but also independently of one another as illustrated in Figure 23. The most common element of an LCSA is environmental life cycle assessment (ELCA or simply LCA). To address the full range of sustainability, the economic and social dimensions also have to be considered. Therefore, the economic elements are included in the life cycle costing (LCC), which helps to evaluate costs occurring in the entire life cycle. This includes production costs, but also costs for transportation, consumer costs, or costs for the disposal of the product. The social elements are covered by social life cycle assessment (SLCA), in which all kinds of social and socioeconomic impacts are analyzed. SLCA has a much shorter history compared to ELCA and this not least because the assessment of social impact is often more complex than the assessment of environmental impact factors as we discuss below.

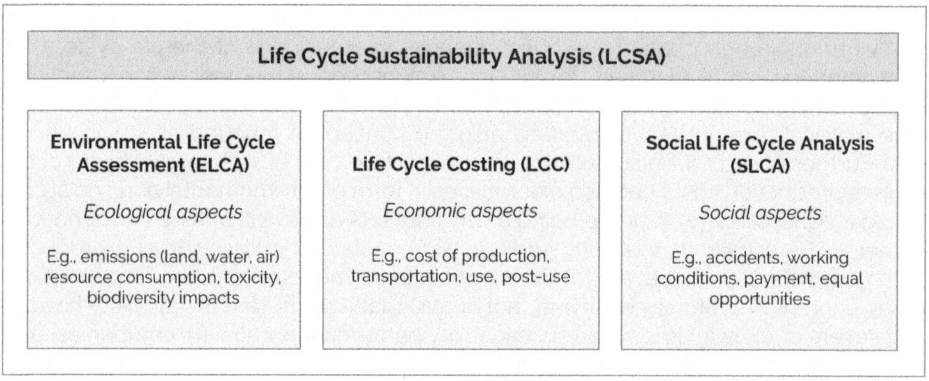

Life Cycle Sustainability Analysis (LCSA)		
Environmental Life Cycle Assessment (ELCA)	**Life Cycle Costing (LCC)**	**Social Life Cycle Analysis (SLCA)**
Ecological aspects	*Economic aspects*	*Social aspects*
E.g., emissions (land, water, air) resource consumption, toxicity, biodiversity impacts	E.g., cost of production, transportation, use, post-use	E.g., accidents, working conditions, payment, equal opportunities

Figure 23: Overview of LCSA elements

Sustainability in business 34: BASF SEEbalance® analysis

The German chemical industry giant BASF has developed its own tools for LCSA. The initial concept of an eco-efficiency analysis was based on ELCA thinking complemented by a total cost calculation resembling an LCC approach. In the ELCA part, environmental impacts of products such as consumption of raw materials and energy, emissions, or toxicity potential are calculated, weighted, and normalized relative to a concrete customer benefit. The result is an environmental fingerprint of the different analyzed products or processes. Cost factors are separately assessed and then included into the final analysis to determine which products are more environmentally friendly and at what costs relative to other products. Later, the tool was further developed into the SEEbalance® analysis (SEE for socio-eco-effectiveness), which also covers societal impacts. The tool thus integrates the various elements of LCSA into one approach and quantifies the three main pillars of sustainability management. The aggregated results are easy to comprehend and communicate. However, each aggregation usually also comes with simplification and potential subjective decisions so that a closer look is often necessary to grasp the full complexity of respective sustainability assessments.

Sources: Saling et al. (2002); Schmidt et al. (2004)

C.6.2.1 Environmental life cycle assessment

ELCA is a method of compiling and assessing the inputs, outputs, and the potential environmental impacts of a product system throughout its life cycle, that is, from the cradle to the grave. Any product or service can be subject of an ELCA—from baby diapers to building materials and from military systems to tourism. The method is standardized, for example, in the standards ISO 14040 and ISO 14044 as part of the standard family on environmental management (ISO, 2006a; ISO, 2006b). ISO 14040 illustrates the following seven principles of ELCA.

- Life cycle perspective: As outlined above, the general idea of ELCA (and also of LCC and SLCA) is to cover all phases of the product life cycle from cradle to grave. The idea is to arrive at a systematic and holistic perspective to identify and possibly avoid a postponement or shifting of environmental burdens from one life cycle stage or process to another.
- Environmental focus: As the name suggests, an ELCA specifically addresses the environmental component of sustainability management while economic and social aspects are covered in LCC and SLCA.
- Relative approach and functional unit: To be able to compare the results of an ELCA of different products, the environmental impact is evaluated in relation to a functional unit that defines what is being studied. The functional unit of a light bulb, for example, might be 1,000,000 lumen-hours of light or the functional unit of a laundry detergent might be 5 kg of clean laundry. Usually, the functional unit is not the product itself (here: the light bulb or a laundry detergent) because there might be different types of product available to reach the desired outcome, that is, the functional unit. It would not make sense, for example, to compare 1 kg of a liquid compact detergent with 1 kg of a powdered detergent simply because they follow an entirely different approach. A functional unit, in this case 5 kg of clean laundry, helps to make both more comparable. The functional unit is thus a reference point, and all analyses in the ELCA are conducted relative to the functional unit.
- Iterative approach: An ELCA follows various phases as outlined below. Later phases in the analysis build upon the results of the earlier phases and can, in turn, be used to adapt preceding analytical steps. Such a process of going back and forth within and between the phases should improve the quality of the entire analysis. For example, the goal and scope of an ELCA can be updated during the analysis. If necessary, data cannot be obtained for a certain process in a defined system, the approach might need adjustments with regard to the system boundaries (e.g., leaving out or devaluing certain aspects for which data quality or availability is insufficient).
- Transparency: An ELCA should be transparent with an open, comprehensive, and understandable presentation of information to enable critical reviews by internal or external experts including various stakeholder groups.
- Comprehensiveness: An ELCA should consider all relevant aspects of the natural environment to allow identifying and addressing potential trade-offs. However, this does not yet include social and economic aspects as these are covered in separate assessments, if desired and applicable. Furthermore, covering every conceivable impact is likely not possible.
- Priority of scientific approach: The procedures and decisions in an ELCA should be based on natural science. If respective findings are not available, the analysis should be based on social or economic science, on international conventions, and only if everything else fails, on value choices such as opinions or preferences.

According to ISO 14040 and ISO 14044, an ELCA is carried out in four consecutive but interrelated steps building on an iterative approach within and between the phases to make sure that the data is comprehensive. The first step is the definition of goals and scope of the assessment, the second step is the compilation of a life cycle inventory, the third step contains the life cycle impact assessment followed by the fourth step of life cycle interpretation.

The objective of the definition of goals and scope as the first step is to select an appropriate functional unit and clearly define the goal and scope of the study. This includes determining the reasons for carrying out the study, describing its intended use, and providing details on the approach to conduct the study. To specify the functional unit, practitioners need to clearly define the function of the product, that is, the role that the product plays for consumers. Functional units are often based on volume, weight, or quantity. An ELCA for a laundry detergent, for example, might define the functional unit as 5 kg of clean laundry. To define a valuable functional unit, five steps are proposed: (1) Describe the product by its properties including the product's social utility. (2) Determine the relevant market segment. (3) Determine the relevant product alternatives. (4) Define and quantify the functional unit in terms of the obligatory product properties required by the relevant market segment. (5) Determine the reference flow for each of the product systems, that is, the output from processes in a given product system that are necessary to achieve the functional unit. For example, how much of a specific laundry detergent (e.g., liquid detergent or a powdered detergent) measured in grams is required to arrive at 5 kg of clean laundry. In other words, the reference flow defines how much resources are needed for one functional unit. Apart from defining the functional unit, another important aspect of the first step it to define the system boundaries, that is, which processes should be covered in the assessment. That means, it has to be decided which data is required, which assumptions are being made, and which specific life cycle stages should be assessed. To be able to gather the relevant data in the next steps, it is necessary to define the product system. That means all interconnected processes in the entire life cycle of the respective product (or products, if an ELCA is used to compare various alternatives) have to be identified.

Task C6-1

Identify potential functional units for ELCAs of products from different industries: clothing, agriculture, automotive, construction, financial services. Come up with some ideas and discuss the difficulties you encounter!

In the second step, the compilation of the life cycle inventory, all relevant data on energy and material inputs and environmental releases are collected. The product and its constituents are described and exchanges between the product system and the environment are identified. These exchanges, that is, the elementary flows, include inputs from nature (e.g., extracted raw materials, land used) and outputs to nature (especially emissions to air, water, and soil). The amounts of elementary flows exchanged by the product system and the environment are in reference to a functional unit as previously defined. Inventory data in an ELCA is limited to physical quantities that are ideally measured or, if measurement is not possible, estimated based on models, prior measurements, and published data. Data sources can be diverse including, for example, parts or task lists, material flow sheets, purchasing lists, waste inventories, emission registers, heat meters, and so on. Such information often comes from company internal sources but it might also be obtained from external sources. Nowadays, there are, for example, specialized commercial and open access databases for life cycle data, and other sources such as official statistics might be used as well. The resulting life cycle inventory is the basis to evaluate comparative environmental impacts or potential improvements.

The life cycle impact assessment as the third step then transfers inventory data into environmental impact potentials by evaluating the magnitude and significance of environmental impacts associated with the elementary flows compiled during the previous phase. Causal pathways link the inventory flows through scientifically proven processes to potential impacts on ecosystems, resources, and human health. This usually includes a classification and a characterization process. In the classification process, certain impact categories are defined, such as climate change, ozone depletion, or resource depletion. These impact categories are an aggregation of negative impacts caused by the used or emitted substances. For example, the outcome "greenhouse gas emissions" can be classified into the impact category of global warming. For some impact categories, such as global warming and ozone depletion, there is a consensus on acceptable characterization factors. For other impact categories, such as resource depletion, consensus is still being developed. In the following characterization process, the elementary flows are brought into a relation to the impact categories. The idea is to find out how significant the impact of substances from the inventory process is on the relevant impact categories. For example, we know that the emission of 9,000 tons of CO_2 and 5,000 tons of methane both have an impact on the atmosphere. A life cycle impact assessment determines which of the two has a greater impact and what implications they have for global warming. Using science-based characterization factors, a life cycle inventory analysis calculates the impacts of each environmental release on various impact categories. For the impact category of global warming, for example, we know that CO_2 is the largest single contributor to climate change, which is why the impact of other greenhouse gases is usually calculated relative to the impact of CO_2. The characterization factors for the global warming potential of CO_2 is thus "1," for methane (CH_4) up to 30 (i.e., methane has a global warming potential that is up to 30 times larger than that of CO_2), or nitrous oxide (N_2O) up to 300 (IPCC, 2021).

Sustainability in society 20: Glass, plastic, or aluminum? Show me the ideal bottle!

Do you prefer drinking from a plastic bottle, from a glass bottle, or from an aluminum can? Disposable or reusable? What is the best alternative from an environmental point of view? This question is a typical use case for an ELCA, and packaging materials were among the first products that were compared in such assessments. The answer to this question is, as often the case, not straightforward as it depends on various factors. More or less unanimously, various ELCA studies found that single-use glass bottles have a worse environmental performance than most alternatives. Reusable solutions are usually better than disposable solutions. Over long transport distances, light and compact plastic bottles may be beneficial if the return rate and the recycling quota are high enough. Glass bottles can be beneficial if they are reused often enough because producing new bottles either from glass waste or from new raw materials is an energy-intensive process. An increased recycling of plastic bottles can also significantly reduce climate with larger bottles being more sustainable than smaller ones because they require less material per unit of content. Furthermore, there might also be trade-offs with regard to the impact categories. Plastic bottles, for example, can be favorable when looking at global warming or acidification but aluminum cans have a smaller impact on water (eutrophication) and are potentially less ecotoxic. Also, specific production techniques or raw materials can change the equation, for example, when looking at plastic bottles produced from fossil or bio-based resources as well as from virgin or recycled material. Overall, the results of an ELCA can depend significantly on the main assumptions and parameters of the respective use case (e.g., recycling quota, transport distance). For drinking water, by the way, the most ecofriendly option by far is to drink tap water from your own reusable container wherever possible instead of bottled water no matter in what form.

Source: Sandin et al. (2020)

In sum, classification helps to assign environmental interventions into impact categories, and characterization helps to determine the significance of the impact of the environmental interventions. Impact categories are then further classified into midpoint impact categories and endpoint impact categories. Midpoint impact categories—or simply midpoints—indicate and quantify environmental problems at an intermediate point between environmental interventions and the final damage to relevant areas of protection. These final damages are referred to as endpoint impact categories. Global warming in itself, for example, is not an endpoint but it can have a negative impact on ecosystem quality as an endpoint. In ELCAs, midpoints help to reduce complexity and, with this, the amount of forecasting and assumptions because each midpoint can potentially have an impact on several endpoints. In a nutshell, elementary flows (e.g., greenhouse gas emission) have a negative impact on certain impact categories as midpoints (e.g., climate change) which, in turn, negatively influence certain endpoints (e.g., ecosystem quality as global warming leads to the extinction of species, extreme weather events, etc.). Figure 24 illustrates another example of the relationships between elementary flows, midpoints, and endpoints.

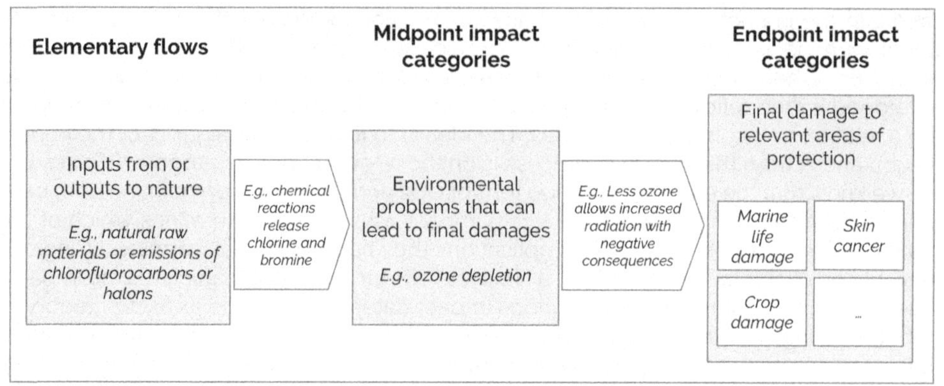

Figure 24: Relationship between elementary flows, midpoints, and endpoints in an ELCA

In the fourth and final stage, life cycle interpretation, the findings of the previous two phases are combined with the defined goal and scope in order to reach conclusions or recommendations. This step should be an ongoing process during the assessment to help guide the other phases. It includes discussions of inventory analysis and impact assessment results. The entire process of an ELCA can be conducted using specialized software tools that offer structured data processing.

C.6.2.2 Life cycle costing

LCC as the economic counterpart to ELCA summarizes all costs from the life cycle of a product that are borne by one or more actors involved in the life cycle, such as farmers, producers, consumers (e.g., Rebitzer & Hunkeler, 2003; Wagner & Lewandowski, 2018). LCC differs from conventional cost accounting in the sense that it aims at assessing the costs attributed to a particular product system and is not limited to the boundaries of a certain company. Therefore, it includes all costs related to the entire life cycle of the production, the use, and the end-of-life of a product that are actually paid for by stakeholders. Just as in an ELCA, the system boundaries thus can go beyond a single company. An important question related to LCC is whether or not to include not only internal but also external costs. External costs derive from negative externalities (see again Chapter B.3.1) and are thus entirely outside the economic system. They cover the monetized effects of environmental and social impacts that are not directly billed to a company or its stakeholders that are in contact with the product. Since external costs are usually related to the natural and social system, but not directly to the economic system, they are often not included in LCC. Thus, an LCC usually covers all cost that are related to real money flows. This includes costs paid for by stakeholders directly involved in the product system but it can also include costs borne by third parties outside of the product system value chain (e.g., cost for waste removal if the product is not properly disposed or recycled or indirect health costs). However, monetarized environmental or social impacts are usually not included in an LCC, because these should be covered in an ELCA and SLCA. In sum, an LCC basically covers all costs that are not already part of ELCA or SLCA. This includes cost for raw materials, energy, or labor, costs for transport, use, and disposal as well as expenses for utilizing knowledge (e.g., patents), transaction costs (e.g., information flows), or marketing.

An LCC can be used to understand the cost drivers of an entire product system by avoiding a shortsighted view on a single company. Therefore, it helps to identify potential trade-offs, for example, if a product is very cost-efficient in production but expensive in disposal because it contains cheap but toxic materials. It thus allows for a holistic evaluation of costs beyond production prices. The general approach of LCC is similar to that of an ELCA as it refers to the same product system boundaries, a functional unit, and defines indicators that are quantifiable, measurable, and monitorable. A main difference to ELCA (and also SLCA, see below) is that the single unit of measurement in an LCC is a monetary value (measured in any currency). Therefore, the life cycle impact assessment stage is not included in an LCC because inventory data does not have to be classified and categorized. Instead, the aggregated data directly provides a measure of impact through a standardized (i.e., monetarized) value. Consequently, an LCC only consists of the remaining three steps introduced above (i.e., definition of goal and scope, compilation of a life cycle inventory, life cycle interpretation). While there are a number of industry guidelines for LCC (e.g., ISO 15686-5 for buildings and constructed assets) there is not yet a uniform standard.

Task C6-2

Compare the idea of ELCA (and SLCA, after reading the next sub-chapter) with that of LCC. In how far can an LCC (and not only ELCA and SLCA) be a relevant tool in sustainability management? How can an LCC help a company to become more sustainable?

C.6.2.3 Social life cycle assessment

SLCA is "a methodology to assess the social impacts of products and services across their life cycle" (UNEP, 2020, p. 20) and can thus be regarded as the social counterpart of ELCA. It is also largely based on the ISO 14040 framework and includes the same four phases of defining goals and scope of the assessment, compiling a life cycle inventory, conducting a life cycle impact assessment followed by a life cycle interpretation. In theory, an SLCA may be conducted on any kind of product, even those that are knowingly harmful to society (e.g., chemical weapons). Like ELCA and LCC, an SLCA can help to compare the impact of products (here: social impacts), analyze the consequences of decisions, and identify potential trade-offs. While an ELCA focuses on collecting information on (mostly) physical quantities and an LCC on monetary values relevant in a product life cycle, an SLCA instead collects information on often rather complex social interactions.

In the first phase, that is, the definition of goal and scope of the assessment, the same questions are asked as in an ELCA. A central aspect is again to identify the functional unit as reference point for the assessment. A specific challenge for SLCAs in this regard is that information from the life cycle inventory are often more difficult to relate to the functional unit in an SLCA compared to an ELCA. In ELCAs, most inventory data are expressed in quantitative terms as elementary flows are usually physical. SLCA, in contrast, often relies on information about process attributes or characteristics that cannot be expressed per unit of process output. Such qualitative information, therefore, cannot easily be summarized per functional unit in later phases of the assessment. Despite these issues, it is nevertheless necessary to define a functional unit as basis for the modeling of product life cycle and the entire product system.

Similar to an ELCA, the aim of the second phase, (social) life cycle inventory, is the collection of relevant data related to social impact. The inventory data is normalized per functional unit if possible, that is, when quantifiable data is available. Relevant information could be, for example, how many working hours are necessary to arrive at the functional unit, at what wages, and so on. This data is necessary for all processes in the product life cycle and product system. In case of qualitative data, the relevant processes will be identified without linking them quantitatively to the functional unit. Even for rather simple products, the amount of potentially available data is vast as any product usually involves various life cycle steps and increasingly complex supply chains. Thus, data collection can be a very time-consuming process when looking at the various stakeholders and social impact categories that are potentially affected. It is therefore usually necessary to prioritize, for example, by focusing on key social issues identified in the literature or by identifying hot spots in the product's life cycle. Social hotspots are defined as "processes located in a region (e.g. country) where a situation occurs that may be considered a problem, a risk, or an opportunity, in relation to a social issue that is considered to be threatening social well-being or that may contribute to its further development" (UNEP, 2020, p. 60) and which should thus be prioritized in an SLCA. Qualitative and quantitative data can be obtained through site-specific data collection (e.g., site specific data on working hours or wages), dedicated databases for SLCA (similar to those databases for ELCA), or through generic data (e.g., average wages in certain countries or regions). Typical data sources for SLCAs include generic risk or reputation data, supplier's self-assessments, social audits, employee surveys, focus groups and interviews, or observations. Thus, the data quality can vary significantly. More than in ELCA, such data can be subjective, based, for example, on employee reports of their perceived degree of control over their schedules and working environment. Despite their subjective nature, such sources can be appropriate if such reports are relevant for the social outcomes of interest.

Sustainability in society 21: Assessing social, environmental, and economic sustainability – The complex task of LCSA

In their textbook chapter on LCSA, Wagner and Lewandowski (2018) illustrate the application of the method for the production of ethanol-based biofuels for the European market. They specifically compare the two alternatives of ethanol produced from Brazilian sugar cane versus from European miscanthus. The main difference between the two alternatives lies in the location of the biomass production (miscanthus in Europe, sugar cane in Brazil), in the mode of transport as well as the transport distance, and in the conversion technology (e.g., production from miscanthus is comparably energy intensive).

In the first phase of the analysis, the functional unit for the analysis was defined as one gigajoule of energy, and the system boundaries covered the cultivation of the biomass including production of fertilizers, transportation processes from the field to the plants and on to the end user, the conversion of biomass into ethanol, and the final use. For the second phase of life cycle inventory analysis, the authors defined climate change, fossil fuel depletion, eutrophication, and acidification as the most important environmental midpoint impact categories for the ELCA while concentrating on the stakeholder group of "workers" for the social impacts with the midpoint categories health and safety, discrimination, and child labor for the SLCA. For the LCC analysis, material and labor cost where included. For the life cycle inventory analysis, data was collected, for example, from literature search, online databases (e.g., ILO for labor conditions and commercial databases for data on material and energy flows), from company and/or government online resources, and from measurements and stakeholder interviews. In the third phase, relevant for the ELCA and SLCA part, data from the life cycle inventory analysis was then translated into environmental and social impact potentials with the aim to aggregate data and make it comparable.

In the fourth and final stage, life cycle interpretation, the analysis of the results of the LCSA illustrates the potential trade-offs between the alternatives and different sustainability aspects. The ELCA showed that the overall environmental performance is best for sugar cane due to its low demand for fertilizers and its low energy needs despite the long transport distances. The LCC analysis showed that Ethanol produced from miscanthus comes with highest production costs due to the higher wages in Europe and the more expensive production technologies. Interestingly, transport cost for sugar cane ethanol are relatively low because it can be transported by ship. From the SLCA, the authors deduce that miscanthus-based ethanol is the most beneficial alternative from a social viewpoint because the working conditions in sugar cane plantations are comparably poor with low wages, only seasonally available work, and potential human rights violations such as child labor. For the European alternative, the working conditions are instead well-defined. Overall, there is thus no ideal biofuel, and the analysis shows how both alternatives can improve their sustainability performance based on the respective hotspots that were identified.

Source: Wagner and Lewandowski (2018)

The third phase of social life cycle impact assessment aims "at calculating, understanding and evaluating the magnitude and significance of the potential social impacts of a product system throughout the life cycle of the product" (UNEP, 2020, p. 80). To systemize data aggregation, social life cycle impact assessment distinguishes between inventory indicators (e.g., remuneration), midpoint impact categories (e.g., fair salary), and category endpoints (e.g., social equity). Similar to ELCA, the idea is that data on social activities (i.e., inventory indicators) are causally linked via intermediary social effects (i.e., midpoint categories) to social consequences (i.e., category endpoints). Category endpoints (e.g., human well-being) may have several midpoint impact categories (e.g., consumer health, worker health), which again may have several inventory indicators (e.g., occupational health, workplace stress, excess work). Different from ELCA, the aggregation is usually not based on natural science (as illustrated for characterization processes above) but is rather based on social or economic science, international conventions, or value choices. An SLCA often includes both positive and negative impacts and indicators of the product life cycle because positive impacts are often important for social sustainability (e.g., paying above minimum wages or providing health care for workers) and to encourage performance beyond mere compliance with national laws, international conventions, and so on.

While especially the UNEP (2020) provides some extensive guidelines for SLCA, there is no uniform standard comparable to ISO 14040/44. A challenge in conducting an SLCA is that inventory indicators and impact categories are not standardized. The latter are usually derived from a stakeholder perspective by first identifying all relevant stakeholders for the respective product system. For each stakeholder group, a list of potential impact categories is derived. For example, for the stakeholder groups of consumers, potential impact categories might be health and safety, consumer privacy, transparency, and end-of-life responsibility but such lists can be subjective. This can also be problematic because SLCA cannot rely as extensively as ELCA on quantitative data and scientifically proven facts and interrelations. Overall, research and practice of SLCA is rather fragmented, and there is an increased attention and thus also a certain consensus only for health- and worker-related indicators, while other upstream and downstream (i.e., toward the beginning and the end of the supply chain or product life cycle) consequences of organizational conduct have not been focused on (Kühnen & Hahn, 2017).

C.6.3 Carbon accounting

With the particular relevance of climate change and global warming, greenhouse gas emissions are of central concern for sustainability management. Companies around the world nowadays regularly define targets for themselves to reduce greenhouse gas emissions. To be able to set targets, relevant information needs to be available from carbon accounting. Therefore, carbon accounting has materialized into its own area of sustainability accounting. Although it is usually referred to as carbon accounting, the respective tools and procedures do not exclusively focus on CO2 emissions but on greenhouse gases in general. Usually one of the first questions in carbon accounting is where did the emissions take place? Answering this question is relevant, for example, to determine responsibilities, identify main emission sources and levers to reduce emissions, and avoid missing relevant emissions as well as double counting. A common distinction in carbon accounting in this regard is between scope 1, scope 2, and scope 3 emissions.

C.6.3.1 Emission scopes

Following the greenhouse gas emissions protocol (WRI & WBCSD, 2004; 2011) and from the perspective of the company in focus, scope 1 emissions are direct emissions from company-owned or company-controlled operations. This includes, for example, emissions from production processes or equipment (e.g., vehicles, furnaces, or boilers). scope 2 as well as scope 3 emissions are indirect emissions because they occur beyond the boundaries of the respective company. Scope 2 emissions stem from electricity, steam, or other sources of energy used by but produced outside of the company. If a company, for example, buys electricity from a utilities company, the greenhouse gases emitted in producing the electricity are counted as scope 2 emissions (e.g., the emission from burning coal for electricity production). For the utilities company itself, however, they are scope 1 emissions. The same applies if a company produces its own electricity in company-owned facilities. Scope 3 emissions, finally, are all other types of indirect emissions that occur upstream or downstream in the supply chain. They are a consequence of the operations of another company that is not owned or controlled by the company in focus. Examples are emissions from the production of purchased or the use of sold goods, emissions from business travel or employee commuting (if this does not take place in company-owned vehicles), emissions from leased assets, or upstream emissions from electricity purchases which occur, for example, when mining coal or as transmission losses. Figure 25 provides an overview of this classification with further categories and examples.

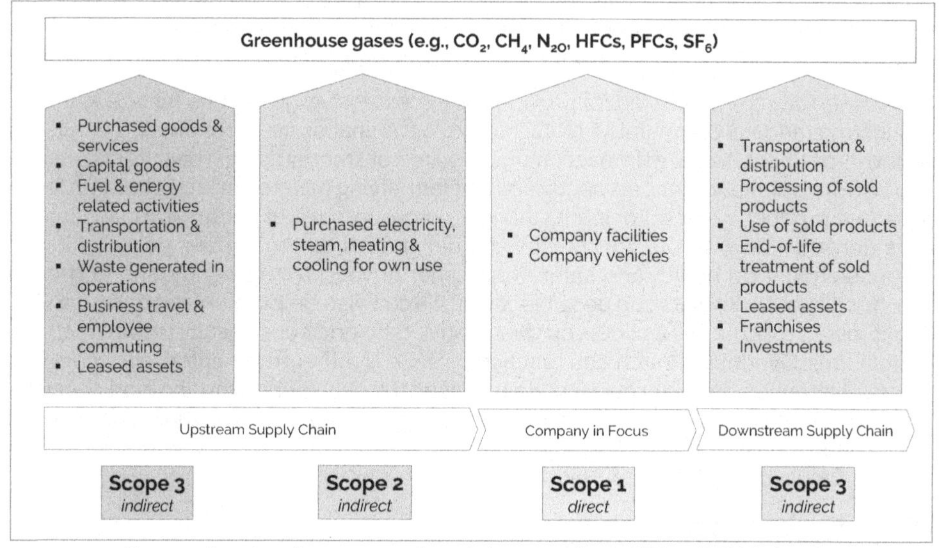

Figure 25: Overview of scope 1, 2, and 3 emissions according to WRI and WBCSD (2011)

Now consider the supply chain of electricity produced from natural gas as an example (adapted from WRI & WBCSD, 2011 with fictive numbers) as illustrated in Figure 26. In this process, electricity is produced from natural gas extracted by Company A that sells the gas to Company B where it is burned to generate energy. The energy is then distributed by Company C to Company D via an electricity grid. We assume that the extraction of gas sets free 10t of CO2e for the amount of gas necessary to produce 100 megawatt hours (MWh) of electricity. Burning the gas to generate electricity produces 100t of CO2e. Ten percent of the 100 MWh electricity are lost in the distribution system of Company C and the remaining 90 percent (or 90 MWh) reach the customer, Company D, that consumes the energy. In sum, 110t of CO2e incur overall for 90 MWh of used electricity. Now let us have a look at the carbon data of all four companies. For the gas mining Company A, the 10t of CO2e from the gas extraction are classified as scope 1 as they are direct emissions from company-owned or company-controlled operations. The 100t of CO2e from the burning of the gas in Company B are indirect scope 3 emissions from processing of sold products (i.e., the gas). From the perspective of Company B, the same 100t of CO2e from the burning of the gas are direct scope 1 emissions, because we have changed the perspective. Company B itself burns the gas so that the respective emissions directly occur in company-owned or company-controlled operations. Another 10t incur as scope

3 emissions from the extraction of gas in Company A as fuel- and energy-related activities. Company C does not have any direct scope 1 emissions from this process. For this company, the 10t of CO2e lost in the distribution system are in scope 2, because they are emissions from purchased energy. Furthermore, Company C has significant scope 3 emissions: 1t of CO2e from the extraction (10t overall x 10 percent for the generated electricity that is consumed/lost in Company C) and 99t of CO2e from the entire generation of electricity sold to Company D (110t overall for extraction and burning of gas x 90 percent of the generated electricity that is sold to Company D). At the customer, Company D, there are again no scope 1 emission but 90t of CO2e emissions in scope 2 from the generation of the purchased energy. Furthermore, Company D has to account for 20t of CO2e emissions in scope 3 as fuel- and energy-related activities: 11t from the electricity lost in the system (110t overall for extraction and burning of gas x 10 percent of lost electricity) and 9t from extraction of the gas necessary for the electricity bought by Company D (10t overall x 90 percent for the generated electricity that is consumed by Company D). All scope 1, 2, and 3 emissions taken together for each individual company (A, B, C, and D) sum up to the 110t of CO2e emissions which occur in the entire system so that the total number per company always indicates the total emissions without neglecting or double counting certain parts. This total number would still sum up to 110t of CO2e even if the supply chain in our example would be entirely different, for example, a completely integrated company which extracts, produces, and then distributes the electricity for consumption in its own factories.

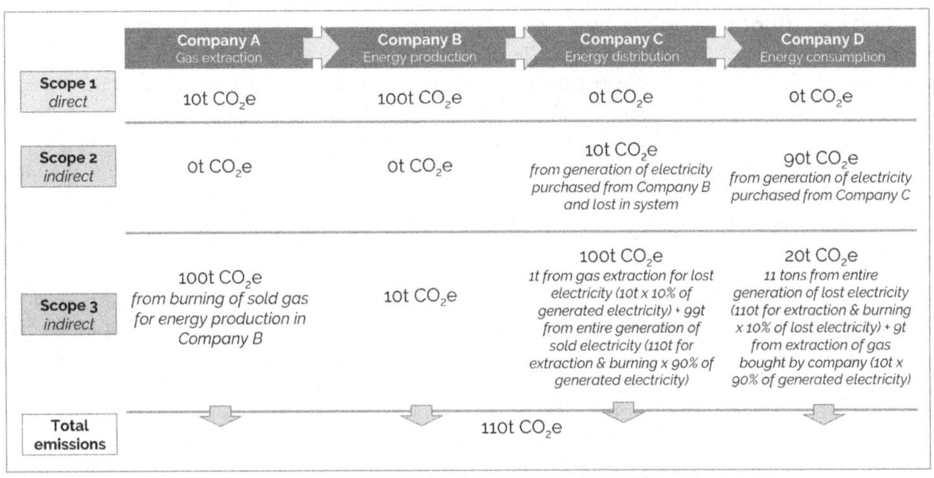

Figure 26: Example adapted from WRI and WBCSD (2011)

The example also illustrates why the distinction in the different scopes is relevant from a sustainability management perspective as it points to the important levers for all companies to reduce their greenhouse gas emissions. Company A could, for example, improve its processes so that less emissions occur during the extraction of the gas. However, since the scope 1 emissions of Company A are relatively small compared to the entire emissions, the entire product and business model of Company A might be subject to a critical analysis. This situation is typical for the entire fossil fuel industry in which only 100 companies worldwide are responsible for the mining of all fossil fuels that account for 71 percent of the entire greenhouse gas emission worldwide from 1988 until 2017 (Griffin, 2017). Interestingly, the scope 1 emissions of all these companies are relatively small compared to the overall emission generated by those fossil fuels, because the mining companies do not burn the fuels themselves but sell them to downstream supply chain customers. Only if no fossil fuels would be extracted and burned at all, could the scope 3 emissions of Company A be cut more drastically. For Company B, the bulk of emissions is in scope

1, which in this case directly indicated that the core business of this company is not climate friendly. If the company would be able to generate energy from renewable sources, the direct carbon footprint in scope 1 would be significantly better. Company C can also gain some relevant insights. Its emissions are largely in scope 3, indicating that its wider business activities—here the distribution of energy from gas—offer room for reducing greenhouse gas emissions. For Company D, finally, there is the supposedly easy option of switching to renewable energies, and this would immediately and drastically cut the scope 2 emissions of the company.

The example also illustrates some of the challenges in carbon accounting. For any given company, scope 1 emissions are relatively easy to measure. Of course, there have to be adequate accounting information systems collecting and assessing the relevant data (e.g., on the amount and types of energy consumed) to be able to calculate emission from such data. Setting up and maintaining such systems is often in itself a substantial task but it can usually be done largely independent of any other actors (apart, e.g., from companies which supply relevant software products or consultancy services). Data on scope 2 emissions are also often relatively easy to obtain as they mainly cover greenhouse gas emissions from energy production, which is a well-researched field. Data on scope 3 emissions, however, require extensive and often highly complex data from actors up- or downstream in the supply chain, for example, on materials or processes. Obtaining such data is often difficult or prone to uncertainties or inaccuracies. Nevertheless, especially information on scope 3 emissions are often very informative. Take the example of an investment company. Such a company has no own production facilities, and the energy consumption for office buildings and other company-owned assets is often relatively small. Accordingly, scope 1 and 2 emissions are likely to be small compared to a manufacturing company. If such a company wants to have a positive impact in the battle against climate change, it can of course buy renewable energy or encourage its employees to switch off the lights and computers when going to lunch. If the same company, however, finances the extraction of fossil fuels or new coal power plants, its scope 3 emissions will be very high and point to a much more important lever for reducing greenhouse gas emissions.

Beyond this general classification into different scopes of emissions, companies usually face a number of questions and challenges in carbon accounting and—eventually—carbon reporting, such as how to deal with complex company structures and shared ownership, how do deal with outsourced or leased operations and with acquisitions and divestments, how to identify emission sources, or what activities are necessary for data collection. Several standards and guidelines provide guidance for organizations to answer such questions. One of the most well-known documents in this regard is the greenhouse gas protocol (WRI & WBCSD, 2004) that provides requirements and guidance for preparing greenhouse gas emissions inventories on the corporate level. It outlines standardized approaches and principles to arrive at a true and fair view of carbon accounting. Other widespread standards with similar aims are, for example, ISO 14064-1 that provides guidance at the organization level for quantification and reporting of greenhouse gas emissions, the DEFRA guidance on measuring and reporting environmental impacts in the United Kingdom, or the IPCC methodology for greenhouse gas inventories.

In the end, however, the system of different scopes on which most carbon accounting activities are based is not fail-safe. Let us again use some illustrative examples. Assume that in year 1, a company emits 5 million tons of CO2e from an energy-intensive facility (e.g., a steel mill). Since the facility is company owned, the emissions are classified in scope 1. In the next year, the company outsources the facility into a joint venture with another company that also brings one of its own facilities into the new business. While the emissions of the respective facilities remain unchanged, they now count as scope 3 emissions because the steel mill in the joint venture does not count as a company-owned facility.

While the entire CO_2e balance remains unchanged, the picture for an uninformed outsider changes significantly, and most investors, for example, still largely consider scope 1 and scope 2 emissions in their evaluations. Or consider the example of a company that produces oral care products. For this company, calculations of greenhouse gas emissions can include the use phase of the products at the end consumer. The end consumer, for example, brushes her teeth using water and electricity. Depending on the underlying assumptions (e.g., energy sources, water temperature, electricity losses), this can lead to significant scope 3 emissions which can distort the picture of emissions at the respective company if the scope 3 emissions then dwarf the scope 1 and 2 emissions from regular business activities.

Data from carbon accounting can be used to inform decisions at various units of analysis. On a company level, it can inform strategic and tactical decisions in sustainability management as illustrated above and inform the decision makers and stakeholders within and beyond company boundaries. Furthermore, a specific element in carbon accounting are product carbon footprints that measure of the total amount of greenhouse gas emissions directly and indirectly accumulated over the life stages of a product (Gao et al., 2014; Kronborg Jensen, 2012). Product carbon footprints are thus a specific form of ELCA and can be used, for example, by product designers or supply chain managers to improve products, by marketers to inform customers, or potentially even by public authorities to regulate carbon emissions at the product level. Finally, a carbon footprint can even be calculated at the individual level based on lifestyle and consumption patterns of a person as part of the overall ecological footprint (see Chapter B.6.1).

Task C6-3

Take a look at the sustainability report of a utility company, a consumer goods company, and a company from the financial service industry and determine the scopes of greenhouse gas emissions that these companies report. Do you see any differences in what is reported by the companies? Also, compare the amounts of CO_2e of the different scopes reported and explain the differences with respect to the different industries the companies belong to.

C.6.3.2 From carbon accounting to carbon management and carbon offsetting

At this point it makes sense to broaden the view and think about the question of what to do with the information gathered and prepared through carbon accounting instruments. One area of application within a company are greenhouse gas reduction targets. To be able to set targets, relevant information needs to be available from carbon accounting. Greenhouse gas (or carbon) emissions reduction targets can be expressed either in relative or in absolute terms. Relative targets (also referred to as intensity targets) define a certain benchmark against which they measure their emissions. This can be, for example, net sales ("improve energy efficiency indexed to net sales by 30 percent"), production volumes or time ("reduce emissions by 25 percent for each ton of product output/minute of production"), or relative emissions per product ("reduce the energy consumption of our products by 30 percent"). Absolute targets directly express targets without any second measurement such as net sales or production volumes for absolute emissions ("reduce emissions by 1 million t of CO_2e") or measured in time ("reach zero emissions/become carbon neutral by 2035"). For any goal—absolute or relative—to be effective, it has to be specific, measurable, and with a clearly defined time horizon.

The Science Based Targets initiative (SBTi) provides extensive guidance on how to develop targets and a path to reduce company greenhouse gas emissions in line with the Paris Agreement goals. The initiative is a partnership between the CDP, the UN Global Compact, the WRI, and the WWF. According to the SBTi, targets "are considered 'science-based' if they are in line with what the latest climate science says is necessary to meet the goals of the Paris Agreement—to limit global warming to well-below 2°C above pre-industrial levels and pursue efforts to limit warming to 1.5°C" (SBTi, 2021a). The SBTi updates its criteria regularly based on advancements of scientific knowledge especially from climate science. To develop targets in accordance with the SBTI, companies have to choose a base year against which changes are being measured. The base year should be representative of the typical greenhouse gas emissions of the company in the past with sufficient data on scope 1, 2, and 3 emissions. The target year should cover between five and 15 years into the future. The company then needs to set the boundaries for measuring emissions based on the greenhouse gas protocol. Furthermore, it has to determine how to treat subsidiaries and different emissions especially from scope 3 depending, for example, on how significant these emissions are relative to the overall emissions from all scopes and on the industry to which the company belongs. The SBTi provides ranges for reduction goals based on the ambition of the company, that is, whether it wants to target the goal of limiting climate change well below 1.5° or 2°C.

Task C6-4

Do some Internet research and identify carbon emission targets by different companies. Do the companies set absolute or relative targets, or both? Are any of these approaches better, and if so: why and under which circumstances? Also compare carbon emission targets across different industries and among companies that belong to the same industry. What do you see, and what do you think?

Ultimately, such targets are a means toward the end of improving a company's emissions performance—or sustainability performance in general, of course, if the targets cover further aspects other than greenhouse gas emissions—as they allow measuring progress. The ways and instruments for improving sustainability performance are vast and usually depend on the respective industry, products, business model, and other company-related factors. We cover numerous options throughout this entire book by looking at different stakeholders and functional areas. Companies nowadays often announce plan to achieve net zero emissions or become climate neutral. Economic activities, however, inevitably involve a certain amount of greenhouse gas emissions. Thus, to achieve net zero emissions, companies either have to implement measures to remove greenhouse gases from the atmosphere and permanently store them (also referred to as neutralization) or they have to offset any remaining residual emissions through compensation. Respective carbon offsetting schemes and initiatives gather investments from companies or individuals to finance environmental projects. Such projects aim, for example, at promoting clean energy technologies in the Global South, planting trees to reduce CO_2, or buying carbon credits from emission trading schemes (see Chapter B.3.2.3). The underlying idea is that these investments balance out the emissions generated by individuals or companies by reducing greenhouse gas emission in other areas. This way, individuals or companies can offset their entire carbon footprint or single activities such as a flight. For example, a one-way trip in economy class from Delhi in India to San Francisco in the United States in a modern aircraft generates around 2.5t of CO_2e according to various carbon emissions calculators available on the Internet. In theory, offsetting the emission from this flight by investing in projects that reduce the same amount of emissions elsewhere would make this flight "carbon neutral." Because all individuals or businesses inevitably emit a certain amount of greenhouse gases, carbon offsetting can be a relevant tool to help reduce emissions.

However, carbon offsetting comes with various challenges and limitations. Interestingly, for example, the price for carbon offsetting can differ significantly when looking at different projects and providers. At the time of publishing this book in early 2022, the price to offset 2.5t of CO_2e for the above-mentioned flight from Delhi to San Francisco ranged from anywhere between USD 40 and 220 from various providers and for different projects or ways of offsetting. Sometimes, these different prices can be explained by the fact that there are all kinds of ways to reduce emissions with very different price tags. However, some projects are cheap simply because they do not deliver what they promise. Thus, if carbon offsetting schemes are supposed to truly contribute to the reduction of greenhouse gas emissions, they need to fulfill certain criteria outlined by Broekhoff et al. (2019):

- First, they need to adhere to the principle of additionality, that is, the greenhouse gas reducing activity (e.g., a planted tree, a new solar stove in the Global South, or the withdrawal from an emission permit from an emissions trading scheme) should not have happened without the offsetting.
- Second, projects should not overestimate their emission reduction potential.
- Third, results from offsetting projects should be long-term so that they reduce greenhouse gases not only temporarily. A classic example of nonpermanence would be trees that are planted to be harvested already in a few years. Initially, growing trees reduces CO_2. If they are then cut and, for example, burned, the CO_2 would be released into the atmosphere again.
- Fourth, claims to reduce greenhouse gas emissions must be exclusive to a specific reduction investment. This means that no more than one offset credit is issued for the same reduction and any double use of projects is avoided.
- Fifth and finally, offsetting projects should not significantly contribute to any other sustainability-related harms.

Unfortunately, many projects do not live up to all these criteria, which leads to severe criticism. Furthermore, carbon offsetting is sometimes criticized for offering greenwashing opportunities for polluters who do not want to engage in their own activities for greenhouse gas reductions or who do not want to change an entirely unsustainable business model (e.g., Hogson & Nauman, 2021). Due to these challenges and problems, carbon offsetting is usually regarded as a matter of last resort for those emission that cannot be reduced through actual reduction measures from the areas of eco-efficiency, eco-effectiveness, or sufficiency (see Chapter A.4). Similar to the waste hierarchy discussed in Chapter C.4.1, the first measure should thus be to reduce emissions before considering carbon offsetting. In its net-zero standard for companies, the SBTi consequently defined corporate net-zero as "reducing scope 1, 2, and 3 emissions to zero or to a residual level that is consistent with reaching net-zero emissions at the global or sector level in eligible 1.5°C-aligned pathways [before] neutralizing any residual emissions at the net-zero target year and any GHG emissions released into the atmosphere thereafter." (SBTi, 2021b, p. 8). According to this definition, compensation or offsetting cannot be used to reach net-zero targets. Instead, it can be a supplementary tool to help reducing emissions outside of a company's own value chain.

Task C6-5

Identify different providers for offsetting and compensation projects on the Internet. What do they do to offset greenhouse gas emissions? What information can you get from the different providers on the aforementioned five criteria for high-quality carbon offsetting schemes? Which one would you prefer for offsetting your own greenhouse gas emission and why?

KEY
TAKEAWAYS

- LCSA consists of ELCA, LCC, and SLCA that can be used to inform various aspects of sustainability management.
- ELCA is carried out in the four steps of defining goals and scope of the assessment, compiling a life cycle inventory, conducting a life cycle impact assessment, and performing a life cycle interpretation.
- LCC does not include a life cycle impact assessment; SLCA is less standardized than ELCA and often cannot rely as extensively as ELCA on quantitative data and scientifically proven facts.
- Scope 1 emissions are direct emissions while scopes 2 and 3 cover different types of indirect emissions; differentiation is relevant to identify levers for improvements and avoid double counting of emissions.
- Carbon emissions reduction targets can be expressed as relative targets and as absolute targets; the SBTi provides guidance on how to develop respective targets.
- Carbon offsetting can be used to balance out emissions by investing in environmental projects but they can be problematic if they do not meet certain quality criteria.

C.7 Sustainability management control

LEARNING GOALS

After reading this chapter you will be able to ...

- ... explain the relations between sustainability management control, sustainability accounting, and sustainability reporting.
- ... differentiate various types of codes of conduct and critically reflect on their usefulness and applicability.
- ... illustrate the content of the UN Global Compact and ISO 26000 as examples for codes of conduct.
- ... explain the general approach of management systems and management system standards.
- ... illustrate the content and procedures of ISO 14001, EMAS, and SA8000 as examples of management system standards.
- ... explain the sometimes subtle differences between—and potential hybrid forms of—codes of conduct, management systems, and management system standards.
- ... critically reflect on audits and certification processes.
- ... explain different types of sustainability balanced scorecards.
- ... outline the development of a sustainability balanced scorecard.

Introduction to Chapter C.7: Screencast
Watch an introduction to the chapter here:

As illustrated earlier, sustainability management control covers the use of management tools to influence sustainability-related organizational behavior. This chapter illustrates various management tools for sustainability, namely codes of conduct, management systems, and the sustainability balanced scorecard. Note that while these tools are widespread and thus covered here in this book, there might be other sustainability management tools complementing or substituting these elements of sustainability management control. Before we jump into discussing the three mentioned tools, let us briefly outline the main differences and similarities of codes of conduct and management systems as two related elements of sustainability management.

In a nutshell, codes of conduct are about what (not) to do in organizational contexts. Thus, they more or less directly describe certain forms of behavior that are deemed appropriate or not. Management systems tackle a different aspect of sustainability in companies and provide guidelines of how to implement certain aspects of sustainability. They usually do not, however, set specific standards or performance goals. Finally, some management systems or codes of conduct exist as hybrids between the two approaches and combine elements of what (not) to do with guidelines on how to implement such behavior. Codes of conduct and management systems can be set up by different entities and actors. Companies themselves or industry associations, for example, can devise their own approach of what (not) to do and how to implement respective behavior. Codes of conduct or standards for management systems can also be created and monitored by governmental or multilateral bodies, NGOs, or technical organizations. We will discuss different example throughout the next two subchapters. Often, the question of who is the driving force behind a specific sustainability management tool already has some implications for the credibility and legitimacy of the respective tool. Furthermore, we can distinguish tools or initiatives according to their thematic focus (e.g., focusing on environmental or social issues), their sectoral focus (i.e., tools or standards for certain industries), and superordinate tools or initiatives (i.e., tools or standards which are widely applicable beyond certain industries and without a narrow focus on specific aspects of sustainability). Examples for all these categories are discussed in the next chapters and throughout this book.

Task C7-1

Throughout this book, we discuss various sustainability-related management tools, and there are many more standards, codes, labels, etc., available to choose from. Some examples are listed below. Without going into details of the nature and content of the examples below: Find out who stands behind the respective tool (i.e., who created and currently manages it) and whether their focus is thematic or sectoral or superordinate. You can refer to other parts of this book or, if the respective instrument is not explicitly mentioned, carry out some Internet searches.

Eco-Management and Audit Scheme (EMAS), Ethical Trading Initiative, Forest Stewardship Council (FSC), Global Sullivan Principles, ISO 14001, ISO 26000, Marine Stewardship Council (MSC), OECD Guidelines for Multinational Enterprises, SA8000, UN Global Compact

C.7.1 Codes of conduct

Codes of conduct (sometimes also referred to as code of ethics) are sets of commitments that define certain attitudes, behaviors, or actions with regard to certain issues or toward a range of stakeholders. While they do not necessarily have to cover sustainability-related topics, most codes of conduct do include certain environmental, social, ethical, or governance issues and are thus regularly discussed as an element of sustainability management.

C.7.1.1 Content and forms

As an element of soft law, that is, as a quasi-legal instrument without legally binding force, there are no regulations or any form of standardization of what could or should be included in a code of conduct. However, there are certain elements from the realm of sustainability management which are often found in many codes of conduct. The following range of topics is not exhaustive and of course not all codes of conduct include all these aspects. Some cover only a few isolated issues while others approach the topic of sustainability more holistically depending on the preferences of the issuer of the code of conduct. In Chapter B.5.1, we already introduced the three dimensions of ESG (environmental, social, and [corporate] governance), and we will refer to these in this chapter as well when illustrating the potential sustainability-related content of codes of conduct. Furthermore, a typical distinction can be made with regard to whether the content of a code of conduct regulates issues within or beyond a company's boundaries. For the environmental dimension of ESG, typical aspects that are often included in a code of conduct aiming at issues within a company's boundaries are, for example, energy management and climate protection, waste prevention and water management, regulating resource use and pollution emissions, or protecting biodiversity and preventing harm to animals. Beyond a company's boundaries, a code of conduct may try to influence environmental performance and behavior of partners along the value chain, foster product stewardship, and regulate investments, credits, and insurances for environmental issues, to name a few. For the social dimension within company boundaries, especially responsibilities toward own employees are part of many codes of conducts, for example, payment issues or work time models, training and education, employment rights, operational safety and health protection, or equal opportunities and gender diversity. Similar issues might also be relevant beyond company boundaries when looking at working conditions and human rights along the value chain or at issues of consumer protection. Interestingly, the governance dimension of ESG is especially prevalent in many codes of conduct especially with regard to the omnipresent compliance issues covering aspects of anti-corruption policies, political influence, the handling of taxes and subsidies, or regional responsibilities related to cultural issues.

Apart from the very heterogeneous content, there are also many different forms of codes of conduct. According to Bondy et al. (2008), codes of conduct can be categorized along several features as illustrated in the following. First, codes of conduct can be devised by companies (typically for themselves and their employees or for their suppliers), by industry associations (for their members), by inter-governmental actors (such as the UN Global Compact introduced below), through a multi stakeholder process (such as the ISO 26000 introduced below), or even for entire professions (such as the Hippocratic Oath for physicians).

Sustainability in business 35: Responsible Care as an industry code of conduct

Responsible Care is an initiative by the International Council of Chemical Associations—the most important association of the global chemical industry. At its core, the program commits companies to various sustainability-related goals and activities such as the continuous improvement of the environmental, health, safety and security knowledge and performance, the efficient use of resources, the minimization of waste, or an active stakeholder management. Almost all large companies in the global chemical industry have subscribed to its principles. Companies can sign the Responsible Care principles and by doing so they voluntarily make a commitment to uphold its principles. With these characteristics, Responsible Care is an example of an industry code of conduct. Notably, subscribing to such a code of conduct does not prevent companies from additionally having their own codes of conduct—which should then of course not contradict the guidelines expressed by Responsible Care.

Self-regulation programs such as Responsible Care, in which industry associations set codes that usually go beyond government regulations to control their collective action, are prevalent. While they can set agreed minimum standards and thus potentially create a level playing field among those committed to the code, critics argue that voluntary self-regulation in the form of such codes and initiatives often falls short of its goals. For Responsible Care, studies on the earlier phases of the program suggest that companies that subscribed to the code even raised their pollution intensity compared to companies that did not join the program. This indicates that effective industry self-regulation requires explicit sanctions and third-party verification complementing the code of conduct itself. Over time, Responsible Care was extended to include, for example, a management framework, self-assessment webtools, and performance indicators.

Sources: European Chemical Industry Council (2021); Gamper-Rabindran and Finger (2013); King and Lenox (2000)

Second, codes of conduct may differ with regard to the nature of their content. Some codes may be rather aspirational and sometimes even philosophical in describing what a company (or any other entity) wants to achieve (e.g., "We seek to create a work environment of mutual trust and respect, in which diversity and inclusion are valued."), they may be regulatory and prescribe certain rules of behavior (e.g., "Child labor is unacceptable in our company and supply chain. Any potential or confirmed case of child labor is immediately reported."), or they can contain both elements. A common distinction in this regard is between principle-based codes and rule-based codes. Principle-based codes are typically short lists of general statements that can cover a wide variety of issues. These statements usually do not target specific behaviors or actions but are instead meant to guide behavior more generally in a variety of contexts. Thus, they are rather flexible and relevant over longer periods of time because they express expectations as yardsticks instead of regulating behavior more precisely. Therefore, they also require individuals to think before acting to ensure their behavior is in line with the code. Rule-based codes are typically large lists of more specific statements and behavioral commitments as they tell individuals more precisely what they can or cannot do. Other than principle-based codes, these instructions provide a clear indication of expected behavior, which is also easier to measure. However, it is unlikely that, in a complex environment, every situation in every area of behavior can be influenced by exact rules. Consequently, there will be gaps in such codes. Furthermore, they must be constantly updated to address omissions and changing situations. Effective codes therefore often combine elements of principle- and rule-based codes of conduct.

Third, codes of conduct may have different target audiences, for example, in restricting or guiding company (or employee) behavior, in influencing other actors such as suppliers, or in being a model code of conduct which acts as an example for others. Fourth, they may be comprehensive or selective in the breadth of covered topics. Fifth, any code of conduct is generally voluntary and nobody can force an individual or company to adhere to a certain code. Nevertheless, a code can also have certain mandatory characteristics. An industry code of conduct can, for example, be mandatory for the members of a certain industry association. If a company is not willing to sign the respective association's code of conduct, it might not be allowed to join. Finally, codes of conduct are not static instruments. They can often be modified by their issuer at least on paper rather easily. Thus, many codes of conduct exist in their second, third, or even more recent edition.

C.7.1.2 Applicability and usefulness

In their overview article, Bondy et al. (2008) provide a summary of potential benefits and limitations of codes of conduct as an element of sustainability management. On the benefit side, they mention that codes of conduct are flexible instruments, which can be uniquely tailored to the given circumstances and needs while being relatively inexpensive to set up. If set up as industry or multistakeholder codes, they can potentially even provide a level playing field among competitors and might mitigate the need for governmental regulation or intervention. Furthermore, other than most company-own codes of conduct, however, they provide a more consistent and standardized picture of (minimum) expectations by internal and external stakeholders. A potential benefit of a company's own code of conduct is that already by virtue of creating the code, the company recognizes the issues expressed in the code as relevant, at least superficially. Having a code can create pressure to follow through on commitments by formalizing and publishing these commitments. Furthermore, if the respective code is truly meant as an instrument of sustainability management, the resulting changes are driven from within the company and thus likely to be more successful where there is an intention to implement.

On the limitations side, many codes of conduct lack accountability mechanisms in terms of monitoring and sanctions. While the setup, for example, of a company code of conduct can be easy, implementation and enforcement may be more extensive if a company is really serious about following through. Adopters of codes of conduct are thus often already leaders in sustainability whereas in other companies, codes of conduct might merely exist as a piece of paper without being applied in daily business. They might even be unknown to a majority of employees. If they do not include complaints procedures or whistleblower protection, codes of conduct are less likely to be taken seriously. With regard to their content, on the one hand, codes written by a company or also by an industry association often receive little input from outside groups. They might then be incomplete in the sense that they do not cover all aspects that are relevant to external stakeholders, especially if the company did not engage in external consultation when drafting the code. Multistakeholder codes, on the other hand, typically determine a bare minimum of acceptable commitments to stakeholders as they are usually derived in a process of bargaining, negotiating, and compromising between multiple actors who have to align their potentially diverging interests. If the respective actors who should be influenced by the codes do not see benefits of using the code, implementation is less likely.

In sum, we can note that codes of conduct themselves cannot change a company's or employee's behavior and the extent and density of a code of conduct is not necessarily connected to its effectiveness and efficiency. Instead, the success or failure of a code depends on the company's desire, ability, and available resources to implement the commitments and rules laid out in the code. Furthermore, principles such as respect, fairness, or sustainability are always ambiguous, and they have to be translated into everyday behavior. Thus, codes of conduct have to be backed by further aspects such as training and monitoring, and they have to be implemented in informal elements such as corporate culture. If, however, formal structures like incentive instruments counteract the words of the code, they will likely be ineffective and ignored. Bondy et al. (2008) therefore posit that the effectiveness of a code lies in its implementation and administration. While a good code of conduct, with a clear language, strong commitments, and a base philosophy similar to the one of the adopting company, is more likely to produce effective initiatives, it still cannot determine if a company will successfully engage in sustainability management. The authors argue that the participation of organization members in the development (or revision) of a code of conduct can encourage commitment. Furthermore, a follow-through in terms of a detection of violations, discipline of employees found in breach, and consistency between the policy and action can facilitate successful implementation. Finally, there will likely always be new issues and areas that have not been regulated in a code of conduct or, in case of principle-based codes, the respective expectations have to be translated into behavior in specific situations. Thus, promotion of active and critical engagement with problematic situations might often be more important than "blind" compliance.

Sustainability in business 36: Why codes of conduct failed at Enron

Before going bankrupt, Enron was a large energy conglomerate in the United States with nearly 30,000 employees, revenues exceeding USD 100 billion, annual profits exceeding USD 1 billion, and a market capitalization of about USD 65 billion. The company had investment grade ratings (i.e., with a relatively low risk of default) and it had been named as one of the "100 Best Companies to Work for in America", as one of America's "Most Innovative Companies," and its board of directors made it into the "Top Five Corporate Boards" list. However, it was also a massive scam because the success of the company was based on extensive balance forgery. In 2002, Enron became the largest business failure at that time. The entire market value was destroyed, employee pensions of about USD 2 billion were lost, and several managers were eventually sentenced to fines and up to 24 years of prison. And all that despite the fact that Enron was considered a good corporate citizen who donated large amounts of money to good causes and despite the fact that there was a seemingly decent system of checks and balances in place. The company had a compliance officer and a hotline to report misbehavior and: a code of ethics! In its final version this code was 64 pages long—you can still find copies of it on the Internet. Guidelines and statements in this company code of conduct determined, for example:

"It is very important that you understand the scope of those policies and learn the details of every one that relates to your job."

"... highest ethical standards ..."

"Moral as well as legal obligations will be fulfilled openly, promptly, and ... will reflect pride on the Company."

"Employees will ... not use information for their personal benefit."

"Relations with ... customers, stockholders, governments, employees, suppliers, press, and bankers will be conducted in honesty, candor, and fairness."

In the case of Enron, however, these were all empty phrases and the true incentives counteracted the words in the code. At Enron, the clear focus was on the share price and on short-term profits. Stock tickers were visible in the lobby, in the elevators, on computers, and so on. There was a high amount of equity options for many employees and in the year 2000 alone, the top 200 managers earned USD 1.4 billion. Risk affinity was promoted and the ruthless top management was regarded the prototype of a desirable employee. All these incentives worked against the code of conduct while external and internal control mechanisms were insufficient or had no effect.

Source: McLean and Elkind (2003); R. R. Sims and Brinkmann (2003)

Task C7-2

Do companies need their own code of conduct? What kind of code is most useful under which circumstances? Under which circumstances could a company think of using/signing an overarching code of conduct (or similar initiatives)?

C.7.1.3 The UN Global Compact and ISO 26000

In 1999, the UN secretary general at that time, Kofi Annan, proposed at the World Economic Forum in Davos that "you, the business leaders gathered in Davos, and we, the United Nations, initiate a global compact of shared values and principles, which will give a human face to the global market" (UN Secretary General, 1999). The idea of shared principles and values already hints at core elements of a code of conduct, and in 2000, the UN Global Compact was launched as a voluntary multistakeholder initiative that enlists corporations in support of 10 universal principles. It does not regulate corporate behavior but provides basic ideas of what is regarded as universally valid values. These ideas are codified in 10 general principles as the core of the UN Global Compact (https://www.unglobalcompact.org/what-is-gc/mission/principles):

Human Rights

1. Businesses should support and respect the protection of internationally proclaimed human rights; and
2. make sure that they are not complicit in human rights abuses.

Labor

3. Businesses should uphold the freedom of association and the effective recognition of the right to collective bargaining;
4. the elimination of all forms of forced and compulsory labor;
5. the effective abolition of child labor; and
6. the elimination of discrimination in respect of employment and occupation.

Environment

7. Businesses should support a precautionary approach to environmental challenges;
8. undertake initiatives to promote greater environmental responsibility; and
9. encourage the development and diffusion of environmentally friendly technologies.

Anti-Corruption

10. Business should work against corruption in all its forms, including extortion and bribery.

Rasche (2013) provides an overview of viewpoints on the UN Global Compact. Critics argue that these principles are rather vaguely formulated, lack clarity, and provide just a minimum standard, which we discussed above as well as a potential drawback for multistakeholder codes of conduct. Furthermore, it is argued that there might be a free rider problem as it is comparably easy to join the UN Global Compact while there is a potential lack of monitoring, sanctions, and enforceable rules. Proponents, however, argue that the principles are rather meant as a yardstick for exchange and not meant as a benchmark. Furthermore, they allow addressing a broad target group of small and large companies from any industry or region of the world while the focus beyond the principles is on learning and continuous improvements.

In 2020, more than 10,000 business participants signed the UN Global Compact (UN Global Compact, DNV GL, 2020). To improve sustainability management, the UN Global Compact is more than just the codes laid out in the 10 principles (e.g., Rasche, 2013). It provides a variety of engagement mechanisms such as working groups and local networks operating in almost 100 countries around the world to initiate dialogue with other stakeholders and facilitate learning. The idea is to take global solutions and best practices downstream for replication and push innovative local solutions upstream for dissemination. Through such elements, it aims at continuous improvement processes regarding social and environmental performance. Against this background, companies also have to report on their progress regularly with regard to the 10 principles or they are dispelled from the initiative. The UN Global Compact offers several forms of disclosure to accommodate different levels of engagement, which makes it easier for smaller companies and for those who started with their activities more recently. However, in an earlier publication, the UN Global Compact itself noted that often, "CEOs and board members are making meaningful commitments to sustainability progress at high percentages. From there, there's a drop-off – sometimes fairly steep – in the number of companies that are following through with actions to implement, measure and communicate sustainability" (UN Global Compact, 2013, p. 12). This again shows that merely having or subscribing to a code of conduct does not automatically induce change to the positive. In the same study, however, the UN Global Compact found that the companies that were committed longer to the UN Global Compact took more action than those that joined rather recently. These results were later corroborated by Schembera (2018), who also showed that strong local networks positively affect the relationship between the duration of membership and the level of implementation of the principles.

Task C7-3

How could the rules of the UN Global Compact be changed so that critics would be satisfied? Do you see any drawbacks of such changes?

Another interesting example of a code of conduct is the international guideline ISO 26000. In contrast to the UN Global Compact, the ISO 26000 guideline offers no opportunities for participation or interaction. Instead, it is an extensive document that outlines in detail the social responsibilities of organizations. It is supposed to be suitable for any kind of private, public, and nonprofit organizations worldwide. In its core, ISO 26000 "provides guidance on the underlying principles of social responsibility, recognizing social responsibility and engaging stakeholders, [as well as] the core subjects and issues pertaining to social responsibility" (ISO, 2010a, p. vi). ISO 26000 can be regarded as prototypical multistakeholder code of conduct. It was developed in a lengthy process over roughly nine years involving almost 500 experts from more than 80 countries and from various stakeholder groups (R. Hahn & Weidtmann, 2016). The outcome of this process was a document of approximately 100 pages, which already indicates that it is an entirely different code of conduct compared, for example, to the UN Global Compact with its brief 10 principles.

ISO 26000 begins with some brief outlines of the scope of the standard (i.e., for which types of organizations it is useful as outlined above), an overview of core terms and definitions, the historic development and main characteristics of social responsibility and sustainable development, as well as seven general principles of social responsibility (see overview of the entire guideline in Figure 27). These principles include accountability, transparency, ethical behavior, respect for stakeholder interests, respect for the rule of law, respect for international norms of behavior, and respect for human rights. For the latter, for example, ISO 26000 states that human rights should be respected and promoted, and organizations should take steps to protect human rights when they are not. Furthermore, organizations are called to respect international norms of behavior in situations where the law does not provide for adequate protection of human rights. Apparently, these general principles of social responsibility are a core aspect of ISO 26000 as a code of conduct. However, the standard becomes more explicit as it also introduces six core subjects of social responsibility: human rights, labor practices, the environment, fair operating practices, consumer issues, and community involvement and development. These core subjects are laid out on about 50 pages in the document, which illustrates the depth of content that ISO 26000 provides to potential users. In the respective chapter, the standard provides deeper guidance, concrete ideas and recommendations of possible actions, and best practice examples and cases. For the core subject of human rights, for example, it describes concrete actions and expectations on how to avoid complicity, on resolving grievances, on discrimination and vulnerable groups, on civil and political rights, and on many more issues.

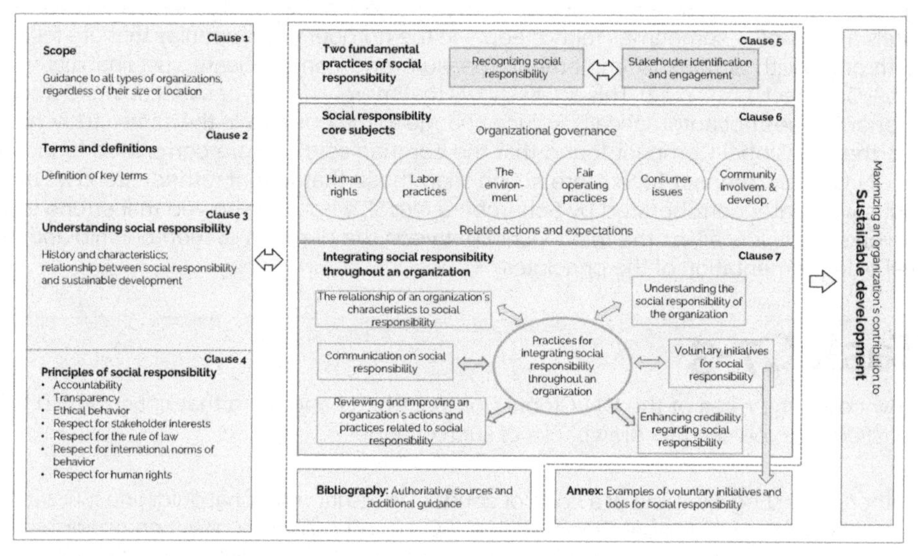

Figure 27: Schematic overview of ISO 26000 according to ISO (2010b), reproduced with permission

Task C7-4

How would you characterize the UN Global Compact, ISO 26000, and the Enron code of conduct according to the following dimensions (where possible, conduct some Internet research if necessary): issuer of the code, nature of the content (principle-based codes and rule-based codes), comprehensiveness of the content, target audience, degree of voluntariness (and for whom)?

Other than for the UN Global Compact, it is not possible to evaluate how many companies or other organizations use the principles and guidelines of ISO 26000 because companies cannot subscribe to or join the standard. Whether or not ISO 26000 is successful in reaching its goal of providing guidance on the social responsibility of organizations is thus difficult to judge. In fact, the standard itself clearly states that it "is not a management system standard. It is not intended or appropriate for certification purposes or regulatory or contractual use. Any offer to certify, or claims to be certified, to ISO 26000 would be a misrepresentation of the intent and purpose of the International Standard" (ISO, 2010a, p. vi). This statement and its implicit differentiation between codes of conduct and management system standards brings us directly to the topic of the next section: management systems for sustainability (where we will also briefly return to ISO 26000 in Chapter C.7.2.2).

C.7.2 Management systems for sustainability

Management systems provide procedures of how to implement certain aspects of management (e.g., environmental management, quality management, etc.) into the strategy and daily operations of an organization. They coordinate and systemize organizational activities by using defined and documented control and feedback mechanisms. Often, the procedures and details of respective management systems are outlined in certain management system standards, that is, standards that illustrate how management systems should be set up. These standards are usually certifiable, that is, organizations can engage auditors who document the organizations compliance with a certain standard and then issue a certificate to document this compliance. However, companies can also set up management systems without relying on external audits and certifications, for example, if they do not want to explicitly document their compliance with certain standards for other actors to see. Management systems and management system standards are not restricted to sustainability issues and, in fact, classic examples stem from the area of quality management. However, management systems are widespread in sustainability management as illustrated in this section.

C.7.2.1 Introduction into management system (standards)

In sustainability management, management systems typically cover ecological or social aspects of management or they combine them in integrated systems. The general idea of such systems is to establish a process for the control and continuous improvement of products, processes, or entire organizations (see R. Hahn, 2012). Such processes are also known as the plan-do-check-act cycle as illustrated in Figure 28.

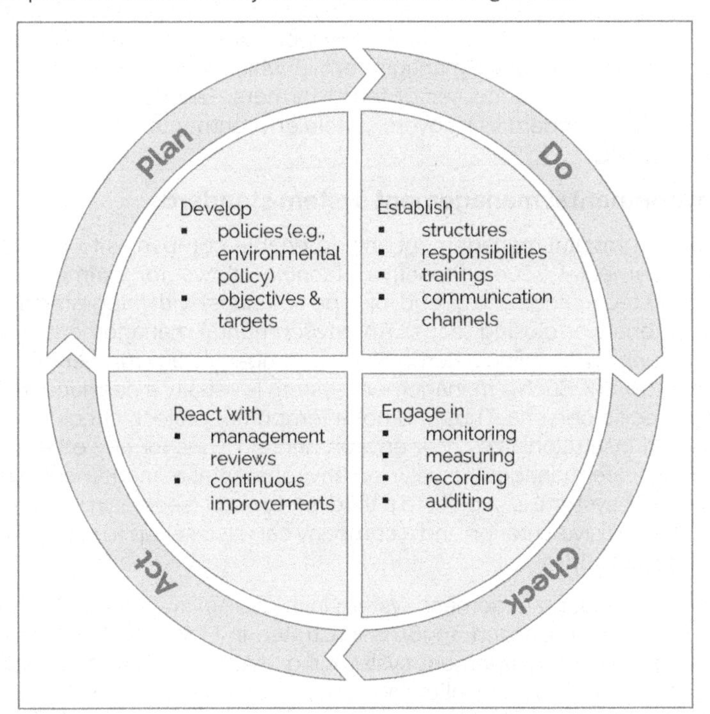

Figure 28: Generic outline of a plan-do-check-act cycle

In contrast to input or output standards, they can help to standardize complex issues such as a comprehensive and organization-wide quality management, environmental management, or social responsibility. Input or output standards provide specific instructions on the aspects that are to be standardized, for example, product specifications, emission limits, or customer satisfaction goals. Such input or output standards, however, can only be used to verify an existing status ex post and they can be used only for very specific issues. Standards that aim at codifying more extensive topics, such as general approaches for environmental or social management, have to be on an abstract level, because concrete detailed instructions on certain input or output parameters would not be generally applicable for different companies in different situations. Therefore, management systems standards are used to develop policies in organizations on certain topics and subsequently to put these policies into practice via targets using an organizational structure, systematic processes and associated resources, measurement and evaluation methodology, and a review process—or in other words: a plan-do-check-act cycle. In sum, management systems (standards) allow the introduction of even complex and possibly also highly context-dependent issues into (standardized) management processes.

The most widely used management system standard is ISO 9001 for quality management systems. The first management systems in the area of sustainability management were environmental management systems and widespread standards are, for example, ISO 14001 or the European EMAS (Eco-Management and Audit Scheme). More recently, dedicated standards for special topics such as energy management (ISO 50001) have also emerged. In the social dimension of sustainability, respective standards are usually less widespread than environmental management system standards but some well-known examples are SA8000 for social accountability, ISO 45001 for occupational health and safety, or AA1000 for stakeholder engagement. All these mentioned standards are industry independent, that is, they can be used irrespective of the industry a company is acting in. Other standards, such as those published by the Forest Stewardship Council (FSC), are industry specific. The FSC aims at promoting responsible forest management. It includes a certification program for forest management in which independent auditors evaluate the planning and practice processes of forest farmers. The FSC can be regarded as a holistic sustainability standard as it covers certain environmental aspects as well as social issues of sustainability.

C.7.2.2 Environmental management system standards

Systematic environmental management should enable companies to proactively tackle corporate environmental issues. Proactive planning allows, for example, to substitute expensive added technologies (e.g., end-of-pipe solutions) with integrated solutions (e.g., substituting materials or closing loops). An environmental management system should support such planning. It defines elements of a company's environmental management and how it should work. Such a management system is usually a permanent element and not bound to specific persons. Thus, it is not a temporary project, check, or singular program but instead institutionalizes how environmental issues (or any other relevant area as outlined above) are managed. Usually, an environmental management system (or any other management system) is subject to a third-party audit (see again Chapter C.3.2). This, however, is not a decisive criterion and a company can also set up a management system without any external audits.

A typical environmental management system includes several elements that mirror the plan-do-check-act cycle (Janzen, 1996) as illustrated in Figure 29. Similar elements can be found in almost any management system (e.g., social management system, quality management system) so that the following aspects can be applied to other management systems as well. Starting point is usually an overarching system of goals for the respective organization. For an environmental management system this means that the company should have a general idea of what it wants to achieve with regard to the environment. These goals are usually framed rather long-term and present global visions such as "become carbon neutral until year X" or "protect biodiversity." These goals are then translated into specific and measurable objectives (e.g., "reduce absolute carbon emissions from production processes by 20% in two years) and accompanied by policies (i.e., general sets of rules or guidelines) and programs (i.e., concrete steps to execute policies). These objectives are pursued by means of integrating environmental management into the company's daily business. To achieve this, environmental management has to be codified in the organization, that is, there should be an environmentally oriented operational and organizational structure. This structure defines, for example, the allocation of responsibilities, resources, or tasks. The human resource management then has to support this structure by means of providing guidance for environmental awareness or by offering training programs and so on. Furthermore, a planning and controlling system needs to be in place, which allows steering the company across departments and functions and avoid silo mentality. The entire action is supported by an environmental accounting system which provides support to environmental information systems in gathering and assessing environmental impacts and performance. Furthermore, the system also covers environmental reporting—at least to company internal stakeholders—to allow measuring the achievement of targets and enable adaptations where necessary. If desired (or mandated by a certain environmental management system standard or general laws and regulations), the reporting can also be extended to external stakeholders.

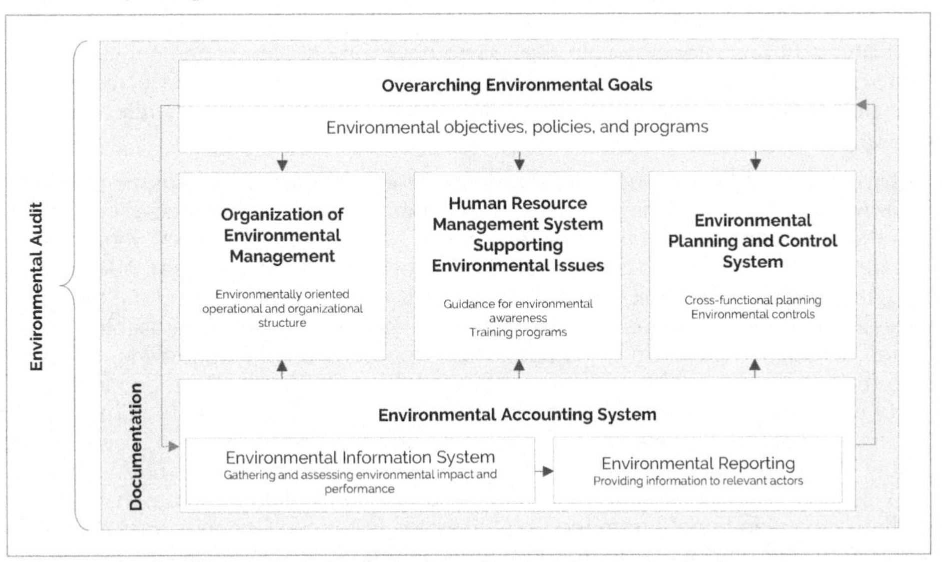

Figure 29: Typical elements of an environmental management system

The goals (and subsequently the objectives, policies, and programs) of the management system guide the activities of the company and should be monitored in the accounting systems. The information from these systems is used to guide management activities and can be used to adjust the goals, for example, when certain targets have been met. All elements and procedures mentioned so far should be well documented in the company so that they are independent of any single person (who might leave the company at any point of time) and thus become an integral part of the company's management approach. If the company decides to have its environmental management system externally audited (e.g., to signal compliance with an environmental management system standard to customers or other actors), an auditor scrutinizes the existing structures, systems, and processes of the environmental management system.

Implementing and maintaining such a system obviously requires certain resources and causes costs and investments. Setting up an environmental information system might require, for example, investments in specialized tools or software, devising training programs requires the input of specialists, and so on. Apart from such initial investments, which can differ significantly depending on the organizational background (e.g., previous activities and existing measures or planned extent of the management system), such systems also produce ongoing costs. These can be divided into fixed costs which are largely unrelated to the company size (e.g., IT cost or registration fees with standard setting institutions), internal costs to implement, administer, and potentially report on the management system (e.g., internal audits or employee working hours to collect data), and external costs which are incurred by employing external experts to support the implementation of a management system (e.g., for employee training or consulting services).

However, environmental management systems are also connected with various benefits for the implementing organization as summarized by Weiss et al. (2017). An improved environmental performance can directly lead to cost reductions, for example, through a more efficient use of resources. Furthermore, indirect costs might be avoided through risk minimization as an environmental management system allows the assessment of operational procedures and legal compliance. Sometimes, authorities or insurance companies provide advantages to organizations with certified environmental management systems such as reductions in inspections, taxes, or insurance premiums. Beyond cost reductions, improved relations to internal stakeholders can lead to improved employee morale or stronger awareness of teams while improved external stakeholder relations can enhance credibility and transparency. Finally, having an environmental management system can lead to competitive advantages if it results in improved market access and increased market share, for example, when customers value and reward the awarded certifications (see again Chapter C.3.2).

The two most well-known auditable standards for environmental management systems are EMAS and ISO 14001. The European EMAS standard was first introduced in 1993 and since then has been subject to larger revisions in 2001 and 2009. The first version of the ISO 14001 standard was published in 1996, with revisions in 2004 and 2015. Beyond ISO 14001, there is an entire family of related standards under the umbrella of the ISO 14000 series of standards. ISO 14001 itself describes the core elements of a certifiable environmental management system while additional supporting standards provide, for example, further guidelines on implementation (ISO 14004 and ISO 14005), on ecodesign (ISO 14006), or on environmental cost accounting (ISO 14052 and ISO 14053). Over time, the two standards improved their applicability for small- and medium sized enterprises. In 2021, roughly 4,000 firms with more than 10,000 facilities were registered with EMAS while ISO 14001 is much more widespread with almost 350,000 certificates and more than 550,000 facilities (according to data from the EMAS register, European Commission, n.d., and the ISO survey, ISO, n.d.). Both standards, EMAS and ISO 14001, are fairly similar and compatible with each other as they both describe how environmental management systems (as illustrated above) should be designed and implemented. They both describe a normed model of an environmental management system and aim at continuous improvement of corporate environmental performance. As both are pure management system standards, however, performance improvement is merely an underlying aim and thus not subject to performance audits or, in other words, companies that implement environmental management system standards do not have to prove performance improvements. The environmental management systems implemented according to these standards are nevertheless subject to third-party verification, and the logos of the standards can be used by the respective companies to inform stakeholders of their compliance with the standards. The main difference between ISO 14001 and EMAS is that the latter mandates increased transparency with the public in the form of a regular environmental statement. Furthermore, EMAS facilitates the assessment of environmental impacts and emphasizes the continuous improvement of environmental performance by means of core indicators from six areas of environmental performance, namely energy efficiency, material efficiency, water, waste, biodiversity, and emissions. Other than EMAS and ISO 14001, there are various specific management system standards in the ecological domain such as for energy management (ISO 50001) or for water efficiency management (ISO 46001).

With this knowledge on management systems and management system standards in mind, it makes sense to briefly return to ISO 26000. Organizations using ISO 26000 cannot document their compliance with the standard to outsiders as the standard is not suitable as a basis for external certification. Thus, it is not a management system standard as these standards are always certifiable. A company own management system, however, does not necessarily have to follow a management system standard and, thus, it does not have to be externally audited. Instead, companies can also set up management systems without relying on external audits and certifications, for example, if they do not want to explicitly demonstrate their compliance with certain standards to other actors. Thus, the code of conduct outlined in ISO 26000 could potentially be the basis of a company own management system for social responsibility, despite the fact that ISO 26000 itself is not a management system standard. In this case, a company would set up its own documented control and feedback mechanisms to implement the principles of ISO 26000. However, because ISO 26000 only briefly sketches how a management system for social responsibility can be implemented, it does not provide adequate guidance in this regard (see again Figure 29). Interestingly, some national standards have been developed based on ISO 26000, which provide further guidance on respective management systems and are certifiable, for example, ONR 192500 in Austria, INTE 35-01-01 in Costa Rica, CSN 01 0391 in the Czech Republic, or DS 49001 in Denmark. Apparently, the differences between the various forms of standards, codes, and systems are sometimes rather subtle. Nevertheless, such subtle differences can be relevant in practice if, for example, a company not only wants to use a management system to improve its own operations but also signal compliance to different stakeholders by means of a certificate.

Sustainability in research 11: King, Lenox, and Terlaak's 2005 article on ISO 14001 certifications

In their 2005 article, published in the Academy of Management Journal, Andrew A. King, Michael J. Lenox, and Ann Terlaak explored the use of environmental management systems and respective ISO 14001 certifications to reduce information asymmetries. They analyzed data from a sample of 7,899 manufacturing firms in the United States, with 46,052 observations from the years 1995 to 2001.

The results suggest that companies with physically distant buyers (i.e., companies that sell their B2B goods to customers far away) or foreign buyers increasingly rely on ISO 14001 certifications. The authors argue that the opportunities for using ISO 14001 as a tool to signal environmental competencies are larger when there is a physical or cultural distance between seller and buyer, because with increasing distance there is reduced information transfer and, thus, transaction costs increase. Against this background, an ISO 14001 certificate can be an effective signal to reduce information asymmetries. Interestingly, also companies that are vertically integrated and have long-term relationships with their buyers more often use respective certificates. Here, the authors argue that the risk of supplier moral hazard increases with ongoing relationships, which raises the need for the buyer to monitor the supplier's environmental performance.

With regard to performance effects of environmental management systems and their certification, the study finds, perhaps not surprisingly, that organizations with an ISO 14001 certification more likely have a functioning environmental management system. Furthermore, the authors show that the adoption of an environmental management system has a positive effect on a company's environmental performance. However, the study also found that companies with an ISO 14001 certificate tended to have lower environmental performance than their peers in their industry. The authors conclude that a certificate is a good signal for an otherwise difficult to observe attribute of an organization or, in other words, an ISO 14001 certificate is a reliable signal for the existence of an environmental management system. Furthermore, while having an environmental management system is associated with performance improvements, the actual certification process may then rather be a symbolic act.

Source: King et al. (2005)

C.7.2.3 Social (and integrated) management system standards

A well-known standard from the social domain of sustainability is SA8000, a voluntary standard for production facilities. SA8000 aims at promoting and enforcing universal labor standards in a world where national labor laws are often weak or not sufficiently enforced. Initiated in 1997 by the independent not-for-profit organization Social Accountability International, this internationally applicable and auditable standard is the oldest of its kind for social sustainability issues. As other standards, it has seen several development steps over time with the current version being published in 2014. SA8000 follows the structure of other well-known and certifiable standards such as ISO 9001 or ISO 14001. Similar to the ISO (for ISO 14001 and other ISO standards) or the European Commission (for EMAS), Social Accountability International and its sister organization, Social Accountability Accreditation Services, accredit and regularly assess qualified organizations as certification (or auditing) bodies. These certification bodies (e.g., the French Bureau Veritas, the German TÜV, or the British BSI Group) offer their services to organizations who would like to become certified according to SA8000. Companies can have their own facilities certified according to SA8000, and each facility needs its own certificate (i.e., it is not possible to have one SA8000 certificate for several facilities of one company). Furthermore, Social Accountability International offers various supplementary services through its corporate program such as guides, toolkits, trainings, webinars, and so on. Furthermore, it offers a so-called social fingerprint rating system, which is designed to help companies measure and improve social performance either in their own company or in their supply chain.

Interestingly, SA8000 is not "just" a management system standard. Instead, it combines a management system standard covering the typical plan-do-check-act elements as well as certification processes and audits with a code of conduct on social and especially labor issues. The normative basis of SA8000 are the UN Universal Declaration of Human Rights, the UN Convention on the Rights of the Child, and conventions of the International Labour Organization from which the standard derived the following fundamental requirements. These all have to be met by a facility that aims to be certified (Social Accountability International, 2014):

1. Child labor: No workers under the age of 15 (sometimes 14); remediation of any child found working.
2. Forced labor: No forced labor; no lodging of deposits or identity papers.
3. Health and safety: Safe and healthy work environment; steps to prevent injuries; regular health and safety worker training; system to detect threats to health and safety; access to bathrooms and potable water.
4. Freedom of association and right to collective bargaining: Right to form and join trade unions and bargain collectively; if law prohibits this, facilitate parallel means of association and bargaining.
5. Discrimination: No discrimination; no sexual harassment.
6. Discipline: No corporal punishment, mental or physical coercion, or verbal abuse.
7. Working hours: Comply with law but no more than 48 hours per week with at least one day off for every seven-day period; voluntary overtime paid at premium rate and not to exceed 12 hours per week on a regular basis; overtime may be mandatory if part of a collective bargaining agreement.
8. Remuneration: Wages must meet the legal and industry standards and be sufficient to meet the basic needs of workers and their families; no disciplinary deductions.

The standard and its supplementary guidance document explain these requirements in detail and thus clearly indicate what (not) to do in organizational contexts, like in a code of conduct. Furthermore, it describes how facilities must go beyond simple compliance to integrate the standard into management systems and practices by means of policies, procedures, communication, and management reviews just as in other management system standards.

Task C7-5

What do you think are the main areas of application for SA8000? For which types of companies is SA8000 suitable and for which types is it not? For example, in which geographical regions or industries does it make sense to have a facility certified? Does it make more sense to have a facility certified in Canada versus in Vietnam? And is it more helpful in the financial service industry than in the textile industry or vice versa? What other factors could be relevant (e.g., position in the supply chain or size of the facility) and why?

Figure 30 illustrates the typical process of implementing SA8000 in a facility (Rasche & Gilbert, 2012). Usually, a company that chooses to get certified first familiarizes itself with the requirements. Choosing a certification body early in the process can be helpful in this process as the respective organizations often also provide additional services on the way to an accreditation. An initial self-assessment of the facility can show gaps, which then need to be filled by implementing the SA8000 requirements. The company then usually begins with setting up the different elements of a management system and, if necessary, adjusts its processes to meet the standard requirements. At this point in time, the certification body can conduct a preaudit to uncover any blind spots or potential problems before the official audit. This official audit process should then ideally start once management is certain that the facility meets the minimum requirement. A certificate is granted for three years, and it includes follow-up visits in the form of surveillance audits during this time. In the monitoring period, the company itself should conduct internal reassessments to make sure that all requirements are still met and ideally engage in continuous improvements. In case a surveillance audit reveals deviations from the standard requirements standard requirements, the company has to engage in corrective actions to deal with any nonconformities. For critical nonconformities, for example, the company has only a brief time frame (e.g., one week) to provide a corrective action plan or an existing certificate will be withdrawn.

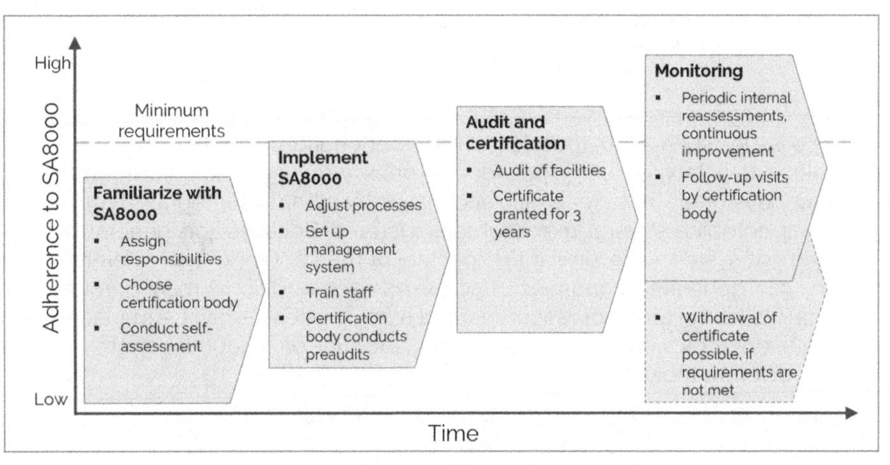

Figure 30: Typical process of SA8000 implementation

Despite its long history and publicity—SA8000 is well-known among sustainability experts worldwide—the standard is still not very widely used. In 2021, just about 5,000 facilities worldwide were certified according to data from Social Accountability Accreditation Services (2021). This might be due to various barriers of implementing SA8000 as outlined by Sartor et al. (2016) based on their extensive review of the literature. It might be difficult, for example, for some facilities to get a certificate in the first place because of a lack of internal expertise, difficulties to communicate standards to workers, or difficulties in aligning the requirements with local contingencies. Managing the certificate might be challenging because many customers have only poor knowledge of the standard. Furthermore, adhering to the SA8000 requirements could reduce the flexibility of the facility and hinder companies in quickly responding to changes in customers' demands. Overall, meeting the SA8000 requirements is often associated with relatively high costs, for example, when modifications of processes are necessary or for additional compensation for overtime or higher wages in general. This might be especially relevant in the Global South if there is a gap between the SA8000 requirements and local practices required by law. Finally, obtaining an SA8000 certificate itself induces consulting, certification, and auditing costs.

However, Sartor et al. (2016) also list various potential benefits of implementing SA8000. For the business function of purchasing, SA8000 provides benefits from a stronger collaboration of the certified company with its suppliers, which allows for a deeper knowledge and easier control of the supply chain. The improved communication along the supply chain can also reduce information asymmetries. For the production department, SA8000 can induce process improvements and also product quality improvements at the certified facilities as a result of the alignment of processes with the requirements of the standard. Several empirical studies analyzed by Sartor et al. (2016) indicate potential increases in productivity and decreases in work accidents. Improved working conditions can also improve employee satisfaction and subsequently reduce staff turnover and absenteeism. From a marketing perspective, having an SA8000 certificate can lead to image improvements, improved stakeholder relationships, and potentially also facilitate market expansion.

Task C7-6

Discuss the potential barriers and benefits of SA8000. When or why might they be relevant? How could the benefits be reaped and the barriers be overcome? How could other stakeholders facilitate the distribution of SA8000 and its requirements? When looking at the barriers and benefits, why do you think SA8000 is far less widely used than ISO 14001 and EMAS?

Other than SA8000, there are various other management system standards on social or governance issues such as AA1000 for stakeholder engagement, ISO 45001 for occupational health and safety, or ISO 37001 for anti-bribery management. Furthermore, companies nowadays often try to reap efficiency gains by means of integrated management systems that combine several management systems. Because the general processes of management systems are similar irrespective of the content of the different systems, companies can generate economies of scope as each additional management system usually requires less in terms of resources, and many processes can be managed collectively for different topics (e.g., setting up training facilities or accounting systems that can be used for different topics).

Sustainability in business 37: The S.E.E.D.S. management system at Vaillant

The German Vaillant group is a multinational company in the fields of heating, ventilation, and air conditioning technology. The company has an extensive management system approach for sustainability through its company own S.E.E.D.S. program—"Sustainability in Environment, Employees,

Development & Products and Society"—which integrates these focal areas. The program follows the classic plan-do-check-act approach, with its steps of setting sustainability strategies and deriving targets, conducting sustainability activities, measuring performance, and reviewing. Targets are defined in all focal areas. For environment, for example, CO2 emissions, energy consumption, or waste consumption; for development & products, for example, the share of efficient and renewable technologies of product sales; for employees, for example, the number of accidents at work; and for society, for example, the supplier adherence to the principles of the UN Global Compact. The company develops specific measures based on these targets and continuously monitors the results, and all sustainability activities are linked with the company's core business. The company-own integrated management system includes certifications for ISO 9001 (quality management), ISO 14001 (environmental management), and ISO 45001 (health and safety management) in all production and development sites. From an operational perspective, the company's sustainability management department is the nucleus of the sustainability activities. It reports directly to the CEO and is supported by "S.E.E.D.S ambassadors" in all functional departments. A health, safety, and environment forum with respective managers from the various manufacturing sites is in constant exchange with the sustainability department which, itself, consults the company's sustainability board that consists of representatives from the top management levels together with partners from sustainability management. As part of their reporting activities, Vaillant regularly publishes sustainability progress reports with facts on its objectives and performance.

Sources: Vaillant Group (2021a); Vaillant Group (2021b)

C.7.2.4 Audits and certification processes

Management system standards are subject to audit processes which certify compliance with the standard requirements. An audit in general can be described as a checklist-based control system. Audits and certifications are not restricted to management system standards but can cover other aspects of sustainability management (or management in general) as indicated throughout this book. An audit can come in different forms. A legal compliance audit assesses the compliance of an entity or its procedures or products with laws. A performance audit assesses the compliance of business, process, or product performance with certain threshold values or goals. A system audit assesses compliance with requirements for process instructions, codes of behavior, and guidelines. The latter type of audit is relevant for the domain of management system standards. In the process of auditing management system standards, a company often initially conducts internal first party audits to check its status quo and reveal potential gaps (see again Chapter C.3.2 on the differentiation between first-, second-, and third-party audits). The actual certification is then carried out by a specialized third party, that is, the certification body. The general task of a certification body is, thus, to confirm whether and to what extent certain outcomes (processes, performances, systems, etc.) are in accordance with the respective standard.

A prototypical audit process is conducted in various successive steps. First, the audit process has to be initiated. For a third-party audit, this means that the company who seeks certification has to identify a certification body. Both sides then prepare for the audit and develop an audit plan, answering questions such as what is being audited, by whom, and when. The preparation includes compiling documents for the review. In case of management system standards, this covers the different elements of the respective management system. The certification body then assigns the relevant tasks to its auditors and determines the audit sequence. The audit itself can then cover different aspects and be of varying depths (e.g., pure desk research, additional on-site visits, plausibility checks, interviews, etc.) depending on regulations and guidelines made by the standard setter. Based upon the findings, the auditor generates an audit conclusion, which is presented to the subject of the audit, that is, usually the company seeking certification. Furthermore, a formal audit report is distributed and, if applicable, a certificate is granted. The certification body might also give further counsel and advice on potential areas for improvement and might follow up on actions and corrective actions.

While such processes are often extensive, the quality of any audit depends on the general design of the respective audit system, and perfect safety cannot be guaranteed. Müller (2006) discusses determinants for the credibility and quality of audit processes. In general, higher audit quality is achieved when the certification body exhibits greater expertise, is highly independent, and conducts the audit with great intensity. Inexperienced certification bodies are less likely to uncover inconsistencies and the same applies to low intensity audits (e.g., merely scanning through some documents instead of thoroughly doing on-site checks). Furthermore, if a certification body is dependent on its counterpart, that is, on the company that is being audited, this can lead to insufficiently conducted audits. Such a dependence can occur, for example, if certification bodies and certified companies are in a direct and potentially long economic relationship. To avoid such problems, Müller (2006) describes various incentives for standard-compliant testing. One approach would be to increase the probability of detecting insufficient audits. The accreditation body, that is, the entity that grants certification bodies the right to conduct audits (e.g., Social Accountability Accreditation Services for SA8000 as described above) could conduct unannounced inspections at the certification bodies or shorten its inspection intervals. Furthermore, the accreditation body could itself conduct random tests at certified cites to check whether the certificate was rightfully issued. However, such measures would increase the cost of the entire system, a cost which would then likely be passed on to the companies desiring certification. Another option would be to safeguard the independence of the certification bodies. For some standards, for example, companies cannot freely choose a certification body themselves. Instead the appointment and payment of a certifier is made by an independent institution, which can prevent dependencies and personal relationships. A mandatory change of the certification body at regular intervals can also avoid dependencies, with the downside that specific expertise of certain companies is lost due to such mandatory changes. Finally, the reputation of the certification body could also be a lever to increase audit quality. If, for example, insufficient audit qualities are made public, this could incentivize auditors to conduct proper audits. This would depend, however, on the likelihood of detecting malpractices by the accreditation body. How any of these measures are implemented can vary significantly between different standards or regulations.

Sustainability in business 38: Certified, yet unsafe – The case of Ali Enterprises in Pakistan

On September 11, 2012, nearly 300 workers died in a catastrophic fire in a factory owned by Ali Enterprises in Karachi, Pakistan. Locked emergency exits and barred windows prevented workers from leaping to safety. All this happened only weeks after the facility received an SA8000 certification by the RINA company, an Italian certification body. RINA itself, however, did not conduct the audit. It subcontracted a local company that was not accredited to conduct SA8000 audits. This tragic incident is unfortunately not an isolated case, and it shows the limits of audits and certification processes either due to structural reasons (e.g., conflict of interests or insufficient standards and rules which provide loopholes) or due to criminal intent (e.g., deceiving people and processes or circumventing rules). RINA later argued that the company was compliant with the SA8000 standard at the time of the audit while evidence would suggest that this was no longer the case at the time of the fire. Critics, however, doubt that any auditor has ever laid foot into the factory—or if they did they most likely looked the other way. After the event, SA8000 was significantly revised with regard to facilities' safety measures and Social Accountability International withdrew all certificates issued by RINA. Despite the incident, SA8000 is widely regarded as an exemplary standard for social sustainability but the more general verdict of many experts is that "auditing is not enough—we must do more" (Crates, 2019).

Sources: Clean Clothes Campaign (n.d.); European Center for Constitutional and Human Rights (2016); Walsh and Greenhouse (2012)

C.7.3 Sustainability balanced scorecard

C.7.3.1 General approach of a balanced scorecard

A the balanced scorecard is a tool in strategic planning and performance management at the business unit level. Historically, managers were mainly interested in financial performance measures to guide their decisions. Kaplan and Norton (1992) revolutionized the thinking about performance metrics by introducing a more "balanced" view of performance by adding further performance elements beyond financial metrics. Their idea was to complement the financial perspective with three other perspectives: customers, internal business processes, and learning and growth. The financial perspective indicates whether the transformation of a strategy leads to improved economic success. The customer perspective defines the market segments in which the business competes. This includes the customer value proposition through which the company or business unit aims to achieve a competitive advantage. The perspective of internal business processes identifies those processes that enable the company to meet the expectations of customers and shareholders. The learning and growth perspective describes the necessary infrastructure required to achieve the objectives of the other three perspectives in terms of employees (qualification, motivation) and information systems. Each perspective contains four kinds of information (Kaplan & Norton, 2007): Objectives (i.e., high level organizational goals), measures (i.e., how progress for the respective objective is measured), targets (i.e., specific target values for each measure), and initiatives (action programs developed to achieve objectives). This should allow the linking of long-term strategic objectives with short-term actions but also to link financial and nonfinancial measures (e.g., addressing customer complaints) of firm success. Thus, the overall idea is to allow monitoring short-term actions and results not only from a financial perspective, but also from the three additional perspectives. Furthermore, the balanced scorecard also helps to evaluate long-term strategy in light of recent performance and it enables companies to modify strategies.

The four perspectives relate to each other in a cause-and-effect chain, which can be illustrated by a strategy map, that is, a framework that helps to link the intangible assets of a firm to the tangible values created for stakeholders. An example of such a causal chain would be that measures to improve human, information, or organizational capital (learning and growth perspective) can have a positive effect, for example, on operations management processes, customer management processes, or on innovation processes (internal perspective). These processes can then, in turn, positively influence the customer value proposition through improved product attributes such as price or quality, improved customer relationships, and improved image (customer perspective). Eventually, this all leads to long-term shareholder value through improved cost structure, increased asset utilization, new revenue opportunities, and so on (financial perspective). The purpose of a balanced scorecard is thus to formulate a hierarchic system of strategic objectives in the four perspectives, derived from the business strategy and aligned toward the financial goals. Furthermore, all four perspectives can also be interlinked in a network-like structure instead of in a strict hierarchical structure (Kaplan & Norton, 2007), which better demonstrates that all four perspectives are interrelated, and also relate to the overall vision and strategy of the firm. Based on a causal system of objectives, corresponding measures are formulated in all four perspectives.

A balanced scorecard contains lagging and leading indicators. Lagging indicators indicate whether a strategic objective in a perspective is achieved. Such indicators are output measures as they result from implementing activities that impact leading indicators. These leading indicators, in turn, are more immediately measurable compared to lagging indicators so that they allow predictive measurement. Customer satisfaction, for example, is a lagging indicator while the percentage of orders fulfilled on time is a leading indicator.

While the traditional balanced scorecard deliberately included nonfinancial perspectives and indicators, it is not yet sustainability focused. Here, the sustainability balanced scorecard comes into play.

C.7.3.2 Sustainability balanced scorecard types

The idea of a sustainability balanced scorecard takes the integration of nonfinancial dimensions one step further and explicitly also integrates environmental and social aspects. The overall idea is to consider sustainability as a vital aspect of management, which needs to be considered when making various managerial decisions because it directly or indirectly influences almost all areas of operation in a company. Consequently, Figge et al. (2002) argue that there are three major advantages of integrating sustainability into general management approaches:

- Economically sound sustainability management is robust to economic crises because it does not consist of mere add-on measures that are abandoned in case of economic hard times. Instead, the costs for achieving sustainability objectives are perceived as contributing to the economic success.
- If sustainability management contributes to the economic success of a company, this can help to disseminate the idea of sustainability in business as financially successful and sustainable companies can act as role models for others.
- Integrating ecological and social aspects of sustainability in general management approaches helps to holistically embrace the idea of sustainability so that companies do not turn a blind eye to the (seemingly) nonfinancial aspects of sustainability.

A sustainability balanced scorecard can facilitate the integration of all three sustainability dimensions (i.e., economic, social, and ecological) into general management approaches especially because it allows management to consider seemingly "soft factors" such as environmental or social objectives. There are, however, numerous ways of integrating sustainability aspects in a balanced scorecard. In their extensive literature review, Hansen and Schaltegger (2016) map these options along two main dimensions as illustrated in Figure 31: (1) The design of the balanced scorecard hierarchy and (2) the design of the balanced scorecard performance perspectives.

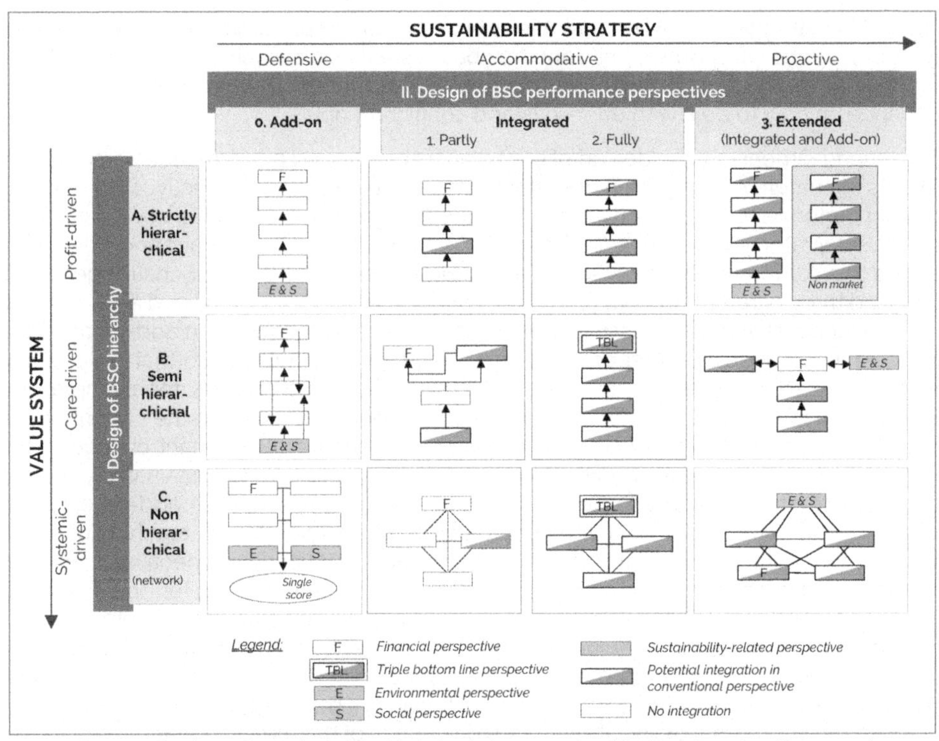

Figure 31: Typology of generic sustainable balanced scorecard architectures based on Hansen and Schaltegger (2016, p. 205), reproduced with permission

The first dimension, hierarchy, reflects the hierarchy between individual performance perspectives and related strategic objectives, that is, the above-mentioned financial perspective, the customer perspective, the internal business processes, the learning and growth perspective, and potentially a fifth sustainability perspective (see the second dimension below). The authors identified three main approaches in the literature. First, the strictly hierarchical approach emphasizes the need for a top-down arrangement of performance perspectives in which all nonfinancial goals have to be directly or indirectly linked to the financial goals. This approach is very common, and it illustrates an instrumental perspective of sustainability management in which sustainability activities are linked to economic and competitive advantages (see also Chapter A.3.4). Accordingly, these approaches can be found in purely profit-driven organizational value systems in which success is measured in terms of money. In the second, semi-hierarchical approach, nonfinancial objectives exist in their own right as there does not have to be an explicit link to the financial perspective. This approach thus relates to a broader stakeholder approach following a triple bottom line perspective instead of a more limited shareholder perspective. While this apparently better captures the general idea of sustainable development (compared to hierarchical approaches), it also means that there are not always strict causal relationships, which makes management more complex as there might be, for example, conflicting interests in the different perspectives. Therefore, managers likely have to move from a "maximizing approach" (i.e., maximizing the achievement of objectives) to a "satisfying approach," and this might require more fundamental changes in business thinking. Semi-hierarchical balanced scorecards can usually be found in organizations with a care-driven value system in which shareholder value is balanced against the interests of other legitimate stakeholders. Third, the nonhierarchical (or network) approach goes even further and replaces linear cause-and-effect chains and hierarchy entirely with a network-like structure, where all perspectives are interrelated and affect each other. Hansen and Schaltegger (2016) find that this approach is rather uncommon and poorly investigated. It comes with some significant drawbacks such as a difficulty in maintaining focus and the risk of a lack of commitment to organizations and people because it provides no guidance on how to deal with trade-offs and conflicting goals.

The second dimension, the design of the balanced scorecard performance perspectives, reflects the nature of integration of sustainability-related strategic objectives into the four existing performance perspectives of a balanced scorecard. It describes how sustainability-related strategic objectives are integrated into a balanced scorecard and how this is related to a company's sustainability strategy. Here again, Hansen and Schaltegger (2016) identified three different approaches: (1) add-on architectures, (2) integrated architectures, and (3) extended architectures. First, balanced scorecards following an add-on architecture add a sustainability perspective to the other four perspectives so that the sustainability balanced scorecard covers five perspectives. Some companies, for example, add an environmental perspective or a community perspective to illustrate the importance of the respective objectives. Such an extra perspective can be a significant change to the existing balanced scorecard, and it allows for the pursuit of multiple sustainability-related strategic objectives and their individual management. However, such add-on architectures can also be regarded as a defensive tactic as this is the least far-reaching option. It does not integrate sustainability goals holistically, and additional perspectives can easily be eliminated especially if there are only poor linkages to the existing four perspectives. The second option, integrated architectures, aim for a partial or complete integration of sustainability aspects into some or all of the four perspectives. The idea is to link the sustainability perspective with core management processes and therefore to create business and societal value. Partly integrated sustainability balanced scorecards cautiously integrate environmental or social aspects in one or few of the existing balanced scorecard perspectives. A partial integration often happens at the internal business processes perspective with the integration of sustainability aspects that are directly related to production processes such as environmental protection, environmental tax payments, energy efficiency, or occupational health and safety objectives. With a broad integration, sustainability aspects are included in all conventional balanced scorecard perspectives. The learning and growth perspective, for example, may be extended with objectives reflecting green capabilities or intellectual capital and the customer perspective could cover sustainability-related image. Integrated architectures can be regarded as accommodative sustainability strategies in which companies accept responsibilities for sustainable development and try to meet stakeholder expectations. Third and finally, extended architectures combine elements of the other two architectures so that they both integrate and add an additional perspective. The focus is usually on integration while an add-on is only necessary when objectives cannot be integrated in any other perspective. An additional sustainability perspective is introduced to capture strategic objectives with very long time horizons that do not or not sufficiently contribute to short-term financial success. This third option can be regarded as the most progressive as it enables short-term as well as long-term financial and nonfinancial success.

Task C7-7

The CEO of a company that does not yet have a strong sustainability agenda sees the need for integrating sustainability further into her organization. Some internal stakeholders, especially some of the other members of the board of directors, are skeptical about sustainability management and fear that extended sustainability activities will only drive costs. The CEO wants to implement sustainability aspects into the balanced scorecard to bring the topic forward. She asked you for your advice on how to proceed. What are the benefits and drawbacks of the different sustainability balanced scorecard designs for the company? Which design would you eventually suggest and why? Would your suggestion be different if the company was an industry leader in sustainability?

C.7.3.3 Developing a sustainability balanced scorecard

To get a better idea of what it means to include sustainability into balanced scorecard approaches, we will now illustrate an exemplary application of such an integration based on Figge et al. (2002) for an extended, strictly hierarchical sustainability balanced scorecard. The first step is to identify a business unit for which the sustainability balanced scorecard should be developed. Because a balanced scorecard does not formulate strategies but instead describes and translates them into objectives, measures, and targets, a general strategy should already exist for the business unit. Large companies are usually comprised of different business units with independent strategies. In smaller companies, the business unit level may be identical with the corporate level. Next, all pertinent and potentially strategically relevant sustainability aspects that affect this business unit need to be identified and listed in step two. These aspects are then translated into causally linked objectives and indicators in a third step. Since this first step is usually rather obvious, the following explanations focus specifically on steps two and three.

After identifying the strategic business unit, the sustainability exposure of the business unit has to be assessed as a second step. To do so, it is usually practical to separately identify potentially strategically relevant environmental and social aspects due to their often quite heterogeneous nature. The aim of this step is to generate a comprehensive and business unit specific profile of sustainability aspects. To be able to list all relevant environmental aspects, it is helpful to compile a list of different types of environmental interventions along the product life cycle. This specifically includes different types of emissions (to air, water, and soil) including radiation, waste and waste heat, material and energy input, noise and vibrations, and direct interventions on nature and landscape. While social aspects can generally be identified in a similar way, it is usually not possible to come up with such a comprehensive classification of aspects for social sustainability because social aspects tend to be quite diversified. Furthermore, social aspects are often value-laden and a matter of preferences of different actors. It can thus be helpful to identify social issues by focusing on relevant stakeholder groups and their claims based on existing frameworks such as those depicted in Figure 9 or Figure 10 in Chapter B.1.

The third step of determining the strategic relevance of the identified sustainability aspects is the core step in any (sustainability) balanced scorecard. Here, the verbally formulated strategy of a business unit is translated into causally linked objectives and indicators. To achieve this, two stages of strategic relevance can be distinguished:

(1) For strategic core issues, lagging indicators have to be defined that indicate whether the objectives in this specific perspective have been achieved. For the financial perspective, this could be, for example, revenue or productivity growth; for the customer perspective, this could be indicators such as market share, customer satisfaction, or cus-

tomer retention; for the internal business processes perspective, for example, innovation or operation processes; for the learning and growth perspective, employee retention, productivity, or satisfaction; and for an added nonmarket perspective, indicators such as legitimacy or freedom of action. The fact that there is an added sustainability (nonmarket) perspective illustrates the "add-on" part of the extended architecture in this example, and we will later add the "integrated" part as well. Furthermore, the types of lagging indicators for this perspective already point to the hierarchical nature of the sustainability balanced scorecard in this example as (perceived) legitimacy of the business unit is not a sustainability indicator in its own right but rather a nonmarket prerequisite for financial success (see again Chapter B.1.2).

(2) Performance drivers show how the desired results in each perspective are to be achieved. They are represented by business-specific leading indicators. If employee satisfaction is a strategic core issue (and lagging indicator) in the learning and growth perspective, for example, employee health and safety can be a sustainability-related performance driver in the same perspective. Similarly, energy efficiency, water efficiency, and material efficiency can be performance drivers for the strategic core issue of production processes (with the lagging indicator of production cost) in the internal business processes perspective. In the customer perspective, a sustainable image can be a performance driver of the strategic core issue of customer satisfaction. All these sustainability-related performance drivers are directly integrated in the existing perspectives illustrating the integrated part of the extended architecture in this example. Furthermore, the added nonmarket perspective can also have their own performance drivers. Child labor, for example, can be a nonmarket indicator that influences the sustainability image, which again illustrates the hierarchical nature of this example (i.e., child labor is included as an indicator because it potentially influences the image and thus customer satisfaction and, eventually, the financial success of the business unit).

To check whether all important sustainability aspects have been met, Figge et al. (2002) suggest answering the following questions while going through the four perspectives:

- Does the sustainability aspect represent a strategic core issue (lagging indicator)?
- Does the sustainability aspect contribute significantly to a strategic core issue and therefore represent a performance driver (leading indicator)?
- What is the substantial contribution of the performance driver to the achievement of the strategic core issue?

The result is a strategic map as exemplarily depicted in a simplified way in Figure 32 for a fictitious craft brewery that produces organic beer. The aim of the company is to increase the return on capital employed (ROCE) by improving its customers' willingness to pay which, in turn, is influenced by customer satisfaction and customer retention. In this strictly hierarchical design, all aspects and indicators have to be directly or indirectly linked with the financial perspective, which also indicated the initially instrumental nature of sustainability in this company. The strategic core issues and performance drivers of the lower level have to contribute to the objectives of the higher level perspective to establish cause-and-effect chains. Furthermore, you can also directly see the extended architecture of this specific sustainability balanced scorecard as there are elements of the add-on architecture (i.e., the added nonfinancial perspective) and of the integrated architecture (i.e., water efficiency or employee safety as sustainability-related elements in the traditional perspectives). Any strategic aspect of the added nonmarket perspective has to be linked directly or indirectly to the financial perspective.

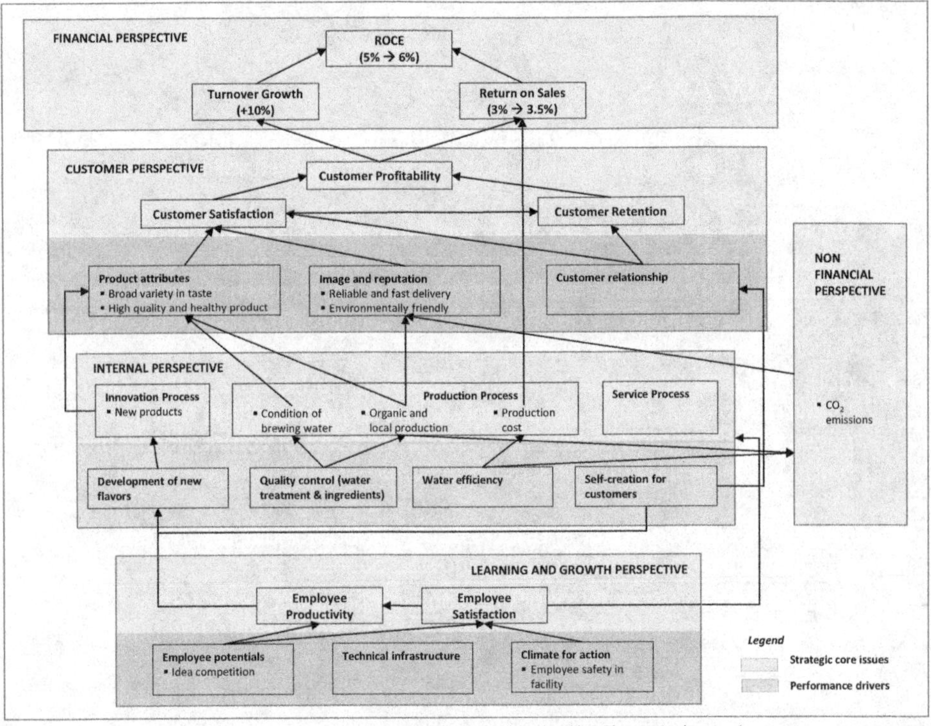

Figure 32: Example of a strategic map (inspired by Figge et al., 2002)

Task C7-8

Follow the step-by-step approach introduced above. (1) Identify a business unit for a company (or think of a fictitious company) in an industry for which you have some solid knowledge. What is the general strategy and vision/mission of this business unit? Based on this starting point: Develop the outline of a sustainability balanced scorecard. You may choose from any of the architectures discussed above. (2) Identify the sustainability exposure separately for strategically relevant environmental aspects and social aspects. For environmental aspects, refer to the list of emissions (to air, water, and soil) including radiation, waste and waste heat, material and energy input, noise and vibrations, and direct interventions on nature and landscape. For social aspects, identify stakeholder groups and the social claims and issues brought up by them. (3) Determine the strategic relevance of the identified sustainability aspects by identifying lagging indicators for strategic core issues and leading indicators for performance drivers.

KEY TAKEAWAYS

- Sustainability management control, sustainability accounting, and sustainability reporting interact in a continuous process of accountability to improve sustainability performance over time.
- While codes of conduct are about what (not) to do in organizational contexts, management systems provide guidelines of how to implement certain aspects of sustainability; management systems standards codify how certain management systems should be designed and are certifiable; hybrid forms and combinations of these different elements exist.
- Codes of conduct provide instructions on what (not) to do, and they can be distinguished based on their issuer, the nature of their content, their target audiences, the breadth of topics they cover, their level of voluntariness; any code has to be backed by further aspects of sustainability management to be effective.
- The UN Global Compact and ISO 26000 are both multistakeholder codes of conduct with very different depths and approaches.
- Management systems introduce a plan-do-check-act cycle to the respective management area they cover, and respective standards provide guidelines for such systems and are certifiable.
- ISO 14001 and EMAS are well-known and widely used environmental management system standards while SA8000 is much less prevalent but nonetheless well-known for a social management system standard that includes elements of a code of conduct.
- Audits are checklist-based control systems used to investigate compliance with certain issues but the quality of audit processes might differ depending on the circumstances.
- A sustainability balanced scorecard is a tool to integrate sustainability aspects into strategic planning; different types of sustainability balanced scorecards can be distinguished based on the design of their hierarchy and of their perspectives.
- To develop a sustainability balanced scorecard, the strategically relevant sustainability aspects of a business unit have to be identified and lagging as well as leading indicators have to be derived.

C.8 Sustainability reporting

LEARNING GOALS

After reading this chapter you will be able to ...

- ... differentiate various forms of sustainability reporting.
- ... explain different types of materiality.
- ... explain the different elements and principles of the GRI standards for sustainability reporting.
- ... explain the relevance of and procedures for climate-related disclosure according to the CDP.
- ... explain the idea of integrated reporting as well as its potential benefits and drawbacks.
- ... discuss the relevance as well as different types of assurance in sustainability reporting.

Introduction to Chapter C.8: Screencast
Watch an introduction to the chapter here:

C.8.1 Introduction to sustainability reporting

Sustainability reporting "provides and substantiates information about the status and progress of corporate sustainability towards internal and external stakeholders through formalized means of communication" (Hahn & Kühnen, 2013, p. 7). Sustainability reporting nowadays has a firm place in the standard repertoire of sustainability management. The vast majority of large multinational companies but also many smaller companies regularly publish a sustainability-related report (KPMG, 2020). Topic-wise, sustainability reporting usually covers multiple aspects and dimensions of sustainability (i.e., ecological, social, and potentially also economic aspects). The term sustainability report is widely used but other terms such as CSR report, corporate citizenship report, nonfinancial report, and so on are usually used interchangeably. Apart from reports covering multiple dimensions of sustainability, also one-dimensional reports (e.g., reports focusing only on the environment like those necessary for an EMAS; see Chapter C.7.2.2) are still sometimes found. Probably the most important form of one-dimensional reports are annual financial reports. Such reports are, however, not usually covered by the term sustainability reporting. They are also not discussed in this chapter, because annual financial reports have a long tradition in management and accounting, and they are usually heavily regulated through reporting frameworks such as the International Financial Reporting Standards (IFRS) or through national standards such as the Generally Accepted Accounting Principles (GAAP) in the United States. However, financial reports nowadays also frequently include sustainability issues and thus extend beyond the narrow focus on the financial dimension only. Reports that provide a truly integrated picture of holistic value creation are called integrated reports (see Chapter C.8.3 below), while those that report on the three dimensions of sustainability side by side are called combined reports. Figure 33 provides an overview of these different forms of sustainability reporting. Considering the format, sustainability reporting is not restricted to publishing annual or biannual reports of any form in print, as a PDF file, or as a dedicated website. Sustainability reporting can also come in form of investor presentations, face-to-face meetings with different stakeholders, internal magazines or the company Intranet, press releases, social media activities, and so on. Such channels are, however, highly diverse and context specific. Therefore, this chapter will concentrate on dedicated reports on sustainability issues.

Reporting related to sustainability issues	
In the form of	*covering*
Integrated or combined reports	Three sustainability dimensions (financial, ecological, and social in one report)
Specialized sustainability, CSR, corporate citizenship etc. reports	Two sustainability dimensions (ecological and social; financial usually not covered)
Isolated environmental or social reports	One sustainability dimension (ecological or social)

Figure 33: Sustainability reporting concepts and terms

In sustainability reporting, we can distinguish between producers and users of information. Information producers are mainly the reporting organizations themselves who collect and validate information based on their internal (sustainability) accounting systems, which are then finally disclosed to the public. Furthermore, a company can involve different service providers, for example, software providers to enable or improve the collection and processing of data as well as auditors and consultants to compile and edit reports or to provide external assurance. On the side of information users, a whole variety of stakeholders might be interested in a company's sustainability reporting, such as investors, communities, civil society, suppliers, or governments. Especially regulators and investors are increasingly interested in sustainability information, and the pressure to disclose adequate information is increasing in many areas as we have already discussed in other chapters (e.g., Chapters B.3 and B.5) and will further illustrate below. Furthermore, information from a company's sustainability reporting is often used by specialized data providers such as rating agencies (see Chapter B.5.3) that aggregate the information and make it available in an abbreviated form.

The general idea of sustainability reporting is that it ideally sets a chain reaction in motion. For adequate reporting to take place, companies first need to engage in sustainability accounting to be able to disclose sustainability information. Potentially, sustainability accounting could already lead to an improvement of sustainability performance when following the famous idiom of management scholar Peter Drucker: "What gets measured gets managed." In a world where sustainable development is increasingly relevant, stakeholders such as investors or customers could then better reward companies with a superior sustainability performance and put pressure on those that lag behind. As always, however, reality is more complicated and sustainability reporting is not a direct proxy for progress in corporate sustainability. The reasons are manifold. For example, the measurement of sustainability performance is often not standardized, incomplete, or at least comes with substantial leeway for companies on how to approach sustainability accounting. This is also an outcome of the high complexity of sustainability with regard to the various subtopics and issues (see, e.g., the 169 subgoals of the SGDs, Chapter A.2.3). For example, the often extremely scattered and opaque supply chains make it difficult to holistically assess sustainability performance (see Chapter C.3) and other challenges. Furthermore, in many cases, sustainability reporting is either entirely voluntary or the content and form of reporting is only loosely regulated—especially compared to the strict specification for financial reporting. However, sustainability reporting as a topic is evolving rapidly so that it will be interesting to see how it can contribute to sustainability performance in the future.

Sustainability in research 12: Gray, Kouhy, and Laver's 1995 article on sustainability reporting

In their article "Corporate social and environmental reporting: A review of the literature and a longitudinal study of UK disclosure", Rob Gray, Reza Kouhy, and Simon Lavers depict sustainability reporting (or corporate social reporting, as they term it) already back in 1995 as a practice that is gaining legitimacy both in politics and in society, and that has definitely proven to be the case by now. Nevertheless, the authors also argue that sustainability reporting lacks a systematic framework, which allows companies to structure self-reports to their individual needs. In this regard, the past 25 years have brought some progress around the world as we will illustrate in this chapter, but to some extent, their verdict is still valid today.

Based on past research, Gray and colleagues showed that sustainability reporting may be related to company size and industry. In addition, factors such as country, capital intensity, and firm age were identified as significant influencing factors for the popularity of sustainability reporting. The authors illustrate two modes of sustainability reporting at that time—both of which can still be found today: sustainability reporting (1) as a supplement within the confines of conventional disclosure and (2) as an independent report to document the company's impact on environment and society.

In their article, the authors add a theoretical lens to sustainability reporting research. They note that sustainability reporting can be explained primarily in the context of stakeholder theory, legitimacy theory, and political economy. Against this background, the authors interpreted the development of sustainability reporting over a 13-year period in the UK. They posit that the disclosure of community, employee, social, and environmental data has increased, while disclosure of customer data has not changed significantly. The authors refer to political economy, which states that economic and political systems are interdependent, to explain the high rate of employee data disclosure, as the influence of the state via certain employee-related laws has increased during this period. Furthermore, they explained trends in the disclosure of environmental or safety data with reference to stakeholder theory (according to which the interests of various actors are incorporated into corporate action) and legitimacy theories (according to which companies seek a value system congruent with society). With these theoretical explanations, Gray, Kouhy, and Lavers significantly influenced following generations of sustainability reporting research until today.

***Source:* R. Gray et al. (1995)**

One of the first questions (and challenges) for companies on sustainability reporting usually is what to report. As you have seen throughout this book, sustainability management is a vast topic covering the entire spectrum of company activities with a multitude of affected stakeholders, and it would be impossible even for smaller companies to report on every sustainability issue that could potentially be relevant. Thus, companies have to decide what issues are most relevant. Here, the concept of materiality comes into play (e.g., Baumüller & Schaffhauser-Linzatti, 2018; Reimsbach et al., 2020). For financial accounting, the International Accounting Standards Board defined that "Information is material if omitting, misstating or obscuring it could reasonably be expected to influence decisions that the primary users of general purpose financial statements make on the basis of those financial statements, which provide financial information about a specific reporting entity" (IASB, 2018). According to this understanding of (financial) materiality, sustainability information is only material—and thus should be reported—if it has a potential influence on the financial performance of a company. If, for example, climate change leads to risks for the business model or operation of a company, such aspects would be material. That means a poor sustainability performance would not be material per se and thus not subject to disclosure, even if it had drastic consequences for some stakeholders or society at large. A poor sustainability performance only becomes material if it would at the same time increase financial risks or impair financial performance, for example, due to consumer boycotts, investor reactions, or regulations. In sum and if applied to sustainability topics, the idea of financial materiality follows a very narrow instrumental perspective of sustainability management. Beyond this narrow perspective, other concepts of materiality are more compatible with the normative notion of sustainable development and sustainability management. Nonfinancial materiality (also double materiality or stakeholder materiality) broadens the perspective. The Global Reporting Initiative (GRI), for example, defines topics as material when they "represent [an organization's] most significant impacts on the economy, environment, and people" (GRI, 2021a, p. 8) This goes beyond the focus on financial performance and investors to include the impact a company has on other stakeholder groups from a triple bottom line perspective.

C.8.2 Regulations and standards for sustainability reporting

The landscape of regulations for reporting is heterogeneous. In some countries, for example, China and India, state-owned companies are required to regularly disclose information about their CSR performance. In many other countries, especially environmental emissions (e.g., in the United States, Canada, Israel, or Japan) or governance information have to be disclosed. Furthermore, many stock exchanges around the world recommend or even require listed companies to disclosure certain sustainability information (see ESG guidance database: https://sseinitiative.org/). Overall, the topic of sustainability reporting is progressing rapidly and new regulations are appearing regularly. Recently, for example, the China Securities Regulatory Commission revised its guidelines, now requiring company reports to consolidate environmental and social information (Peiyuan, 2021). One of the most important developments in recent years, with regard to its impact on the number of companies and also with regard to the reporting requirements, is probably the proposal for the European Corporate Sustainability Reporting Directive (CSRD) published in 2021 (European Commission, 2021). According to the directive, most companies with more than 250 employees will have to report on sustainability-related risks, sustainability targets, and likely also on various ESG issues even with specific indicators following the idea of double materiality. Furthermore, the directive includes a mandatory requirement for limited external assurance (see Chapter C.8.5 below) on the provided information. The directive is scheduled to be finalized in 2022 and will be effective from 2024 on.

Nevertheless, sustainability reporting is still often voluntary or covered only by rather unspecific and general reporting requirements without much specifications regarding form or content, especially compared to the highly regulated topic of financial reporting. Therefore, voluntary standards try to fill the gap and provide guidance on what and how to report. By far the most well-known sustainability reporting standard worldwide comes from the GRI. The GRI was founded in 1997 with the mission to providing organizations with a common standard to follow when reporting their sustainability impacts. The first version of the GRI guidelines was launched in 2000, with revisions published in 2002, 2006, and 2013. Initially, the entire GRI guidelines on all sustainability issues were published in one document. Since 2016, the GRI publishes its standard in a modular form so that single elements can be updated or added more easily. The entire system of GRI standards (i.e., the different modules) comprises three elements (see GRI, 2021a):

- The universal standards GRI 1, GRI 2, and GRI 3 are relevant for all organizations and their sustainability reports. GRI 1 explains general requirements and principles for sustainability reporting. GRI 2 illustrates the information that should generally be disclosed by an organization with respect to organizational details, governance, and sustainability-related strategy, policies, and practices. These aspects do not cover any specific performance indicators but instead enable the reader to gain a general understanding of the company background and its approach with regard to sustainability. GRI 3 outlines in detail how a company should determine and disclose material topics.
- The various sector-specific standards (GRI 11, GRI 12, GRI 13, ...) apply to specific industries and cater to the fact that many sustainability issues are highly context specific. Companies should use the sector standard that applies to their specific sector. GRI 11, for example, provides information to companies in the oil and gas sector about their likely material topics. However, the list of sector standards is not exhaustive, and for

many industries, sector specific standards do not exist, yet.

- The topic standards provide guidance on how to report specific information on different sustainability topics. After determining material topics based on GRI 3 and potentially a sector-specific standard, companies should refer to the specific guidance of the respective topic standards. The 200 series (GRI 201, GRI 202, ...) covers economic issues such as procurement practices (GRI 204) or anti-corruption (GRI 205). These two exemplary issues from the economic dimension demonstrate that the economic-oriented topic standards do not aim at replacing traditional financial reporting guidelines (such as IFRS) but rather at complementing them. The 300 series (GRI 301, GRI 302, ...) covers environmental issues such as water (GRI 303) or waste (GRI 306). Finally, the 400 series (GRI 401, GRI 402, ...) covers social issues such as health and safety (GRI 403) or rights of indigenous peoples (GRI 411). Other than the general disclosures outlined in GRI 2, these topic standards also provide specific performance indicators that enable a company to report on the various aspects of its sustainability performance.

When applying the GRI standards, companies are urged to comply with eight general reporting principles described in GRI 1 (2021a, pp. 20-24):

- Accuracy: Information shall be correct and sufficiently detailed to allow an assessment of the organization's impacts.
- Balance: Information shall be reported in an unbiased way and provide a fair representation of the organization's negative and positive impacts.
- Clarity: Information shall be presented in a way that is accessible and understandable.
- Comparability: Information shall be selected, compiled, and reported consistently to enable an analysis of changes in the organization's impacts over time and an analysis of these impacts relative to those of other organizations.
- Completeness: Information shall be sufficient to enable an assessment of the organization's impacts during the reporting period.
- Sustainability context: Information shall present an organization's impacts in the wider context of sustainable development.
- Timeliness: Information shall be reported on a regular schedule and made available in time for information users to make decisions.
- Verifiability: Information shall be gathered, recorded, compiled, and analyzed in such a way that it can be examined to establish its quality.

Task C8-1

Compare the sustainability reports from two companies from the same industry by referring to the GRI principles. What do you think they have done well, and where do you see room for improvements? Do you, as a report user, feel well informed about the two companies' sustainability performance and activities or would you require additional (or maybe less) information? If necessary, consult the GRI 1 standard (freely available via the website of the GRI) for more information on the principles.

The typical procedure for compiling and publishing a sustainability report is outlined by the GRI as follows. First, companies should familiarize themselves with the reporting principles of GRI 1 to gain an understanding of the general requirements. All companies are then required to disclose the general information outlined in GRI 2. For the specific performance indicators and further reporting details on different sustainability issues, companies should then conduct a materiality analysis according to GRI 3 and, if possible, based on applicable sector-specific standards. The idea of this step is to determine which topics are material and should thus be covered in the report. The sustainability report should disclose information for the respective topic standards for each material topic or provide reasons for omissions. Each sustainability report prepared in alignment with the GRI includes a content index to enable easy detection of the various issues covered in the report.

To gain a better understanding of the breadth and depth of information that companies are required to report in accordance with the GRI standards, let us have a closer look at the topic-specific standards. Topic-specific standards cover requirements on topic management disclosures and on topic disclosures. Topic management disclosures provide information on how the company manages the respective material topic, while topic disclosures are specific performance indicators to be reported on the respective material topic. GRI 306 on waste, for example, contains two substandards on topic management disclosures (306-1 and 306-2) and three substandards on topic disclosures (306-3, 306-4, 306-5) (GRI, 2021b). GRI 306-1 asks companies to describe their inputs, activities, and outputs and whether these impacts relate to waste generation. GRI 306-2 requires information on actions taken to prevent waste generation and processes used to collect and monitor waste-related data. According to GRI 306-3, companies have to report on the total weight of waste generated in metric tons as well as a breakdown by composition of the waste. GRI 306-4 asks for information on the total weight of waste diverted from disposal in metric tons and again a breakdown by composition of the waste. Furthermore, different steps of recovery operations (preparation for reuse, recycling, and other operations) have to be disclosed separately for hazardous and nonhazardous waste. GRI 306-5 requires similar information for waste directed to disposal, again with details on different disposal operations (incineration with and without energy recovery, landfilling, and other options). Each of these substandards comes with requirements (i.e., what to report), recommendations (i.e., brief and general hints on how to report), and guidance (i.e., extensive advice and background information). This in-depth view into one of the topic-specific standards already illustrates the complexity of sustainability as a management topic and, consequently, of the complexity of adequately disclosing information to stakeholders.

Beyond the GRI, other international organizations such as the Sustainability Accounting Standards Board (SASB) as well as more traditional accounting actors such as the International Accounting Standards Board (IASB—which is responsible for the IFRS), some national reporting guidelines (e.g., the German Sustainability Code [Deutscher Nachhaltigkeitskodex]), or sector- or issue-specific frameworks (see Chapter C.8.3) provide guidance on different aspects of sustainability reporting. Overall, many experts expect worldwide regulations and standardizations to continue to develop dynamically. In 2020, for example, several large standardization organizations active in the field of sustainability reporting (including the GRI) issued a statement of intent to work together toward comprehensive corporate reporting (CDP et al., 2020). Also, governments around the world have recognized reporting as an instrument that is comparably easy to implement from a regulatory point of view.

C.8.3 Special topics and approaches in sustainability reporting

A part from a holistic view on sustainability as displayed in the GRI standards, some specific reporting standards, initiatives, and tools exist that aim at delving deeper into certain sustainability aspects such as climate change or human rights, which we will cover exemplarily in the following. A significant player in this regard is the CDP (formerly the Carbon Disclosure Project), a nongovernmental organization with the mission of collecting and publishing climate-related company data. Each year, the CDP sends out extensive questionnaires to thousands of companies asking for information on their climate strategy, key figures, risks, emissions, and so on. Data that is released by companies is available free of charge on the CDP's homepage. To exert pressure on companies to disclose information, the CDP publishes the names of those companies that do not participate in its questionnaire surveys, and it has secured the backing of several hundred investors and major buyers worldwide. Over time, the CDP broadened its target group to also include cities, states, and regions as potential information providers. Furthermore, the CDP nowadays also collects data on forests and deforestation as well as on water.

The relevance of the CDP for sustainability reporting can easily be expressed by numbers: In 2021, more than 13,000 companies worth more than 60 percent of global market capitalization disclosed data through the CDP (CDP, 2021b). The questions in the three surveys on climate change, forests, and water security are developed and adapted annually where necessary. In 2021, the climate questionnaire for companies, for example, covered questions on governance issues, risks, and opportunities, business strategy, targets and performance, emission data including detailed breakdowns, energy, carbon pricing, and some further aspects. The CDP evaluates the answers and, as a result, calculates and releases scores on a scale from A to D- (and "F" for companies that fail to disclose sufficient information). In 2020, about 277 (out of 9,526) disclosing companies were included in the climate change A list, 16 (out of 687) in the forests A list, and 106 (out of 2,934) in the water security A list. Companies can receive detailed benchmark reports from the CDP to compare themselves with peer companies. Especially because the topic of climate change is currently of paramount importance in our society, climate-related disclosure is likely to remain an important domain in sustainability reporting. This is also expressed by some other high level initiatives in this regard. In 2015, for example, the representatives from the largest economies worldwide as well as from important central banks initiated the establishment of a Task Force on Climate-Related Disclosure (TCFD; see TCFD, 2020). The TCFD develops recommendations for climate-related disclosures, and not only have various nations already made a public commitment to mandating disclosure according to the TCFD regulations, the CDP questionnaire is now aligned with the TCFD regulations as well.

Another topic that has gained some attention in the last years—albeit at a much slower pace than climate-related disclosures—is human rights reporting. Increasing regulations and pressure to improve human rights in worldwide supply chains (see Chapter C.3.3) has brought this topic into the public sphere so that specific guidelines have emerged here as well. The UN Guiding Principles Reporting Framework (Shift Project Ltd. & Mazars LLP, 2015) provides a framework and guidance on how to report on human rights issues. It encourages companies to publicly disclose their commitments for human rights and information on how these commitments are implemented and report on various specific issues such as how stakeholder engagement is organized or how the company assesses its impact and tracks performance on relevant human rights issues. Similar to the proliferation of certified environmental management systems versus social management systems, however, dedicated human rights reporting is much less prevalent than climate reporting. At the same time, this does not necessarily mean that only very few companies report on human rights issues at all. Instead, human rights topics can also be covered by general sustainability reports, for example, following the GRI standards that also quite broadly cover human rights topics (e.g., GRI 408 on child labor, GRI 409 on forced and compulsory labor, or GRI 411 on rights of indigenous people).

Another way of approaching sustainability reporting is not to focus on specific topics but to instead approach reporting in a holistic manner. The idea of integrated reporting promises such a comprehensive approach by accounting for a broad base of relevant capitals. According to the International Integrated Reporting Council (IIRC), this includes financial capital but it also explicitly covers manufactured, intellectual, human, social and relationship, as well as natural capital. The idea of integrated reporting is to promote the understanding of the interdependencies between these capitals and "improve the quality of information available to providers of financial capital to enable a more efficient and productive allocation of capital" (IIRC, 2021, p. 2). The general idea behind this approach is that company value is nowadays by and large influenced not by physical and financial assets but instead by other factors such as knowledge or reputation. One main assumption is, thus, that sustainability is a means to create value, which follows an instrumental perspective of sustainability management. Against this background, integrated reporting recognizes, among others, the relevance of social and natural capital to create financial value and thus calls for an integration of economic, environmental, and social perspectives in company reporting. However, while this value creation relates broadly to all the types of capital listed above, the underlying assumption is that the creation of value enables financial returns to providers of financial capital so that materiality in integrated reporting is understood more in terms of financial materiality than double materiality.

Other than, for example, the GRI standards, the IIRC's International Integrated Reporting Framework is not a full-blown standard with concrete guidance on metrics and content. Instead, it provides a general outline and principles for integrated reporting. Seven guiding principles, which are in many ways pretty similar to the aforementioned GRI principles, illustrate how an integrated report should be prepared and presented (see IIRC, 2021, pp. 25-37):

- Strategic focus and future orientation: Illustrate how the company creates value in the short, medium, and long term and how this affects the different capitals.
- Connectivity of information: Provide a holistic picture of the combination, interrelatedness, and dependencies between the different factors of value creation.
- Stakeholder relationships: Provide insight into relationships with key stakeholders and how the company considers and responds to their legitimate interests.
- Materiality: Disclose information about matters that substantively affect the organization's ability to create value.
- Conciseness: Provide sufficient context without disclosing irrelevant information.
- Reliability and completeness. Include all material matters in a balanced way (i.e., positive and negative aspects) and without material error.
- Consistency and comparability. Present information consistently over time in a way that enables comparison with other relevant organizations.

Furthermore, eight general content elements briefly explain what an integrated report should cover without, however, providing details on specific topics as it is the case in the GRI topic standards (see IIRC, 2021, pp. 38-48):

- Organizational overview and external environment: Illustrate what the organization does and under which circumstances it operates.
- Governance: Illustrate how the company's governance structure supports its ability to create value.
- Business model: Illustrate the business model and how the company transfers input into output.
- Risks and opportunities: Illustrate the specific risks and opportunities that affect the company's ability to create value.
- Strategy and resource allocation: Illustrate the company's objectives and how it wants to achieve them.
- Performance: Illustrate to what extent the company has achieved its strategic objectives and the effects on the different types of capital.
- Outlook: Illustrate challenges and uncertainties and their potential implications for the company's business model and future performance.
- Basis of preparation and presentation: Illustrate how the company determines what to include in the report.

Overall, the current framework of the IIRC thus provides an overview of a reporting philosophy with a general approach instead of being a full-blown reporting standard. Integrated reporting as a disclosure practice is not uncontested in practice and academia. Kannenberg and Schreck (2019) as well as Villiers et al. (2017) highlight the different arguments and viewpoints in their reviews of the literature. On the one hand, advocates of integrated reporting argue that it improves the quality of information available to external stakeholders (mostly investors) as well as accessibility of nonfinancial information, and thus enables more efficient capital allocation. Furthermore, companies are stimulated to include sustainability in management processes if they are regarded as value relevant (i.e., "integrated thinking"). Drawbacks are, on the other hand, the potentially high costs for developing and implementing integrated reporting systems, especially because integrated reporting calls for a deep connection of the different types of capitals. Companies are supposed to transparently show (ideally based on quantifiable connections), how the different types of capitals relate to value creation, which might be difficult with regard to data gathering and quantification of nonfinancial information. Furthermore, integrated reporting applies a mainly instrumental view of sustainability through its investor-focused approach. Thus, companies risk ignoring other stakeholder groups in their reporting compared to the idea of double materiality in other reporting formats. This could lead to less sustainability information being disclosed if this information is not regarded as material in the narrow sense of the concept.

Importantly, most of the mentioned standards and initiatives are not mutually exclusive but can be combined. For example, a company disclosing information to the CDP can use the respective data on climate change issues also for its GRI reports, an integrated report can also be in accordance with the GRI, and so on.

C.8.4 Credibility and assurance of sustainability information

Because sustainability reporting is still mostly voluntary or only loosely regulated, an important question focuses on the reliability of the published information, especially if there are no uniform standards, checks, and balances. An increasingly important practice in sustainability reporting is therefore the external assurance of published information. Annual financial reports have been subject to mandatory external assurance by audit companies practically since inception. That means, an external third-party (i.e., the auditing company) checks whether the financial information supplied by a company in their annual report is accurate—also referred to as "true and fair view." In sustainability reporting, assured information has been the exception rather than the norm for many years, not least because utilizing the services of an external auditor is costly. Nowadays, however, an increasing number of companies and especially the majority of large multinationals around the world have at least some of the information in their reports assured (KPMG, 2020). This trend is expected to continue because, for example, investors or rating agencies value reliable information or because new regulations such as the European CSRD call for external assurance. If done properly, an external audit can improve the confidence in the disclosed information through increasing transparency and credibility. Furthermore, respective audit processes and the know-how of assurance companies can help to identify improvement potentials in the reporting processes and potentially also in the underlying aspects of sustainability management and thus eventually improve the quality of information. A respective audit process in sustainability reporting roughly follows the same procedures as most audit processes for other subjects as well (see again Chapter C.7.2.4). In the beginning, the auditor usually tries to gain an overview of the sustainability management at the client company to conduct a preliminary risk analysis and thereby to determine the steps necessary to provide an assurance statement. The respective to-be-assured qualitative or quantitative information are then reviewed. Typically, an auditor also reconstructs the aggregation of data and conducts data analysis in samples. If, for example, the client asked for assured information on carbon emissions, the auditor may check how emission data was collected, calculated, and aggregated from different facilities in the company. In the end, the respective text parts of the sustainability report (or the sustainability-related information in any other type of report) are critically reviewed, for example, to ensure that there are no misleading statements. The final outcome of this entire process is then the independent assurance statement and, additionally, usually a more extensive report and feedback presentation for the client.

Sustainability in business 39: Sustainability in business 39: Volkswagen's 2014 sustainability report in light of the diesel emissions scandal

Sustainability reports can be an efficient tool for communicating sustainability efforts and performances to a variety of stakeholders. Furthermore, they can be a valuable tool to improve company internal procedures and foster continuous improvements. However, they are not a panacea, and they might even be used for outright greenwashing. Volkswagen's 2014 sustainability report was published in May 2015, just months before the famous diesel emissions scandal became public. In the report, which was written based on the GRI standards, the company highlights that it is "driving forward the development of solutions that range from highly efficient, eco-friendly diesel ..." (p. 37) and that it "boost[s] efficiency and reduce emissions in diesel engines" (p. 111). The report was assured with a limited assurance statement in which the audit company PricewaterhouseCoopers recommended to especially improve the materiality analysis. The consequences of inaccurate reporting are immediately visible when looking at the evaluation of Volkswagen's sustainability performance by third parties. Respective ratings and appraisals often rely to a large extent on company internal information (see Chapter B.5.3). In September 2014, for example, the company was supposedly the most sustainable car manufacturer worldwide, according to the DJSI. Just one month later, the scandal became public and Volkswagen was expelled from the index. Maybe a bit tragically, most employees likely did not know about the illegal events at Volkswagen and other automotive companies, and the employees at Volkswagen's sustainability department assumedly put significant efforts into improving the company's sustainability performance.

Sources: Fry (2015); Makortoff (2015); Volkwagen AG (2015)

In general, there are two types of assurance processes leading to two different types of assurance statements: Limited assurance and reasonable assurance. The main difference between these two forms of assurance is the extent of an auditor's engagement that is needed to come to a verdict about the information that is to be assured. The result of a limited assurance engagement is expressed in negative form regarding the conclusion and the reasonable assurance statement in positive form. Let us have a look at two fictive and generic examples to illustrate the differences more clearly. A limited assurance statement of an auditing company could read like this: "Nothing has come to our attention that causes us to believe that internal control at the audited company is not effective, in all material respects, based on the relevant criteria." This form of negative opinion ("nothing has come to ... is not effective") basically excludes fundamental failures in the assurance process. The certainty with which the auditor makes its statement is thus limited, because the audit process only has to confirm that there were likely no major flaws in the reported information and in the assurance process. A reasonable assurance statement is expressed with a positive form of opinion such as: "In our opinion internal controls at the audited company are effective in all material respects, based on the relevant criteria." This statement conveys more confidence because the respective audit processes usually rely on more evidence being collected and more tests or tasks being conducted than for limited assurance. The auditor needs to reduce the risk of making a false statement to acceptable levels and thus engages in more extensive audit processes compared to a limited assurance engagement. Potential tasks an audit company can conduct during their assurance engagement are, for example, conducting internal interviews with management and employees or external interviews with other stakeholders as well as site visits, reviewing of internal and external documents, or scrutinizing internal data system (Gürtürk & Hahn, 2016). However, also a reasonable assurance statement can of course never be an absolute assurance. Since reasonable assurance engagements are more intensive compared to limited assurance engagements, they are also costlier. In sustainability reporting, negative assurance statements are thus much more prevalent, also because sustainability information is generally often quite complex compared, for example, to financial information. Finally, an assurance statement is not a direct indicator of sustainability performance as the assurance process only scrutinizes the quality and accuracy of the disclosed information and not the quality of the sustainability management or sustainability performance per se (Reimsbach et al., 2018). In other words, even the world's most unsustainable company can have its sustainability report assured, and it can receive a reasonable assurance if all disclosed information is correct and reliable.

Task C8-2

Read the assurance statements of two recent sustainability reports. Do you see any differences in the assurance process or in the tasks conducted by the auditing company? What can you learn from these statements and what not? For example, what did the assurers do to come to their verdict, and is there anything else that could be done to improve confidence in the disclosed information and in the assurance process? What information from the sustainability reports was subject to assurance? Do you find a limited or a reasonable assurance statement?

KEY TAKEAWAYS

- Sustainability reporting can cover anything from one to all three pillars of sustainability, depending on the reporting format.
- Materiality defines which information should be disclosed. Financial materiality has to be distinguished from nonfinancial materiality—the main distinguishing element are the addressees of reporting.
- The GRI standards are comprised of universal standards, sector-specific standards, and topic standards. They also cover eight general principles for sustainability reporting.
- The CDP is the most important actor for climate-related reporting. It annually sends out extensive questionnaires and scores companies according to their reporting efforts.
- Integrated reporting aims at disclosing the interdependencies of different types of financial and nonfinancial capital for value creation.
- Reported sustainability information can be externally assured to increase confidence. The two main forms are limited and reasonable assurance.

C.9 Sustainable business models and alternative forms of organizations3

LEARNING GOALS

After reading this chapter you will be able to ...

- ... describe different types of sustainable business models and how they contribute to sustainable development.
- ... explain challenges and barriers toward sustainable business model innovation.
- ... explain the peculiarities of cooperatives, public–private partnerships, and social enterprises as alternative forms of organizations and why they might be especially well-suited to contribute to sustainable development.
- ... differentiate between different business models of social enterprises.
- ... discuss challenges of the different organizational forms as drivers of sustainability.

Introduction to Chapter C.9: Screencast
Watch an introduction to the chapter here:

C.9.1 Sustainable business models

What makes a company (more) sustainable? The answer could be, for example, improving internal processes to reduce the company's environmental footprint or improving its social sustainability through supplier development or higher social standards in own factories. Very often, however, mere incremental improvements of internal processes only provide small levers to shape a company's sustainability impact. Especially if a company builds upon an inherently unsustainable business model, such changes and improvements are not sufficient, as they do not tackle the core of the problem. For example, if an oil extracting company improves its processes of oil extraction to be more environmentally friendly and emit less CO2, this company might be able to cut its scope 1 emissions (see again Chapter C.6.3.1). However, the major environmental impact does not come from the CO2 generated during the extraction phase but from burning it as fuel or when plastics made from fossil fuel are incinerated at the end of their product life. Thus, improved extraction processes alone cannot change this. Similar challenges often occur with many social issues. A focal company which, for example, designs and sells electronic devices may set up programs to improve health and safety procedures or worker remuneration within its own company boundaries. If, however, the company relies on suppliers to produce devices that use large amounts of conflict minerals, such internal social changes may only cover a fraction of the true social sustainability impacts (see again Chapter C.3.1). These examples illustrate why it is relevant to scrutinize the sustainability of the entire business model.

A business model describes how a company is doing business, that is, how it implements its business strategy and translates it into business processes. Richardson (2008) summarizes three main elements of a business model: value proposition, value creation and delivery, and value capture. The value proposition defines the product, the target customers, and how the company plans to win customers and gain a competitive advantage. The value creation and delivery system describes how a company aims to create and deliver the previously defined value to its customers by defining the relevant resources and capabilities, the organizational processes in the supply chain, and the company's position in that chain. The aspect of value capture, finally, illustrates how a company generates revenues and—eventually—profit. A sustainable business model picks up on these

3 *This chapter was coauthored by Rüdiger Hahn and Carolin Waldner.*

elements. Sustainability is thus intended to be integrated already in the value creation, possibly beyond a narrow view on direct customers by creating value for various stakeholders (Freudenreich et al., 2020). Furthermore, sustainability should be part of value creation by reducing negative social and environmental impacts and by eventually capturing positive social and environmental value for multiple stakeholders. Accordingly, Shakeel et al. (2020) summarize a sustainable business model as a "business model that integrates [a] multistakeholder view [and] aims at the creation of monetary and nonmonetary value for stakeholders and holds a long-term perspective." (p. 8)

Bocken et al. (2014; 2019) synthesized the following eight—in parts slightly overlapping—sustainable business model archetypes. Beyond these archetypes, some even more fine-grained classifications of sustainable business models distinguish can be used for analytical purposes or as inspiration for sustainable business model development (Lüdeke-Freund et al., 2018, e.g., identify 45 sustainable business model patterns).

- Maximize material and energy efficiency: Such business models achieve more with fewer resources while generating less waste, emissions, and pollution (see again Chapter A.4.2). Efficiency-focused business models of this type can come, for example, in form of lean or low-carbon manufacturing or via increased product functionality to reduce the total number of products required. Positive impacts come in form of enhanced efficiency and resource use, which can at the same time lead to cost savings. Negative side effects might be that such business models often generate only incremental change and may lead to rebound effects (see again Chapter A.4.5).
- Closing resource loops: Such business models aim to reduce material input by turning waste into resources (see again Chapter A.4.3). Examples are closed-loop and circular economy approaches, elements of reuse, recycle, and remanufacture, or industrial symbiosis systems. On the positive side, such business models reduce waste by turning waste into valuable input material, which can even lead to entirely new revenue streams. On the negative side, they may lead to more material use due to potentially quicker sales cycles and to sustained (instead of reduced) waste streams if waste is regarded as valuable.
- Substitute with renewables and natural processes: Such business models replace nonrenewable with renewable resources. Examples are providers of clean renewable energy or business models that build upon environmentally friendly materials and production processes. A positive impact is that such business models reduce the reliance on finite resources and contribute to an overall green economy. However, the necessary products and processes might have a significant negative footprint, such as a lack of recyclability (e.g., certain types of batteries or solar-panels), or an extended use of bio-based products that could lead, for example, to deforestation or conflict with food supply chains.
- Deliver functionality not ownership: Such business models provide services instead of physical products to satisfy users' needs (see again Chapters B.6.3 and C.1.2). Examples are various types of product-, use-, or result-oriented product service systems. These types of business models can encourage a more sustainable behavior of producers and consumers and reduce the need for physical goods (and thus resources). A potential negative side effect, however, is a rebound effect when the overall product use is increased, for example, because it is easier and less costly to use a certain product.
- Adopt a stewardship role: Such business models engage with all stakeholders along the supply chain to ensure their well-being. Examples are certified products or processes such as Fairtrade or MSC products (upstream stewardship, because this mainly aims toward the beginning of the supply chain) or retailers removing certain products from their shelves (downstream stewardship, because this mainly aims toward the

end of the supply chain). Typical positive impacts of such business models are that they help to ensure the long-term viability of supply chains and contribute to protecting the environment. Again, however, rebound effects might occur, for example, when people consume more of an environmentally or socially friendly product and thus neutralize or even overcompensate the positive impacts.

- Encourage sufficiency: Such business models provide solutions to reduce consumption (see again Chapter A.4.4). Examples can be found in slow fashion, in second-hand markets for used goods and in collaborative consumption, in durable products, or in frugal innovations (see Chapter C.5.3). Positive effects of business models of this type are that they actively reduce consumption and, from a business perspective, may lead to loyal long-term customer relationships. However, such approaches often come with a price premium which often confines respective products to a niche market. Moreover, they might be difficult to scale because prevalent consumer habits of buying products at a fast pace are difficult to overcome.
- Repurpose for society/environment: Such business models seek to create social or environmental benefits beside being financially sustainable (see the topic of social enterprises in Chapter C.9.2). Examples are social enterprises and other hybrid business models as discussed in-depth below. When successful, such approaches can harmonize sustainability thinking with business motives, which then can deliver positive sustainable value to society and companies. Current market logics, however, often do not favor such approaches.
- Develop sustainable scale-up solutions: Such business models deliver sustainable solutions on a large scale to maximize sustainability benefits. Examples are collaborative approaches to scaling up such as open innovation platforms, franchising approaches for sustainable enterprises, or sustainable crowdfunding (see also Chapter C.9.2). Approaches of this type can potentially create change through the scaling of sustainable solutions. A strong focus on scalability might also, however, detract from sustainability purposes and can lead to negative sustainability impacts, if scaled-up approaches eventually prove to be unsustainable.

Task C9-1

Find real-life examples for the various business model archetypes. What do the companies implementing these models do differently compared to companies implementing conventional business models? What is their value proposition, how do they create and deliver value, and how do they capture value?

The creation of (sustainable) business models is often a purposeful process of innovation. Business model innovation describes a holistic transformation of a company's core business logic rather than focusing on the innovation of isolated products. Sustainable business model innovation, therefore, describes the creation of "modified and completely new business models [that] can help develop integrative and competitive solutions by either radically reducing negative and/or creating positive external effects for the natural environment and society" (Schaltegger, Hansen, & Lüdeke-Freund, 2016, p. 3). Such innovations are often subject to significant challenges as described by Schaltegger, Lüdeke-Freund, and Hansen (2016). The development of sustainable niche market business models into sustainable mass market business models often requires convincing potential customers to change their own habits (e.g., changing to product service systems instead of buying products or paying higher prices for more durable products). Furthermore, it requires opening new communication and distribution channels to address and reach potential customers beyond a formerly often clearly defined target group. A move toward mass markets might be especially difficult if niche companies could previously yield higher margins, which might not be realistic in larger markets with more cost pressure from consumers. A transformation of formerly conventional mass market business models into more sustainable mass market business models can be similarly difficult. Here again, customers have to be convinced to accept changes to products they are familiar with. The same applies to other actors in the supply chain which, for example, have to adapt to a more efficient use of materials or to new collaborations with suppliers. Bocken and Geradts (2020) illustrate how different institutional barriers can inhibit such innovation processes. First and foremost, a focus on maximizing shareholder value is regarded as detrimental for sustainable business model innovation as it leads to uncertainty avoidance and short-termism. Such institutional barriers arguably lead to a focus on exploiting existing business models instead of approaching sustainable business model innovations. Consequently, companies often revert to standard innovation processes, conventional resource planning, incentive systems focused on the short term, and on financial performance metrics. Companies that are able to break free of this logic and balance shareholder and stakeholder value, however, seem to have better chances for sustainable business model innovation as they more easily embrace ambiguity and value long-term business sustainability. The authors argue that this can lead to an enabling innovation structure that embraces sustainability through the development of peoples' capabilities as well as incentive schemes and performance metrics for sustainability. In addition, the literature offers various tools for sustainable business model innovation. Bocken et al. (2013), for example, offer a value mapping tool to support sustainable business modelling while Lüdeke-Freund et al. (2018) identify a multitude of sustainable business model patterns as a source of inspiration to help companies integrate sustainable value creation in their core business.

Sustainability in business 40: Choice editing as an approach to more sustainable business stewardship

The adoption of a stewardship role was identified above as an approach to sustainable business models. Retail companies are in an exceptional position in the supply chain to take over a stewardship role with a downstream view on the supply chain as they are an important gatekeeper between producers and consumers. Retail companies (as well as any other company) can engage in choice editing. That is, they can actively limit the choices available to their customers by not offering certain products in their stores as a way of using the design of value propositions and sales channels of a business model to promote more sustainable consumer behavior. In recent years, choice editing has been increasingly discussed in sustainability management, and there are numerous examples in which retailers use choice editing and thus force more sustainable consumption patterns upon their customers. Already in 2015, the London-based department store Selfridges stopped sales of disposable plastic bottles of which the company previously sold more than 400,000 per year. In 2021, the German discount chain Aldi announced its intention to entirely ban meat products that stem from indoor breeding of animals from its stores by 2030. For retailers, choice editing can be an approach to stewardship that is directly connected to their business model, because providing customers with a certain choice of goods is indeed the core purpose of retailing. However, producing companies can also engage in choice editing. In 2006, for example, the German multinational firm Henkel took over Alba, a Brazilian producer of adhesives. Some of Alba's products were prone to misuse as cheap drugs for glue sniffing with severe health effects. Immediately after the takeover, Henkel therefore began to develop alternative products and introduced them to the market already shortly after the takeover to entirely replace the former products and prevent misuse. In all these cases, "value" is not regarded as a short-term concept but instead focuses on the long-term perspective and on different stakeholders.

Sources: Höppner (2021); Ogleby (2016); WBCSD (2008)

C.9.2 Alternative forms of organizations

In the context of sustainability management, alternative forms of organizations beyond purely profit-driven perspectives can provide some interesting avenues for sustainable organizational practices. Respective organizations often experiment with collaborative organizational mechanisms that allow them to address societal challenges. Many alternative forms of organizations embed sustainability-oriented goals in their logic of for-profit and market-based businesses. Hence, they often operate at the crossroads between the private, public, and civil society sectors (see again Chapter B.4.1) and are sometimes referred to as hybrid organizations (Battilana & Lee, 2014). The concept of organizational hybridity refers to the combination of underlying organizational logics that would conventionally not be pursued together. Hybrid organizations often, for example, combine mission-driven elements of nonprofit organizations with profit-driven practices of commercial enterprises. While such combinations are highly complex, they can also be a source of creativity and are therefore a potentially important way of bringing together market-oriented organizations with sustainability-related goals. Examples of such alternative forms of organizations include cooperatives, cross-sector partnerships, and social enterprises, as further illustrated in this chapter.

Sustainability in research 13: Pache and Santos' 2013 article on hybrid organizing

Hybrid organizational structures unite competing logics in a single structure and thus represent different perspectives. In the 2013 article "Inside the hybrid organisation: Selective coupling as a response to competing institutional logics", Anne-Claire Pache and Filipe Santos argue that today's pluralistic, institutional environment increases the urgency of such forms of organization. According to the authors, dilemmas stemming from competing logics are considered as the major challenge in those companies. The authors address this issue by explaining challenges of hybrid organizations and developing strategies to resolve these conflicts.

In early institutional research, conflict resolution in hybrid structures is based on decoupling and compromise strategies. The decoupling strategy supports symbolic practices that are expected by one logic, whereby the organization is exclusively focused on implementing another logic. A for-profit company, for example, might extensively advertise a supposed sustainability focus by highlighting certain philanthropic projects without really engaging in core aspects of sustainability management. The compromise strategy deals with the attempt to comply with institutional rules, but only to a minimum standard, to create a balance between conflicting expectations of external actors. Both approaches, however, can lead to internal conflicts, and external stakeholders tend to critically reflect corporate actions. Nevertheless, various hybrid organizations successfully navigate in their environment. The authors conducted an inductive comparative case study of four such social enterprises. Based on an analysis of extensive archival data and 62 interviews, Pache and Santos show that the organizations combined competing commercial and social logics by selectively linking them. They argue that selective coupling is a form of combining different logics, which can reduce internal conflicts and secure external support in the long term. In conclusion, the authors argue that companies meet the demands of external actors by combining competing logics especially when stakeholder interests become more pluralistic. If a company is able to create a perfect combination, it can strongly differentiate itself from the competition and achieve its long-term legitimacy.

Source: Pache and Santos (2013)

Cooperatives are community-based organizations that pursue the goal of serving the socio-economic needs of their members. Such organizations have a long tradition and can be traced back to medieval times when, for example, peasants collaborated in growing crops to achieve the most efficient harvesting outcomes and share the risk of crop losses. During industrialization and the labor movement in the 18th century, cooperatives were further introduced as alternatives to purely commercially oriented factory structures. Putting decent working and living conditions in the focus, cooperatives later spread to different sectors, such as milling and banking (Forno, 2013). Nowadays, many different forms of small and large cooperatives exist. A prominent example are producer or worker cooperatives in developing countries, which are owned and controlled by local smallholder farmers. Local ownership and local control of the business activities as well as the combined bargaining power enable these cooperatives to remain autonomous and self-organized (Tefera et al., 2017; Webb & Cheney, 2014). Coffee cooperatives, for example, are comprised of smallholder coffee farmers who voluntarily join their forces to sell their coffee beans on the global market and ensure the economic and social well-being of their local communities. By collaborating in the cooperative, the farmers also improve their access to resources and are able to, for example, participate in business training activities or share equipment for harvesting and processing the coffee beans. Moreover, the individual farmer, who is member of a cooperative, is not as vulnerable to market risks or dependent on particular buyers. Hence, they can also start to invest in long-term and more environmentally friendly production practices, such as crop rotation, natural fertilizers, and mixed cultivation. This way, cooperatives in developing countries do not only improve the economic and social welfare of their members, but might also have a positive long-term impact on the environment (Mazzarol et al., 2018; Webb & Cheney, 2014).

Credit cooperatives are another prominent example of alternative forms of organizations (Cutcher & Mason, 2014; Goglio & Kalmi, 2017). Cooperative banks, such as The Co-operative Bank in the UK, the National Cooperative Bank in the U.S., or the Volksbanken/Raiffeisenbanken in Germany, were founded in the 18th century with the aim of serving people and small businesses—initially mostly in rural areas—by offering credits with low interest rates. In contrast to private banks, cooperative banks are owned and managed by their members, that is, the customers who hold shares in the bank or have deposits with them. Hence, the customers, as members of the cooperative, vote for the board of directors. This participatory system ideally ensures that the cooperative banks prioritize their customers' needs. However, the member-oriented value system often also limits the amount of profits generated by the bank as its members are mostly individuals and small firms, while large industry players usually have their financial deposits in private banks. The total amount of money invested in cooperative banks is therefore much smaller compared to private banks, which also limits the overall social and environmental impact that cooperative banks can have.

Sustainability in business 41: The Mondragon cooperative

One of the most well-known and largest cooperatives worldwide is the Mondragon Group founded in Spain in 1956 as a membership-based production company mainly selling paraffin heaters. While many production cooperatives maintain a local membership structure, Mondragon decided to think big in its business model. Particularly in the 1990s and early 2000s, the cooperative started to respond to the ongoing economic globalization by building its own production plants abroad. This way, the company aimed to stay competitive on a global market and increase its market shares. Consequently, the Mondragon Group grew significantly in the past decades. Today, it is one of the largest Spanish companies, with over 80,000 employees, activities in almost all countries of the world, and with operations in diverse subsectors of manufacturing, retail, finance, and knowledge. The Mondragon Group houses various cooperatives under its organizational roof that are operating in accordance with the International Cooperative Alliance, an NGO that represents the global movement of cooperatives and sets guidelines for these organizations. Mondragon stresses that this means that their community focus is still at the center of organizational activities, represented by its corporate focus on "human promotion" and "social development."

While Mondragon is frequently highlighted as positive example of multinational cooperatives, its internationalization was not without critique. Researchers recently found, for example, that the internationalization led to a global labor hierarchy within the Mondragon Group, in which the interests and decisions of the headquarters seem to outweigh those of subsidiaries abroad. The headquarters' distribution of power and interests therefore impeded the participatory and member-focused practices that are an inherent part of the cooperative model.

Sources: Centro Corporativo de Mondragon (2021); Errasti et al. (2017) ; Flecha and Ngai (2014)

Overall, the member-oriented and collaborative structure of cooperatives comes with opportunities for the generation of social welfare and sustainable development, because they usually focus on a long-term perspective instead of merely short-term profits. However, this alternative form of organizations also comes with a range of challenges, as illustrated by Cook (1995). Problems might arise, for example, from the frequently unclear or undefined property rights in cooperatives. Newer members might benefit from entering a cooperative later than others, because their investment is smaller, but they nevertheless obtain the full benefits. Another challenge in cooperatives arises when the investment portfolio does not reflect each member's risk preferences. Consequently, some members have to take more risk than they are comfortable with, which may negatively influence the performance of a cooperative.

A second alternative form of organizations are public–private partnerships. As the name suggests, these organizations are cross-sector partnerships between actors from the public and private sector, which agree to provide public services and create societal welfare while sharing financial, social, and human resources. Ideally, the overall objectives of the partnership should not be in conflict with the partners' individual organizational goals and the collaboration has to be formally contracted. Like cooperatives, public–private partnerships have a long history of implementing society-oriented projects in areas such as urban planning and education programs. Combining the strengths of public and private actors brings opportunities for both parties. Public organizations benefit, for example, from accessing the expertise, skills, and technological innovation of private actors, while private actors benefit, for example, from mitigating risks and tapping into governmental resources and guarantees. To avoid failure, Osei-Kyei et al. (2017) suggest that the partnerships should follow some basic principles, including focusing on long-term goals and ensuring effective risk management.

Public–private partnerships have the potential to tackle to the sustainability issues that the public and civil society sectors alone fail to address, because they formally bind private companies to contribute to public goals and combine the partners' respective strengths (N. Wang & Ma, 2021). An example of a public–private partnership is the BioCarbon Fund (Baroudy & Hooda, 2011; Syiem et al., 2020). This cross-national fund from the governments of the United Kingdom, the United States, Norway, and Germany aims at lowering the greenhouse gas emissions from deforestation in developing countries. Businesses from small subsistence farmers to multinational corporations play an important role in land use. Therefore, the BioCarbon Fund brings together public and private actors in order to change to sustainable sourcing and land management practices. The private partners contribute by mobilizing financial resources and providing livelihood opportunities for the local communities.

However, public–private partnerships also bear potential risks (Anopchenko et al., 2019), such as a high managerial complexity that comes with large projects involving diverse partners and different interests. The private partner, for example, might have to carry the full financial risks and burdens while at the same time being confronted with high governmental restrictions. The public partner, in turn, faces the risk of a possible bankruptcy of the private partner and full responsibility as a consequence. Public–private partnerships face frequent criticism as they are often delayed or miss their financial targets. In a literature review, Languille (2017) summarized that many public–private partnerships rarely meet their expectations in practice. Instead, a lack of accounting mechanisms and incentives often leads to inefficiency. An example is public–private schools in the Global South, which are supposed to include children from low-income households into a high-quality education system. In reality, however, these schools are often located in urban areas that attract high-income families, while the poor children still attend public schools with scarce resources.

A third alternative form of organizations are social enterprises, also referred to as social businesses, social ventures, sustainable enterprises, or enterprises for the public good (Ostertag et al., 2021; Vedula et al., 2021). These types of organizations pursue a social or environmental mission while simultaneously engaging in commercial activities to sustain their business operations (Battilana & Lee, 2014). From their extensive review of the literature, Saebi et al. (2019) distinguish four different types of social enterprises by differentiating two main criteria: the social or environmental mission and the commercial activities. Regarding the social or environmental mission, the social enterprise can create a sustainability-related value for their beneficiaries or with their beneficiaries. The former is usually the case when companies generate some form of commercial revenue to cross-subsidize their engagement for the environment or for people in need. In the latter case, the beneficiaries are seen as part of the value creation process (e.g., as employees), so that the social mission is achieved with the beneficiaries. With regard to the commercial activities of social enterprises, Saebi et al. (2019) distinguish between differentiated and integrated approaches. In the differentiated approach, social and commercial value creation are independent from each other. Commercial profits are generated completely unrelated to the social or environmental mission, but they are used to fund this mission. In the integrated approach, commercial and social value creation are entangled, for example, when beneficiaries are the paying customers of the social enterprise's products or services, which are then usually provided to them for a low price.

This differentiation results in four types of social enterprises as illustrated in Figure 34: The first is the two-sided value model in which the commercial profits cross-subsidize the social value. An example is the shoe manufacturer TOMS, which donates one pair of shoes to a child in need for each pair sold to regular paying customers. In this model, commercial activities are differentiated from the social mission and beneficiaries are recipients outside of the value creation process. Second, the market-oriented work model, which also cross-subsidizes the social value creation by differentiated commercial activities. In this case, however, social value is generated with beneficiaries. The German social enterprise Auticon, for example, employs autistic people as IT consultants. The beneficiaries (i.e., people on the autism spectrum) are thus part of the value creation process. The commercial value in this business model is differentiated, as companies pay Auticon for its IT services to access the specific skills of people with autism. The third type is the one-sided value model, which combines an integrated commercial value creation with beneficiaries as customers and a social value creation for beneficiaries. Such business models are prevalent in many social enterprises in the Global South. People in remote rural areas, for example, are offered products that improve their health or living standards. These people are thus paying customers who do not actively engage in value creating processes. In the fourth type, the social-oriented work model, beneficiaries are both customers and at the same time employees in the social enterprises. The commercial value creation is thus integrated, and the beneficiaries are part of the value creation process. As such, this type is a combination between the market-oriented and the one-sided value model. A prominent example is the company VisionSpring, which sells high quality glasses to the poor communities for affordable prices, while employing people from these communities in their sales department (Saebi et al., 2019).

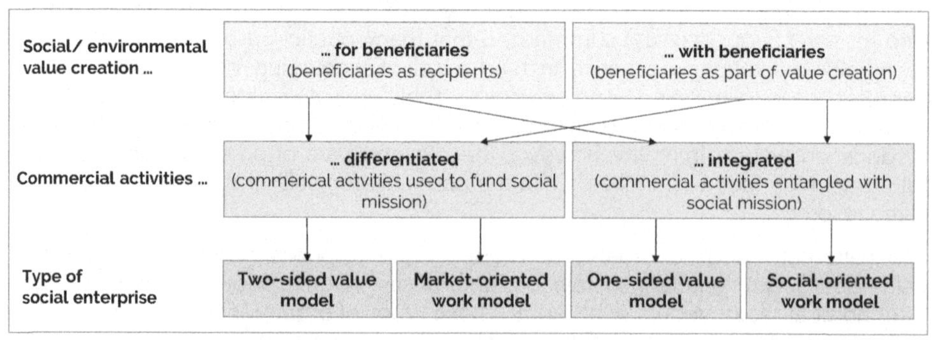

Figure 34: Different business models of social enterprises (own figure based on Saebi et al., 2019)

Despite the different approaches of social enterprises, a common goal is to use market-based activities to address needs in society. The profit- and growth-orientated commercial activities therefore serve as a means to reach the sustainability-related mission of social enterprises (R. Hahn & Ince, 2016). The range of different sustainability-related missions of social enterprises is vast—from solving local problems to overcoming market failures that other actors, such as commercial businesses, public institutions, or nonprofit organizations, leave unattended. By definition of their sustainability-related goals, social enterprises are inherently more sustainable than purely commercial firms (Zahra et al., 2009).

Sustainability in business 42: Fighting food waste with "Too Good To Go"

Food waste is one of the major challenges of our society: On a global level, 1.3 billion tons of food are wasted per year, which equals one-third of all food produced for human consumption. Food waste is both an environmental problem as it is responsible for six percent of the global greenhouse gas emissions, and at the same time a social problem, considering that around two billion people face food insecurity worldwide. The prevention of food waste is therefore an important target for social enterprises, which the Danish company Too Good To Go (TGTG) aims to tackle. With a platform business model, TGTG connects local restaurants and supermarkets that have surplus food at the end of the day. With the TGTG smartphone app, restaurants and supermarkets can offer high quality surplus food—or food that has reached its "best before" date—in the form of food boxes. Customers purchase food boxes online and pick them up. The price per box depends on the quality and amount of food but is generally a lot more affordable than the regular items. For each box sold, TGTG keeps a fixed amount of revenues to cover their expenses and sustain their business.

TGTG was founded in 2016 in Copenhagen and has successfully spread to 14 European countries in the first five years of business activities, including large markets such as France, Germany, and the United Kingdom. Along with their app service, TGTG has initiated "the food waste movement" to achieve a reduction of food waste on four levels: households, businesses, schools, and public affairs. While the former three aim to inspire individuals and organizations to reduce their waste directly at home, at work, or in school, the latter aims at driving change in food supply chains through regulations and policies, to which TGTG wants to contribute. This way, TGTG primarily creates social value in the form of positive impact on the environment (less waste and reduced greenhouse gas emissions in the food value chain), which means that beneficiaries are not part of the value creation process (social value for beneficiaries). Their commercial value creation is primarily based on regular customers who buy food boxes, that is, a differentiated commercial value creation. TGTG's primary business model is therefore, based on the typology of Saebi et al. (2019), a two-sided value model. However, considering that TGTG also sees people with low income as their target group, who otherwise cannot afford high-quality restaurant food, they can also be clustered as one-sided value model (social value creation for beneficiaries and integrated commercial value creation).

Sources: FAO et al. (2020); Too Good To Go International (n.d.); Vo-Thanh et al. (2021)

The goal duality of social enterprises (i.e., the combination of sustainability-related and commercial goals) comes with several advantages. Doherty et al. (2014) identified, for example the increased independence of the organization through its commercial activities as an advantage, and Waldner (2020) found that the communication of the social mission helps to maintain a positive reputation and stakeholder support due to their social orientation. However, balancing a social mission with commercial goals may also lead to organizational tensions (Smith & Lewis, 2011). Such tensions derive from contradictory elements that organizational actors have to attend to. These contradictions can come from external sources, such as diverse and oftentimes conflicting stakeholder demands, for example, from investors, customers, employees, and beneficiaries. Tensions may also stem from internal sources, for example, when the organizational members try to balance elements of profit-oriented and mission-driven organizational values and norms. When leaders of social enterprises face such tensions in the form of conflicting stakeholder demands or different organizational values, they may have difficulties to make the most effective decision for the enterprise's future. Hence, tensions pose challenges for the leaders in social enterprises, who have to decide, for example, who to hire (the person with a business background or the person with expertise in the social field), how to communicate the dual identities to stakeholders (focusing on financial independency or social value creation), or which performance metrics to use to measure success and growth (e.g., financial measures that show short-term success and are easy to quantify, or social impact measures that oftentimes are ambiguous and long-term oriented) (Smith et al., 2013). If not addressed properly, such tensions are likely to result in an imbalance of the social and commercial goals, which may threaten the organization's legitimacy and ultimately bears the danger of mission drift, that is, an inconsistency perceived by the stakeholders between the organization's actions and its stated mission. Mission drift usually occurs in the form of a loss of focus on the social mission for the gain of financial performance (Grimes et al., 2019).

Sustainability in society 22: Benefit Corporations and B Corp certifications

In 2010, Benefit Corporations (B Corps) were introduced in the United States to classify social enterprises. The idea was to enable organizations to put their social or environmental mission in focus while at the same time allowing financial growth and a limited profit distribution. Today, in some countries such as Italy, Colombia, and most states of the United States, "Benefit Corporation" is a registered legal form as addition to other legal forms such as Limited Companies (Ltd.).

However, many other countries do not have legal structures for social enterprises. Nevertheless, social enterprises in these countries can still obtain a B Corp certification through an assessment, during which the social and environmental impact of the social enterprise is evaluated. Social enterprises that want to become a B Corp, that is, obtain the B Corp certificate, thus need to demonstrate that they are able to balance social and financial goals through high standards of social and environmental performance, transparency, and legal accountability. The evaluation process is administered by the nonprofit organization B Lab with reassessment every three years. B Corp certifications can help social enterprises in terms of reputation, stakeholder support, and network access. According to B Lab, there are currently over 3,500 certified B Corps in more than 70 countries including, for example, ice cream producer Ben & Jerry's, the e-commerce platform Etsy, and outdoor gear retailer Patagonia.

Sources: Moroz et al. (2018); Villela et al. (2021)

Generally, mission drift is associated with negative outcomes for the social enterprise, such as a decline of the organization's authenticity, which may result in a lack of stakeholder support, or even organizational failure (Battilana & Lee, 2014). Social entrepreneurs can be surprisingly creative to ensure the stability of their sustainability-oriented mission and avoid mission drift. Some, for example, integrate participatory governance mechanisms that allow their employees or customers to influence the organization's decision making. One example is the online bank Tomorrow Bank, which invites all stakeholders, including employees, customers, and potential customers, to share their ideas, feedback and requests via a publicly available virtual whiteboard. Many social enterprises also include a constraint in their governance structure, which forbids them from distributing profits to their shareholders. This mechanism serves to avoid profit-maximizing behavior (Defourny, 2014). To improve legitimacy and the general working conditions of social enterprises, some countries have developed specific legal forms for organizations that qualify as social enterprises.

Another challenge many social enterprises face is access to the financial market. While securing investments such as bank loans and venture capital is important for any kind of venture, social enterprises face particular challenges, considering that they are oftentimes associated with unfavorable risk and return characteristics because they are not (primarily) guided by the aim of maximizing financial returns. However, at the same time, donors and investors of nonprofit organizations may refrain from investing in social enterprises due to their commercial activities. Against this background, some specialized options of financing have evolved in the last couple of years. One example is social banks, that is financial institutions that specifically provide funding to organizations that aim to create social value. Another option for social enterprises to obtain funding are impact investments that specifically aim to create a measurable social or environmental impact and financial returns at the same time (see Chapter B.5.2). Social venture capital and venture philanthropy are similar investing instruments in which private investors provide capital for social projects. These options usually center on using venture capital methods to achieve a positive social impact while providing a high level of nonfinancial support. Finally, social enterprises can also obtain funds through sustainability-oriented crowdfunding (see Chapters B.5.2 and B.5.4).

Task C9-2

Find three examples of social enterprises. Which type of social enterprise model (according to Saebi et al., 2019) do they apply? How do they differ in their approach to create economic and social/environmental value? Where do you see the main challenges for these businesses to achieve their goals?

Faces of sustainability 10: Muhammad Yunus

The Nobel Peace Prize Laureate of 2006, Muhammad Yunus, is a serial social entrepreneur. The economist was born in 1940 in Bengal (today Bangladesh) and was educated in the United States. Being confronted with poverty and famine in his home country Bangladesh, he was eager to act based on the idea that businesses can be an important tool to solve societal problems. He started to experiment by lending money to poor women. The loans were meant to help the women start their own businesses. Because they had all paid back their loans, he founded the first microcredit institution in 1983, the Grameen Bank. Microcredits are small loans for poor people at reasonable interest rates. Regular banks often dismiss such small loans, as the transactions costs as well as the risk that the poor will not be able to repay the loans are high. In Yunus' opinion, however, microcredits are an important mechanism for people to start a business and find a way out of poverty, which would ultimately lead to an improvement in human rights and social justice. The role of women was of particular importance for Yunus, as he sees them as the engines of their families. According to him, women who earn money are likely to invest it in their children's health and education as well as their households, which improves the living conditions of the whole family. The microcredits of Grameen Bank are therefore primarily directed toward women.

In 2006, Yunus received the Nobel Prize for his engagement. The Grameen Bank is nowadays frequently used as a prime example for social entrepreneurship and for its combination of business and social logics that aim to create a systemic change to reduce poverty in the Global South. However, his ideas are not uncontested. Over the last decade, critical voices accused Yunus' Grameen Bank or more specifically the idea of microcredits of having led many small business owners into a debt trap. Nevertheless, the attention that Muhammad Yunus drew to poverty in developing countries and the shortcomings of the money-centered worldview are largely undisputed.

Sources: Karim (2008); Ford (2013); Parker et al. (2014)

KEY TAKEAWAYS

- Sustainable business models can be differentiated into eight archetypes: Maximize material and energy efficiency; Closing resource loops; Substitute with renewables and natural processes; Deliver functionality not ownership; Encourage sufficiency; Repurpose for society/environment; Develop sustainable scale up solutions.
- Developing sustainable niche market business models into sustainable mass market business models as well as transforming conventional mass market business models into sustainable mass market business models is challenging and prone to different institutional barriers such as a focus on maximizing shareholder value.
- Alternative organizational forms combine the logic of for-profit businesses with social and environmental aspects in their organizational structure and can, therefore, be important tools to foster sustainability. Cooperatives are community-based organizations which pursue the goal to serve the socioeconomic needs of their members. Public–private partnerships are collaborations between actors of the public and private sectors. Social enterprises are organizations that pursue a social or environmental mission while engaging in commercial activities.
- Social enterprises can apply four business model archetypes: a one-sided and a two-sided value model as well as a market-oriented and a social-oriented work model.
- Social enterprises often face limitations in accessing financial resources, and they are challenged by their goal multiplicity, by the need to balance different identities and stakeholder expectations, and by the danger of mission drift.

C.10 Digitalization and sustainability management

LEARNING GOALS

After reading this chapter you will be able to ...

- ... illustrate different environmental, social, and governance challenges stemming from digitalization.
- ... explain opportunities of various digital technologies to foster sustainability and sustainability management.
- ... discuss how respective technologies can generally be used to influence behavior.
- ... explain the idea of corporate digital responsibility (CDR).
- ... illustrate areas for environmental, social, and governance CDR.

Introduction to Chapter C.10: Screencast
Watch an introduction to the chapter here:

The topic of digitalization with its potential benefits and drawbacks for sustainability in society and in organizations is vast because, at least potentially, it affects all elements of human life and corporate functions. Digital technologies can enhance but also impede environmental sustainability, and respective digital innovations can help as well as hinder social advancement, for example, through exclusion or inclusion of disadvantaged groups in society as outlined throughout this chapter. Due to the breadth of relevant issues, however, this chapter can only give a brief introduction into this extensive topic by highlighting exemplary aspects of digitalization as a challenge for and as an enabler of sustainability and sustainability management.

C.10.1 Digitalization as a challenge for sustainability and sustainability management

Challenges of digitalization for sustainability and sustainability management come to the fore in all three sustainability-related aspects of ESG (environment, social, governance; see Chapter B.5.1). On the environmental side, digital technologies contribute an increasing share to global greenhouse gas emissions. For example, the mining of Bitcoins, probably the most well-known digital currency, is expected to produce more greenhouse gases than the entire states of the Czech Republic and Qatar combined—and that is not even from worldwide Bitcoin mining but only the share of respective operations in China (Jiang et al., 2021). Overall, the information and communication technology sector is estimated to contribute up to four percent of global greenhouse gas emissions, and they are expected to increase further (Freitag et al., 2021). Another prominent sustainability challenge of digitalization is the generation of large amounts of electronic waste, that is, discarded electrical or electronic equipment. While electronic devices, and with this eventually also electronic waste, have been produced for decades, the amount of such waste is increasing fast as such devices are nowadays replaced at a high pace and electronic gadgets and components can be found in almost every part of our daily lives. As most electronic components contain some toxic materials, inadequate disposal poses serious environmental risks to water, soil, and air. Given that recycling quotas are still low, with a worldwide average of less than 20 percent of all electronic waste being collected and recycled (Forti et al., 2020), this translates into risks not only for nature but also for human life, for example when toxic materials dissolve into groundwater resources and so on. Furthermore, also the extraction and mining of new materials and metals needed for the production of digital technologies is often connected to severe environmental problems (n.a., 2021).

Sustainability in society 23: The dirty side of producing digital technologies

Digital devices have entered almost every part of our daily lives. They all require electronic components, and these require materials such as cobalt and lithium. These materials are known for sustainability problems especially during the early life cycle phases of mining and extraction, with severe environmental damages for the affected regions. Cobalt, for example, is a critical base material used in batteries or to produce superalloys. Large parts of the world's cobalt are mined in the Democratic Republic of Congo and is often extracted by artisanal miners, that is, people who are not officially employed but instead work independently, usually by hand, to mine cobalt for a subsistence living. Apart from environmental problems especially in unofficial and largely unregulated mines, the mining of cobalt also incurs a heavy social cost. While it may have a positive impact on local living standards, there are significant negative health effects for the workers, many of whom are still children. Some companies actively try to improve the situation, but complex supply chains and other issues prove to be difficult hurdles. Interestingly, especially digital technologies such as blockchain could be one way to improve sustainability standards of extracting such materials by enabling the transparent tracing of materials. Another critical component particularly of batteries is lithium. Mining lithium often requires large quantities of water in otherwise arid areas such as the sand flats in northern Argentina or Chile, or it requires large amounts of energy, both of which have a significant negative environmental impact. As with cobalt, the pressure is high either to improve the sustainability performance of lithium mining, to technically substitute it with other material in respective products, or to reduce the necessary amounts of new lithium by improving the recyclability of old products.

Sources: Banza Lubaba Nkulu et al. (2018); Bazilier and Girard (2018); Nogrady (2020); n.a. (2021)

The production and disposal of electronic waste also leads to significant social challenges. Inadequate disposal and recycling harms the health and safety of millions of adults and children working in the informal waste sector, especially in the Global South (World Health Organization, 2021), and the mining of new materials and metals is connected to severe social issues such as child labor, exploitation, and health risk (Banza Lubaba Nkulu et al., 2018). Beyond risks and problems related to materials used in electronic devices, Trittin-Ulbrich et al. (2021) illustrate additional social issues of digitalization related to the actual delivery and use of respective tools and technologies in and around organizations. They illustrate that many Internet companies and providers of digital platforms are often in a monopoly-like situation and make use of a low paid precarious labor force while often neglecting workers' rights by putting employees under constant surveillance. Also many seemingly sustainability-compatible business models from the sharing economy (see again Chapter B.6.3) have received criticism when, for example, flexible working arrangements for people who deliver certain services offer little payment or social benefits while being highly insecure (also Etter et al., 2019). Moreover, the application of many digital services themselves may cause direct problems. The use of inadequately or sometimes just carelessly programmed algorithms amplifies discrimination by reinforcing stereotypes resulting in unfair treatment, for example, of certain people applying for a job (Köchling & Wehner, 2020). Finally, addiction to social media has become a widespread phenomenon in recent years.

Apart from environmental and social problems, governance issues also arise when looking at issues of data security, data privacy, and so on. We regularly hear news about cyberattacks, leaked passwords, and illegal sales of private and confidential information. Basically, every individual of our globalized society that does not live in total isolation leaves digital traces everywhere, and it is difficult—if not impossible—to control them or even recognize what kind of data is being collected. These traces of data can be used to monitor an individual's beliefs, attitudes, and behavior to an extent most people cannot even imagine. Furthermore, our personal but publicly or semi-publicly available data (i.e., accessible for certain private or public companies and governmental actors) can at least partly be used also in the real world, for example, for facial recognition or other means of identification. Consequently, personal privacy and confidentiality is at risk from private companies and governmental actors—or partly from both if they willingly or unwillingly cooperate. In China, for example, data from hundreds of millions of surveillance cameras are analyzed with facial recognition software and artificial intelligence. This technology supports the Chinese surveillance state and is not only used to fight crime or control outbreaks during the COVID-19 pandemic but also to control ethnic minorities (Qiang, 2019). In a technologically similar example, the London police uses live facial recognition for real-time identity checks in public areas to identify criminal suspects automatically with the aim of increasing safety and efficiency (Bradford et al., 2020), which illustrates that the circumstances of using respective technologies can make a significant difference in our perception of such applications. Digitalization might even contribute to destabilizing entire societies via the seemingly ubiquitous fake news. Critics even warn that "fake news is not an unintended consequence of social media, but a central part of social media business models and a key source of revenue" (Trittin-Ulbrich et al., 2021, p. 8).

Task C10-1

As an individual, you do not only own physical goods but you also the right of your own personal data. How far are you willing to resign this right and give away your data (a) for higher social goods such as less crime and increased security on the streets (b) for your own personal gain in exchange for free digital services? Try to find out which companies have access to what kind of your personal data when looking through some of the apps installed on your smartphone!

Sustainability in business 43: Facebook and the Cambridge Analytica data scandal

Internet firms and social media platforms make extensive use of algorithms to collect and analyze data, which can then be used to influence users in their attitudes and behavior. In 2018, a data scandal of hitherto unprecedented scale surfaced when a whistleblower revealed that the data analytics company Cambridge Analytica used extensive personal information of almost 90 million Facebook users without their authorization or knowledge. The data was used, among others, in Donald Trump's 2016 presidential campaign to selectively target voters with news to influence their voting behavior. This campaign might have included content that was later allegedly connected to a potential Russian campaign that aimed at disrupting the presidential election. Later it became known that Facebook apparently knew about the unauthorized harvesting of data already in 2015, but it did not alert users and took only limited steps to recover or secure personal data. Facebook CEO Mark Zuckerberg testified to the United States congress, and the company admitted to mishandling data of millions of customers. It was later fined USD 5 billion as part of a settlement over claims of mishandling data.

Sources: Berghel (2018); Cadwalladr and Graham-Harrison (2018); Isaak and Hanna (2018); Ma and Gilbert (2019)

C.10.2 Digitalization as an enabler of sustainability and sustainability management

The other side of the coin is that digitalization also offers many opportunities to improve sustainability and foster sustainability management. Digital communities and social media platforms enable stakeholders to make themselves heard and actively engage with corporate as well as public decision makers and hold them accountable for their decisions as news about wrongdoings can nowadays spread faster than ever. Digitalization has empowered entire social movements and, for example, climate change activists, indigenous influencers, or victims of abuse use digital technologies to speak up, spread the word, and push sustainability-related topics. Furthermore, digital services can often substitute physical goods or services (e.g., videoconferences can replace some physical meetings and thus save travel emissions). If the respective digital solutions create less environmental impact—which could be determined, for example, through life cycle sustainability assessment (see Chapter C.6.2)—they can contribute to ecological sustainability. Similarly, services such as e-healthcare that use digitalization to deliver health care services can improve access to health care, for example, in underserved regions.

Task C10-2

Think about digital versus physical goods and services and find examples where digital solutions substitute physical solutions. What are the sustainability impacts of the digital solutions and of the physical solutions, respectively? Under which circumstances are digital solutions more sustainable?

Significant positive potential for sustainability from digitalization lies in tools and technologies which enable more sustainable processes and behavior across the entire life cycle of products and in the respective supply chains. An important lever for sustainability is the increased transparency enabled through digital technologies because transparency can help to identify sustainability issues and enable oversight to tackle related problems. Against this background, McGrath et al. (2021) provide an extensive overview of potential solutions, including the following:

- Tracking and surveillance technologies: Such systems tend to automate data gathering processes in supply chains so that companies are, for example, no longer reliant on input from suppliers. The authors illustrate in an example how satellite surveillance is used to monitor agricultural supply chains and identify, for example, undesired or even illegal deforestation. Focal companies can use this data to target problem areas and engage with suppliers to stop such activities. Other examples are solutions for smart agriculture to increase crop yields or smart transport packages using digital tags and sensors to monitor and report their status. Respective data (e.g., on location, temperature, humidity, or weight) can be used, for example, to improve sustainable route finding in logistics or to avoid waste and defective goods. Such technologies can also be used to incentivize certain sustainability-related behaviors, for example, careful or energy-efficient driving of truck drivers, but of course the potential problems of such measures are also evident (e.g., data security, privacy issues).
- Dialogic technologies: Digital technologies can be used to enable dialogue between different actors in a supply chain. In supplier management, for example, noncompliance with certain sustainability criteria can be automatically flagged to enable feedback loops and the development of corrective action plans. Furthermore, social and environmental data might be shared with external stakeholders such as customers or NGOs to receive feedback and increase trust, which directly relates to the next type of technologies: data dissemination technologies.
- Data dissemination technologies: Data dissemination technologies enable sharing of information in different formats. An example of such technologies are QR codes (QR = quick response). Such codes, which you also find at the beginning of each chapter in this book providing a link to the screencasts, can easily be printed on products to be scanned by customers with their smartphone. A website can then, for example, provide sustainability-related information on materials used in the product or on manufacturing issues or sources of raw materials. If linked to other technologies such as blockchain (see next bullet point), the connected information might be especially valuable due to an increased level of security. Furthermore, such codes can also be used as a tracking technology, for example, to incentivize the return of old products in exchange for deposits or discounts.
- Blockchain technology: A blockchain is a digitally shared database of transactions or events that are linked through cryptographic methods. Blockchains guarantee a

single version of truth in an otherwise trustless environment so that there is no need for third-party verification of the respective data (see also Pournader et al., 2020). The potential of blockchain technology for sustainability management is extensive (see also Pournader et al., 2020; Saberi et al., 2019) and lies especially in its strength in improving traceability and transparency along with the speed of information transfer among multiple and unrelated actors. It can enable information flows on social and environmental conditions across entire supply chains that would otherwise be lost in the different tiers. For example, information about social or environmental conditions in the phase of raw material extraction or during the cultivation of agricultural goods can be entered into a blockchain and thus transported reliably and fast through the supply chain until the final disposal of the product, where the respective information on the materials that were utilized can be used for reduction or recycling purposes. Such improved traceability can thus help to contribute to more social sustainability by conveying information on human rights or fair wages to buyers and users of goods. It can also be used to improve ecological sustainability by transferring respective environmental information, for example, on environmentally friendly sourcing or production techniques, or by ensuring that certificates from carbon offsetting schemes are used only once and stem from reliable reduction sources (see Chapter C.6.3.2). However, there are various barriers that currently hinder a broad dissemination or pose other problems as discussed, for example, by Babich and Hilary (2020) and Saberi et al. (2019). They illustrate that implementing blockchain technology comes at a comparably high cost as new information technology tools as well as the respective know-how are needed. Furthermore, while data transferred through blockchain technology is incorruptible and thus trustworthy, the reliability of the data relies on the accuracy of the input into the blockchain. Therefore, a weak point is the information creation as it still happens in the physical world.

Sustainability in business 44: IBM's pilot project on sensor-monitored, blockchain-based sustainable water management

Water is a scarce resource in many regions, and sustainable water management is a challenge. In partnership with the nonprofit organization Freshwater Trust and the sensor provider SweetSense, tech giant IBM implemented a pilot system for sustainable groundwater management in California. Sensors transmit real-time data on water extraction in the Sacramento San Joaquin River Delta and the information is then recorded in a blockchain. Farmers, regulators, and other actors can access the information via a web-based dashboard and groundwater use permits can be traded among market actors. For example, a farmer who does not need the entire amount of allocated water can sell excess permits to another farmer. The system also allows the implementation of smart contracts that are automatically executed when certain conditions are met, for example, when certain water levels or price levels are reached. Similar systems are being developed not only for groundwater use but also for waste water management to monitor water quality. Once a company performs a treatment to clean waste water, sensors measure the water quality and send the results to the blockchain. Once the data is recorded in the blockchain, it is traceable and unforgeable so that, for example, authorities can monitor waste water quality in real time and pay benefits or collect fines.

Sources: W. Henry et al. (2020); Kathri (2021); Wolfson (2019)

McGrath et al. (2021) illustrate that the respective digital technologies can often be used either with a control orientation or with a relational orientation. With a control orientation, companies use digital technologies mainly to ensure compliance, for example, of suppliers, with certain standards or procedures. The aim is to improve efficiency and verifiability of processes and to process results by rendering human input unnecessary or at least simplifying it. With a relational orientation, digital technologies are used to initiate and simplify communication between different actors with the aim of improving trust and data sharing as important prerequisites to foster sustainability management. This often facilitates (and sometimes requires) more long-term partnerships, and a focus is usually on less but better data for improved mutual planning and collaboration between actors.

McGrath et al. (2021) further argue that while some technologies might lean more toward one or the other orientation (e.g., dialogic technologies to relational orientation and tracking and surveillance to control orientation), the important question is rather how companies want to use them and with what purpose, and to keep in mind that neither orientation is per se good or bad. Instead, both come with certain advantages and disadvantages. The control orientation, on the one hand, mainly promises improved data security, centralized control, and with this also fast and efficient means to gather data. A relational orientation, on the other hand, provides a more developmental focus for mutual sustainability improvements of different actors. At the same time, it might reduce the amount of data to be collected and analyzed by focusing on depth and quality (instead of breath and volume) of data. On the downside of control orientation, for example, lies the risk of administrative burdens and cost for buying and maintaining the necessary technological infrastructure to cope with the generated amount of data or the risk of producing a negative sense of surveillance that might lead to reluctance of willing participation in such activities. For a relational orientation, respective activities incur time and cost for developing trust and improving relations. For such approaches to be successful, it is furthermore often necessary to reduce the amount of control between actors, and increased data sharing might be associated with an increased risk of losing intellectual property.

C.10.3 Elements of corporate digital responsibility

Building on the idea of corporate social responsibility as introduced in Chapter A.2.4, corporate digital responsibility (CDR) has emerged as a stand-alone concept (e.g., Herden et al., 2021; Lobschat et al., 2021). Initial attempts to define the concept describe CDR as the "extension of a firm's responsibilities which takes into account the ethical opportunities and challenges of digitalization" (Herden et al., 2021, p. 17). CDR is of course relevant for the information technology sector and for companies with digital business models but it is also relevant for any other type of company as long as they use digital data or technologies. Potential areas of application of CDR vary among corporations. Herden et al. (2021) structure topics relating to CDR along the three sustainability-related dimensions of ESG, and the following overview provides an extract of an even wider array of potential topics that corporations have taken or should take responsibility for. For environmental CDR, the authors specifically highlight:

- Reduction of energy and carbon footprint: As outlined above, information and communication technology can leave a significant ecological footprint. Efforts should thus be made to reduce this footprint. In many cases, digital services can be superior to conventional products or services when looking at their environmental impact (e.g., when video conferences reduce the need for business travel). Nevertheless, respective products should be based on efficient technologies, and potential rebound effects should be monitored and if possible avoided.
- Deal with electronic waste: Companies are urged to implement responsible recycling practices for digital waste, which could utilize many of the concepts and approaches illustrated in Chapter C.4.3.
- Use digital systems as a means to facilitate sustainability efforts: Finally (and not discussed by Herden et al., 2021), companies should not only avoid negative environmental effects from digital technologies in a reactive manner but also to actively use them to foster sustainability as outlined in the preceding subchapter.
- For social CDR, Herden et al. (2021) highlight, among others, the following aspects:
- Digital well-being: To avoid mental and physical problems from the use of digital technologies (e.g., addiction to social media), companies are expected to encourage responsible use and support users in finding a right balance between using digital

technologies and staying connected to the real world.

- Digital empowerment: To avoid an increasing digital divide between more and less digitally literate people, companies could engage in digital empowerment by raising awareness and providing respective education.
- Digital inclusion: The implementation of digital technologies should not prevent unserved or underserved people from completing important tasks or from participating in basic activities. The authors refer to the example of providing certain services mainly or even exclusively online such as job application processes, governmental services, or even health applications such as booking an appointment for a COVID-19 vaccination during the recent pandemic.
- Unbiased artificial intelligence: If companies use or develop artificial intelligence, they should ensure that it does not discriminate against any specific groups of people or specific individuals, and they should monitor self-learning processes of artificial intelligence to avoid misconduct. Furthermore, and connected to the topic of digital empowerment and digital inclusion, companies should make sure that people understand the underlying algorithms so that they can comprehend conclusions or recommendations given by artificial intelligence.
- Digital surveillance: A common demon many people associate with digital technologies is an unavoidable surveillance. Companies should thus make sure that advances in encryption, data security, and data anonymity offer protection also to technologically less savvy people.
- Digital freedom: Due to the fact that fundamental digital infrastructures are often within the sphere of influence of private companies, there is also a responsibility for supporting digital freedom as an element of human rights. Companies should take precautions that the data and privacy of users are protected or, if that is not possible, they should inform users about any third parties such as governments who potentially have access to private information.

For governance CDR, finally, Herden et al. (2021) illustrate, among others, the following aspects:

- Data ownership and privacy: Companies should have clear and understandable data ownership and privacy policies.
- Data responsibility and stewardship: Because companies collect and use data, they should handle it responsibly, and they are accountable to data owners.
- Data security: Companies should only collect as much data as is necessary to deliver a certain service. At the same time, companies should take all measures to guarantee data safety including continuous reviews of technical infrastructure and training of employees.
- Robot ethics: Companies that create robots or artificial intelligence must abide by the laws of robotics that provide fundamental yardsticks of behavior for robots and their creators.

Many companies indeed already apply such elements of self-regulatory CDR as awareness in society about the benefits and challenges of digitalization is rising. However, from a current perspective it seems unlikely that the wish for extensive CDR will be satisfied by voluntary measures alone. As is the case with sustainability management in general, multiple stakeholders will have to exercise pressure or create incentives to foster CDR throughout the entire business sphere.

Task C10-3

Identify two companies of your choice with business models strongly anchored in the digitalized technologies: One large multinational and one small or medium-sized company. Develop a first outline of a CDR program for both companies. Prioritize different measures according to their relevance for the respective company and justify your prioritization. In what ways do your ideas for the programs of the two companies differ and why?

KEY TAKEAWAYS

- Digital technologies, for example, use and produce a large amount of energy and electronic waste, they may result in social problems such as low paid work or an amplification of discrimination, and they may be connected to governance issues such as data security or data privacy.
- Digital tools and technologies such as tracking and surveillance technologies, dialogic technologies, data disseminating technologies, and blockchain technology may enable more sustainable processes and behavior.
- Digital technologies can be used either with a control orientation (i.e., to ensure compliance) or with a relational orientation (i.e., to initiate and simplify communication between different actors).
- CDR describes responsibilities of companies regarding ethical opportunities and challenges of digitalization.
- Environmental CDR includes reducing energy and carbon footprint, dealing with digital waste, and using digital systems as a means to facilitate sustainability efforts.
- Social CDR includes, for example, digital well-being, digital empowerment, digital inclusion, unbiased artificial intelligence, digital surveillance, and digital freedom.
- Governance CDR includes, for example, data ownership and privacy, data responsibility and stewardship, data security, and robot ethics.

Glossary

4R framework: Illustrates several alternatives (reuse, repair, remanufacture, recycle) of what to do with a product after its useful life

Active (investment) approach: Capital providers engage with the investees to drive social and ecological topics and standards

Attitude-behavior gap: Describes the failure to translate intentions into action, that is, consumer attitudes do not always lead to actual behavior

Balanced scorecard: Tool in strategic planning and performance management; combines financial perspective, customer perspective, internal business processes perspective and learning and growth perspective to link long-term strategic objectives with short-term actions

Base (or bottom) of the pyramid (BoP): Refers to the bottom-tier of the world income pyramid

Benefit Corporations (B Corps): Legal business form in the United States that enables organizations to put a social or environmental mission in focus while allowing a limited profit distribution; additionally: certification system for Benefit Corporations worldwide

Best-in-class approach: Option in sustainable finance; focuses investment objects that are relatively more sustainable compared with their peers, e.g., the most sustainable companies in an industry

Boomerang effect: See Rebound effect

BoP 1.0: First evolution of BoP business models focusing on the poor as an underserved customer group with the aim of selling to them

BoP 2.0: Second evolution of BoP business models focusing on integrate the BoP as a resource for value co-creation

BoP 3.0: Second evolution of BoP business models that aims more consequently at encouraging self-management, capacity building, and sharing of skills and knowledge

Brundtland definition: Definition of sustainable development by the UN World Commission on Environment and Development (chaired by Gro Harlem Brundtland) saying that "Sustainable development is development that meets the needs of the present without compromising the ability of future generations to meet their own needs" (WCED, 1987, p. 41)

Business case for sustainability: Assumption that it pays off for a company to be sustainable; widespread argument for sustainability management

Business model: Describes how a company implements its business strategy and translates it into business processes

Business model innovation: Describes a holistic transformation of a company's core business logic

Civil society: Referred to as the "third sector" (next to market sector and state); includes broad variety of actors that can neither be subsumed as market actors nor as governmental actors

Civil society organizations: Organizations from the civil society sector that form around a common cause, interest, or idea; e.g., religious groups or loosely organized movements

Civil society push: Determinant for sustainability-oriented innovation – Society can induce normative pressure on other actors to act more sustainably

Closed loop systems: See also Cradle to cradle; systems implementing the strategy of eco-effectiveness in which ideally all waste materials become input resources; such systems can come in the form of biological loops or technological loops

Cooperatives: Community-based organizations which pursue the goal of serving the socio-economic needs of their members

Code of ethics: See Codes of conduct

Codes of conduct: Sets of commitments that define certain attitudes, behaviors, or actions with regard to certain issues or toward a range of stakeholders

Collaborative consumption: A special form of consumption in which ownership is usually replaced by access to resources

Command-and-control instruments: Governmental interventions that prescribe certain outcomes and directly influence behavior of individuals or firms

Communal economies: A type of collaborative consumption; allow the exchange of less tangible assets such as time, skills, money, experience, or space among peers or they allow the exchange of unused or only sporadically used physical items of owners.

Corporate citizenship: Term frequently but ambiguously used to describe corporate efforts in and for society; usually voluntary philanthropic activities by corporations such as donations

Corporate digital responsibility (CDR): The "extension of a firm's responsibilities which takes into account the ethical opportunities and challenges of digitalization" (Herden et al., 2021, p. 17)

Corporate responsibility: See Corporate social responsibility

Corporate social responsibility: The "responsibility of an organization for the impacts of its decisions and activities on society and the environment" (ISO, 2010a, p. 3)

Corruption perceptions index: Index indicating the perceived level of corruption in the public sector; published by the NGO Transparency International

Cost push: Determinant for sustainability-oriented innovation – Increasing prices for raw materials lead to optimized resource usage or substitution of materials by relying on innovation

Cradle to cradle: See also Closed-loop systems; by closing technical or biological material cycles, natural resources should no longer be lost through disposal

Cradle to grave: Counterpart of the "Cradle to cradle" approach in the sense of a linear view on product from raw material extraction to disposal

Credence quality: Type of product attribute; consumer has no knowledge or information to make a judgement about such attributes

Critical sustainability: See quasi-sustainability

Cross-sector partnerships: A company and at least one partner from the nonprofit sector work together

Crowdfunding: Way of obtaining funds by raising usually small amounts of money from a large number of people over the Internet

Deceptive pricing: Pricing practices that try to obscure the true cost of a product

Decommoditization: Practice in (sustainable) supply chain management; "explicitly treating a supplier and/or entire chain that provides a commodity (lots of substitutes/competition mainly on price) as if it supplied a rare/strategic input." (Pagell et al., 2010, p. 64)

Decoupling: Refers to breaking the link between (positive) human development and (negative) ecological impact

Degree of compromise: Construct from sustainability marketing; purchase or usage of sustainable products might involve some form of compromise for the individual

Degree of confidence: Construct from sustainability marketing; illustrates how convinced an induvial is of the sustainability benefits of a product

Design for the environment: Approaches that aim at reducing the overall impact of a product on human health and the environment

Design for sustainability: See Design for the environment

Double materiality: See Nonfinancial materiality

Downcycling: Value of the original material can only partly be restored, recycling process results in lower-grade materials

Earth overshoot day: Exact day in each year when humanity's demand for ecological resources exceeds the Earth's regenerative capacity

Eco-design: See Design for the environment

Eco-efficiency: Strategy to decouple economic development from environmental burden; aims at a relative decoupling through the quantitative reduction of resources and emissions in products or processes

Eco-innovation: "All measures of relevant actors (firms, politicians, unions, associations, churches, private households) which develop new ideas, behavior, products and processes, apply or introduce them and which contribute to a reduction of environmental burdens or to ecologically specified sustainability targets." (Rennings, 2000, p. 322)

Ecological sustainability: See quasi-sustainability

EMAS: European auditable standard for environmental management systems

Emotional appeal: Type of message in marketing – Tries to reach the targeted individual by establishing an emotional connection

Environmental life cycle assessment (ELCA): Element of the life cycle sustainability assessment – Method of compiling and assessing the inputs, outputs, and the potential environmental impacts of a product system throughout its life cycle

Environmental management system: Includes several elements which mirror the plan-do-check-act cycle with regard to the environment (see also Management system)

Environmental management systems standards: Standards that illustrate how management systems should be set up regarding the ecological dimension of sustainability

Endpoint impact categories: Classification category in an environmental life cycle assessment – Endpoint impact categories reflect the final damage to relevant areas of protection

ESG: Stands for "environmental, social, and (corporate) governance" as three common elements of sustainability management

Excessive pricing: Pricing practices that exceed a fair price

Experiences attribute: Types of product attribute; respective attributes can only be fully assessed after the purchase

External stakeholders: Stakeholders outside of a company such as suppliers or customers

Externality: Either a cost or benefit that an individual has to incur even though they did not agree to it

Fees or taxes: Type of market-based instrument in form of monetary fees that are directly applied to the amount of pollution generated by a certain source

Financial materiality: "Information is material if omitting, misstating or obscuring it could reasonably be expected to influence decisions that the primary users of general purpose financial statements make on the basis of those financial statements, which provide financial information about a specific reporting entity" (IASB, 2018)

First-party audit: Internal audit conducted by people who work at the audited organization itself

Focal firm: Central company in a supply chain which shapes large parts of the supply chain through its decisions

Frugal innovations: Type of innovation especially prevalent at the BoP – "a product, service or a solution that emerges despite financial, human, technological and other resource constraints, and where the final outcome is less pricey than competitive offerings (if available) and which meets the needs of those customers who otherwise remain unserved" (Simula et al., 2015, p. 1568)

Functional unit: Reference point that helps to compare the results of an environmental life cycle assessment of different products; the functional unit is the desired outcome and different types of products can potentially be used the desired outcome

Glass ceiling: Describes artificial barriers that prevent women form moving up the hierarchical latter in a company

Global South: Term used to describe lower-income countries mostly in Africa, Asia, Latin America, and Oceania

Government failure: Situation in which government cannot act efficiently or ensure an optimal outcome

Governmental support: Governmental interventions that aims at changing the priorities that actors assign to sustainability issues due to financial support

Greenhouse gas protocol: Document which provides requirements and guidance for preparing greenhouse gas emission inventories on the corporate-level; outlines standardized approaches and principles to arrive at a true and fair view in carbon accounting

Greenwashing: "The act of misleading consumers regarding the environmental practices of a company (firm-level greenwashing) or the environmental benefits of a product or service (product-level greenwashing)" (Delmas & Burbano, 2011, p. 66)

GRI: Global Reporting Initiative; publishes the most well-known sustainability reporting standard worldwide; founded in 1997

GRI standards: See GRI

Human Development Index: Composite measure of average achievement in key dimensions of human development

Hybrid organizations: Alternative forms of organizations that embed sustainability-oriented goals in their structure; often operate at the crossroads between the private, public, and civil society sector

Impact investing: "Investments made with the intention to generate positive, measurable social and environmental impact alongside a financial return" (Hand et al., 2020, p. 74)

Inbound transport: Element in logistics – The transport leading into the warehouse or retail stores

Industrial symbiosis networks: Companies in a certain region collaborate by exchanging material and energy to reduce the intake of virgin raw materials and the output of waste

Information requirements: Governmental interventions that aim at changing the priorities that actors assign to sustainability issues due to, e.g., corporate disclosure requirements

Institutional voids: Absence of specialized intermediaries, regulatory systems, and contract-enforcing mechanisms

Instrumental stakeholder theory: Regards stakeholders as instrumental to a company's financial success; similar in its assumptions to the business case for sustainability as it puts the company´s financial goals in the center of thinking

Integrated management systems: Combination of several management systems

Integrative stakeholder theory: Links the three perspectives of descriptive, instrumental, and normative stakeholder theory

Intention-behavior gap: See Attitude-behavior gap

Intergenerational justice: Element of sustainable development describing the aspiration of giving future generations a voice and allowing them to meet their needs

Internal stakeholders: Stakeholders within a company such as owners or shareholders, employees, and managers

Internalizing negative externalities: Externalities are given a price in production and consumption

Intragenerational justice: Element of sustainable development describing the aspiration of meeting the needs of the present

IPAT-equation: Equation that illustrates the human impact on ecological systems; Impact = Population x Affluence x Technology

ISO 14001: Certifiable standard for environmental management systems

ISO 14040 and ISO 14044: Standards for environmental life cycle assessment

ISO 14064-1: Standard that provides guidance at the organization level for quantification and reporting of greenhouse gas emissions

ISO 26000: International guideline which "provides guidance on the underlying principles of social responsibility, recognizing social responsibility and engaging stakeholders, [as well as] the core subjects and issues pertaining to social responsibility" (ISO, 2010a, p. vi); can be regarded as a prototypical multistakeholder code of conduct

John Rawls's Theory of Justice: Famous work of ethics by philosopher John Rawls which can serve as an ethical reference of intragenerational justice

Just-in-time-delivery: Element in logistics – Aligning of material orders from suppliers with a manufacture´s production schedules

Kant's Categorical Imperative: "Act only according to that maxim whereby you can at the same time will that it should become a universal law" (Kant, 1993, p. 30)

Lagging and leading indicators: Components of a balanced scorecard; lagging indicators are output measures which indicate whether a strategic objective in a perspective is achieved; leading indicators are more immediately measurable and thus allow predictive measurement

Leaky pipelines: Describes the phenomenon that women often "leak out" before reaching management positions

Legitimacy: "Generalized perception or assumption that the actions of an entity are desirable, proper, or appropriate within some socially constructed system of norms, values, beliefs, and definitions" (Suchman, 1995, p. 574)

Life cycle costing: Element of the life cycle sustainability assessment – Summarizes the costs occurring in the entire life cycle that are related to real money flows; not limited to the boundaries of a certain company

Life cycle impact assessment: Third step of the environmental life cycle assessment; transfer of inventory data into environmental impact potentials by evaluating the magnitude and significance of environmental impacts associated with the elementary flows compiled during the life cycle inventory; also applied in social life cycle assessment

Life cycle inventory: Second step of the environmental life cycle assessment; collection of all relevant data on energy and material inputs and environmental releases; limited to physical quantities which are measured or estimated; also applied in social life cycle assessment

Life cycle sustainability assessment (LCSA): Tool for information gathering in sustainability accounting; aims at assessing the sustainability impacts of products along their entire life cycle

Limited assurance: Type of assurance in (nonfinancial) reporting; a limited assurance statement is expressed in negative form

Logistics: Process of how resources are stored and transported from tier to tier in a supply chain

Management systems: Provide procedures of how to implement certain aspects of management into the strategy and daily operations of an organization; coordinate and systemize organizational activities by using defined and documented control and feedback mechanisms

Management system standards: Standards that illustrate how management systems should be set up; certifiable and widespread in sustainability management

Market failure: Situation of inefficient distribution of goods and services in the free market

Market-based instruments: Governmental interventions that aim at encouraging more sustainable behavior through market signals

Market pull: Determinant for sustainability-oriented innovation – Changes in demand incentivize companies to innovate sustainably

Marketing myopia: Situation in which companies are too focused on producing and selling products without actually asking what the customer wants

Midpoint impact categories: Classification category in an environmental life cycle assessment – Indicate and quantify environmental problems at an intermediate point between environmental interventions and the final damage to relevant areas of protection

Mission drift: An inconsistency perceived by the stakeholders between an organization's actions and its stated mission; usually occurs in the form of a loss of focus on the social mission for the gain of financial performance

Modern slavery: "Situations of exploitation that a person cannot refuse or leave because of threats, violence, coercion, deception, and/or abuse of power" (International Labour Organization, 2017, p. 9)

Moral appeal: Type of message in marketing – Aims at triggering people´s sense of right and wrong

Negative criteria: Option in sustainable finance; certain investment options are excluded from the investment universe

Negative externalities: A cost or benefit that an individual has to incur even though they did not agree to it; the overall social cost originating from production or consumption are not included in market prices

Negative rights: Element of human right which have to be always obeyed and establish passive duties to refrain from certain behavior

Neutralization: Remove greenhouse gases from the atmosphere and permanently store them

Nonfinancial materiality: Topics are defined as material in reporting when they "represent [an organization's] most significant impacts on the economy, environment, and people" (GRI, 2021a, p. 8); focus not only on financial performance

Nongovernmental Organization / NGO: Nonprofit, voluntary citizens' group with common interests

Normative stakeholder theory: Puts stakeholder at the center of thinking and asks for the purpose of business in society by bringing a moral perspective to stakeholder theory

Norm-based screening: Option in sustainable finance; considers investment objects when they are in accordance with certain international standards and norms

Offsetting: Financing of measures to reduce greenhouse gas emissions outside of a company's own value chain to balance out emissions generated by the companies

Operational optimization: Type of Sustainability-oriented innovation – Approach that builds upon a given set of needs and tries to satisfy them more efficiently than before

Organizational transformation: Type of Sustainability-oriented innovation – Activities that aim at providing novel goods, services, and business models thus moving toward a fundamental shift in an organization's mindset

Outbound transport: Element in logistics – The transport from the facilities to the customers

Passive approach: Option in sustainable finance; investors do not actively engage with the investment object

Pay gaps: Differences in average wages between different groups

Personal norms: Norms rooted in the individual in the form of values, assumptions, or beliefs

Plan-do-check-act cycle: Process of management systems for the control and continuous improvement of products, processes, or entire organizations; can help to standardize complex issues

Planetary boundaries: Concept that illustrates nine boundaries within which humanity can continue to develop on Earth

Policy instruments: Instruments used by states or state-like actors to achieve certain outcomes or encourage or restrict certain behaviors of others

Positive criteria/positive screening: Option in sustainable finance; choosing investments that achieve certain (minimum) standards

Positive rights: Element of human right which require collective duties to actively satisfy them instead of merely avoiding harm

Post-use costs: Part of Total consumer costs; costs for collecting, storing, and disposing or recycling products at the end of their life cycle

Predatory pricing: Pricing practices of charging prices significantly below the market rate to force competitors out of the market

Price fixing: Two or more competing market actors collude to fix prices above the market rate

Primary stakeholders: Stakeholder that are directly affected by a company´s operations and thus have major interest in its activities

Private governance: Substitute or supplement to governmental regulations

Product carbon footprints: Method in environmental life cycle assessment for measuring the total amount of greenhouse gas emissions directly and indirectly accumulated over the life stages of a product

Product life cycle: Describes all stages through which a product passes; often starts with the extraction of raw materials and ends with the disposal or reuse or recycling of the products or materials

Product-oriented service: Type of product service system – Provide additional value to physical goods through supplementary services.

Product service systems: Consist of physical goods which are combined with intangible services to fulfill customer needs

Public-private partnerships: Cross-sector partnerships between actors from the public and private sector, which agree to provide public services and create societal welfare while sharing financial, social, and human resources

Purchasing power parities: Rates of currency conversion that try to equalize the purchasing power of different currencies

Quasi sustainability: Understanding of sustainability; builds upon the principle of prudence and on not passing critical levels or critical boundaries

Race to the bottom: Situation in which governments reduce standards further and further to attract businesses

Rational appeal: Type of message in marketing – Focuses on the self-interest of the customers

Reasonable assurance: Type of assurance in (nonfinancial) reporting; a reasonable assurance statement is expressed in positive form

Rebound effect: Describes a situation of stagnating or rising overall impacts despite increased efficiency, effectiveness, or sufficiency

Recycling: Product is broken down into its parts to gain materials which are then to be used again

Redistribution markets: Allow consumers or peers to redistribute products or tangible assets from where they are not needed to where they are needed

Refurbishing: Restoring an old product and bringing it up to date

Regulatory pull: Determinant for sustainability-oriented innovation – Governments provide incentives to voluntarily act in a certain way

Regulatory push: Determinant for sustainability-oriented innovation – Sustainability-related specifications from governmental institutions require companies to change their approaches and behaviors

Remanufacturing: Using parts from a discarded product to replace broken parts in another product

Repair: Maintaining a defective product so that it can be used again with its original function

Repurposing: Using parts from a discarded product for a new function

Result-oriented service: Type of product service system – Customer neither owns nor uses the physical good but pays for a result only

Reusing: Product which is still in good condition can be used by another person or organization in its original function

Reverse logistics: "Refers to the sequence of activities required to collect the used product from the customers for the purpose of either reuse or repair or re-manufacture or recycle or dispose of it" (Agrawal et al., 2015, p. 76)

SA8000: Voluntary standard for individual production facilities; aims at promoting and enforcing universal labor standards; combines a management system standard with a code of conduct on social and especially labor issues

Science Based Targets initiative (SBTi): Partnership between various NGOs and other actors; provides guidance on how to develop targets and a path to reduce company greenhouse gas emissions in line with the Paris Agreement goals

Scope 1 emissions: Direct emissions from company-owned or company-controlled operations from the perspective of the company in focus

Scope 2 emissions: Indirect emissions from the perspective of the company in focus; include emissions that stem from electricity, steam, or other sources of energy used by but produced outside of the company

Scope 3 emissions: All other types of indirect emissions (not already covered by scope 2 emissions) that occur upstream or downstream in the supply chain from the perspective of the company in focus

Search attribute: Type of product attribute; respective attributes can be evaluated prior to purchase

Second-party audit: External audit in which a company directly conducts an audit at its suppliers

Secondary stakeholders: Stakeholders that have no direct interest or formal claim, but some form of reasonable influence

Sharing economy: Puts the exchange and rental of resources (instead of ownership) at the center of thinking

Social management system standards: Standards that illustrate how management systems should be set up regarding the social dimension of sustainability

Social banks: Financial institutions that specifically provide funding to organizations that aim to create social value

Social enterprises: Pursue a social or environmental mission while simultaneously engaging in commercial activities to sustain their business operations; also referred to as social businesses, social ventures, sustainable enterprises, or enterprises for the public good

Social hotspots: "Processes located in a region (e.g. country) where a situation occurs that may be considered a problem, a risk, or an opportunity, in relation to a social issue that is considered to be threatening social well-being or that may contribute to its further development" (UNEP, 2020, p. 60) and which should thus be prioritized in a social life cycle analysis

Social life cycle assessment (SLCA): Element of the life cycle sustainability assessment – Analysis of all kinds of social and socioeconomic impacts; comparably new form of life cycle analysis partly due to the complexity of assessing social impact

Social norm: General perceptions of acceptable behavior in and by peer groups

Social venture capital: Private investors provide capital for social projects; usually center on venture capital methods to achieve a positive social impact while providing a high level of nonfinancial support

Soft law: Quasi-legal instruments which have no legally binding force

Sphere of (organizational) influence: "Range/extent of political, contractual, economic or other relationships through which an organization has the ability to affect the decisions or activities of individuals or organizations" (ISO, 2010a, p. 4)

Stakeholder materiality: See Nonfinancial materiality

Stakeholders: "Any group or individual who can affect or is affected by the achievement of the organisation's objectives" (Freeman, 1984, p. 46)

Strong sustainability: Understanding of sustainability; idea to live only from the "interest" of natural capital and to use only those natural goods and services that are continuously added without diminishing the natural capital stock

Sufficiency: A behavior-based concept that aims for appropriate levels and forms of consumption

Sustainability accounting: Gathering of sustainability-related information for transparency and decision-making purposes

Sustainability balanced scorecard: Integrates environmental and social aspects in a balanced scorecard approach (see also balanced scorecard)

Sustainability management control: Use of management tools to influence sustainability-related organizations behavior; aims at integrating sustainability information into management decision-making to foster more sustainable behavior

Sustainability marketing: "Planning, organizing, implementing and controlling [of] marketing resources and programs to satisfy consumers' wants and needs, while considering social and environmental criteria and meeting corporate objectives" (Belz & Peattie, 2012, p.29)

Sustainability-oriented innovations: "involves making intentional changes to an organization's philosophy and values, as well as to its products, processes or practices, to serve the specific purpose of creating and realizing social and environmental value in addition to economic returns" (Adams et al., 2016, p. 181)

Sustainability ratings: Assess the sustainability performance of companies or entire countries

Sustainability reporting: Disclosure of sustainability-related information to internal and external stakeholders

Sustainability themed investments: Option in sustainable finance; investors seek to invest in certain areas they connect with sustainability

Sustainable business model: A "business model that integrates [a] multistakeholder view [and] aims at the creation of monetary and non-monetary value for stakeholders and holds a long-term perspective." (Shakeel et al., 2020, p. 8)

Sustainable business model innovation: Describes the creation of "modified and completely new business models [that] can help develop integrative and competitive solutions by either radically reducing negative and/or creating positive external effects for the natural environment and society" (Schaltegger, Hansen, & Lüdeke-Freund, 2016, p. 3)

Sustainable consumption: "The use of goods and services that respond to basic needs and bring a better quality of life, while minimising the use of natural resources, toxic materials and emissions of waste and pollutants over the life cycle, so as not to jeopardise the needs of future generations" (UNEP, 2010, p. 12).

Sustainable Development Goals / SDGs: See UN Sustainable Development Goals (SDGs)

Sustainable finance taxonomy: Classification system in sustainable finance that establishes a list of environmentally sustainable economic activities

Sustainable human resource management: Focuses on fostering employees' sustainable behavior at work to improve a company's sustainability performance and about what a company can, could, or should do for its employees

Sustainable supply chain management: "The strategic, transparent integration and achievement of an organization's social, environmental, and economic goals in the systemic coordination of key interorganizational business processes for improving the long-term economic performance of the individual company and its supply chains" (Carter & Rogers, 2008, p. 368) or "the management of material, information and capital flows as well as cooperation among companies along the supply chain while taking goals from all three dimensions of sustainable development, i.e., economic, environmental and social, into account which are derived from customer and stakeholder requirements." (Seuring & Müller, 2008, p. 1700).

Systems building: Type of Sustainability-oriented innovation – Innovations that require a rather radical shift in the sense that they require thinking beyond the boundaries of a single organization

Technology push: Determinant for sustainability-oriented innovation – New technologies open avenues for new business models, product, and processes

Third-party audit: External audit which is conducted by an auditing organization independent of any specific customer-supplier relationship

Total customer costs: Combines various types of cost for the end consumer of a product; includes purchase price, transaction costs, use costs, and post-use costs

Tradeable permits: Type of marked-based instrument that aims at achieve a cost-efficient reduction of burdens by regulating the amount of pollution

Transaction costs: Part of Total consumer cost; usually nonmonetary costs including search and information costs

Triple Bottom Line: Defines ecological, economic, and social sustainability as three pillars of sustainability

UN Global Compact: Voluntary multistakeholder initiative that enlists corporations in support of ten general principles; does not regulate corporate behavior but provides basic ideas of what is regarded as universally valid values

UN Principles for Responsible Investment: UN initiative that addresses investors around the world and encourages them to sign six aspirational principles

UN Sustainable Development Goals (SDGs): 17 global sustainability-related goals set by the United Nations General Assembly in 2015 to be achieved by 2030

Upcycling: "A process of converting materials into new materials of higher quality and increased functionality" (Ellen MacArthur Foundation, 2013, p. 25); sometimes also used when materials maintain value and thus similar to recycling

Use costs: Part of Total consumer costs; occur by using a product and relevant especially for long-lasting products

Use-related services: Type of product service system – Ownership of a physical good stays with the provider who makes the good available for customers to use

Value-based screening: Option in sustainable finance; investments are excluded based on personal or religious values

Venture philanthropy: See Social venture capital

Virgin material: New material brought into production processes

Visionary pull: Determinant for sustainability-oriented innovation – Pull factors from within the market sector; strong company-internal vision and normative impetus toward sustainability

Waste hierarchy: Classification of options for dealing with by-products and waste; consists of reduce, reuse, recycle, and sometimes recover

Weak sustainability: Understanding of sustainability; main goal is to keep the total sum of anthropogenic capital and natural capital constant by substitution

Wicked problem: A problem that is difficult to solve due to its complexity and/or incomplete and potentially contradictory requirements

Zero waste and package free shops: Specialized supermarkets selling unpackaged food and other items

References

Adams, L., Ni Luanaigh, A., Thomson, D., & Rossiter, H. (Aug. 2018). Measuring and reporting on disability and ethnicity pay gaps (Research report 117). Manchester, UK. Equality and Human Rights Commission.

Adams, R., Jeanrenaud, S., Bessant, J., Denyer, D., & Overy, P. (2016). Sustainability-oriented Innovation: A Systematic Review. International Journal of Management Reviews, 18(2), 180–205.

Adebiyi-Abiola, B., Assefa, S., Sheikh, K., & García, J. M. (2019). Cleaning up plastic pollution in Africa. Science, 365(6459), 1249–1251.

Agrawal, S., Singh, R. K., & Murtaza, Q. (2015). A literature review and perspectives in reverse logistics. Resources, Conservation and Recycling, 97, 76–92.

Ahmad, K. (2001). Drug company sued over research trial in Nigeria. The Lancet, 358(9284), 815.

Ahonen, S. (2018, December 18). New Bangladesh Minimum Wage. https://sus-a.com/index.php/new-bangladesh-minimum-wage/2018/

Aknin, L. B., Whillans, Ashlyey, V., Norton, M. I., & Dunn, E. W. (2019). Happiness and Prosocial Behavior: An Evaluation of the Evidence. In J. F. Helliwell, R. Layard, & J. D. Sachs (Eds.), World Happiness Report 2019 (pp. 66–85). Sustainable Development Solutions Network.

Alcott, B. (2005). Jevons' paradox. Ecological Economics, 54(1), 9–21.

Allen, M. R., Dube, O. P., Solecki, W., Aragón-Durand, F., Cramer, W., Humphreys, S., Kainuma, M., Kala, J., Mahowald, N., Mulugetta, Y., Perez, R., Wairiu, M., & Zickfeld, K. (2018). Framing and Context. In V. Masson-Delmotte, P. Zhai, H.-O. Pörtner, D. Roberts, J. Skea, P. R. Shukla, A. Pirani, W. Moufouma-Okia, C. Péan, C. Pidcock, S. Connors, J. Matthews, Y. Chen, X. Zhou, M. I. Gomis, E. Lonnoy, T. Maycock, M. Tignor, & T. Waterfield (Eds.), Global Warming of 1.5°C. An IPCC Special Report on the impacts of global warming of 1.5°C above pre-industrial levels and related global greenhouse gas emission pathways, in the context of strengthening the global response to the threat of climate change, sustainable development, and efforts to eradicate pove (pp. 49–91).

Al-Shammari, M., Rasheed, A., & Al-Shammari, H. A. (2019). CEO narcissism and corporate social responsibility: Does CEO narcissism affect CSR focus? Journal of Business Research, 104, 106–117.

American Marketing Association. (2017). Definitions of Marketing. American Marketing Association. https://www.ama.org/the-definition-of-marketing-what-is-marketing/

Anand, U. (2015, August 1). India has 31 lakh NGOs, more than double the number of schools. The Indian Express. https://indianexpress.com/article/india/india-others/india-has-31-lakh-ngos-twice-the-number-of-schools-almost-twice-number-of-policemen/

Andrew, B. (2008). Market failure, government failure and externalities in climate change mitigation: The case for a carbon tax. Public Administration and Development, 28(5), 393–401.

Angrick, M., Burger, A., & Lehmann, H. (2013). Factor X: Re-source - designing the recycling society. Eco-efficiency in industry and science: Vol. 30. Springer.

Anopchenko, T., Gorbaneva, O., Lazareva, E., Murzin, A., & Ougolnitsky, G. (2019). Modeling Public—Private Partnerships in Innovative Economy: A Regional Aspect. Sustainability, 11(20), 5588.

Argenti, P. A. (2004). Collaborating with Activists: How Starbucks Works with NGOs. California Management Review, 47(1), 91–116.

Arrhenius, S. (1896). On the Influence of Carbonic Acid in the Air upon the Temperature of the Ground. Philosophical Magazine and Journal of Science, 41(251), 237–276. https://www.rsc.org/images/Arrhenius1896_tcm18-173546.pdf

Arts, W. A., & Gelissen, J. (2010). Models of the Welfare State. In F. G. Castles, S. Leibfried, J. Lewis, H. Obinger, & C. Pierson (Eds.), The Oxford Handbook of the Welfare State. Oxford University Press. https://doi.org/10.1093/oxfordhb/9780199579396.003.0039

Asioli, D., Aschemann-Witzel, J., & Nayga, R. M. (2020). Sustainability-Related Food Labels. Annual Review of Resource Economics, 12(1), 171–185.

Auger, P., & Devinney, T. M. (2007). Do What Consumers Say Matter? The Misalignment of Preferences with Unconstrained Ethical Intentions. Journal of Business Ethics, 76(4), 361–383.

Austin, J. E. (2000). The collaboration challenge: How nonprofits and businesses succeed through strategic alliances. A Drucker Foundation leaderbook. Jossey-Bass. http://www.loc.gov/catdir/bios/wiley043/99088237.html

Ayres, R. U. (2007). On the practical limits to substitution. Ecological Economics, 61(1), 115–128.

Babich, V., & Hilary, G. (2020). OM Forum—Distributed Ledgers and Operations: What Operations Management Researchers Should Know About Blockchain Technology. Manufacturing & Service Operations Management, 22(2), 223–240.

Bajaj, V. (2010, April 21). C. K. Prahalad, Proponent of Poor as Consumers, Dies at 68. The New York Times. https://www.nytimes.com/2010/04/22/business/22prahalad.html

Bansal, P., & Roth, K. (2000). Why Companies Go Green: A Model of Ecological Responsiveness. Academy of Management Journal, 43(4), 717–736.

Bansal, P., & Song, H.-C. (2017). Similar But Not the Same: Differentiating Corporate Sustainability from Corporate Responsibility. Academy of Management Annals, 11(1), 105–149.

Banza Lubaba Nkulu, C., Casas, L., Haufroid, V., Putter, T. de, Saenen, N. D., Kayembe-Kitenge, T., Musa Obadia, P., Kyanika Wa Mukoma, D., Lunda Ilunga, J.-M., Nawrot, T. S., Luboya Numbi, O., Smolders, E., & Nemery, B. (2018). Sustainability of artisanal mining of cobalt in DR Congo. Nature Sustainability, 1(9), 495–504.

Barnett, M. L. (2019). The Business Case for Corporate Social Responsibility: A Critique and an Indirect Path Forward. Business & Society, 58(1), 167–190.

Barnett, M. L., Hartmann, J., & Salomon, R. M. (2018). Have You Been Served? Extending the Relationship between Corporate Social Responsibility and Lawsuits. Academy of Management Discoveries, 4(2), 109–126.

Baroudy, E., & Hooda, N. (2011). Sustainable land management and carbon finance: the experience of the BioCarbon Fund. In E. Wollenberg, M.-L. Tapio-Bistrom, M. Grieg-Gran, & A. Nihart (Eds.), Climate Change Mitigation and Agriculture (pp. 123–130). Routledge.

Battilana, J., & Lee, M. (2014). Advancing Research on Hybrid Organizing – Insights from the Study of Social Enterprises. Academy of Management Annals, 8(1), 397–441.

Baumeister, S. (2018). We Are Still In! Conference report from the 2018 Ceres Conference. Journal of Cleaner Production, 196, 183–184.

Baumüller, J., & Schaffhauser-Linzatti, M.-M. (2018). In search of materiality for nonfinancial information—reporting requirements of the Directive 2014/95/EU. Sustainability Management Forum | NachhaltigkeitsManagementForum, 26(1-4), 101–111.

Bayer AG. (2021, February 25). Annual Report 2020. Leverkusen, Germany. https://www.bayer.com/sites/default/files/2021-02/Bayer-Annual-Report-2020.pdf

Bazilier, R., & Girard, V. (2018, May 17). Artisanal mines: potentially positive effects on local living standards. GlobalDev Blog. https://globaldev.blog/blog/artisanal-mines-potentially-positive-effects-local-living-standards

bbc.com. (2021, April 9). South Korea beauty brand sorry for 'paper bottle' label fail. https://www.bbc.com/news/world-asia-56687585

BCI. (2019, May 7). Better Cotton Principles and Criteria V2.1. Chatelaine, Switzerland. https://bettercotton.org/wp-content/uploads/2019/06/Better-Cotton-Principles-Criteria-V2.1.pdf

BCI. (2020). Better Cotton Initiative - 2019 Annual Report. https://stories.bettercotton.org/2019AnnualReport/index.html

Bedford, C., & Morhaim, S. (2002). The Next Industrial Revolution. Baltimore, MD. Earthome Productions. https://vimeo.com/20372160

Belz, F., & Peattie, K. J. (2012). Sustainability marketing: A global perspective (2. ed.). Wiley.

Bento, N., Gianfrate, G., & Thoni, M. H. (2019). Crowdfunding for sustainability ventures. Journal of Cleaner Production, 237, 117751.

Berger, I. E., Cunningham, P. H., & Drumwright, M. E. (2004). Social Alliances: Company/Nonprofit Collaboration. California Management Review, 47(1), 58–90.

Berghel, H. (2018). Malice Domestic: The Cambridge Analytica Dystopia. Computer, 51(5), 84–89.

Berliner, D., & Prakash, A. (2015). "Bluewashing" the Firm? Voluntary Regulations, Program Design, and Member Compliance with the United Nations Global Compact. Policy Studies Journal, 43(1), 115–138.

Bhatti, Y., Ramaswami Basu, R., Barron, D., & Ventresca, M. J. (2018). Frugal Innovation - Models, Means, Methods. Cambridge University Press.

Bishu, S. G., & Alkadry, M. G. (2017). A Systematic Review of the Gender Pay Gap and Factors That Predict It. Administration & Society, 49(1), 65–104.

BlackRock, Inc. (2021). About BlackRock. https://www.blackrock.com/sg/en/about-us

Bloom, N., Liang, J., Roberts, J., & Ying, Z. J. (2015). Does Working from Home Work? Evidence from a Chinese Experiment. The Quarterly Journal of Economics, 130(1), 165–218.

Bocken, N., Boons, F., & Baldassarre, B. (2019). Sustainable business model experimentation by understanding ecologies of business models. Journal of Cleaner Production, 208, 1498–1512.

Bocken, N., & Geradts, T. H. (2020). Barriers and drivers to sustainable business model innovation: Organization design and dynamic capabilities. Long Range Planning, 53(4), 101950.

Bocken, N., & Short, S. (2016). Towards a sufficiency-driven business model: Experiences and opportunities. Environmental Innovation and Societal Transitions, 18, 41–61.

Bocken, N., Short, S., Rana, P., & Evans, S. (2013). A value mapping tool for sustainable business modelling. Corporate Governance: The International Journal of Business in Society, 13(5), 482–497.

Bocken, N., Short, S., Rana, P., & Evans, S. (2014). A literature and practice review to develop sustainable business model archetypes. Journal of Cleaner Production, 65, 42–56.

Boll, C., & Lagemann, A. (2018). Gender pay gap in EU countries based on SES (2014). European Commission.

Bondy, K., Matten, D., & Moon, J. (2008). Codes of conduct as a tool for sustainable governance in MNCs. In A. Crane, D. Matten, & L. J. Spence (Eds.), Corporate social responsibility: Readings and cases in a global context (pp. 432–455). Routledge.

Botsman, R., & Rogers, R. (2011). What's mine is yours: How collaborative consumption is changing the way we live. Collaborative consumption. Collins.

Bradford, B., Yesberg, J. A., Jackson, J., & Dawson, P. (2020). Live Facial Recognition: Trust and Legitimacy as Predictors of Public Support for Police Use of New Technology. The British Journal of Criminology, Article azaa032. Advance online publication. https://doi.org/10.1093/bjc/azaa032

Braungart, M., McDonough, W., & Bollinger, A. (2007). Cradle-to-cradle design: creating healthy emissions – a strategy for eco-effective product and system design. Journal of Cleaner Production, 15(13-14), 1337–1348.

Bris, A. (2021, March 19). Danone's CEO has been ousted for being progressive – blame society not activist shareholders. The Conversation. https://theconversation.com/danones-ceo-has-been-ousted-for-being-progressive-blame-society-not-activist-shareholders-157383

Brix-Asala, C., Hahn, R., & Seuring, S. (2016). Reverse logistics and informal valorisation at the Base of the Pyramid: A case study on sustainability synergies and trade-offs. European Management Journal, 34(4), 414–423.

Broekhoff, D., Gillenwater, M., Colbert-Sangree, T., & Cage, P. (2019, November 13). Securing Climate Benefit: A Guide to Using Carbon Offsets. Stockholm Environment Institute; Greenhouse Gas Management Institute. https://www.offsetguide.org/pdf-download/

Brønn, P. S., & Brønn, C. (2018). Sustainability: A wicked problem needing new perspectives. In H. Borland, A. Lindgreen, F. Maon, J. Vanhamme, V. Ambrosini, & B. P. Florencio (Eds.), Business Strategies for Sustainability (pp. 3–18). Routledge.

Brown, T. J., & Dacin, P. A. (1997). The Company and the Product: Corporate Associations and Consumer Product Responses. Journal of Marketing, 61(1), 68–84.

Bulloch, G. (2018). The Intrapreneur: Confessions of a Corporate Insurgent. Unbound.

Bureau of Democracy, Human Rights, and Labor. (2021, January 20). Non-Governmental Organizations (NGOs) in the United States. U.S. Department of State. https://www.state.gov/non-governmental-organizations-ngos-in-the-united-states/

Busch, T., Bruce-Clark, P., Derwall, J., Eccles, R., Hebb, T., Hoepner, A., Klein, C., Krueger, P., Paetzold, F., Scholtens, B., & Weber, O. (2021). Impact investments: a call for (re) orientation. SN Business & Economics, 1(2).

Cadwalladr, C., & Graham-Harrison, E. (2018, March 17). Revealed: 50 million Facebook profiles harvested for Cambridge Analytica in major data breach. The Guardian. https://www.theguardian.com/news/2018/mar/17/cambridge-analytica-facebook-influence-us-election

Carlos, W. C., & Lewis, B. W. (2018). Strategic Silence: Withholding Certification Status as a Hypocrisy Avoidance Tactic. Administrative Science Quarterly, 63(1), 130–169.

Carroll, A. B. (2008). A History of Corporate Social Responsibility: Concepts and Practices. In A. Crane, D. Matten, A. McWilliams, J. Moon, & D. S. Siegel (Eds.), The Oxford Handbook of Corporate Social Responsibility (pp. 19–46). Oxford University Press.

Carter, C. R., & Rogers, D. S. (2008). A framework of sustainable supply chain management: moving toward new theory. International Journal of Physical Distribution & Logistics Management, 38(5), 360–387.

CDP. (Feb. 2021a). Transparency to transformation - A chain reaction: CDP Global Supply Chain Report 2020. London, UK, New York, NY. CDP. https://6fefcbb86e61af1b-2fc4-c70d8ead6ced550b4d987d7c03fcdd1d.ssl.cf3.rackcdn.com/cms/reports/documents/000/005/554/original/CDP_SC_Report_2020.pdf?1614160765

CDP. (2021b, October 14). CDP reports record number of disclosures and unveils new strategy to help further tackle climate and ecological emergency. https://www.cdp.net/en/articles/media/cdp-reports-record-number-of-disclosures-and-unveils-new-strategy-to-help-further-tackle-climate-and-ecological-emergency

CDP, CDSB, GRI, & IIRC, S. (Sep. 2020). Statement of Intent to Work Together Towards Comprehensive Corporate Reporting.

Centro Corporativo de Mondragon. (2021). About Us. https://www.mondragon-corporation.com/en/about-us/

Changing Markets Foundation. (May 2018). The false promise of certification: How certifcation is hindering sustainability in the textiles, palm oil and fisheries industries. https://changingmarkets.org/wp-content/uploads/2018/05/The-False-Promise-Full-Report.pdf

Chatterji, A. K., Durand, R., Levine, D. I., & Touboul, S. (2016). Do ratings of firms converge? Implications for managers, investors and strategy researchers. Strategic Management Journal, 37(8), 1597–1614.

Chopra, S. (2019). Supply chain management: Strategy, planning, and operation (Seventh edition, global edition). Pearson.

Christian, C., Ainley, D., Bailey, M., Dayton, P., Hocevar, J., LeVine, M., Nikoloyuk, J., Nouvian, C., Velarde, E., Werner, R., & Jacquet, J. (2013). A review of formal objections to Marine Stewardship Council fisheries certifications. Biological Conservation, 161, 10–17.

Clausen, J., Fichter, K., & Winter, W. (2011). Theoretische Grundlagen für die Erklärung von Diffu-sionsverläufen von Nachhaltigkeitsinnovationen. Borderstep Institut. https://www.borderstep.de/wp-content/uploads/2014/07/Clausen-Fichter-Winter-Theoretische_Grundlagen_fuer_die_Erklaerung_von_Diffusionsverlaeufen_von_Nachhaltigkeitsinnovationen-2011.pdf

Clean Clothes Campaign. (n.d.). Time Line of the Ali Enterprises Case. Amsterdam, Netherlands. https://cleanclothes.org/safety/ali-enterprises/time-line-for-the-ali-enterprises-case

Clémençon, R. (2016). The Two Sides of the Paris Climate Agreement. The Journal of Environment & Development, 25(1), 3–24.

Closing the Loop, Fairphone, & Call2Recycle. (Sep. 2020). Making a business case for African battery recycling. Closing the Loop; Fairphone; Call2Recycle. https://www.closingtheloop.eu/sites/default/files/2020-10/CTL-Whitepaper-Business-Case-Battery-Recycling-20200930.pdf

Competition & Markets Authority. (2021, September 21). Environmental claims on goods and services. https://www.gov.uk/government/publications/green-claims-code-making-environmental-claims/environmental-claims-on-goods-and-services

Cook, M. L. (1995). The Future of U.S. Agricultural Cooperatives: A NeoInstitutional Approach. American Journal of Agricultural Economics, 77(5), 1153–1159.

Crane, A., Matten, D., Glozer, S., & Spence, L. J. (2019). Business ethics: Managing corporate citizenship and sustainability in the age of globalization (5th edition). Oxford University Press.

Crane, A., Palazzo, G., Spence, L. J., & Matten, D. (2014). Contesting the Value of "Creating Shared Value". California Management Review, 56(2), 130–153.

Crates, E. (2019, July 26). Auditing is not enough – we must do more. Chartered Institute of Procurement & Supply. https://www.cips.org/supply-management/analysis/2019/july/auditing-is-not-enough/

Crouch, D. (2018, September 1). The Swedish 15-year-old who's cutting class to fight the climate crisis. The Guardian. https://www.theguardian.com/science/2018/sep/01/swedish-15-year-old-cutting-class-to-fight-the-climate-crisis

Cutcher, L., & Mason, P. (2014). Credit unions. In M. Parker, G. Cheney, V. Fournier, & C. Land (Eds.), Routledge companions in business, management and accounting. The Routledge companion to alternative organization (pp. 277–290). Routledge.

Cuvelier, L., & Pinson, L. (Jan. 2021). One year on: BlackRock still addicted to fossil fuels. Reclaim Finance; Urgewald. https://reclaimfinance.org/site/wp-content/uploads/2021/01/OneYearOnBlackRockStillAddictedToFossilFuels.pdf

Dai, J., Montabon, F. L., & Cantor, D. E. (2014). Linking rival and stakeholder pressure to green supply management: Mediating role of top management support. Transportation Research Part E: Logistics and Transportation Review, 71, 173–187.

Dalla Via, N., & Perego, P. (2018). Determinants of Conflict Minerals Disclosure Under the Dodd-Frank Act. Business Strategy and the Environment, 27(6), 773–788.

Daniel J. Edelman Holdings Inc. (2021). Edelman Trust Barometer 2021. https://www.edelman.com/sites/g/files/aatuss191/files/2021-01/2021-edelman-trust-barometer.pdf

Defourny, J. (2014). From third sector to social enterprise: A European research trajectory. In J. Defourny (Ed.), Social enterprise and the third sector: Changing European landscapes in a comparative perspective (pp. 33–57). Routledge.

Delmas, M. A., & Burbano, V. C. (2011). The Drivers of Greenwashing. California Management Review, 54(1), 64–87.

Dembek, K., Sivasubramaniam, N., & Chmielewski, D. A. (2020). A Systematic Review of the Bottom/Base of the Pyramid Literature: Cumulative Evidence and Future Directions. Journal of Business Ethics, 165(3), 365–382.

UN, Department of Economic and Social Affairs, Population Division. (2019). World Population Prospects 2019: Highlights. Statistical Papers - United Nations (Ser. A), Population and Vital Statistics Report. United Nations. https://population.un.org/wpp/Publications/Files/WPP2019_Highlights.pdf

Depping, A., & Walden, D. (2021, March 9). German Supply Chain Law: RegE (Government Draft Law), FAQ and EU. https://www.lexology.com/library/detail.aspx?g=9e474dfd-6abd-49c0-98b1-141a6c00de66

Deutsche Umwelthilfe. (2011, July 7). Danone führt Verbraucher mit Werbung für Joghurtbecher aus Biokunststoff in die Irre [Press Release]. https://www.duh.de/presse/pressemitteilungen/pressemitteilung/danone-fuehrt-verbraucher-mit-werbung-fuer-joghurtbecher-aus-biokunststoff-in-die-irre/

Diamond, J. M. (2006). Collapse: How societies choose to fail or succeed. Penguin Books.

Doherty, B., Haugh, H., & Lyon, F. (2014). Social Enterprises as Hybrid Organizations: A Review and Research Agenda. International Journal of Management Reviews, 16(4), 417–436.

Dolega, P., Buchert, M., & Betz, J. (2020). Ökologische und sozio-ökonomische Herausforderungen in Batterie-Lieferketten: Graphit und Lithium. Darmstadt, Germany. Oeko-Institut. https://www.oeko.de/fileadmin/oekodoc/Graphit-Lithium-Oeko-Soz-Herausforderungen.pdf

Domenech, T., & Davies, M. (2011). Structure and morphology of industrial symbiosis networks: The case of Kalundborg. Procedia - Social and Behavioral Sciences, 10, 79–89.

Donaldson, T., & Preston, L. E. (1995). The Stakeholder Theory of the Corporation: Concepts, Evidence, and Implications. Academy of Management Review, 20(1), 65–91.

Dosi, G., & Nelson, R. R. (2010). Technical Change and Industrial Dynamics as Evolutionary Processes. In B. H. Hall & N. Rosenberg (Eds.), Handbook of the Economics of Innovation. Handbook of The Economics of Innovation, Vol. 1 (Vol. 1, pp. 51–127). Elsevier. https://doi.org/10.1016/S0169-7218(10)01003-8

Dowling, J., & Pfeffer, J. (1975). Organizational Legitimacy: Social Values and Organizational Behavior. The Pacific Sociological Review, 18(1), 122–136.

dpa (2014, August 30). Puma stoppt den Öko-Beutel für Schuhe. Süddeutsche Zeitung. https://www.sueddeutsche.de/wirtschaft/sportartikel-puma-stoppt-den-oeko-beutel-fuer-schuhe-dpa.urn-newsml-dpa-com-20090101-140830-99-02185

Drempetic, S., Klein, C., & Zwergel, B. (2020). The Influence of Firm Size on the ESG Score: Corporate Sustainability Ratings Under Review. Journal of Business Ethics, 167(2), 333–360.

Dyckhoff, H., & Souren, R. (2008). Nachhaltige Unternehmensführung: Grundzüge industriellen Umweltmanagements. Springer-Lehrbuch. Springer-Verlag.

Easterlin, R. A. (2017). Paradox Lost? Review of Behavioral Economics, 4(4), 311–339.

Eccles, R. G. (2020). Do Signatories To The Principles For Responsible Investment Practice What They Preach? https://www.forbes.com/sites/bobeccles/2020/08/04/do-signatories-to-the-principles-for-responsible-investment-practice-what-they-preach/

Eggert, J., & Hartmann, J. (2021). Purchasing's contribution to supply chain emission reduction. Journal of Purchasing and Supply Management, 27(2), 100685.

Ehrenfeld, J., & Gertler, N. (1997). Industrial Ecology in Practice: The Evolution of Interdependence at Kalundborg. Journal of Industrial Ecology, 1(1), 67–79.

Ekhardt, F. (2015, March 11). Nicht die Konzerne – wir selbst sind das Problem. Zeit Online. https://www.zeit.de/wirtschaft/2015-03/naomi-klein-kapitalismus-klimawandel/komplettansicht

Elkington, J. (n.d.). About. Retrieved February 14, 2021, from https://johnelkington.com/about/

Elkington, J. (1999). Cannibals with forks: The triple bottom line of 21st century business. Capstone.

Ellen MacArthur Foundation. (2013). Towards the circular economy: Economic and business rationale for an accelerated transition. https://www.ellenmacarthurfoundation.org/assets/downloads/publications/Ellen-MacArthur-Foundation-Towards-the-Circular-Economy-vol.1.pdf

Ellen MacArthur Foundation. (2021). Universal circular economy policy goals: enabling the transition to scale. Ellen MacArthur Foundation. https://www.ellenmacarthurfoundation.org/publications/universal-circular-economy-policy-goals-enabling-the-transition-to-scale

Ellen MacArthur Foundation, & McKinsey Center for Business and Environment. (June 2015). Growth Within: A Circular Economy Vision for a Competitive Europe. https://www.ellenmacarthurfoundation.org/assets/downloads/publications/EllenMacArthurFoundation_Growth-Within_July15.pdf

Ellerman, A. D., Marcantonini, C., & Zaklan, A. (2016). The European Union Emissions Trading System: Ten Years and Counting. Review of Environmental Economics and Policy, 10(1), 89–107.

Elsner, P., Müller-Kirschbaum, T., Schweitzer, K., Wolf, R., Seiler, E., Désilets, P., Detsch, R., Dornack, C., Ferber, J., Fleck, C., Fröhling, M., Hagspiel, K., Hahn, R., Haupts, C., Hoffmann, C., Krüger, P., Lange, M., Leopold, T., Löscher, M., . . . Kadner, S. (2021). Plastics Packaging in a Closed Loop - Potentials, Conditions, Challenges. Munich, Germany, London, UK. https://www.circular-economy-initiative.de/s/VP_Gesamtbericht_EN

Errasti, A., Bretos, I., & Nunez, A. (2017). The Viability of Cooperatives: The Fall of the Mondragon Cooperative Fagor. Review of Radical Political Economics, 49(2), 181–197.

Etter, M., Fieseler, C., & Whelan, G. (2019). Sharing Economy, Sharing Responsibility? Corporate Social Responsibility in the Digital Age. Journal of Business Ethics, 159(4), 935–942.

European Center for Constitutional and Human Rights. (Nov. 2016). Case report - RINA certifies safety before factory fire in Pakistan. https://www.ecchr.eu/fileadmin/Fallbeschreibungen/CaseReport_Rina_Pakistan.pdf

European Chemical Industry Council. (2021). Responsible Care Management Framework. cefic. https://cefic.org/app/uploads/2019/11/brochure_basic_v9.pdf

European Commission. (n.d.). EMAS Register. https://ec.europa.eu/environment/emas/emas_registrations/register_en.htm

European Commission. (2011, October 25). A renewed EU strategy 2011-14 for Corporate Social Responsibility (COM(2011) 681 final). Brussels.

European Commission. (2021, April 4). DIRECTIVE OF THE EUROPEAN PARLIAMENT AND OF THE COUNCIL amending Directive 2013/34/EU, Directive 2004/109/EC, Directive 2006/43/EC and Regulation (EU) No 537/2014, as regards corporate sustainability reporting (COM(2021) 189 final). Brussels, Belgium.

Regulation laying down supply chain due diligence obligations for Union importers of tin, tantalum and tungsten, their ores, and gold originating from conflict-affected and high-risk areas, May 17, 2017. https://eur-lex.europa.eu/legal-content/EN/TXT/?uri=uriserv%3AOJ.L_.2017.130.01.0001.01.ENG&toc=OJ%3AL%3A2017%3A130%3ATOC

Regulation on the establishment of a framework to facilitate sustainable investment, and amending Regulation 2019/2088 on sustainability-related disclosures in the financial services sector, December 17, 2019. https://data.consilium.europa.eu/doc/document/ST-14970-2019-ADD-1/en/pdf

Eurosif. (2018). European SRI Study 2018. Brussels. http://www.eurosif.org/wp-content/uploads/2018/11/European-SRI-2018-Study.pdf

Evening Standard. (2008). The 1000 London's Most Influential People 2009. https://www.standard.co.uk/hp/front/environment-7283865.html

fairafric. (2021). Our journey, our mission. https://fairafric.com/en/our-journey/

Fairtrade International (Ed.). (2019, April 4). Fairtrade Standard for Small-scale Producer Organizations - Version 2.3. https://files.fairtrade.net/standards/SPO_EN.pdf

Fairtrade International. (2020). Innovation and resilience for a more sustainable world - Annual Report 2019-2020. Fairtrade International. https://files.fairtrade.net/publications/Fairtrade_Annual_Report_2020_web.pdf

FAO, IFAD, UNICEF, WFP, & WHO. (2020). The state of food security and nutrition in the world - Transforming food systems for affordable healthy diets (Vol. 2020). FAO.

Feilhauer, S., & Hahn, R. (2021a). Firm-nonprofit collaboration: Explaining the rationale behind firms' cross-sector partner choices. Long Range Planning, 54(1), 101952.

Feilhauer, S., & Hahn, R. (2021b). Formalization of Firms' Evaluation Processes in Cross-Sector Partnerships for Sustainability. Business & Society, 60(3), 684–726.

Fernández Briseño, D., Chegut, A., Glennon, E., Scott, J., & Yang, J. (2020). Retail Carbon Footprints: Measuring Impacts from Real Estate and Technology. MIT Real Estate Innovation Lab. https://realestateinnovationlab.mit.edu/wp-content/uploads/2021/01/FINAL_Retail-carbon-footprints-report_011221.pdf

Ferrer, M. de. (2021, September 22). Artists hijack billboards to protest the greenwashing of 'Europe's dirtiest bank'. https://www.euronews.com/green/2021/09/22/artists-hijack-billboards-to-protest-the-greenwashing-of-europe-s-dirtiest-bank

Fichter, K., & Arnold, M. G. (2003). Nachhaltigkeitsinnovationen von Unternehmen. Erkenntnisse einer explorativen Untersuchung. In G. Linne & M. Schwarz (Eds.), Handbuch Nachhaltige Entwicklung (pp. 273–285). VS Verlag für Sozialwissenschaften. https://doi.org/10.1007/978-3-663-10272-4_26

Figge, F., Hahn, T., Schaltegger, S., & Wagner, M [Marcus] (2002). The Sustainability Balanced Scorecard - linking sustainability management to business strategy. Business Strategy and the Environment, 11(5), 269–284.

Figge, F., Young, W., & Barkemeyer, R. (2014). Sufficiency or efficiency to achieve lower resource consumption and emissions? The role of the rebound effect. Journal of Cleaner Production, 69, 216–224.

Fiksel, J. (2011). Design for environment: A guide to sustainable product development (2nd ed.). McGraw-Hill Professional; McGraw-Hill.

Fink, L. (2018). A Sense of Purpose. Harvard Law School Forum on Corporate Governance. https://corpgov.law.harvard.edu/2018/01/17/a-sense-of-purpose/

Fink, L. (2020). A Fundamental Reshaping of Finance: Larry Fink's 2020 letter to CEOs. https://www.blackrock.com/corporate/investor-relations/2020-larry-fink-ceo-letter

Fink, L. (2021). Larry Fink's 2021 letter to CEOs. https://www.blackrock.com/corporate/investor-relations/larry-fink-ceo-letter

Flecha, R., & Ngai, P. (2014). The challenge for Mondragon: Searching for the cooperative values in times of internationalization. Organization, 21(5), 666–682.

Flew, A., & Priest, S. (2002). A dictionary of philosophy [3rd ed.]. MacMillan Press. http://search.credoreference.com/content/title/macdphil?institutionId=4361

Florence, N. (2014). Wangari Maathai - Visionary, environmental leader, political activist. Lantern Books.

Ford, L. (2013, May 24). Muhammad Yunus: 'Business is a beautiful mechanism to solve problems'. The Guardian. https://www.theguardian.com/global-development/2013/may/24/muhammad-yunus-business-solve-problems

Forno, F. (2013). Co-Operative Movement. In D. A. Snow, D. Della Porta, B. Klandermans, & D. McAdam (Eds.), The Wiley-Blackwell Encyclopedia of Social and Political Movements (pp. 278–280). Blackwell Publishing Ltd. https://doi.org/10.1002/9780470674871.wbespm055

Forti, V., Baldè, C. P., Kuehr, R., & Bel, G. (2020). The Global E-waste Monitor 2020 - Quantities, flows, and the circular economy potential. Bonn, Germany, Geneva, Switzerland, Rotterdam, Netherlands. United Nations University; United Nations Institute for Training and Research; International Telecommunication Union; International Solid Waste Associatio. http://ewastemonitor.info/wp-content/uploads/2020/12/GEM_2020_def_dec_2020-1.pdf

Frank, T., & Cort, T. (Jan. 2020). Report of Results Global Survey on Sustainability and the SDGs - Awareness, Priorities, Need for Action. Hamburg, Germany. https://www.globalsurvey-sdgs.com/wp-content/uploads/2020/01/20200205_SC_Global_Survey_Result-Report_english_final.pdf

Fraser, I. J., Müller, M., & Schwarzkopf, J. (2020). Dear supplier, how sustainable are you? Sustainability Management Forum | NachhaltigkeitsManagementForum, 28(3-4), 127–149.

Freeman, R. E. (1984). Strategic management: A stakeholder approach. Pitman series in business and public policy. Pitman.

Freeman, R. E. (2014). In Person. https://redwardfreeman.com/in-person/

Freitag, C., Berners-Lee, M., Widdicks, K., Knowles, B., Blair, G. S., & Friday, A. (2021). The real climate and transformative impact of ICT: A critique of estimates, trends, and regulations. Patterns (New York, N.Y.), 2(9), 100340.

Freitas Netto, S. V. de, Sobral, M. F. F., Ribeiro, A. R. B., & Da Soares, G. R. L. (2020). Concepts and forms of greenwashing: a systematic review. Environmental Sciences Europe, 32(1).

Freudenreich, B., Lüdeke-Freund, F., & Schaltegger, S. (2020). A Stakeholder Theory Perspective on Business Models: Value Creation for Sustainability. Journal of Business Ethics, 166(1), 3–18.

Friede, G., Busch, T., & Bassen, A. (2015). ESG and financial performance: aggregated evidence from more than 2000 empirical studies. Journal of Sustainable Finance & Investment, 5(4), 210–233.

Friedman, M. (1970, September 13). The Social Responsibility Of Business Is to Increase Its Profits. The New York Times Magazine, Section SM.

Fry, E. (2015, October 25). VW fooled everyone. Was it the only one? Fortune. https://fortune.com/2015/10/26/emissions-testing-software-cheat-volkswagen-scandal/

Fu, R., Tang, Y., & Chen, G. (2020). Chief sustainability officers and corporate social (Ir) responsibility. Strategic Management Journal, 41(4), 656–680.

fuseproject. (2021). Puma Clever Little Bag. https://www.fuseproject.com/work/puma-clever-little-bag

Gamper-Rabindran, S., & Finger, S. R. (2013). Does industry self-regulation reduce pollution? Responsible Care in the chemical industry. Journal of Regulatory Economics, 43(1), 1–30.

Gao, T., Liu, Q., & Wang, J. (2014). A comparative study of carbon footprint and assessment standards. International Journal of Low-Carbon Technologies, 9(3), 237–243.

Garg, P., & Ramachandran, J. (2019). Hindustan Unilever Limited (A): Growing with India (Harvard Business School Case IMB739-PDF-ENG).

Gerstmeyer, M.-A. (2020, October 30). Was kann das neue „Kleiderkreisel"? Welt. https://www.welt.de/icon/mode/article218922336/Vinted-Was-kann-das-neue-Kleiderkreisel.html

Gharfalkar, M., Court, R., Campbell, C., Ali, Z., & Hillier, G. (2015). Analysis of waste hierarchy in the European waste directive 2008/98/EC. Waste Management (New York, N.Y.), 39, 305–313.

UN Global Compact. (2013). Global Corporate Sustainability Report 2013. UN Global Compact.

UN Global Compact, DNV GL. (2020). Uniting Business in the Decade of Action - Building on 20 Years of Progress. UN Global Compact. https://www.dnv.com/Publications/uniting-business-in-the-decade-of-action-building-on-20-years-of-progress-183983

Global Footprint Network. (2021). Ecological Footprint Explorer. https://data.footprintnetwork.org/

Global Poverty and Inequality in the 20th Century: Turning the Corner? (2001). Economic Round-up(Centenary 2001), 1–52. https://doi.org/10.3316/ielapa.536381064632834

Global Sustainable Investment Alliance. (2021). Global Sustainable Investment Review 2020. Global Sustainable Investment Alliance. http://www.gsi-alliance.org/wp-content/uploads/2021/07/GSIR-2020.pdf

Godfrey, L., Nahman, A., Yonli, A. H., Gebremedhin, F. G., Katima, J. H. Y., Gebremedhin, K. G., Osman, M. A. M., Ahmed, M. T., Amin, M. M., Loutfy, N. M., Osibanjo, O., Oelofse, S., & Richter, U. H. (2018). Africa Waste Management Outlook. United Nations Environment Programme.

Goglio, S., & Kalmi, P. (2017). Credit Unions and Co-operative Banks across the World. In J. Michie, J. R. Blasi, & C. Borzaga (Eds.), Oxford handbooks: Vol. 1. The Oxford handbook of mutual, co-operative, and co-owned business. Oxford University Press.

Gold, S., Hahn, R., & Seuring, S. (2013). Sustainable supply chain management in "Base of the Pyramid" food projects—A path to triple bottom line approaches for multinationals? International Business Review, 22(5), 784–799.

Gond, J.-P., El Akremi, A., Swaen, V., & Babu, N. (2017). The psychological microfoundations of corporate social responsibility: A person-centric systematic review. Journal of Organizational Behavior, 38(2), 225–246.

Gray, B., & Stites, J. (2013). Sustainability through Partnerhsips: A Guide for Executives. Network for Business Sustainability. https://static1.squarespace.com/static/5d5156083138fd000193c11a/t/5d61eaa68728cb0001cf571b/1566698219172/NBS-Partnerships-Executive-Report.pdf

Gray, R., Kouhy, R., & Lavers, S. (1995). Corporate social and environmental reporting: a review of the literature and a longitudinal study of UK disclosure. Accounting, Auditing & Accountability Journal, 8(2), 47–77.

Grayson, D., McLaren, M., & Spitzeck, H. (2014). Social intrapreneurism and all that jazz: How business innovators are helping to build a more sustainable world. Greenleaf.

GRI. (2021a). GRI 1: Foundation 2021. GRI.

GRI. (2021b). GRI 306: Waste 2020. GRI.

Griffin, P. (2017). The Carbon Majors Database – CDP Carbon Majors Report 2017. London, UK. CDP.

Grimes, M. G., Williams, T. A., & Zhao, E. Y. (2019). Anchors Aweigh: The Sources, Variety, and Challenges of Mission Drift. Academy of Management Review, 44(4), 819–845.

Grolin, J. (1998). Corporate legitimacy in risk society: the case of Brent Spar. Business Strategy and the Environment, 7(4), 213–222.

Gürtürk, A., & Hahn, R. (2016). An empirical assessment of assurance statements in sustainability reports: smoke screens or enlightening information? Journal of Cleaner Production, 136, 30–41.

Hahn, R. (2009). The Ethical Rational of Business for the Poor – Integrating the Concepts Bottom of the Pyramid, Sustainable Development, and Corporate Citizenship. Journal of Business Ethics, 84(3), 313–324.

Hahn, R. (2011). Integrating corporate responsibility and sustainable development: A normativeconceptual approach to holistic management thinking. Journal of Global Responsibility, 2(1), 8–22.

Hahn, R. (2012). Standardizing Social Responsibility? New Perspectives on Guidance Documents and Management System Standards for Sustainable Development. IEEE Transactions on Engineering Management, 59(4), 717–727.

Hahn, R. (2013). Host Europe: Advancing CSR and Sustainability in a Medium-sized IT Company. In J. T. Lawrence & P. W. Beamish (Eds.), Globally responsible leadership: Managing according to the UN Global Compact (pp. 414–433). SAGE Publications.

Hahn, R., & Gold, S. (2014). Resources and governance in "base of the pyramid"-partnerships: Assessing collaborations between businesses and non-business actors. Journal of Business Research, 67(7), 1321–1333.

Hahn, R., & Ince, I. (2016). Constituents and Characteristics of Hybrid Businesses: A Qualitative, Empirical Framework. Journal of Small Business Management, 54, 33–52.

Hahn, R., & Kühnen, M. (2013). Determinants of sustainability reporting: a review of results, trends, theory, and opportunities in an expanding field of research. Journal of Cleaner Production, 59, 5–21.

Hahn, R., & Weidtmann, C. (2016). Transnational Governance, Deliberative Democracy, and the Legitimacy of ISO 26000. Business & Society, 55(1), 90–129.

Hahn, T., Pinkse, J., Preuss, L., & Figge, F. (2015). Tensions in Corporate Sustainability: Towards an Integrative Framework. Journal of Business Ethics, 127(2), 297–316.

Haigh, N., & Griffiths, A. (2009). The natural environment as a primary stakeholder: the case of climate change. Business Strategy and the Environment, 18(6), 347–359.

Halme, M., Lindeman, S., & Linna, P. (2012). Innovation for Inclusive Business: Intrapreneurial Bricolage in Multinational Corporations. Journal of Management Studies, 49(4), 743–784.

Hand, D., Dithrich, H., Sunderji, S., & Nova, N. (June 2020). Annual Impact Investor Survey 2020. Global Impact Investing Network. https://thegiin.org/assets/GIIN%20Annual%20Impact%20Investor%20Survey%202020.pdf

Hanke, T. (2021, March 3). Der Danone-Konzernchef ist Opfer seiner eigenen Widersprüche geworden. Neue Züricher Zeitung. https://www.nzz.ch/wirtschaft/der-danone-konzernchef-ist-opfer-seiner-eigenen-widersprueche-geworden-ld.1604672

Hansen, E. G., & Revellio, F. (2020). Circular value creation architectures: Make, ally, buy, or laissezfaire. Journal of Industrial Ecology, 24(6), 1250–1273.

Hansen, E. G., & Schaltegger, S. (2016). The Sustainability Balanced Scorecard: A Systematic Review of Architectures. Journal of Business Ethics, 133(2), 193–221.

Hansen, E. G., & Schmitt, J. C. (2020). Orchestrating cradletocradle innovation across the value chain: Overcoming barriers through innovation communities, collaboration mechanisms, and intermediation. Journal of Industrial Ecology. Advance online publication. https://doi.org/10.1111/jiec.13081

Hansen, E. G., Wiedemann, P., Fichter, K., Lüdeke-Freund, F., Jaeger-Erben, M., Schomerus, T., Alcayaga, A., Blomsma, F., Tischner, U., Ahle, U., Büchle, D., Denker, A., Fiolka, K., Fröhling, M., Häge, A., Hoffmann, V., Kohl, H., Nitz, T., Schiller, C., . . . Kadner, S. (2021, April 29). Circular Business Models: Overcoming Barriers, Unleashing Potentials. Munich, Germany, London, UK. https://www.acatech.de/publikation/circular-business-models-overcoming-barriers-unleashing-potentials/download-pdf?lang=en

Harrington, W., & Morgenstern, R. D. (2007). Economic Incentives Versus Command and Control: What's the Best Approach for Solving Environmental Problems? In G. R. Visgilio & D. M. Whitelaw (Eds.), Acid in the Environment (pp. 233–240). Springer US. https://doi.org/10.1007/978-0-387-37562-5_12

Hart, S. L. (1995). A Natural-Resource-Based View of the Firm. Academy of Management Review, 20(4), 986–1014.

Hart, S. L., & Dowell, G. (2011). A Natural-Resource-Based View of the Firm. Journal of Management, 37(5), 1464–1479.

Hartmann, J., & Moeller, S. (2014). Chain liability in multitier supply chains? Responsibility attributions for unsustainable supplier behavior. Journal of Operations Management, 32(5), 281–294.

Helbig, C., Thorenz, A., & Tuma, A. (2020). Quantitative assessment of dissipative losses of 18 metals. Resources, Conservation and Recycling, 153, 104537.

Henkel AG & Co. KGaA. (n.d.–a). Sustainable Development Goals (SDG): Henkel's Contribution and Activities. Düsseldorf, Germany. https://www.henkel.com/resource/blob/811284/bb7158c356bcffff304976fc8e1046c0/data/henkel-sdg-and-activities-eng.pdf

Henkel AG & Co. KGaA. (n.d.–b). Sustainable Development Goals (SDGs). https://www.henkel.com/sustainability/positions/sustainable-development-goals

Henkel AG & Co. KGaA. (June 2020). Sustainable Development Goals (SDG) - Henkel's Contribution and Activities. https://www.henkel.com/resource/blob/811284/bb7158c356bcffff304976fc8e1046c0/data/henkel-sdg-and-activities-eng.pdf

Henkel AG & Co. KGaA. (2021, November 11). Henkel successfully issued sustainability-linked bonds with a volume of 720 million euros [Press release]. Düsseldorf, Germany. https://www.henkel.com/investors-and-analysts/investor-relations-news/2021-11-11-henkel-successfully-issued-sustainability-linked-bonds-with-a-volume-of-720-million-euros-1419126

Henry, L. A., Buyl, T., & Jansen, R. J. (2019). Leading corporate sustainability: The role of top management team composition for triple bottom line performance. Business Strategy and the Environment, 28(1), 173–184.

Henry, W., Miller, B., & Maewall, S. (2020). Blockchain and IoT - Using cutting edge technologies for wastewater management. Deloitte Development LLC. https://www2.deloitte.com/content/dam/Deloitte/us/Documents/technology/Blockchain_and_IoT_for_Wastewater_Management_POV_121520_Digital.pdf

Herden, C. J., Alliu, E., Cakici, A., Cormier, T., Deguelle, C., Gambhir, S., Griffiths, C., Gupta, S., Kamani, S. R., Kiratli, Y.-S., Kispataki, M., Lange, G., Moles de Matos, L., Tripero Moreno, L., Betancourt Nunez, H. A., Pilla, V., Raj, B., Roe, J., Skoda, M., . . . Edinger-Schons, L. M. (2021). "Corporate Digital Responsibility". Sustainability Management Forum | NachhaltigkeitsManagementForum, 29(1), 13–29.

Herz, S., Vina, A., & Sohn, J. (2007). Development without Conflict: The Business Case for Community Consent. World Resources Institute. https://files.wri.org/s3fs-public/pdf/development_without_conflict_fpic.pdf

Hoang, N. T., & Kanemoto, K. (2021). Mapping the deforestation footprint of nations reveals growing threat to tropical forests. Nature Ecology & Evolution. Advance online publication. https://doi.org/10.1038/s41559-021-01417-z

Hoff, A. (2019, June 10). Dutch child labour due diligence law: a step towards mandatory human rights due diligence. Oxford Human Right Hub. https://ohrh.law.ox.ac.uk/dutch-child-labour-due-diligence-law-a-step-towards-mandatory-human-rights-due-diligence/

Hogson, C., & Nauman, B. (2021, August 31). Carbon offsets: a licence to pollute or a path to net zero emissions? Financial Times. https://www.ft.com/content/cfaa16bf-ce5d-4543-ac9c-9d9234e10e9d

Höppner, S. (2021, July 7). Aldi verzichtet auf Billigfleisch - ein echter Fortschritt? DW. https://www.dw.com/de/aldi-verzichtet-auf-billigfleisch-ein-echter-fortschritt/a-58177191

Hörisch, J., Freeman, R. E., & Schaltegger, S. (2014). Applying Stakeholder Theory in Sustainability Management. Organization & Environment, 27(4), 328–346.

Horwell, V. (2007, September 12). Dame Anita Roddick. The Guardian. https://www.theguardian.com/news/2007/sep/12/guardianobituaries.business

Hsieh, N. (2004). The Obligations of Transnational Corporations: Rawlsian Justice and the Duty of Assistance. Business Ethics Quarterly, 14(4), 643–661.

Hsieh, N. (2009). Does Global Business Have a Responsibility to Promote Just Institutions? Business Ethics Quarterly, 19(2), 251–273.

Huang, D. Z. X. (2021). Environmental, social and governance (ESG) activity and firm performance: a review and consolidation. Accounting & Finance, 61(1), 335–360.

Hubbertz, H. (2006). Corporate Citizenship und die Absorption von Unsicherheit. Sozialwissenschaften Und Berufspraxis, 29(2), 298–314.

Hunt, T [Terry] (2006). Rethinking the Fall of Easter Island. American Scientist, 94(5), 412.

IASB. (2018, October 31). IASB finalises amendments to IAS 1 and IAS 8 regarding the definition of materiality [Press release]. https://www.iasplus.com/en/news/2018/10/definition-of-material

IIRC. (Jan. 2021). International <IR> Framework. https://www.integratedreporting.org/wp-content/uploads/2021/01/InternationalIntegratedReportingFramework.pdf

International Energy Agency. (2021). Global Energy Review 2021. Paris. International Energy Agency. https://www.iea.org/reports/global-energy-review-2021

International Finance Corporation. (Oct. 2019). Global Progress Report of the Sustainble Banking Network: Innovations in Policy and Industry Actions in Emerging Markets. Washington D.C. https://www.ifc.org/wps/wcm/connect/227d98d4-13ae-4742-ae94-fb248b84f0be/SBN%2BGlobal%2BProgress%2BReport_1010.pdf?MOD=AJPERES&CVID=mUhlWWP

International Labour Organization. (2017). Global estimates of modern slavery: Forced labour and forced marriage. International Labour Organization.

International Monetary Fund. (May 2019). Fiscal Policies for Paris Climate Strategies - From principle to practice. IMF Policy Paper. https://www.imf.org/~/media/Files/Publications/PP/2019/PPEA2019010.ashx

International Standardization Organization. (n.d.). ISO Survey. https://www.iso.org/the-iso-survey.html

International Standardization Organization. (2006a). ISO 14040:2006 - Environmental management — Life cycle assessment — Principles and framework. ISO.

International Standardization Organization. (2006b). ISO 14044:2006 - Environmental management — Life cycle assessment — Requirements and guidelines. ISO.

International Standardization Organization. (2010a). ISO 26000:2010(E): Guidance on social responsibility. ISO.

International Standardization Organization. (2010b). Schematic Overview of ISO 26000: PUB100260. https://www.iso.org/files/live/sites/isoorg/files/store/en/PUB100260.pdf

International Transport Forum. (2015). The Carbon Footprint of Global Trade - Tackling Emissions from International Freight Transport. OECD. https://www.itf-oecd.org/sites/default/files/docs/cop-pdf-06.pdf

IPBES. (2019). Summary for policymakers of the global assessment report on biodiversity and ecosystem services. Intergovernmental Science-Policy Platform on Biodiversity and Ecosystem Services. https://doi.org/10.5281/zenodo.3553579

IPCC (Ed.). (2021). Climate Change 2021: The Physical Science Basis. Contribution of Working Group I to the Sixth Assessment Report of the Intergovernmental Panel on Climate Change. Cambridge University Press.

Isaak, J., & Hanna, M. J. (2018). User Data Privacy: Facebook, Cambridge Analytica, and Privacy Protection. Computer, 51(8), 56–59.

Jahan, S. (2016). Human Development Report 2016: Human Development for Everyone. United Nations Development Programme. http://hdr.undp.org/sites/default/files/2016_human_development_report.pdf

Janzen, H. (1996). Ökologisches Controlling im Dienste von Umwelt- und Risikomanagement. Zugl.: Düsseldorf, Univ., Diss., 1996. Controlling-Anwendungen. Schäffer-Poeschel.

Jevons, W. S. (1865). The Coal Question: An Inquiry Concerning the Progress of the Nation, and the Probable Exhaustion of Our Coal Mines. Macmillan & Co.

Jia, Y., Tsui, A. S., & Yu, X. (2021). Beyond Bounded Rationality: CEO Reflective Capacity and Firm Sustainability Performance. Management and Organization Review, 1–38.

Jiang, S., Li, Y., Lu, Q., Hong, Y., Guan, D., Xiong, Y., & Wang, S. (2021). Policy assessments for the carbon emission flows and sustainability of Bitcoin blockchain operation in China. Nature Communications, 12(1), 1938.

John, D. (2011). Grameen Danone Foods – A Case of a Social Business Enterprise. In E. von Kimakowitz, M. Pirson, H. Spitzeck, C. Dierksmeier, & W. Amann (Eds.), Humanistic Management in Practice (pp. 103–118). Palgrave Macmillan UK. https://doi.org/10.1057/9780230306585_8

Jolliffe, D., & Prydz, E. B. (March 2016). Estimating International Poverty Lines from Comparable National Thresholds (Policy Research Working Paper No. 7606). http://documents1.worldbank.org/curated/en/837051468184454513/pdf/Estimating-international-poverty-lines-from-comparable-national-thresholds.pdf

Jonas, H. (1979). Das Prinzip Verantwortung: Versuch einer Ethik für die technologische Zivilisation. Insel Verlag.

Jordan, G. (2001). Shell, Greenpeace and the Brent Spar. Palgrave Macmillan.

Joselow, M. (2021, May 27). Court Orders Shell to Slash Emissions in Historic Ruling. Scientific American. https://www.scientificamerican.com/article/court-orders-shell-to-slash-emissions-in-historic-ruling/

Joyce, T. (2019, September 24). Lidl Belgium U-turn on Fairtrade. http://www.fruitnet.com/eurofruit/article/179795/lidl-u-turn-on-fairtrade

Jung, J. C., & Park, S. B. (2017). Case Study: Volkswagen's Diesel Emissions Scandal. Thunderbird International Business Review, 59(1), 127–137.

Kabengele, C., & Hahn, R. (2021). Institutional and firm-level factors for mobile money adoption in emerging markets–A configurational analysis. Technological Forecasting and Social Change, 171, 120934.

Kahneman, D., & Deaton, A. (2010). High income improves evaluation of life but not emotional well-being. Proceedings of the National Academy of Sciences of the United States of America, 107(38), 16489–16493.

Kannenberg, L., & Schreck, P. (2019). Integrated reporting: boon or bane? A review of empirical research on its determinants and implications. Journal of Business Economics, 89(5), 515–567.

Kant, I. (1993). Grounding for the metaphysics of morals - On a Supposed Rights to Lie Because of Philanthropic Concerns (3. ed.). Hackett.

Kaplan, R. S., & Norton, D. P. (1992). The Balanced Scorecard - Measures that Drive Performance. Harvard Business Review(January-February), 71–79.

Kaplan, R. S., & Norton, D. P. (2007). Using the Balanced Scorecard as a Strategic Management System. Harvard Business Review(July-August), 150–161.

Karim, L. (2008). Demystifying Micro-Credit. Cultural Dynamics, 20(1), 5–29.

Karnani, A. (2008). Help, don't romanticize, the poor. Business Strategy Review, 19(2), 48–53.

Kathri, Y. (2021, September 13). IBM Blockchain Assists Groundwater Pilot in Drought-Prone California. https://www.coindesk.com/markets/2019/02/11/ibm-blockchain-assists-groundwater-pilot-in-drought-prone-california/

Kaufmann, F.-X. (1992). Der Ruf nach Verantwortung. Risiko und Ethik in einer unüberschaubaren Welt. Herder.

Kenber, B. (2021, February 13). Anti-slavery chocolate is taken off ethical list. The Times. https://www.thetimes.co.uk/article/anti-slavery-chocolate-is-taken-off-ethical-list-ghsrh06vs

Khanna, T., & Palepu, K. (2006). Emerging Giants: Building World-Class Companies in Developing Countries. Harvard Business Review, 84(10), 60–70.

King, A. A., & Lenox, M. J. (2000). Industry Self-Regulation Without Sanctions: The Chemical Industry's Responsible Care Program. Academy of Management Journal, 43(4), 698–716.

King, A. A., Lenox, M. J., & Terlaak, A. (2005). The Strategic Use of Decentralized Institutions: Exploring Certification With the ISO 14001 Management Standard. Academy of Management Journal, 48(6), 1091–1106.

Kirchherr, J., Reike, D., & Hekkert, M. (2017). Conceptualizing the circular economy: An analysis of 114 definitions. Resources, Conservation and Recycling, 127, 221–232.

Klein, N. (1999). No logo: Taking aim at the brand bullies. Picador. http://www.loc.gov/catdir/description/hol042/00710214.html

Klein, N. (2014). This changes everything: Capitalism vs. The climate. Simon & Schuster. http://www.h-net.org/reviews/showrev.php?id=43027

Kleindorfer, P. R., Singhal, K., & Wassenhove, L. N. (2005). Sustainable Operations Management. Production and Operations Management, 14(4), 482–492.

Knowles, M. (2019, May 20). Lidl rethinks switch to Fairtrade bananas. http://www.fruitnet.com/eurofruit/article/178753/lidl-rethinks-switch-to-fairtrade-bananas

Koch, S., Krüger, C., Lohmann, J., Müller-Henning, Matthias, Redelfs, Manfred, & Smid, K. (2005). Brent Spar und die Folgen: Zehn Jahre danach. Greenpeace Hintergrund Papier. Hamburg, Germany. Greenpeace e.V. https://www.greenpeace.de/sites/www.greenpeace.de/files/Brent_Spar_und_die_Folgen_1.pdf

Köchling, A., & Wehner, M. C. (2020). Discriminated by an algorithm: a systematic review of discrimination and fairness by algorithmic decision-making in the context of HR recruitment and HR development. Business Research, 13(3), 795–848.

Kölbel, J. F., Heeb, F., Paetzold, F., & Busch, T. (2020). Can Sustainable Investing Save the World? Reviewing the Mechanisms of Investor Impact. Organization & Environment, 33(4), 554–574.

KPMG. (December 2020). The KPMG International Survey of Sustainability Reporting 2020. https://assets.kpmg/content/dam/kpmg/xx/pdf/2020/11/the-time-has-come.pdf

Kronborg Jensen, J. (2012). Product carbon footprint developments and gaps. International Journal of Physical Distribution & Logistics Management, 42(4), 338–354.

Kuchler, M., & Linnér, B.-O. (2012). Challenging the food vs. fuel dilemma: Genealogical analysis of the biofuel discourse pursued by international organizations. Food Policy, 37(5), 581–588.

Kühnen, M., & Hahn, R. (2017). Indicators in Social Life Cycle Assessment: A Review of Frameworks, Theories, and Empirical Experience. Journal of Industrial Ecology, 21(6), 1547–1565.

Kühnen, M., & Hahn, R. (2019). From SLCA to Positive Sustainability Performance Measurement: A TwoTier Delphi Study. Journal of Industrial Ecology, 23(3), 615–634.

Kumar, A., Prakash, G., & Kumar, G. (2021). Does environmentally responsible purchase intention matter for consumers? A predictive sustainable model developed through an empirical study. Journal of Retailing and Consumer Services, 58, 102270.

Kuper, J., & Hojsik, M. (Aug. 2008). Poisoning the poor - Electronic waste in Ghana. Amsterdam, Netherlands. Greenpeace International. https://www.greenpeace.de/sites/www.greenpeace.de/files/GhanaEWaste_FINAL_0.pdf

LaBella, M. J., Sullivan, L., Russel, J., & Novikov, D. (Sep. 2019). The Devil is in the Details: The Divergence in ESG Data and Implications for Sustainable Investing. QS Investors. https://qsinvestorsproduction.blob.core.windows.net/media/Default/PDF/The%20Devil%20is%20in%20the%20Details_Divergence%20in%20ESG%20Data.pdf

Lacayo, R. (2007, October 17). Moguls & Entrepreneurs: William McDonough and Michael Braungart. Time Magazine. http://content.time.com/time/specials/2007/article/0,28804,1663317_1663322_1669931,00.html

Lakner, C., Yonzan, N., Mahler, D. G., Aguilar, R. A. C., & Wu, H. (2021). Updated estimates of the impact of COVID-19 on global poverty: Looking back at 2020 and the outlook for 2021. https://blogs.worldbank.org/opendata/updated-estimates-impact-covid-19-global-poverty-looking-back-2020-and-outlook-2021

Lampikoski, T. (2012). Green, Innovative, and Profitable: A Case Study of Managerial Capabilities at Interface Inc. Technology Innovation Management Review(Nov.), 4–12.

Languille, S. (2017). Public Private partnerships in education and health in the global South: a literature review. Journal of International and Comparative Social Policy, 33(2), 142–165.

Laville, S., & Watts, J. (2019, September 21). Across the globe, millions join biggest climate protest ever. https://www.theguardian.com/environment/2019/sep/21/across-the-globe-millions-join-biggest-climate-protest-ever

Le Manach, F., Jacquet, J. L., Bailey, M., Jouanneau, C., & Nouvian, C. (2020). Small is beautiful, but large is certified: A comparison between fisheries the Marine Stewardship Council (MSC) features in its promotional materials and MSC-certified fisheries. PloS One, 15(5), e0231073.

LeBaron, G., Edwards, R., Hunt, T [Tom], Sempéré, C., & Kyritsis, P. (2021). The Ineffectiveness of CSR: Understanding Garment Company Commitments to Living Wages in Global Supply Chains. New Political Economy, 1–17.

Lebreton, L., Slat, B., Ferrari, F., Sainte-Rose, B., Aitken, J., Marthouse, R., Hajbane, S., Cunsolo, S., Schwarz, A., Levivier, A., Noble, K., Debeljak, P., Maral, H., Schoeneich-Argent, R., Brambini, R., & Reisser, J. (2018). Evidence that the Great Pacific Garbage Patch is rapidly accumulating plastic. Scientific Reports, 8(1), 4666.

Leismann, K., Schmitt, M., Rohn, H., & Baedeker, C. (2013). Collaborative Consumption: Towards a Resource-Saving Consumption Culture. Resources, 2(3), 184–203.

Leitheiser, E. (2021). How domestic contexts shape international private governance: The case of the European Accord and American Alliance in Bangladesh. Regulation & Governance, 15(4), 1286–1303.

Lenton, T. M., Rockström, J., Gaffney, O., Rahmstorf, S., Richardson, K., Steffen, W., & Schellnhuber, H. J. (2019). Climate tipping points - too risky to bet against. Nature, 575(7784), 592–595.

Levitt, T. (1960). Marketing myopia. Harvard Business Review, 38(July-August), 45–56.

Liu, Z., Ciais, P., Deng, Z., Lei, R., Davis, S. J., Feng, S., Zheng, B., Cui, D., Dou, X., Zhu, B., Guo, R [Rui], Ke, P., Sun, T., Lu, C., He, P., Wang, Y [Yuan], Yue, X., Wang, Y [Yilong], Lei, Y., . . . Schellnhuber, H. J. (2020). Near-real-time monitoring of global CO2 emissions reveals the effects of the COVID-19 pandemic. Nature Communications, 11(1), 5172.

Lobschat, L., Mueller, B., Eggers, F., Brandimarte, L., Diefenbach, S., Kroschke, M., & Wirtz, J. (2021). Corporate digital responsibility. Journal of Business Research, 122, 875–888.

Lofstedt, R. E., & Renn, O. (1997). The Brent Spar Controversy: An Example of Risk Communication Gone Wrong. Risk Analysis, 17(2), 131–136.

Lüdeke-Freund, F., Carroux, S., Joyce, A., Massa, L., & Breuer, H. (2018). The sustainable business model pattern taxonomy—45 patterns to support sustainability-oriented business model innovation. Sustainable Production and Consumption, 15, 145–162.

Lülfs, R., & Hahn, R. (2014). Sustainable Behavior in the Business Sphere. Organization & Environment, 27(1), 43–64.

Lyall, S. (2007, September 12). Anita Roddick, Body Shop Founder, Dies at 64. The New York Times. https://www.nytimes.com/2007/09/12/world/europe/12roddick.html

Lynas, M., Houlton, B. Z., & Perry, S. (2021). Greater than 99% consensus on human caused climate change in the peer-reviewed scientific literature. Environmental Research Letters, 16(11), 114005.

Ma, A., & Gilbert, B. (2019, August 23). Facebook understood how dangerous the Trump-linked data firm Cambridge Analytica could be much earlier than it previously said. Here's everything that's happened up until now. https://www.businessinsider.com/cambridge-analytica-a-guide-to-the-trump-linked-data-firm-that-harvested-50-million-facebook-profiles-2018-3

Macbeth, C., Bourguignon, G., Petruzzi McHale, C., Taylor, G., & Cibrario Assereto, C. (2020, October 22). Sustainable Finance: A Global Overview of ESG Regulatory Developments (Alert Memorandum). Cleary Gottlieb. https://www.clearygottlieb.com/-/media/files/alert-memos-2020/sustainable-finance-a-global-overview-of-esg-regulatory-developments.pdf

MacKay, B., & Munro, I. (2012). Information Warfare and New Organizational Landscapes: An Inquiry into the ExxonMobil–Greenpeace Dispute over Climate Change. Organization Studies, 33(11), 1507–1536.

Maehle, N., Otte, P. P., & Drozdova, N. (2020). Crowdfunding Sustainability. In R. Shneor, L. Zhao, & B.-T. Flåten (Eds.), Advances in Crowdfunding (pp. 393–422). Springer International Publishing. https://doi.org/10.1007/978-3-030-46309-0_17

Makortoff, K. (2015, September 29). Volkswagen cut from top sustainability index. CNBC. https://www.cnbc.com/2015/09/29/volkswagen-cut-from-dow-jones-sustainability-ranking.html

Makower, J. (2016). John Elkington and the search for What's Next. https://www.greenbiz.com/article/john-elkington-and-search-whats-next

Mansouri, N. (2016). A Case Study of Volkswagen Unethical Practice in Diesel Emission Test. International Journal of Science and Engineering Applications, 5(4), 211–216.

Marine Stewardship Council. (2020). Celebrating and supporting sustainable fisheries: The Marine Stewardship Council Annual Report 2019 - 20. https://www.msc.org/docs/default-source/default-document-library/about-the-msc/msc-annual-report-2019-2020.pdf

Matten, D. (1998). Management ökologischer Unternehmensrisiken: Zur Umsetzung von Sustainable Development in der reflexiven Moderne. Zugl.: Düsseldorf, Univ., Diss. M-und-P-Schriftenreihe für Wissenschaft und Forschung. M & P Verlag für Wissenschaft und Forschung.

Matten, D., Crane, A., & Chapple, W. (2003). Behind the Mask: Revealing the True Face of Corporate Citizenship. Journal of Business Ethics, 45(1/2), 109–120.

Matten, D., & Moon, J. (2008). "Implicit" and "Explicit" CSR: A Conceptual Framework for a Comparative Understanding of Corporate Social Responsibility. Academy of Management Review, 33(2), 404–424.

Mazzarol, T., Clark, D., Reboud, S., & Mamouni Limnios, E. (2018). Developing a conceptual framework for the co-operative and mutual enterprise business model. Journal of Management & Organization, 24(4), 551–581.

McDonough, W., & Braungart, M. (2002). Cradle to cradle: Remaking the way we make things. New York, NY. North Point Press.

McGrath, P., McCarthy, L., Marshall, D., & Rehme, J. (2021). Tools and Technologies of Transparency in Sustainable Global Supply Chains. California Management Review, 64(1), 67–89.

McLean, B., & Elkind, P. (2003). The smartest guys in the room: The amazing rise and scandalous fall of Enron. Portfolio. http://www.loc.gov/catdir/enhancements/fy0720/2003054944-b.html

McNeil, D. G., Jr. (2011, August 11). Nigerians Receive First Payments for Children Who Died in 1996 Meningitis Drug Trial. The New York Times, A4. http://www.nytimes.com/2011/08/12/world/africa/12nigeria.html

Meadows, D. H., Randers, J., & Meadows, D. L. (2004). Limits to growth: The 30-year update. Chelsea Green Publishing Company. http://www.loc.gov/catdir/enhancements/fy0729/2004000125-d.html

Mestre, A., & Cooper, T. (2017). Circular Product Design. A Multiple Loops Life Cycle Design Approach for the Circular Economy. The Design Journal, 20(sup1), S1620-S1635.

Minter, A. (2016, January 13). The Burning Truth Behind an E-Waste Dump in Africa. Smithonian Magazine. https://www.smithsonianmag.com/science-nature/burning-truth-behind-e-waste-dump-africa-180957597/

Mistlin, A. (2021, May 11). Activists target Liverpool FC sponsor Standard Chartered over fossil fuel links. The Guardian. https://www.theguardian.com/uk-news/2021/may/11/activists-target-standard-chartered-from-all-sides-over-fossil-fuel-links

Mitchell, R. K., Agle, B. R., & Wood, D. J. (1997). Toward a Theory of Stakeholder Identification and Salience: Defining the Principle of who and What Really Counts. Academy of Management Review, 22(4), 853–886.

Mitra, K., Reiss, M. C., & Capella, L. M. (1999). An examination of perceived risk, information search and behavioral intentions in search, experience and credence services. Journal of Services Marketing, 13(3), 208–228.

Molena, F. (1912). Remarkable Weather of 1911: The Effect of the Combustion of Coal on the Climate - What Scientists Predict for the Future. Popular Mechanics Magazine(-March), 339–342.

Monbiot, G. (2017, April 12). Finally, a breakthrough alternative to growth economics – the doughnut. The Guardian. https://www.theguardian.com/commentisfree/2017/apr/12/doughnut-growth-economics-book-economic-model

Moroz, P. W., Branzei, O., Parker, S. C., & Gamble, E. N. (2018). Imprinting with purpose: Prosocial opportunities and B Corp certification. Journal of Business Venturing, 33(2), 117–129.

Müller, M. (2006). Die Glaubwürdigkeit der Zertifizierung von Qualitäts-, Umwelt- und Sozialstandards. Die Betriebswirtschaft, 66(5), 585–601.

n.a. (1995). Brent Spar, broken spur. Nature, 375(6534), 708.

n.a. (2021). Lithium-ion batteries need to be greener and more ethical. Nature, 595(7865), 7.

Neumayer, E. (2013). Weak versus strong sustainability: Exploring the limits of two opposing paradigms (Fourth edition). Edward Elgar.

Nike. (2020, March 8). Nike's response to No Logo (by Naomi Klein) [archived from the original website]. https://web.archive.org/web/20000416175422/http://nikebiz.com/labor/nologo_let.shtml

Nisbet, E. G., & Fowler, C. R. (1995). Is metal disposal toxic to deep oceans? Nature, 375(6534), 715.

Nissen, C., Cludius, J., Graichen, V., & Gores, S. (Dec. 2020). Trends and projections in the EU ETS in 2020: The EU Emissions Trading System in numbers. EIONET report -ETC/CME 3/2020. https://www.eionet.europa.eu/etcs/etc-cme/products/etc-cme-reports/etc-cme-report-3-2020-trends-and-projections-in-the-eu-ets-in-2020/@@download/file/Report_ETS_03_2020_20201218.pdf

Nogrady, B. (2020, May 14). Cobalt is critical to the renewable energy transition - How can we minimize its social and environmental cost? Ensia. https://ensia.com/features/cobalt-sustainability-batteries/

Nordhaus, W. (2020). The Climate Club: How to Fix a Failing Global Effort. Foreign Affairs, 99(3), 10–17.

The Norwegian Nobel Committee. (2004). The Nobel Peace Prize for 2004. Press Release. https://www.nobelprize.org/prizes/peace/2004/press-release/

n-tv.de. (2011, July 26). Danone wird abgemahnt - "Musterbeispiel für Greenwashing". https://www.n-tv.de/ratgeber/Danone-wird-abgemahnt-article3901791.html

Nugent, C. (2021, January 22). Amsterdam Is Embracing a Radical New Economic Theory to Help Save the Environment. Time Magazine. https://time.com/5930093/amsterdam-doughnut-economics/

Oetinger, B. von, & Reeves, M. (2007). Größe verpflichtet. Harvard Business Manager, 28(1), 60–66.

Ogleby, G. (2016, November 7). Choice editing: a crucial next step for the circular economy? Edie Newsroom. https://www.edie.net/news/5/Circular-economy-for-businesses-consumer-choice-editing-Sandy-Rodger/

Ones, D. S., Wiernik, B. M., Dilchert, S., & Klein, R. (2015). Pro-Environmental Behavior. In J. D. Wright (Ed.), International Encyclopedia of the Social & Behavioral Sciences (pp. 82–88). Elsevier. https://doi.org/10.1016/B978-0-08-097086-8.22008-4

Onsongo, E. (2019). Institutional entrepreneurship and social innovation at the base of the pyramid: the case of M-Pesa in Kenya. Industry and Innovation, 26(4), 369–390.

Osei-Kyei, R., Chan, A. P. C., Javed, A. A., & Ameyaw, E. E. (2017). Critical success criteria for public-private partnership projects: international experts' opinion. International Journal of Strategic Property Management, 21(1), 87–100.

Ostertag, F., Hahn, R., & Ince, I. (2021). Blended value co-creation: A qualitative investigation of relationship designs of social enterprises. Journal of Business Research, 129, 428–445.

Ottaviani, J. (2016, April 11). The E-waste Republic. Spiegel Online. https://www.spiegel.de/international/tomorrow/electronic-waste-in-africa-recycling-methods-damage-health-and-the-environment-a-1086221.html

OXFAM. (2020, September 21). Confronting Carbon Inequality - Putting climate justice at the heart of the COVID-19 recovery (OXFAM Media Debriefing). https://assets.oxfamamerica.org/media/documents/Confronting-Carbon-Inequality.pdf

Pache, A.-C., & Santos, F. (2013). Inside the Hybrid Organization: Selective Coupling as a Response to Competing Institutional Logics. Academy of Management Journal, 56(4), 972–1001.

Paech, N. (2007). Directional Certainty in Sustainability-Oriented Innovation Management. In M. Lehmann-Waffenschmidt (Ed.), Sustainability and Innovation. Innovations Towards Sustainability: Conditions and Consequences (pp. 121–139). Physica-Verlag Heidelberg.

Pagell, M., Wu, Z., & Wasserman, M. E. (2010). Thinking differently about purchasing portfolios: An assessment of sustainable sourcing. Journal of Supply Chain Management, 46(1), 57–73.

Park, H. J., & Lin, L. M. (2020). Exploring attitude–behavior gap in sustainable consumption: comparison of recycled and upcycled fashion products. Journal of Business Research, 117, 623–628.

Parker, M., Cheney, G., Fournier, V., Land, C., & Lightfoot, G. (2014). Imagining alternatives. In M. Parker, G. Cheney, V. Fournier, & C. Land (Eds.), Routledge companions in business, management and accounting. The Routledge companion to alternative organization (pp. 55–66). Routledge.

Part, M. (2019). The Greta Thunberg story: Being different is a superpower. Sole Books.

Paterson, T. A., & Huang, L. (2019). Am I Expected to Be Ethical? A Role-Definition Perspective of Ethical Leadership and Unethical Behavior. Journal of Management, 45(7), 2837–2860.

Peattie, K. (2001). Towards Sustainability: The Third Age of Green Marketing. The Marketing Review, 2(2), 129–146.

Pega, F., Náfrádi, B., Momen, N. C., Ujita, Y., Streicher, K. N., Prüss-Üstün, A. M., Descatha, A., Driscoll, T., Fischer, F. M., Godderis, L., Kiiver, H. M., Li, J., Magnusson Hanson, L. L., Rugulies, R., Sørensen, K., & Woodruff, T. J. (2021). Global, regional, and national burdens of ischemic heart disease and stroke attributable to exposure to long working hours for 194 countries, 2000-2016: A systematic analysis from the WHO/ILO Joint Estimates of the Work-related Burden of Disease and Injury. Environment International, 154, 106595.

Peiyuan, G. (2021, July 16). Annual reports in China will now include environmental and social information. Responsible Investor. https://www.responsible-investor.com/articles/annual-reports-in-china-will-now-include-environmental-and-social-information

Peltier, E., & Moses, C. (2021, January 29). A Victory for Farmers in a David-and-Goliath Environmental Case. https://www.nytimes.com/2021/01/29/world/europe/shell-nigeria-oil-spills.html

Peters, J. F., Baumann, M., Zimmermann, B., Braun, J., & Weil, M. (2017). The environmental impact of Li-Ion batteries and the role of key parameters – A review. Renewable and Sustainable Energy Reviews, 67, 491–506.

Petrenko, O. V., Aime, F., Ridge, J., & Hill, A. (2016). Corporate social responsibility or CEO narcissism? CSR motivations and organizational performance. Strategic Management Journal, 37(2), 262–279.

Phillips, M. (2021, June 9). Exxon's Board Defeat Signals the Rise of Social-Good Activists. The New York Times. https://www.nytimes.com/2021/06/09/business/exxon-mobil-engine-no1-activist.html

Pigou, A. C. (2017). The economics of welfare. Classics in economics series. Routledge.

Polimeni, J. M., Mayumi, K., Giampietro, M., & Alcott, B. (2015). The Jevons' paradox and the myth of resource efficiency improvements. Routledge.

Pournader, M., Shi, Y., Seuring, S., & Koh, S. L. (2020). Blockchain applications in supply chains, transport and logistics: a systematic review of the literature. International Journal of Production Research, 58(7), 2063–2081.

Prahalad, C. K. (2004). The fortune at the bottom of the pyramid (1. print). Wharton School Publ.

Prahalad, C. K., & Hammond, A. (2002). Serving the World's Poor, Profitably. Harvard Business Review, 80, 4–11.

Prahalad, C. K., & Hart, S. (2002). The Fortune at the Bottom of the Pyramid. Strategy + Business, 8(26), 54–67.

UN PRI. (2020). PRI Brochure 2020. London, UK. https://www.unpri.org/download?ac=10948

Prieto-Sandoval, V., Alfaro, J. A., Mejía-Villa, A., & Ormazabal, M. (2016). ECO-labels as a multidimensional research topic: Trends and opportunities. Journal of Cleaner Production, 135, 806–818.

Pryshlakivsky, J., & Searcy, C. (2013). Sustainable Development as a Wicked Problem. In S. F. Kovacic & A. Sousa-Poza (Eds.), Topics in Safety, Risk, Reliability and Quality. Managing and Engineering in Complex Situations (Vol. 21, pp. 109–128). Springer Netherlands. https://doi.org/10.1007/978-94-007-5515-4_6

PwC. (2015). Sharing or paring? Growth of the sharing economy. https://www.pwc.com/hu/en/kiadvanyok/assets/pdf/sharing-economy-en.pdf

Qiang, X. (2019). President XI's Surveillance State. Journal of Democracy, 30(1), 53–67.

Rajghatta, C. (2010, April 18). C K Prahalad: Guru of poverty and profit dies at 69. The Times of India. https://timesofindia.indiatimes.com/india/C-K-Prahalad-Guru-of-poverty-and-profit-dies-at-69/articleshow/5826769.cms

Rangan, V. K., & Lee, K. (2016). Grameen Danone Foods Ltd., a Social Business (Harvard Business School Case 511-025).

Rangan, V. K., & Rajan, R. (2007). Unilever in India: Hindustan Lever's Project Shakti--Marketing FMCG to the Rural Consumer (Harvard Business School Case 505-056).

Rankin, J. (2022, January 3). Fury as EU moves ahead with plans to label gas and nuclear as 'green'. The Guardian. https://www.theguardian.com/world/2022/jan/03/fury-eu-moves-ahead-plans-label-gas-nuclear-green

Rasche, A. (2013). The United Nations and Transnational Corporations: How the UN Global Compact Has Changed the Debate. In J. T. Lawrence & P. W. Beamish (Eds.), Globally responsible leadership: Managing according to the UN Global Compact (pp. 33–49). SAGE Publications.

Rasche, A., & Gilbert, D. U. (2012). Social Accountability 8000 and socioeconomic development. In D. Reed, P. Utting, & A. Mukherjee-Reed (Eds.), Routledge studies in development economics: Vol. 93. Business regulation and non-state actors: Whose standards? Whose development? (pp. 68–80). Routledge.

Rawls, J. (1971). A theory of justice. Belknap Press. http://search.ebscohost.com/login.aspx?direct=true&scope=site&db=nlebk&db=nlabk&AN=282760

Rawls, J. (1999). The law of peoples: With "The idea of public reason revisited". Harvard Univ. Press.

Raworth, K. (2017). Doughnut economics: Seven ways to think like a 21st century economist. Chelsea Green Publishing.

Rebitzer, G., & Hunkeler, D. (2003). Life cycle costing in LCM: ambitions, opportunities, and limitations. The International Journal of Life Cycle Assessment, 8(5), 253–256.

Reficco, E., & Gutiérrez, R. (2016). Organizational Ambidexterity and the Elusive Quest for Successful Implementation of BoP Ventures. Organization & Environment, 29(4), 461–485.

Reimer, M., van Doorn, S., & Heyden, M. L. M. (2018). Unpacking Functional Experience Complementarities in Senior Leaders' Influences on CSR Strategy: A CEO–Top Management Team Approach. Journal of Business Ethics, 151(4), 977–995.

Reimsbach, D., Hahn, R., & Gürtürk, A. (2018). Integrated Reporting and Assurance of Sustainability Information: An Experimental Study on Professional Investors' Information Processing. European Accounting Review, 27(3), 559–581.

Reimsbach, D., Schiemann, F., Hahn, R., & Schmiedchen, E. (2020). In the Eyes of the Beholder: Experimental Evidence on the Contested Nature of Materiality in Sustainability Reporting. Organization & Environment, 33(4), 624–651.

Reiner, G., Gold, S., & Hahn, R. (2015). Wealth and health at the Base of the Pyramid: Modelling trade-offs and complementarities for fast moving dairy product case. International Journal of Production Economics, 170, 413–421.

Rennings, K. (2000). Redefining innovation — eco-innovation research and the contribution from ecological economics. Ecological Economics, 32(2), 319–332.

Renwick, D. W., Redman, T., & Maguire, S. (2013). Green Human Resource Management: A Review and Research Agenda International Journal of Management Reviews, 15(1), 1–14.

Research Dive. (2020). Organic Food Market - Report Overview. Research Dive. https://www.researchdive.com/346/organic-food-market

Resick, C. J., Hargis, M. B., Shao, P., & Dust, S. B. (2013). Ethical leadership, moral equity judgments, and discretionary workplace behavior. Human Relations, 66(7), 951–972.

Reuter, M. A., van Schaik, A., & Ballester, M. (2018). Limits of the circular economy: Fairphone modular design pushing the limits. World of Metallurgy – ERZMETALL, 71(2), 68–79.

Richardson, J. (2008). The business model: an integrative framework for strategy execution. Strategic Change, 17(5-6), 133–144.

Riisgaard, L., Lund-Thomsen, P., & Coe, N. M. (2020). Multistakeholder initiatives in global production networks: naturalizing specific understandings of sustainability through the Better Cotton Initiative. Global Networks, 20(2), 211–236.

Rizzi, F., Gusmerotti, N., & Frey, M. (2020). How to meet reuse and preparation for reuse targets? Shape advertising strategies but be aware of "social washing". Waste Management, 101, 291–300.

Robertson, J. L., & Barling, J. (2013). Greening organizations through leaders' influence on employees' pro-environmental behaviors. Journal of Organizational Behavior, 34(2), 176–194.

Rocha, J., Nahi, T., & Hyrske-Fischer, M. (April 2021). How does Faitrade mitigate human rights violations in global supply chains? Fairtrade International. https://files.fairtrade.net/publications/Fairtrade_HRDD_2021.pdf

Rondinelli, D. A., & London, T. (2003). How corporations and environmental groups cooperate: Assessing cross-sector alliances and collaborations. Academy of Management Perspectives, 17(1), 61–76.

Roos, D., & Hahn, R. (2019). Understanding Collaborative Consumption: An Extension of the Theory of Planned Behavior with Value-Based Personal Norms. Journal of Business Ethics, 158(3), 679–697.

S&P Dow Jones Indices. (Jan. 2021a). Dow Jones Sustainability Indices: Methodology. https://www.spglobal.com/spdji/en/documents/methodologies/methodology-dj-sustainability-indices.pdf

S&P Dow Jones Indices. (2021b, January 29). Dow Jones Sustainability World Index: Factsheet. https://www.spglobal.com/spdji/en/idsenhancedfactsheet/file.pdf?calcFrequency=M&force_download=true&hostIdentifier=48190c8c-42c4-46af-8d1a-0cd5db894797&indexId=100013741

Saberi, S., Kouhizadeh, M., Sarkis, J., & Shen, L. (2019). Blockchain technology and its relationships to sustainable supply chain management. International Journal of Production Research, 57(7), 2117–2135.

Sachs, J. D., Kroll, C., Lafortune, G., Fuller, G., & Woelm, F. (2021). Sustainable Development Report 2021. Cambridge University Press.

Sachs, W., & Santarius, T. (Eds.). (2007). Fair future: Resource conflicts, security and global justice :A report of the Wuppertal Institute for Climate, Environmentt and Energy. Zed.

Saebi, T., Foss, N. J., & Linder, S. (2019). Social Entrepreneurship Research: Past Achievements and Future Promises. Journal of Management, 45(1), 70–95.

Sajko, M., Boone, C., & Buyl, T. (2021). CEO Greed, Corporate Social Responsibility, and Organizational Resilience to Systemic Shocks. Journal of Management, 47(4), 957–992.

Saling, P., Kicherer, A., Dittrich-Krämer, B., Wittlinger, R., Zombik, W., Schmidt, I., Schrott, W., & Schmidt, S. (2002). Eco-efficiency analysis by basf: the method. The International Journal of Life Cycle Assessment, 7(4), 203–218.

SAM. (2020). SAM Corporate Sustainability Assessment. Zurich, Switzerland. S&P Global Switzerland SA. https://www.spglobal.com/esg/csa/static/docs/SAM_factsheet_CSA_2020.pdf

Sandberg, J., Juravle, C., Hedesström, T. M., & Hamilton, I. (2009). The Heterogeneity of Socially Responsible Investment. Journal of Business Ethics, 87(4), 519–533.

Sandin, G., Miliutenko, S., & Liptow, C. (2020). Single-use plastic bottles and their alternatives - Recommendations from Life Cycle Assessments. UNEP. https://www.lifecycleinitiative.org/wp-content/uploads/2020/07/UNEP_PLASTIC-BOTTLES-REPORT_29-JUNE-2020_final-low-res.pdf

Sartor, M., Orzes, G., Di Mauro, C., Ebrahimpour, M., & Nassimbeni, G. (2016). The SA8000 social certification standard: Literature review and theory-based research agenda. International Journal of Production Economics, 175, 164–181.

Savourey, E., & Brabant, S. (2021). The French Law on the Duty of Vigilance: Theoretical and Practical Challenges Since its Adoption. Business and Human Rights Journal, 6(1), 141–152.

SBTi. (June 2021a). SBTI Corporate Manual, TVT-INF-002, Version 1.1. https://science-basedtargets.org/resources/files/SBTi-Corporate-Manual.pdf

SBTi. (October 2021b). SBTI Corporate Net-Zero Standard, Version 1.0. https://science-basedtargets.org/resources/files/Net-Zero-Standard.pdf

Schaltegger, S., Hansen, E. G., & Lüdeke-Freund, F. (2016). Business Models for Sustainability. Organization & Environment, 29(1), 3–10.

Schaltegger, S., Lüdeke-Freund, F., & Hansen, E. G. (2016). Business Models for Sustainability. Organization & Environment, 29(3), 264–289.

Schembera, S. (2018). Implementing Corporate Social Responsibility: Empirical Insights on the Impact of the UN Global Compact on Its Business Participants. Business & Society, 57(5), 783–825.

Schmeller, D. S., Courchamp, F., & Killeen, G. (2020). Biodiversity loss, emerging pathogens and human health risks. Biodiversity and Conservation, 1–8.

Schmidt, I., Meurer, F., Saling, P., Kicherer, A., Reuter, W., & Gensch, C.-O. (2004). SEEbalance®: Managing sustainability of products and processes with the socio-eco-efficiency analysis by BASF. Greener Management International, 45, 79–94.

Schoeneborn, D., Morsing, M., & Crane, A. (2020). Formative Perspectives on the Relation Between CSR Communication and CSR Practices: Pathways for Walking, Talking, and T(w)alking. Business & Society, 59(1), 5–33.

Schor, J. B., & Cansoy, M. (2019). The Sharing Economy. In F. F. Wherry, I. Woodward, J. B. Schor, & M. Cansoy (Eds.), The Oxford Handbook of Consumption (pp. 49–73). Oxford University Press. https://doi.org/10.1093/oxfordhb/9780190695583.013.32

Schulz, S. (2021, March 29). Wie Hedgefonds den Kohleausstieg befeuern. Spiegel Online. https://www.spiegel.de/wirtschaft/service/emissionshandel-wie-hedgefonds-den-kohleausstieg-beschleunigen-a-44bf3116-4557-4f05-b1c3-f7a4944f7be3

UN Secretary General. (1999, February 1). Secretary-General proposes Global Compact on Human Rights, Labour, Environment, in adress to World Economic Forum in Davos: Press release SG/SM/6881. https://www.un.org/press/en/1999/19990201.sgsm6881.html

UN Secretary General. (2011, January 28). Twentieth-Century Model 'A Global Suicide Pact', Secretary-General Tells World Economic Forum Session on Redefining Sustainable Development: Press release SG/SM/13372-ECO/186-ENV/DEV/1182. https://www.un.org/press/en/2011/sgsm13372.doc.htm

Sen, S., & Bhattacharya, C. B. (2001). Does Doing Good Always Lead to Doing Better? Consumer Reactions to Corporate Social Responsibility. Journal of Marketing Research, 38(2), 225–243.

Seuring, S., & Müller, M. (2008). From a literature review to a conceptual framework for sustainable supply chain management. Journal of Cleaner Production, 16(15), 1699–1710.

Shakeel, J., Mardani, A., Chofreh, A. G., Goni, F. A., & Klemeš, J. J. (2020). Anatomy of sustainable business model innovation. Journal of Cleaner Production, 261, 121201.

ShareAction. (2020, December 1). Proxy voting records challenge asset managers' responsible investment claims. Press Release. https://shareaction.org/proxy-voting-records-challenge-asset-managers-responsible-investment-claims/

Shift Project Ltd., & Mazars LLP (Eds.). (2015). UN Guidling Principles Reporting Framework. https://www.ungpreporting.org/wp-content/uploads/UNGPReportingFramework_2017.pdf

Shneor, R., Zhao, L., & Flåten, B.-T. (2020). Introduction: From Fundamentals to Advances in Crowdfunding Research and Practice. In R. Shneor, L. Zhao, & B.-T. Flåten (Eds.), Advances in Crowdfunding (pp. 1–18). Springer International Publishing. https://doi.org/10.1007/978-3-030-46309-0_1

Sikka, P. (2021, November 26). Mandatory ethnic pay gap reporting is vital to overcome racial employment discrimination. https://leftfootforward.org/2021/11/prof-prem-sikka-mandatory-ethnic-pay-gap-reporting-is-vital-to-overcome-racial-employment-discrimination/

Sims, R., Schaeffer, R., Creutzig, F., Cruz-Núñez, X., D'Agosto, M., Dimitriu, D., Figueroa Meza, M. J., Fulton, L., Kobayashi, S., Lah, O., McKinnon, A., Newman, P., Ouyang, M., Schauer, J. J., Sperling, D., & Tiwari, G. (2014). Transport. In O. Edenhofer, R. Pichs-Madruga, Y. Sokona, E. Farahani, S. Kadner, K. Seyboth, A. Adler, I. Baum, S. Brunner, P. Eickemeier, B. Kriemann, J. Savolainen, S. Schlömer, C. von Stechow, T. Zwickel, & J. C. Minx (Eds.), Climate Change 2014: Mitigation of Climate Change: Contribution of Working Group III to the Fifth Assessment Report of the Intergovernmental Panel on Climate Change (pp. 599–670). Cambridge University Press.

Sims, R. R., & Brinkmann, J. (2003). Enron Ethics (Or: Culture Matters More than Codes). Journal of Business Ethics, 45(3), 243–256.

Simula, H., Hossain, M., & Halme, M. (2015). Frugal and reverse innovations - Quo Vadis? Current Science, 109(9), 1567–1572.

Singh, N. (2021, March 30). 'Shakti' network powers HUL's rural growth. The Times of India. https://timesofindia.indiatimes.com/business/india-business/shakti-network-powers-huls-rural-growth/articleshow/81750547.cms

Smith, W. K., Gonin, M., & Besharov, M. L. (2013). Managing Social-Business Tensions: A Review and Research Agenda for Social Enterprise. Business Ethics Quarterly, 23(3), 407–442.

Smith, W. K., & Lewis, M. W. (2011). Toward a Theory of Paradox: A Dynamic equilibrium Model of Organizing. Academy of Management Review, 36(2), 381–403.

Social Accountability Accreditation Services. (2021). SA8000 Certified Organisations. http://www.saasaccreditation.org/certfacilitieslist

Social Accountability International. (July 2014). Social Accountability 8000 International Standard: SA8000: 2014. New York, NY. https://sa-intl.org/wp-content/uploads/2020/02/SA8000Standard2014.pdf

Sohn, Y. J., Kim, H. T., Baritugo, K.-A., Jo, S. Y., Song, H. M., Park, S. Y., Park, S. K., Pyo, J., Cha, H. G., Kim, H., Na, J.-G., Park, C., Choi, J.-I., Joo, J. C., & Park, S. J. (2020). Recent Advances in Sustainable Plastic Upcycling and Biopolymers. Biotechnology Journal, 15(6), e1900489.

Sourov, K., & van Hyfte, W. (Nov. 2020). Sovereign Analysis: Natural Capital vs the Nature of Capital. Candriam. https://www.candriam.com/48ff47/siteassets/medias/publications/brochure/corporate-brochures-and-reports/sovereign-report/2021_01_sovereign_sustainability_en_web.pdf

Spangenberg, J. H., Fuad-Luke, A., & Blincoe, K. (2010). Design for Sustainability (DfS): the interface of sustainable production and consumption. Journal of Cleaner Production, 18(15), 1485–1493.

Spitzeck, H. (2013). Normative Versus Instrumental Corporate Responsibility. In S. O. Idowu, N. Capaldi, L. Zu, & A. D. Gupta (Eds.), Encyclopedia of Corporate Social Responsibility (pp. 1768–1770). Springer Berlin Heidelberg. https://doi.org/10.1007/978-3-642-28036-8_210

Starik, M. (1995). Should trees have managerial standing? Toward stakeholder status for non-human nature. Journal of Business Ethics, 14(3), 207–217.

Statista, Inc. (2021, November 4). Value of the sharing economy worldwide in 2014 and 2025. https://www.statista.com/statistics/830986/value-of-the-global-sharing-economy/

Stavins, R. N. (2003). Experience with Market-Based Environmental Policy Instruments. In Handbook of Environmental Economics. Environmental Degradation and Institutional Responses (Vol. 1, pp. 355–435). Elsevier. https://doi.org/10.1016/S1574-0099(03)01014-3

Stefan, A., & Paul, L. (2008). Does It Pay to Be Green? A Systematic Overview. Academy of Management Perspectives, 22(4), 45–62.

Steffen, W., Richardson, K., Rockström, J., Cornell, S. E., Fetzer, I., Bennett, E. M., Biggs, R., Carpenter, S. R., Vries, W. de, Wit, C. A. de, Folke, C., Gerten, D., Heinke, J., Mace, G. M., Persson, L. M., Ramanathan, V., Reyers, B., & Sörlin, S. (2015). Sustainability. Planetary boundaries: Guiding human development on a changing planet. Science, 347(6223), 1259855.

Stephens, J. (2006, May 7). Panel Faults Pfizer in '96 Clinical Trial In Nigeria. Washington Post, A01. http://www.washingtonpost.com/wp-dyn/content/article/2006/05/06/AR2006050601338_pf.html

Stephens, J. (2007, May 30). Pfizer faces criminal charges in Nigeria. Washington Post, A10. http://www.washingtonpost.com/wp-dyn/content/article/2007/05/29/AR2007052902107_pf.html

Stierli, M., Shorrocks, A., Dabies, J. B., Lluberas, R., & Koutsoukis, A. (2015). Global Wealth Report 2015. Credit Suisse. https://publications.credit-suisse.com/tasks/render/file/?fileID=F2425415-DCA7-80B8-EAD989AF9341D47E

Stiglitz, J. E. (2009). Government Failure vs. Market Failure: Principles of Regulation. In E. Balleisen & D. Moss (Eds.), Government and Markets (pp. 13–51). Cambridge University Press. https://doi.org/10.1017/CBO9780511657504.002

Stone, M. (2021, February 8). Why France's new 'repairability index' is a big deal. Grist. https://grist.org/climate/why-frances-new-repairability-index-is-a-big-deal/

Stubbs, W., & Cocklin, C. (2008). An ecological modernist interpretation of sustainability: the case of Interface Inc. Business Strategy and the Environment, 17(8), 512–523.

Suchman, M. C. (1995). Managing Legitimacy: Strategic and Institutional Approaches. Academy of Management Review, 20(3), 571–610.

Supran, G. (2020, October 16). ExxonMobil just attacked our 2017 research study [Tweet]. Twitter. https://twitter.com/GeoffreySupran/status/1317108093419999232

Supran, G., & Oreskes, N. (2017). Assessing ExxonMobil's climate change communications (1977–2014). Environmental Research Letters, 12(8), 84019.

Supran, G., & Oreskes, N. (2020a). Addendum to 'Assessing ExxonMobil's climate change communications (1977–2014)' Supran and Oreskes (2017 Environ. Res. Lett. 12 084019). Environmental Research Letters, 15(11), 119401.

Supran, G., & Oreskes, N. (2020b). Reply to Comment on 'Assessing ExxonMobil's climate change communications (1977–2014)' Supran and Oreskes (2017 Environ. Res. Lett. 12 084019). Environmental Research Letters, 15(11), 118002.

Supran, G., & Oreskes, N. (2021, November 18). The forgotten oil ads that told us climate change was nothing. The Guardian. https://www.theguardian.com/environment/2021/nov/18/the-forgotten-oil-ads-that-told-us-climate-change-was-nothing

Suri, T., & Jack, W. (2016). The long-run poverty and gender impacts of mobile money. Science, 354(6317), 1288–1292.

Syiem, E., Arpac, L., & Khan, S. (2020). Insights and Experiences from the BioCarbon Fund Emission Reductions Projects in the Land-Use Sector. World Bank. https://elibrary.worldbank.org/doi/pdf/10.1596/34499

Tan, J. (2021, April 12). Innisfree criticised for 'false advertising' after plastic found within paper bottle. https://www.marketing-interactive.com/innisfree-criticised-for-false-advertising-after-plastic-found-within-paper-bottle

Tang, Y., Qian, C., Chen, G., & Shen, R. (2015). How CEO hubris affects corporate social (ir)responsibility. Strategic Management Journal, 36(9), 1338–1357.

TCFD. (Oct. 2020). 2020 Status Report. https://assets.bbhub.io/company/sites/60/2020/09/2020-TCFD_Status-Report.pdf

Tefera, D. A., Bijman, J., & Slingerland, M. A. (2017). Agricultural Co-Operatives in Ethiopia: Evolution, Functions and Impact. Journal of International Development, 29(4), 431–453.

Tenner, I., & Hörisch, J. (2020). Crowdfunding for Responsible Entrepreneurship. In H. Pechlaner & S. Speer (Eds.), Responsible Entrepreneurship (pp. 117–134). Springer Fachmedien Wiesbaden. https://doi.org/10.1007/978-3-658-31616-7_6

Tews, K., Busch, P.-O., & Jorgens, H. (2003). The diffusion of new environmental policy instruments. European Journal of Political Research, 42(4), 569–600.

TNS Opinion & Social. (Sep. 2014). Special Eurobarometer 416: Attitudes of European citizens towards the environment. European Commission. https://ec.europa.eu/commfrontoffice/publicopinion/archives/ebs/ebs_416_en.pdf

Tony's Chocoloney. (2020). Tony's Chocoloney annual fair report 2019/2020. Amsterdam. https://tonyschocolonely.com/nl/en/download/annual-fair-report-2019-2020.pdf

Too Good To Go International. (n.d.). The Movement Against Food Waste. https://toogoodtogo.org/en/movement

Transparency International. (2021). Corruption perceptions index 2020. Transparency International Secretariat. https://images.transparencycdn.org/images/CPI2020_Report_EN_0802-WEB-1_2021-02-08-103053.pdf

Trittin-Ulbrich, H., Scherer, A. G., Munro, I., & Whelan, G. (2021). Exploring the dark and unexpected sides of digitalization: Toward a critical agenda. Organization, 28(1), 8–25.

Tukker, A. (2004). Eight types of product–service system: eight ways to sustainability? Experiences from SusProNet. Business Strategy and the Environment, 13(4), 246–260.

Turban, D. B., & Greening, D. W. (1997). Corporate Social Performance and Organizational Attractiveness to Propsective Employees. Academy of Management Journal, 40(3), 658–672.

Turner, M., & Fink, L. (2016, February 2). Here is the letter the world's largest investor, BlackRock CEO Larry Fink, just sent to CEOs everywhere. https://www.businessinsider.com/blackrock-ceo-larry-fink-letter-to-sp-500-ceos-2016-2?r=DE&IR=T

Ulrich, P. (2002). Republikanischer Liberalismus und Corporate Citizenship. In H. Münkler & H. Bluhm (Eds.), Gemeinwohl und Gemeinsinn. Zwischen Normativität und Faktizität (pp. 273–291). Akademie Verlag.

UN. (1948). Universal Declaration of Human Rights, Resolution 217 A (III) of 10.12.1948. UN.

UN. (2011). Guiding Principles on Business and Human Rights - Implementing the United Nations "Protect, Respect and Remedy" Framework (HR/PUB/11/04). New York, NY, Geneva, Switzerland. https://www.ohchr.org/documents/publications/guidingprinciplesbusinesshr_en.pdf

UNDP. (July 2008). Creating Value for all: Stratgegies for Doing Business with the Poor. New York, NY. https://www.rw.undp.org/content/dam/rwanda/docs/povred/RW_rp_Creating_Value_for_All_Doing_Business_with_the_Poor.pdf

UNDP. (2019). Human Development Report 2019: Beyond income, beyond averages, beyond today: Inequalities in human development in the 21st century. United Nations Development Programm. http://hdr.undp.org/sites/default/files/hdr2019.pdf

UNEP. (2010). ABC of SCP - Clarifying Concepts of Sustainable Consumption and Production. Paris, France. https://www.oneplanetnetwork.org/sites/default/files/10yfp-abc_of_scp-en.pdf

UNEP. (2020). Guidelines for Social Life Cycle Assessment of Products and Organizations 2020. UNEP.

United States Environmental Protection Agency. (June 2021). Fast Facts - U.S. Transportation Sector Greenhouse Gas Emissions 1990 –2019: EPA-420-F-21-049. https://www.epa.gov/sites/production/files/2021-06/documents/420f21049.pdf

Urban, K., Schiesari, C., Boysen, O., Hahn, R., Wagner, M [Moritz], Lewandowski, I., Kuckertz, A., Berger, E. S. C., & Reyes, C. A. M. (2018). Markets, Sustainability Management and Entrepreneurship. In I. Lewandowski (Ed.), Bioeconomy - Shaping the transition to a sustainable, biobased economy (pp. 231–286). Springer International Publishing. https://doi.org/10.1007/978-3-319-68152-8_8

US SIF Foundation. (2020). Report on US Sustainable and Impact Investing Trends 2020: Executive Summary. https://www.ussif.org/files/US%20SIF%20Trends%20Report%202020%20Executive%20Summary.pdf

UVA Darden School of Business. (2021). R. Edward Freeman. https://www.darden.virginia.edu/faculty-research/directory/r-edward-freeman

Vaillant Group. (2021a). S.E.E.D.S - The Vaillant Group`s Sustainability Programme. https://www.vaillant-group.com/news-centre/publications/progress-report/s-e-e-d-s-nachhaltigkeitsziele-1610364.html

Vaillant Group. (2021b). S.E.E.D.S Sustainability Targets. https://www.vaillant-group.com/news-centre/publications/progress-report/s-e-e-d-s-nachhaltigkeitsziele-1610364.html

Valentine, S. V. (2016). Kalundborg Symbiosis: fostering progressive innovation in environmental networks. Journal of Cleaner Production, 118, 65–77.

van Gansbeke, F. (2021, March 20). Sustainability And The Downfall Of Danone CEO Faber. Forbes. https://www.forbes.com/sites/frankvangansbeke/2021/03/20/sustainability-and-the-downfall-of-danone-ceo-faber-12/

van Loon, P., McKinnon, A. C., Deketele, L., & Dewaele, J. (2014). The growth of online retailing: a review of its carbon impacts. Carbon Management, 5(3), 285–292.

VanTilburg, J. A. (1994). Easter Island: Archaeology, ecology and culture. British Museum Press.

Vedula, S., Doblinger, C., Pacheco, D., York, J., Bacq, S., Russo, M., & Dean, T. (2021). Entrepreneurship for the Public Good: A Review, Critique, and Path Forward for Social and Environmental Entrepreneurship Research. Academy of Management Annals, Article annals.2019.0143. Advance online publication. https://doi.org/10.5465/annals.2019.0143

Villela, M., Bulgacov, S., & Morgan, G. (2021). B Corp Certification and Its Impact on Organizations Over Time. Journal of Business Ethics, 170(2), 343–357.

Villiers, C. de, Venter, E. R., & Hsiao, P.-C. K. (2017). Integrated reporting: background, measurement issues, approaches and an agenda for future research. Accounting & Finance, 57(4), 937–959.

Vinted. (2021). About. https://www.vinted.com/about

Vis, M., Mantau, U., Allen, B., Essel, R., & Reichenbach, J. (2016). CASCADES - Study on the optimised cascading use of wood (No 394/PP/ENT/RCH/14/7689. Final report). Brussels, Belgium.

Volkwagen AG. (2015, May 5). Sustainability Report 2014. Wolfsburg.

von Carlowitz, H. C. (1713; 2009). Sylvicultura oeconomica (Reprint of 2. ed., Leipzig, Braun 1732). Forstliche Klassiker: Vol. 1. Kessel.

Voss, H., Davis, M., Sumner, M., Waite, L., Ras, I. A., Singhal, D., & Jog, D. (2019). International supply chains: compliance and engagement with the Modern Slavery Act. Journal of the British Academy, 7 (s1), 61–76.

Vo-Thanh, T., Zaman, M., Hasan, R., Rather, R. A., Lombardi, R., & Secundo, G. (2021). How a mobile app can become a catalyst for sustainable social business: The case of Too Good To Go. Technological Forecasting and Social Change, 171, 120962.

Wagner, M [Moritz], & Lewandowski, I. (2018). Life-Cycle Sustainability Assessment. In I. Lewandowski (Ed.), Bioeconomy - Shaping the transition to a sustainable, biobased economy (pp. 260–274). Springer International Publishing. https://doi.org/10.1007/978-3-319-68152-8_8

Waldner, C. J. (2020). In the Centre of Attention: How Social Entrepreneurs Influence Organisational Reputation. Journal of Social Entrepreneurship, in press.

Wallis, M. von, & Klein, C. (2015). Ethical requirement and financial interest: a literature review on socially responsible investing. Business Research, 8(1), 61–98.

Walls, J. L., & Berrone, P. (2017). The Power of One to Make a Difference: How Informal and Formal CEO Power Affect Environmental Sustainability. Journal of Business Ethics, 145(2), 293–308.

Walsh, D., & Greenhouse, S. (2012, December 8). Certified Safe, a Factory in Karachi Still Quickly Burned. The New York Times, Section A, Page 1. https://www.nytimes.com/2012/12/08/world/asia/pakistan-factory-fire-shows-flaws-in-monitoring.html

Wang, C., Ghadimi, P., Lim, M. K., & Tseng, M.-L. (2019). A literature review of sustainable consumption and production: A comparative analysis in developed and developing economies. Journal of Cleaner Production, 206, 741–754.

Wang, N., & Ma, M. (2021). Public–private partnership as a tool for sustainable development – What literatures say? Sustainable Development, 29(1), 243–258.

Wang, Y [Yanling], Xu, S., & Wang, Y [Yanxia] (2020). The consequences of employees' perceived corporate social responsibility: A metaanalysis. Business Ethics: A European Review, 29(3), 471–496.

Watts, J. (2019, March 11). Greta Thunberg, schoolgirl climate change warrior: 'Some people can let things go. I can't'. The Guardian. https://www.theguardian.com/world/2019/mar/11/greta-thunberg-schoolgirl-climate-change-warrior-some-people-can-let-things-go-i-cant

WBCSD. (Nov. 2008). Sustainable Consumption Facts and Trends - From a business perspective. Geneva, Switzerland. https://docs.wbcsd.org/2008/11/SustainableConsumptionFactsAndTrends.pdf

WCED. (1987). Our common future. Oxford paperbacks. Oxford University Press.

Webb, T., & Cheney, G. (2014). Worker-owned-and-governed co-operatives and the wider co-operative movement: Challenges and opportunities within and beyond the global economic crisis. In M. Parker, G. Cheney, V. Fournier, & C. Land (Eds.), Routledge companions in business, management and accounting. The Routledge companion to alternative organization (pp. 88–112). Routledge.

Weiler, A. (2017). Xerox gibt Solid-Ink-Drucker auf. https://www.channelpartner.de/a/xerox-gibt-solid-ink-drucker-auf,3049983

Weimann, J., Knabe, A., & Schöb, R. (2015). Measuring happiness: The economics of well-being. MIT Press.

Weiss, D., Skinner, A., Smyth, M., Slupska, M., Kahlenborg, W., Iraldo, F., Daddi, T., Giocomo, M. R. de, Testa, F., & Melis, M. (2017). Supporting the Evaluation of the Implementation of EMAS - Final Report. Publications Office of the European Union.

Weizsäcker, E. von, Lovins, A. B., & Lovins, L. H. (1997). Factor four: Doubling wealth - halving resource use (reprinted.). Earthscan.

Wernicke, G., Sajko, M., & Boone, C. (2021). How much influence do CEOs have on company actions and outcomes? The example of corporate social responsibility. Academy of Management Discoveries. Advance online publication. https://doi.org/10.5465/amd.2019.0074

Westwater, H. (2020, November 3). Fake billboards target HSBC over 'climate colonialism'. The Big Issue. https://www.bigissue.com/news/environment/fake-fossil-bank-billboards-target-hsbc-over-climate-colonialism/

Wettstein, F. (2005). From Causality to Capability. Journal of Corporate Citizenship, 19, 105–117.

Wettstein, F., & Waddock, S. (2005). Voluntary or Mandatory: That is (not) the Question – Linking Corporate Citizenship with Human Rights Obligations for Businesses. Zeitschrift Für Wirtschafts- Und Unternehmensethik, 6(3), 304–320.

White, K., Habib, R., & Hardisty, D. J. (2019). How to SHIFT Consumer Behaviors to be More Sustainable: A Literature Review and Guiding Framework. Journal of Marketing, 83(3), 22–49.

Wickert, C., & Risi, D. (2019). Corporate Social Responsibility. Cambridge University Press.

Wijen, F., & Chiroleu-Assouline, M. (2019). Controversy Over Voluntary Environmental Standards: A Socioeconomic Analysis of the Marine Stewardship Council. Organization & Environment, 32(2), 98–124.

Wolfson, R. (2019, February 8). IBM Pilots Blockchain and IoT Sensor Solution To Track Sustainable Groundwater Usage In California. Forbes. https://www.forbes.com/sites/rachelwolfson/2019/02/08/ibm-pilots-blockchain-and-iot-sensor-solution-to-track-sustainable-groundwater-usage-in-california/?sh=310fdb383edb

Wong, E. M., Ormiston, M. E., & Tetlock, P. E. (2011). The Effects of Top Management Team Integrative Complexity and Decentralized Decision Making on Corporate Social Performance. Academy of Management Journal, 54(6), 1207–1228.

World Economic Forum. (2021). The Global Risks Report 2021. World Economic Forum. http://www3.weforum.org/docs/WEF_The_Global_Risks_Report_2021.pdf

World Health Organization. (2021). Children and digital dumpsites - E-waste exposure and child health. Geneva, Switzerland. https://www.who.int/publications/i/item/9789240023901

WRI, & WBCSD. (March 2004). The greenhouse gas protocol: A corporate accounting and reporting standard. n.p. World Business Council for Sustainable Development; World Resources Institute.

WRI, & WBCSD. (September 2011). Corporate Value Chain (Scope 3) Accounting and Reporting Standard: Supplement to the GHG Protocol Corporate Accounting and Reporting Standard.

Xerox Corporation. (2016). Xerox® ColorQube® 8580Colour Printer - Evaluator Guide (858EG-022D). https://www.office.xerox.com/latest/858EG-022.PDF

Yaziji, M., & Doh, J. (2009). NGOs and Corporations. Cambridge University Press.

Yeung, P. (2019, May 29). The Toxic Effects of Electronic Waste in Accra, Ghana. Bloomberg. https://www.bloomberg.com/news/articles/2019-05-29/the-rich-world-s-electronic-waste-dumped-in-ghana

Yunus Social Business. (2020). Business as Unusual - How Social Intrapreneurs can Turn Companies into a Force for Good. https://www.yunussb.com/business-as-unusual

Yuriev, A., Boiral, O., Francoeur, V., & Paillé, P. (2018). Overcoming the barriers to pro-environmental behaviors in the workplace: A systematic review. Journal of Cleaner Production, 182, 379–394.

Zahra, S. A., Gedajlovic, E., Neubaum, D. O., & Shulman, J. M. (2009). A typology of social entrepreneurs: Motives, search processes and ethical challenges. Journal of Business Venturing, 24(5), 519–532.

Zawadzki, S. J., Steg, L., & Bouman, T. (2020). Meta-analytic evidence for a robust and positive association between individuals' pro-environmental behaviors and their subjective wellbeing. Environmental Research Letters, 15(12), 123007.

Zeschky, M. B., Widenmayer, B., & Gassmann, O. (2011). Frugal Innovation in Emerging Markets. Research-Technology Management, 54(4), 38–45.

Zeschky, M. B., Winterhalter, S., & Gassmann, O. (2014). From Cost to Frugal and Reverse Innovation: Mapping the Field and Implications for Global Competitiveness. Research-Technology Management, 57(4), 20–27.

Zhao, X., Wu, C., Chen, C. C., & Zhou, Z. (2022). The Influence of Corporate Social Responsibility on Incumbent Employees: A Meta-Analytic Investigation of the Mediating and Moderating Mechanisms. Journal of Management, 48(1), 114–146.

Zimmermann, T., Memelink, R., Rödig, L., Reitz, A., Pelke, N., John, R., & Eberle, U. (2020). Die Ökologisierung des Onlinehandels: Neue Herausforderungen für die umweltpolitische Förderung eines nachhaltigen Konsums. Texte 227/2020. Umweltbundesamt. https://www.umweltbundesamt.de/sites/default/files/medien/5750/publikationen/2020_12_03_texte_227-2020_online-handel.pdf

Made in the USA
Monee, IL
18 September 2024